FUGITIVISM

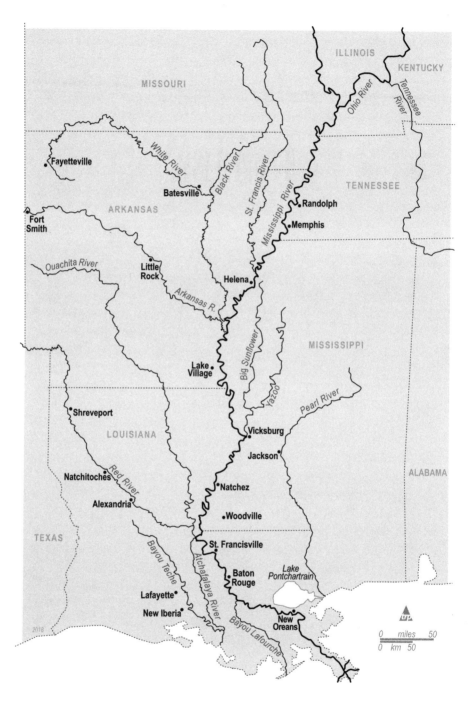

The Lower Mississippi Valley. *Cartography by Tom Paradise.*

FUGITIVISM

*Escaping Slavery
in the Lower
Mississippi Valley,
1820–1860*

S. Charles Bolton

The University of Arkansas Press
Fayetteville
2019

ISBN: 978-1-68226-099-9
eISBN: 978-1-61075-669-3

23 22 21 20 19   5 4 3 2 1

Designed by Liz Lester

♾ The paper used in this publication meets the minimum requirements of the American National Standard for Permanence of Paper for Printed Library Materials Z39.48-1984.

Library of Congress Cataloging-in-Publication Data
Names: Bolton, S. Charles, author.
Title: Fugitivism : escaping slavery in the lower Mississippi Valley, 1820-1860 / S. Charles Bolton.
Description: Fayetteville, AR : The University of Arkansas Press, [2019] | Series: Arkansas history | Includes bibliographical references and index. | Identifiers: LCCN 2018054035 (print) | LCCN 2018056149 (ebook) | ISBN 9781610756693 (electronic) | ISBN 9781682260999 (cloth : alk. paper)
Subjects: LCSH: Fugitive slaves—Mississippi River Valley Region—History—19th century. | Slavery—Mississippi River Valley Region—History—19th century. | Slaves—Southern States—Social conditions.
Classification: LCC E450 (ebook) | LCC E450 .B69 2019 (print) | DDC 306.3/620977—dc23
LC record available at https://lccn.loc.gov/2018054035

Supported by the Gordon Morgan Publication Fund

For Lillie, Ilan, Casimir, Zara, Mari, and Archer

I bathed in the Euphrates when dawns were young,
I built a hut near the Congo, and it lulled me to sleep,
I looked upon the Nile and raised pyramids above it.
I heard the singing of the Mississippi when,
   Abe Lincoln went down to New Orleans,
And I've seen its muddy bosom turn all golden in the sunset.

LANGSTON HUGHES, "The Negro Speaks of Rivers,"
The New Negro: Voices of the Harlem Renaissance,
Edited by Alain Locke, Introduction by Alan
Rampersad (New York: Simon and Schuster, 1992), 141.

CONTENTS

ACKNOWLEDGMENTS

I began to think seriously about runaway slaves in 2006 when James Hill of the National Park Service (NPS), National Underground Railroad Network to Freedom, and Susan Ferentinos of the Organization of American Historians contacted me about a project that the NPS later published as *Fugitives from Injustice: Freedom Seeking Slaves in Arkansas, 1800–1869*. A keynote address to the Arkansas Historical Society in 2008 provided an opportunity to discuss my idea about expanding that project to the Lower Mississippi Valley.

I am grateful to Morris S. Arnold for helping me understand colonial Louisiana and reading a penultimate version of chapter 2, Jake Looney for doing the same with respect to the Arkansas legal system and reading chapter 5, and Vince Vinikas for reading and editing three chapters. Conevery Valenčius read the entire manuscript and offered perceptive suggestions, some of which I ignored until they were reinforced by an anonymous publication referee. Brian Mitchell shared his knowledge of New Orleans at the early stages of the project, and Rod Lorenzen helped me improve the manuscript at the end.

Ottenheimer Library of the University of Arkansas at Little Rock assisted me in many ways. I am also grateful to the staffs of the Benjamin L. Hooks Central Library in Memphis, the Butler Center for Arkansas Studies at the Central Arkansas Library, the UALR Center for Arkansas History and Culture, the Special Collections Room at the Hill Memorial Library at LSU, the Louisiana Collection at Tulane University, and the Historical Archives of the Louisiana Supreme Court at the University of New Orleans. Amanda Paige, a historian in her own right, provided much valuable assistance on this book.

Many thanks to the people at the University of Arkansas Press and to Tom Paradise, cartographer extraordinaire.

On a personal level, I want to thank the parents of the people to whom this book is dedicated: Shannan Venable, Conevery and Matt

Valenčius, and Jesse Bolton and Angie Anderson. Bettina Brownstein encouraged my efforts on this project from beginning to end and served as a role model for the concept that retirement is a good time to do for satisfaction the useful work you used to do for money. I am also grateful for the support of my friends of many decades Gene and Diane Lyons, Judy and Davis Bullwinkle, Jeanne Joblin, and Carla Anderson. Small but very enjoyable portions of the work were done in Ada Hall's kitchen with its wonderful view of Lake Winnebago. The multifarious activities of the Endorfemmes and their menfolk and associates, and the regular meetings of Earl Ramsey's floating poker game, provided a conviviality for which I am grateful.

FUGITIVISM

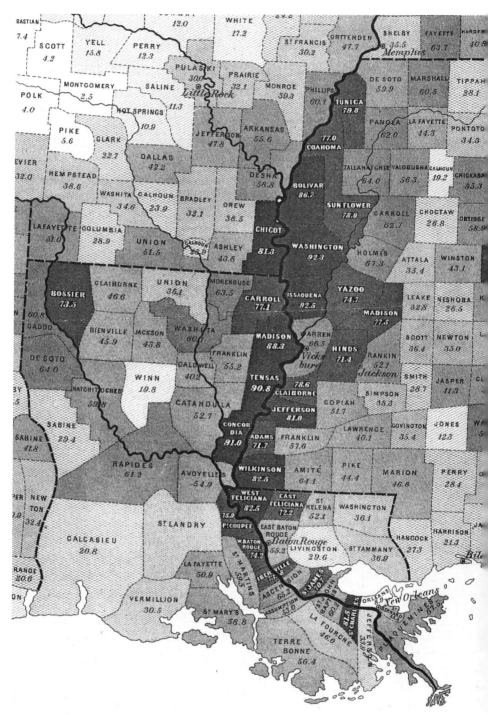

Counties and percentage of enslaved people in 1860. Detail from "Map Showing Distribution of the Slave Population of the Southern States," Washington, 1861. *Library of Congress, Geography and Map Division.*

INTRODUCTION

On page three of the March 6, 1850, edition of Natchez's *Mississippi Free Trader and Gazette*, nestled among the advertisements was the following notice:

> ## RUNAWAY SLAVES.
>
> **$100** REWARD will be paid for the apprehension of two negro fellows, who left the residence of the undersigned, in Ouachita parish, about the 1st of November last; ANTHONY is about 24 years of age, stout built, black complexion; has a scar on his upper lip, has been shot in his right shoulder and arm, and cannot fully straighten his right hand fingers, hangs his head when spoken to. SAM, about 15 years, dark complexion, spare made, and inclined to be knock-kneed. They were brought from Decatur county, Georgia, in February, 1849, and will probably endeavor to return there. Fifty dollars will be paid for either of them if taken out of this state, or twenty-five dollars if taken in this state. Address
> JAMES J. VICKERS,
> Ringgold Post Office,
> feb 27-w1m   Bienville parish, La.

Advertisements such as this one had been common in southern newspapers for more than a century, and they are very good sources of information. Owners included all the details they thought would help in finding their property, and while some of their comments reflect racial stereotyping, we may assume that other details were as accurate as the subscribers could make them. Based on an analysis of many ads, we know nine out of ten of those being sought in most parts of the Lower Mississippi Valley were males like Anthony and Sam. At age fifteen, Sam was a little younger than most of them, who ranged in age from the late teens to the middle thirties. Anthony's "black complexion" suggests his African ancestry and Sam's "dark" skin probably also, but more than a third of the runaways were mixed-race people usually described in various shades of yellow or copper. In New Orleans the word "mulatto" described a person who was half black, and "griffe," one that was one quarter black. Anthony's downcast look when addressed by white people was probably less a personality trait than a conscious attempt to project a false image of submissiveness that was belied by the rebellious act that got him into the papers. Physical descriptions that included gunshot wounds like Anthony's were rare, but about 3 percent of advertised runaways bore permanent marks of punishment. If James Vickers, their owner, was correct, and he probably was, Anthony and Sam were also typical fugitives in that they were heading for someplace in the South rather than to a free state in the North, motivated by the desire to be with friends, lovers, or family or to enjoy the excitement of a city and the fellowship of the black communities to be found there.

Running away from slavery was common enough to become a metaphor for many other kinds of escapes. There were runaway horses, runaway brides, runaway debtors, and the ceremony that followed elopement was sometimes referred to as runaway marriage. A Mississippi woman named Fanny Budlong ran an ad in an Alexandria, Virginia, paper looking for her husband whom she called not only a runaway but also "a drunkard and a Jackson man." The verbal "ran away" was commonly shortened to one word, as in the phrase "he ranaway."[1]

Despite its ubiquitous use, in the past, the present, and in this volume, "runaway" is an inadequate way of describing a person who absented himself or herself from slavery. For one thing, it suggests escapees left some place where they should have remained, as if they fled from battle rather than bondage. It also ignores the fact that they left for a multiplicity of purposes, headed for many different places, and stayed away for varying lengths of time. Historians have attempted to solve this problem by referring to escapees who were gone for an evening or even a day or two as truants and those who sought permanent freedom in southern swamps and forests as maroons. Both terms are useful although not without problems, the one freighted with school-child associations and the other derived from West Indian runaways who achieved a degree of self-sufficiency that was rare in North America. Additionally, there is no word for urban runaways, although the circumstances of their enslavement, the manner of their flight, and quite often their goals, were much different than rural runaways.

The word "fugitivism" used in the title of this book emphasizes not only the ubiquitous nature of slave escapes but also their collective impact on the South. The willingness of slaves to take risks to secure their freedom created an opportunity for slave stealing, a common and profitable crime in the South. Their unwillingness to be captured played an important role in making violence an important aspect of southern culture. And the violence associated with capture and punishment, the autobiographies of successful escapees, and the heartbreaking stories of recapture in the North, all played a role in making slavery so divisive an issue that it led to the Civil War.

The starting point for anyone studying antebellum fugitivism is the comprehensive history by John Hope Franklin and Loren Schweninger, *Runaway Slaves: Rebels on the Plantation*, which came out in 1998. Since then, more specialized works have demonstrated the importance of looking at specific regions of the South, like the Lower Mississippi Valley that is the subject of this one. Larry Eugene Rivers's recent book, *Rebels and Runaways: Slave Resistance in Nineteenth-Century Florida*, shows how the history and geography of that state made the runaway phenomenon somewhat different from other places. When Spain controlled Florida, that country gave freedom to American-owned runaways from Georgia and South Carolina; meanwhile, Spanish-owned slaves were escaping to live in relative freedom with Native Americans. During the antebellum period enslaved people belonging to Florida planters did the same, and Rivers claims that more than a thousand black fugitives fought against the American Army in the Second Seminole War of 1835–1842. Another Florida study, Matthew Clavin's *Aiming for Pensacola: Fugitive Slaves on the Atlantic and Southern Frontier*, tells the intriguing story of how interaction with the Atlantic world, the impossibility of plantation agriculture on sandy soil, and the development of a small industrial sector created a multicultural and multiracial society in which African Americans enjoyed a significant degree of social freedom and economic opportunity. Small wonder then, that enslaved people seeking a better life fled to a city of three thousand people from as far away as New Orleans. Another area of geographic distinction was the coastal region of North Carolina. In *The Watermen's Song*, David S. Cecelski shows how free and enslaved black people played a critical role as sailors who navigated the rivers and coastal waters of the region and fished commercially in them. Slaves who did these jobs were often hired out by their owners, which gave the workers a large amount of freedom as well as the knowledge and skills necessary to escape from bondage and assist others to do the same.[2]

Other recent studies have illuminated specific aspects of fugitivism. Stephanie M. H. Camp's *Closer to Freedom: Enslaved Women & Everyday*

Resistance in the Plantation South shows how women thwarted the web of restraints, including "reveilles, curfews, slave patrols, and laws requiring passes and banning independent travel or meetings," that were a part of daily life for black people on southern plantations. Women fled to distant parts far less often than men, largely because family responsibilities kept them at home, but they regularly engaged in what Camp and other historians call truancy. One form was to leave their cabins in the slave quarters to gather at distant places in the woods, sometimes for religious purposes, at other times to dance and party. Another gender study, *My Brother Slaves: Friendship, Masculinity, and Resistance in the Antebellum South,* by Sergio A. Lussana, discusses the close relationships that made life more bearable for enslaved males and was one reason why, like Anthony and Sam, they often ran off together or assisted others who were living in the woods or on the run. Toward the other end of the runaway scale from Camp's truants were fugitives known as maroons, named after Spanish and French runaways in South America and the West Indies who fled to distant parts where they set up permanent camps and lived self-sufficiently. Such near-independence was rare in the American South, but fugitives did build rude homes for themselves in swamps and forests while subsisting for the most part on food and supplies stolen from plantations. *Slavery's Exiles* by Sylviane A. Diouf is a recent and comprehensive study of the phenomenon.[3]

Steamboat escapes were important in the Lower Mississippi Valley, and Thomas C. Buchanan's *Black Life on the Mississippi: Slaves, Free Blacks, and the Western Steamboat World,* was an especially important source for *Fugitivism.* Environmental aspects, especially the geography of rivers and wetlands, shaped the nature of fugitivism as well as almost everything else in the valley, and Christopher Morris's *The Big Muddy: An Environmental History of the Mississippi and Its Peoples from DeSoto to Hurricane Katrina* is an essential guide to not only the physical environment but also the cultural patterns, economic development, and political change that shaped its last five hundred years of turbulent history.[4]

The Lower Mississippi Valley, as the term is used here, stretches from the mouth of the Ohio River at Cairo, Illinois, to the Gulf of Mexico, encompasses western Tennessee and Mississippi and most of Arkansas and Louisiana, and includes portions of the Arkansas and the Red Rivers that flow in from the west, the Yazoo River that is the eastern boundary of the Mississippi Delta, and the Atchafalaya Basin and Bayou Teche of southern Louisiana.

The area south of Natchez was settled by France in the early eighteenth century and later governed Spain until the Louisiana Purchase. While this study focuses on the antebellum period, it also examines slavery in colonial Louisiana and argues that the difference between the French and Spanish system for hunting runaway slaves, which made capturing them a responsibility of the government, and the Anglo-American practice, which left that up to the public, had important consequences for the South.[5]

Not until the 1820s did the Americans move into the area north of Natchez, but in the 1830s as the Choctaw and Chickasaw were forced from their homelands in Mississippi, the Delta region of that state and adjacent portions of Tennessee and Arkansas joined the former Natchez District of Mississippi and much of Louisiana to become the heart of the Cotton Kingdom. Settlers brought enslaved workers with them, and an internal slave trade arose to supply many more. Walter Johnson's *Soul by Soul: Life inside the Antebellum Slave Market* is one of several studies that explain the importance of that institution, and it also describes the dehumanizing practices associated with the imprisonment and sale of the unwilling immigrants in New Orleans. The same author's *River of Dark Dreams: Slavery and Empire in the Cotton Kingdom* examines all aspects of the region's main industry and provides a slave's-eye view of life on the plantations. In *Flush Times & Fever Dreams: A Story of Capitalism and Slavery in the Age of Jackson*, Joshua D. Rothman analyzes the intense drive for wealth and upward mobility that led American settlers to drive their workers harder and punish them more severely than did masters in the older portions of the South. Sven Beckert's *Empire of Cotton* puts the Mississippi Delta in world-historical perspective as "the chief grower of the industrial world's most important commodity—a kind of Saudi Arabia of the early nineteenth century." However, cotton was not the only crop produced by the enslaved people of the Mississippi Valley, and Richard Follett's *The Sugar Masters, Planters and Slaves in Louisiana's Cane World, 1820–1860* is vital to understanding an industry that utilized steam-powered equipment and factory-like techniques but also demanded intense physical efforts from its male-dominated workforce. State laws and legal records play a vital role in the following chapters, and this book owes much to Judith Kelleher Schafer's *Slavery, the Civil Law, and the Supreme Court of Louisiana.*[6]

Fugitivism looks at runaway slaves from a somewhat different perspective than previous studies, most of which have emphasized their importance as evidence that American slaves resisted slavery. Kenneth Stampp, whose *The Peculiar Institution: Slavery in the Antebellum South*, published in 1956, began the modern study of slavery, declared escape and flight to be "an important form of protest against bondage." Gerald W. Mullin's *Flight and Rebellion: Slave Resistance in Eighteenth-Century Virginia*, which came out in 1972, elaborated the point, demonstrating that "New Negroes" born in Africa rebelled against their enslavement in individual acts of violence and ran away in groups, but acculturated workers, and especially those with special skills, ran away more often and for longer periods, largely because they were able to pose as free blacks. Resistance is also the dominate theme in the books of Franklin and Schweninger, Rivers, Camp, and Diouf. Woven into that interpretation is the concept of "agency," the idea that even though bound by an oppressive system of control and punishment enslaved people exercised a significant degree of control over their own lives. At different times and places, they negotiated with their owners on minor matters, earned money by selling food from their private gardens, maintained significant family and kin-ship relations, conspired together, engaged in religious activities, and kept abreast of the ongoing sectional debate over their status. Still, as Walter Johnson has recently pointed out, agency is "almost always defined as the pursuit of civil rights and economic choice," in other words it assisted in the resistance to the slaveholder oppression.[7]

Important though it is, emphasizing fugitivism as resistance tends to focus more attention on slavery rather than on the slave. *Fugitivism* attempts to give more attention to the individuals than the institution. Running away was certainly a rebellious act, but it was also a choice, and the pull of self-actualization and anticipated happiness was often more important to the decision than the push of exploitation. Viewed objectively, fugitivism was resistance and fugitives were rebels, but from a subjective perspective, runaway slaves were people willing to take dangerous risks to improve their physical, material, and psychological well-being. In doing so they were exercising the entire triad of natural rights that Thomas Jefferson claimed for Americans, "life, liberty, and the pursuit of happiness," and the importance of the first two ought not to overshadow the significance of the third. *Fugitivism* takes a wholistic approach to escape and flight, recognizing that runaways were fighting against slavery, but also paying attention to the physical environment and historical context that influenced their behavior, and emphasizing that flight was often an act that involved ambition as well as defiance of authority.

Separate chapters among those that follow discuss the impact of fugitivism on southern society and culture. One understudied aspect is the runaway phenomenon as it developed in urban areas, a subject to which Richard C. Wade gave some attention half a century ago in his classic *Slavery in the Cities*. *Fugitivism* looks closely at rural slaves who fled to the cities, urban slaves who left their owners but not their city, and those who fled from both. New Orleans is discussed at length, but the relatively understudied city of Memphis is also emphasized, and the smaller urban centers of Baton Rouge, Natchez, Vicksburg, and Little Rock get their share of attention. Also, while much has been written about southern violence, and slavery is usually mentioned in that regard, this is the first study to illustrate the important role that blacks who fled and whites who chased them played in helping to make violence a regional characteristic. The stealing of slaves, heretofore largely ignored, also gets a full treatment. It was a common crime whose perpetrators lured risk-taking people away from their owners by pretending to help them escape. Finally, *Fugitivism* for the first time shows how fugitives from the Mississippi Valley played a role in heightening the sectional conflict that led to the Civil War.[8]

Much of the evidence for this study comes from newspapers published in the Lower Mississippi Valley. Franklin and Schweninger based most of their work on runaway slave advertisements and an extensive collection of local court records. They rejected entirely the many autobiographies published by runaway slaves who escaped to the North, and the interviews with ex-slaves done by WPA workers funded by the New Deal. The former have been criticized because they were published by abolitionists and sometimes edited to reflect the interests of that group, and the latter because of the perhaps faulty memory of the aged interviewees and the possibility they were influenced by the people who asked the questions. In the last several decades, however, historians have begun to place more emphasis on both the autobiographies and the interviews, arguing that there is no reason to believe they are less reliable than the traditional documents written by white people, and that the voices of slaves are essential to understanding slavery. Stephanie Camp, Walter Johnson, Larry Eugene Rivers, and Edward E. Baptist, whose *The Half Has Never Been Told* has much to say about the Lower Mississippi Valley, have used them extensively and effectively. With respect to *Fugitivism*, however, fugitive slave autobiographies have an important limitation. The successful escapees who wrote them while living in northern states or Canada are a small and unrepresentative percentage of the runaway population, almost all of whom left only for brief periods, stayed out as long as possible without going far, or tried to get somewhere else in the South. Anthony and Sam, for example, fled from Bienville Parish in northwest Louisiana, which is about the same distance from Ohio as it is from Georgia, yet their goal was not the free state to the north but the slave state to the east.

Fugitivism draws on anecdotal evidence from more than 3,000 runaway slave advertisements taken from newspapers published in New Orleans, Natchez, Vicksburg, Memphis, and Little Rock and quantitative data collected from a representative sample of 1,396 of them, but its major source is news stories about fugitives and attempts to get them back. They were written by newspapermen who wanted to sell papers and were not above sensationalizing a story, but the content was important to their readers, and we may assume that most of the facts were as accurate as the reporters could make them. Runaway slave advertisements were posted by owners who described people who had escaped or by jailors who described those that had been caught. Newspaper articles offer evidence about what happened between the plantation and the jail and sometimes escapes that ended in success. They also tell us about white attitudes toward fugitivism, public policies designed to control it, and how criminals made money from it.

By far the most important paper in the antebellum Lower Mississippi Valley was the New Orleans *Daily Picayune*, which began publication in January 1837 and has continued down to the present, merging with the *Times-Democrat* in 1914 and changing its title to the *Times-Picayune* in 1937. The *Picayune* brought to New Orleans the "penny press" journalism of the 1830s, which published news stories designed for the general public rather than only people interested in politics and foreign affairs. The *Picayune* sold on the streets for the price of its namesake, a coin worth 1/16th of a Spanish dollar or 6 ¼ cents, well under other papers that were going for 10 cents a copy. Editors George W. Kendall and Francis A. Lumsden hired reporters to cover local news, including activity in the city's courts, and write about it in short articles laced with humor and satire. They also delivered national and international news faster than their competitors by utilizing an express system of horses, steamboats, and trains before the telegraph became available in 1848. Kendall fought as a volunteer in the Mexican War and sent articles to the *Picayune* on a regular basis, becoming the nation's first war correspondent and helping the newspaper earn a national reputation. Most important here, is the *Picayune*'s role as a regional newspaper that reprinted local stories taken from papers throughout the Lower Mississippi Valley, many of them no longer extant.[9]

Readers of the following pages will see that they contain a large amount of quoted material, which is used because I believe it conveys an important sense of antebellum culture and historical reality. For the same reason, the wording, spelling, and punctuation have been left as they appeared in the original text, adding only a few words in brackets that seemed necessary for understanding the meaning of a particular sentence.

CHAPTER 1

The Honest Growler
and Absentee Slaves

ON FEBRUARY 16, 1853, the *New-York Daily Times*, a newspaper less than four years old that would soon shorten its name to the *New York Times*, published a long report titled "The South" by "Yeoman," who had recently traveled extensively in the region. It was the first in a series of fifty such articles that would appear over the next year and a half, averaging about 2,400 words each. The author was Frederick Law Olmsted, who would in a few years design and construct New York's Central Park and later urban green spaces in other major American cities and earn a reputation as the father of American landscape architecture, but who was also an outstanding travel writer and is still a major source for anyone trying to understand the South on the eve of the Civil War. Olmsted had much to say about runaway slaves, in part because they were important to his own economic perspective on slavery but also because the southerners talked about them a lot. Offering the best summary was an elderly black man who lived along the Mississippi River between Woodville and Natchez, Mississippi. He explained to the journalist the purpose of a set of wooden stocks standing along a public road: They are "for slaves that 'misbehave bad,'" he said, "and especially those that run away. Heaps of runaways o' dis country, suh. Yes suh, heaps o'n em round here."[1]

Fred, as he called himself, was born in 1822 in Hartford, Connecticut, where his father was a well-to-do merchant, and one of his ancestors had been an original settler almost two hundred years before. Beyond grammar school, his formal education involved living with a series of ineffective clergyman tutors and a single semester at Yale but reading and a passion for firsthand experience made up for the lack of classroom time. One early source of learning was accompanying his parents on tours of

New England and New York state in horse carriages on annual summer vacations, during which Fred developed a love of rural scenery and a deep interest in agriculture. In 1843, at the age of twenty-one, he joined the crew of a merchant ship bound for China, hoping for adventure and a firsthand view of the exotic culture of the Far East; unfortunately, however, he was almost constantly sick, unable to spend much time ashore, and under the control of a brutal captain whose crew nearly mutinied on the return trip home. Back in Connecticut, Olmsted decided on a career in farming, anxious to demonstrate the effectiveness of scientific agriculture, and in 1848 his father bought him a dilapidated farm on Staten Island in New York, which in less than a year he turned into a model of productivity and beauty, improving the land and the crops, renovating the nine-room house, and landscaping the grounds. The following year, he took a break from farming and embarked on a walking trip in the British Isles and Europe with his brother, John H. Olmsted, and their friend, Charles L. Brace, soon to become a well-known reformer noted for sending children from New York's slums to live in rural homes. Olmsted took extensive notes that he later turned into *Walks and Talks of an American Farmer in England,* a travel book that discussed the social structure and economy of the country and praised the beauty of its countryside and the charm of its rural communities.[2]

The Olmsted family carriage rides in the Northeast and his perambulations in England were important to Frederick's development as a landscape architect, but they also created a standard by which he judged the South, which always came off badly. His brief career in the merchant marine was also a formative experience, something that became clear in an article he published in the *American Whig Review* in December 1851. He was responding to a news item in the *Times* about a sea captain who repeatedly whipped a young cook who claimed to be too sick to work, had the man's lacerated back washed in saltwater, and deprived him of food and water until he died. The *Times* was outraged at the captain, at an admiralty court that let him off with a fine, and at the first mate of the vessel who claimed the sailor deserved the punishment. Olmsted was sympathetic to the victim, but he believed that such punishment was a necessary evil. Citing his own experience, he agreed that seamen were whipped mercilessly and even capriciously, but argued the punishments were necessary to provide low-class recruits with the skills and discipline needed at sea. In his opinion, young men who were accustomed to the savage world of urban slums lacked self-control and were immune to rational persuasion. He summed up the analysis in a phrase that would be echoed in his judgment on the punishment of slaves: "Trained like brutes, they must yet be driven like brutes." He suggested that the situation might be improved by giving young sailors an apprentice-like status that would bind captains to be responsible for their welfare and creating schools where they could learn nautical skills before they went to sea.[3]

Olmsted's interest in the South and his career as a traveling correspondent grew out of discussions with a circle of intellectually active and socially concerned friends about the sectionalism that seemed to be tearing the country apart. Many of his companions were ardent abolitionists, but while Fred was opposed to slavery, he thought it "an unfortunate circumstance for which the South was in no way to blame" and that ending the institution immediately would be impossible. Instead he supported the free-soil position that would prohibit its expansion into the territories. He was a strong opponent of the Fugitive Slave Act of 1850 that made it easier for southerners to catch escaped slaves in the North. In fact, he said he would not only "take in a fugitive slave" but even "shoot a man that was likely to get him." It was apparently Charles Brace who suggested that Olmsted should get firsthand knowledge of the South and introduced him to Henry Raymond, editor of the *New York Daily Times*. Raymond was familiar with *Walks and Talks of an American Farmer in England*, which had been published in New York and well received by the public, and the editor quickly agreed to hire Olmsted and commission him to tour the regions and report on what he found there.[4]

Raymond's charge to Olmsted was a general one, but Fred had a clear idea of what he wanted to do. His would be a factual account "of observations on Southern Agriculture & general economy as affected by Slavery," and include information on "the conditions of the slaves" as well as the "hopes & fears of sensible planters & gentlemen." He also planned to turn his newspaper articles into a book. Characteristically, he accomplished what he set out to do. Upon his return from the South, he did additional research in libraries to supplement what he had learned there and added extensive comments reflecting his own views, including those on the worsening sectional crisis. As we shall see, this material was also influenced by his prejudice in favor of the northern society, particularly that of New England.[5]

Olmsted's experience in the South began on December 10, 1852, when the newly commissioned journalist, now thirty years old, checked into Gadsby's Hotel in Washington, DC, to spend the first night of what turned out to be two trips to the South, which together involved about thirteen months of travel through all the slave states except Arkansas, Florida, and Missouri. He spent a few days in the nation's capital and visited a farm in Maryland before going on to Virginia where he visited Richmond, Petersburg, and Norfolk, traveling mostly by train and spending three weeks in the state. He crossed into North Carolina on January 7, 1854, and over the next five weeks visited Raleigh and Fayetteville, rode a steamboat down the Cape Fear River to Wilmington and continued by train south to Charleston, South Carolina, and Savannah, Georgia, and then west to Columbus, Georgia, and on to Montgomery, Alabama, from where a steamboat carried him down the Alabama River to Mobile, and another one along the Gulf Coast to New Orleans, where he arrived about February 18. He traveled by steamboat up the Red River as far as Natchitoches and back to New Orleans and from there up the Mississippi River to Memphis, stopping at Vicksburg along the way. After one night in Memphis, he returned home mostly by stagecoach across the northern piedmont portions of Mississippi and Alabama and the western backcountry of Georgia, the Carolinas, and Virginia. The details of most of that journey are unrecorded, but it took a little more than two weeks. The entire trip included about three and a half months in the South, a month of which was spent in the Lower Mississippi Valley, less than a week of it in New Orleans.[6]

Within seven months of his return home, the indefatigable Olmsted left again, this time with his brother John for an extended journey on horseback through Texas that was hoped would cure John's worsening tuberculosis. They left New York on November 10, 1853, on the way to Baltimore and then Wheeling, Virginia (now West Virginia), from where they took steamboats down the Ohio River and the Mississippi River to New Orleans, stopping along the way at Lexington, Kentucky, and making a side trip to Nashville, Tennessee. From New Orleans, it was another boat trip up the Red River to Natchitoches, where they acquired horses, a mule, and other supplies for a five-month "saddle trip" across the eastern portion of Texas, visiting Austin on the way to the Mexican border at Eagle Pass and then riding back via Houston and the Louisiana cities of Lake Charles, Opelousas, and Lafayette. At the mouth of the Red River, John, whose health had not been improved by the dry Texas air as was hoped, took a boat trip down to New Orleans, while Fred continued on horseback up the eastern side of the Mississippi River through Bayou Sara and Natchez. Having spent another month or so coming and going in the Mississippi Valley, he rode out of Natchez to the northeast through Jackson, Mississippi, and Tuscaloosa, Alabama, along the Tennessee-South Carolina border, up through Richmond, Virginia, and reached home at the end of July, nine months after leaving it.[7]

Olmsted's first trip to the South was the basis for fifty lengthy articles published in the *Times* in 1852 and 1853 in a series titled "The South" and signed Yeoman, a pen name that reflected both the author's interest in agriculture and his commitment to the American political doctrine of republicanism. In 1856, he published *A Journey in the Seaboard Slave States*, based on the articles that covered his travels from Virginia through Louisiana. The second trip yielded fifteen additional letters to the *Times* and a travelogue titled *A Journey Through Texas; or, A Saddle Trip on the Southwestern Frontier*, which was written mostly by John based on Fred's notes and published in 1857. Fred's two return trips furnished the material for a series of ten letters published in the *New York Daily Tribune* in 1857, and that same year he used them for a third volume that appeared in 1860 with the title *A Journey in the Back Country*. Eventually the collective 1,732 pages of this trilogy were condensed and edited under Olmsted's direction by the journalist Edwin R. Goodloe into *The Cotton Kingdom*, originally published in two volumes in 1861, which has become a classic of southern history widely read and cited down to the present.[8]

In the early pages of *A Journey in the Seaboard Slave States*, Olmsted described himself as an "honest growler" for whom a critical approach to any subject was part of his nature, but he also claimed to be free of any "partisan bias."[9] Southerners might be excused for thinking the growling sometimes became more like biting and reflected a northern viewpoint. For example, *The Cotton Kingdom* contained this summary of southern domesticity: "Nine times out of ten . . . I slept in a room with others, in a bed which stank, supplied with but one sheet, if with any; I washed with utensils common to the whole household; I found no garden, no flowers, no fruit, no tea, no cream, no sugar, no bread, . . . no curtains, no lifting windows (three times out of four absolutely no windows)." He was similarly critical of the service and the food in most of the hotels where he stayed, the failure of trains and steamboats to depart on time, the nearly impassable condition of many roads, and the lack of education of much of the white population. An objective analysis might have excused some of this because of the rural nature of the South and the recent settlement of its southwestern portion, but Olmsted did not take that into account. Nor did he think that economic deprivation was the problem. "Nowhere in Georgia were people as poor as they were on Cape Cod in Massachusetts, yet there is hardly a poor woman's cow on the Cape that is not better housed and more comfortably provided for than a majority of the people of Georgia."[10]

Olmsted was also critical of the southern master class. Most of them did not display much more generosity of spirit or live much better than ordinary farmers. Despite their alleged "broad, generous, lavish, bountiful and luxurious . . . open-handed hospitality of character," he claimed they never failed to charge him for a night's stay. Their homes were often made of hewed logs, floored with puncheon boards, and lacked glass in their windows; and they served him mostly bacon, greens, and "pone." The very wealthy planters sometimes lived in stately mansions with attractive grounds and ran well-organized plantations, but Olmsted found them excessively materialistic and fundamentally undemocratic. Those in South Carolina were a "decayed and stultified people" with "an absurd state and sectional pride" and "a profound contempt of everything foreign except despotism." A Yale graduate well known to Fred and his friends turned out to believe in democracy only because it allowed him and his social class the opportunity to dominate their society and receive the greatest benefit from the economy. Above all, however, Olmsted blamed them for not doing more to educate and uplift their enslaved workers. Despite that, his critique of slavery was less negative than one might have expected.[11]

Olmsted came to believe southern slaves were reasonably well fed and housed and treated humanely. Whipping and similar forms of coercion and punishment, he felt were necessary to make slaves work in the cotton fields just as they were necessary to turn the English lower classes into effective sailors. Paraphrasing his comments on low-class sailors, he wrote that "slavery has come to us from a barbarous people, and naturally, barbarous means have to be employed in order to maintain it." His descriptions of the enslaved at work and play sometimes displayed an ugly racism that might seem to justify their bondage. For example, in South Carolina he and a friend watched a group at work under the direction of an overseer who rode among them carrying a whip and "constantly directing and encouraging them." When he turned his back, they slacked off, and overall, to Fred's eyes they were "clumsy, awkward, Gross, elephantine in their movements; pouting, grinning, and leering at us; sly, sensual, and shameless, in all their expressions and demeanor." He found the whole scene revolting, seemingly bothered as much by the inefficiency as anything else.[12]

Despite his racism, Olmsted could accept the enslavement of African Americans only on a temporary basis. He thought black people were potentially as intellectually and morally capable as everyone else, although they were lacking "in those elements of character that were required for social interaction with whites, which should forever prevent us from trusting [them] with social munities [privileges] with ourselves." If social, and perhaps political equality as well, were beyond them, he thought freedom was not, and they should be prepared to receive it. Responding in part to what he saw in the South, Olmsted became increasingly committed to the idea that it was society's responsibility to uplift its underprivileged and under civilized (as he would have put it) members whether they were sailors, slaves, or impoverished northern workers. Fred was not an abolitionist, but he had a strong commitment to other forms of social reform.[13]

Olmsted's major criticism of southern slavery was that it was bad for the South. Again and again, he argued that slave labor cost more and produced less than free labor, whether black or white. What modern historians see as resistance to slavery, he thought of as inefficiency. Slaves hired out by their owners in Virginia, for example, earned for their owners about the amount that free laborers were paid, but they required constant supervision and still broke tools, damaged livestock, and feigned illness to get out of work. In addition, they ran away from their owners, who had to waste time, energy, and often money to get them back. They also had to be housed, clothed, and taken care of when they were too young or too old to work. Lacking any real incentive, enslaved workers produced poor-quality goods and delivered inefficient service, creating standards of quality for the South that would not be accepted in the North. He blamed white southerners for using their money to buy slaves rather than spend it on public education, improved transportation, and other public facilities that would benefit society. Slavery did not elevate the standard of living in the South, except perhaps for very wealthy planters; instead it kept the region in a crude, frontier-like condition.[14]

Olmsted's first discussion of runaway slaves took place less than two weeks after leaving Washington. He was at a farm belonging to Nathaniel Crenshaw, a Quaker, who employed Irish workers rather than slaves, explaining that he did it both out of conscience and in the interest of good management. Crenshaw was opposed to slavery but said he was not an abolitionist; he would not help a slave to escape nor would he return a fugitive to his owner. He claimed to know two enslaved people who had escaped to the North and done very well for themselves. One of them was a man who had been a free black in Virginia but then re-enslaved when he could not prove his status. He ran away, started a business in a northern city, and fifteen years later was worth $10,000. The other was a woman who was also free but feared re-enslavement. She went to Philadelphia and nearly starved to death at first but eventually came to own four houses in the city.[15]

Crenshaw said he might have solved his labor problem by hiring slaves as many of his neighbors did, but the cost was about the same and the black workers sometimes became discontented and ran away. They hid in nearby swamps, stole corn and livestock from nearby farms, and occasionally slept in the cabins of the slaves who lived on them. Runaways able to remain free until the end of the lease period often returned to their owners, who had lost nothing when their rented property escaped from a lessee, and they were sometimes so happy that the slaves had not died or "gone to Canada" that they did not punish them and hired them out the following year. White men hunted the fugitives, but Crenshaw thought they were not very successful.[16]

Further south Olmsted learned about escapees who attempted to live on their own permanently. This was in the Great Dismal Swamp that runs along the coast of Virginia and North Carolina and at that time was about thirty miles long and ten miles wide. The area had a long history as a refuge for maroons, as Olmsted learned from Joseph, "a jaded looking Negro who proved to be a very intelligent and good-natured fellow" and was owned by a church that rented him out to work at making shingles, one element of the thriving lumber business that went on there. A decade earlier there had been many of them, according to Joseph. "Children were born, bred, lived, and died here," and there were still people in the swamp who were native to it. In recent years, however, they had been hunted by professional slave catchers, who arrested anyone who did not have a pass from their owners or papers proving they were free. They collected a reward for runaways whose owners could be found and sold those who were unclaimed. They used dogs in the chase and shot their prey if they did not surrender. But, as Joseph put it, "some of 'em would rather be shot than be took." Joseph told Olmsted that he had heard of three or four maroons killed in a single day. Those who were left supported them- selves by stealing food from nearby plantations and sometimes working in lumber camps alongside hired-out slaves. According to him, it was easy to distinguish a runaway from a rented slave because the former looked scared and hungry and were close to naked. "What a life it must be," wrote Olmsted, "born outlaws; educated self-stealers; trained from infancy to be constantly in dread of the approach of a white man as a thing more feared than wild-cats or serpents, or even starvation."[17]

At the end of January 1854, Olmsted spent three days on a rice plan- tation near Savannah, Georgia, owned by Richard J. Arnold, a former Rhode Island merchant who had married a southern woman and moved there to run the estate she had inherited. Olmsted stayed at White Hall, one of four plantations that the Arnolds owned in the area and the only one Richard managed personally. It was remarkably well organized and efficiently operated, something the correspondent thought might be related to Arnold's New England work ethic and business acumen. The workforce at White Hall was organized into groups of twenty or so led by an African American "driver," but each hand, men and women alike, was assigned an individual task each day based on a specific measure of what constituted a reasonable day's work for that job. Under the task system, twenty field hands might be required to dig five hundred feet of ditches or hoe a half an acre of rice or use an ox team to plow one acre. Skilled slaves had other quotas, a cooper, for example, was required to produce eighteen barrels a week. Instead of working from sunrise to sunset task workers could quit when the assigned job was accomplished, which sometimes might be early in the afternoon. The required amount of daily output for different tasks had over time become standard on all the plantations in the area and represented something like a contract between master and slave. The bosses enforced their side of the bargain by whipping, the workers by leaving the job. As Olmsted put it, the settled amount for each task was a "proscriptive right" and attempts to increase it would risk "a general stampede to the 'swamp'—a danger the slave can always hold before his master's cupidity."[18]

Olmsted reached New Orleans in the latter part of February and while there visited Fashion, a sugar plantation twenty miles up the Mississippi River that was owned by Richard Taylor, who was an acquaintance of his and the son of former president Zachary Taylor. Fashion included nine hundred acres of cultivated land and another three hundred of swamp and woodland, and it was worked by nearly two hundred enslaved people. In the fall of 1852 it produced 650 barrels of sugar and 1,200 barrels of molasses. Taylor discussed with Olmsted the financial risks involved in the capital-intensive industry that required both expensive machinery and a large workforce, and gave him a tour of the facility, giving the journalist material for several articles in the *Times*. His gracious host also provided Olmsted with transportation back to New Orleans in a horse and buggy driven by a house servant named William, who proved to be a valuable source in his own right. As Olmsted explained to his readers, his driver was very open and talkative and "as he expressed great affection and respect for his owner, I felt at liberty to question him on some points upon which I had always previously avoided conversing with slaves."[19]

William was from Virginia, having been taken from there twenty years earlier when he was thirteen and brought across the Blue Ridge Mountains to Louisville and then down to Louisiana by steamboat. He was sold to the owner of the same plantation where he now lived and had been sold two times along with it. He said slaves in that neighborhood were seldom sold unless they were runaways. It had been very painful for him to be taken away from his mother, and he would like to see her again but was uninterested in moving back, having become used to Louisiana, learned French, and come to know many people where he lived. He said Fashion was the best plantation in the state and that the slaves there were well housed, clothed, and fed. They had Sundays off, were allowed their own gardens, and often received "presents." Still, the blacks who lived in New Orleans, both the slaves and those who were free, were "better off" than those in the country, "they make more money, and it is 'gayer' there, and there is more 'society.'" William also had clear ideas about what he would do if he were free. First, he would work a year to get money for a house and some land. Then he would make a short trip to Virginia and back. After that he would get married and support his family by growing garden vegetables to sell in New Orleans. He had no doubt about his ability to make it as a free man. He would work all the time because he would be doing it "for myself." William claimed that the other black people on the plantation felt the same way. Olmsted was impressed with William but skeptical about his ability to function as a free man, largely because the enslaved man could not understand why the New Orleans area needed levees to keep river water out and New York City did not. Given that William's failure was more related to a lack of education than intelligence, and that the question is hardly a good test of one's ability to get along in the world, we may safely conclude that Olmsted's judgment was based on the man's race more than his answer.[20]

Two weeks after leaving Fashion, Olmsted was on a large cotton plantation on the Red River, probably one of the four owned by Meredith Calhoun, all of them located on the Red River in Rapides Parish, Louisiana. "Calhoun's Landing," which served the complex, was on the site of the present city of Colfax, in what is now Grant Parish. The correspondent was shown around one of the plantations by the resident manager, a well-educated man whose "love of nature and the *bucolic* life" made him something of a kindred spirit. Without irony, Olmsted wrote that this fellow viewed slavery as an integral part of agriculture in much the same way that the Roman poet Virgil viewed animal husbandry, and he thought that abolition was as unnatural to the former as vegetarianism would have been to the latter. Out in the fields he watched as black men dug ditches, with the owner's expectation that they would complete thirty to forty feet of a trench five feet wide at the top, four feet wide at the bottom, and four feet deep each day. The plowing was done by women driving both single and double teams of mules, and Olmsted did not think that men could have done it any better. Children planted corn in already plowed fields, one group dropping seeds in the furrow at regular intervals and a second hoeing dirt over them, the whole "moving across the field in two parallel lines with a considerable degree of precision." Writing about the scene, the correspondent noted that slaves in the southwest were worked much harder than those in other parts of the South, displaying both his concern for efficiency and his racism: "They are obliged to keep constantly and steadily moving, and the stupid, plodding, machine-like manner in which they move is painful to witness." Black drivers supervised field hands closely, shouting at them and cracking whips, although the whip ends touched the slave only lightly if at all. This was the gang labor system, which had originated in the tobacco fields of Virginia and Maryland in the colonial period and was effective for the growing and harvesting of cotton. Unlike the task system, it required working "from day clean to first dark" under close supervision and with the constant threat of corporal punishment for slowing down.

Even when the cracker at the end of the whip did not touch the skin, its noise reminded victims that serious violence was an ever-present possibility. The system reminded Olmsted of his days in the merchant marine. Asked whether it bothered him to administer physical punishment, one overseer replied: "It's my business, and I think nothing of it. Why, Sir, I wouldn't mind killing a negro more than I would a dog." He had never done it, but many overseers had. Once when a field hand attempted to hit him with a hoe, he had fired a pistol at him, but it misfired. He did shoot and wound a slave who ran away from him. Normally he did not carry a gun, but he always had a bowie knife with him.[21]

Out riding with this man (or perhaps a different overseer working for Calhoun, Olmsted is not clear), the correspondent witnessed "the severest corporal punishment" he saw in the South. Crossing a gully, they found an eighteen-year-old black woman hiding in the bushes at the bottom. Asked why she was not at work, Sam's Sal, as she called herself, said her father had locked her in the cabin that morning, and it was a long time before she was able to loosen a board and get out—apparently too late to join the crew, at least without being punished. Not believing the story, the overseer dismounted and "struck her thirty or forty blows with his tough, flexible, 'raw-hide' whip." Then he asked her to tell the truth, and she repeated the same story. This time he ordered her to raise up her clothes and lie on the ground and "continued to flog her across her naked loins and thigh" while she remained "writhing, groveling, and screaming." The punishment was carried out in a business-like manner, without any display of emotion on the part of the overseer, and a fifteen-year-old boy who was with the two men appeared to be irritated only by the interruption of the ride. Later they learned that Sal had worked in the morning but snuck off after the midday meal without being missed—something that had never happened before. Asked if the punishment had to be so severe, the overseer claimed that anything less would have encouraged her to do it again, and others would follow that example. He said that when he had first come to this plantation running away for a few days or a week was quite common, the slaves saying it was "hell to be on his place," but gradually they had become accustomed to "his ways." There were fewer flights at the present, in part because he punished those that did not leave, by making them work on Sundays, for example. Other enslaved people had stopped giving food and shelter to the escapees and sometimes even helped to capture them.

While Sam's Sal's whipping was the worst one that Olmsted witnessed. He was certain such things were quite common, and he justified them in a dispassionate manner. Returning to his naval analogy, he argued that corporal punishment was even more necessary for slaves than for sailors, because they had much more opportunity to run and hide, and because having not signed up for the work they were doing had no moral obligation to do it.[22]

On his way back to the North after the Texas trip, Olmsted parted with his brother John in New Orleans and Olmsted traveled by horseback up the eastern side of the Mississippi River. On May 30, 1854, he found food and lodging at what he later called "a first-rate cotton plantation," probably Evermay near Port Gibson in Claiborne County, Mississippi, one of the largest in the state with nearly thirteen hundred acres of land under cultivation. The owner, Benjamin Smith, spent most of his time in Lexington, and it was the resident overseer who showed Fred around. The visit was particularly significant because, as Olmsted put it, "this was the only large plantation that I had an opportunity of seeing at all closely, over which I was not chiefly conducted by an educated gentleman and slave owner by whose habitual impressions and sentiments my own were probably somewhat influenced." He also later met a merchant from the area in New York City who told him that Evermay was managed in much the same way as other Mississippi plantations.

Cotton and corn were the principal crops grown at Evermay, the former for sale and the latter used to feed the enslaved workers. Meat for the plantation came from the estimated two hundred hogs who lived in the nearby swamp. The 135 slaves included 67 who worked in the fields on a regular basis, although some of them were nursing mothers counted as half-hands because they left the field four times a day to feed their children. In addition, there was a team of specialists that made the plantation largely self-sufficient: "3 mechanics (blacksmith, carpenter and wheelwright), 2 seamstresses, 1 cook, 1 stable servant, 1 cattle-tender, 1 hog-tender, 1 teamster, 1 house servant (overseer's cook), and one midwife and nurse." The field hands worked from sunup until sundown, about sixteen hours in the summer, with only a brief rest for the midday meal, although they were sometimes allowed to stop at 8:00 in the morning on Saturday and they never worked on Sundays. Olmsted rode through fields where women hoed cotton without looking up lest they draw the attention of the driver who used his whip frequently, "sometimes allowing the lash to fall lightly upon their shoulders." A child carrying a calabash served water to the workers. The regular food allowance of each worker was a half a bushel of corn per week and four pounds of pork a week, supplemented by eggs from chickens raised by the slaves and vegetables from their gardens. At Christmas, each family got a barrel of molasses as well as tobacco, coffee, and calico cloth; and during the year some of them were able to buy other things with money made by selling lumber cut in the swamp on Saturdays and Sundays. Despite what the overseer believed was the generous treatment that the workforce received on this plantation, slaves did attempt to escape. "He had no runaways out at this time," but not long ago he was whipping a man who turned around, tried to stab him, and then fled. He had dogs, however, "trained on purpose to run after niggers, and never let out for anything else" and they soon caught the fugitive, who was later sold to someone going to Texas. The dogs made escape difficult, but not impossible, in part because they could not pick up a scent after it rained. Runaways usually remained in the neighborhood, however, to be close to families, and were eventually caught. He had never had anyone gone for more than a few months.[23]

Dogs were an important part of slave control throughout the South. Joseph, Olmsted's source of information on the Dismal Swamp, told him that a variety of breeds were used, among them bloodhounds, foxhounds, and bulldogs, and sometimes mongrels as well. They were kept away from black people as puppies and then taught to chase a running man by being rewarded with meat when the quarry climbed a tree. Later they were trained to follow the scent from an article of clothing. In the North Carolina *Fayetteville Observer*, the journalist read an article about a "pack of ten hounds, trained for hunting runaways" that had been auctioned off for a total sum of $1,540, the most expensive canine going for $301 and the lowest for $75. Always interested in the economic cost of slave ownership, Olmsted noted that "a man who would pay these prices must anticipate frequent occasion to use his purchase." Olmsted heard more about professional slave catchers in northern Alabama. There they used not only specially trained dogs but also horses trained to leap fences when in hot pursuit. These men were paid $10 to $20 a day and up to $200 for prolonged hunts. If the slaveholder refused to pay, they let the slave go free rather than put him in jail where the owner could get him back for a small fee. The dogs they used were mixed breeds, often partly Spanish bloodhound, and they were trained as puppies to chase blacks. Olmsted's source said he had heard that "old, keen ones kept chained until needed led the packs and could follow a trail several days old unless it had rained."[24]

By the time he came back from Texas, the hunting of runaway slaves was familiar to Olmsted. One night, camping out near Jackson, Mississippi, he was awakened by sounds coming from a nearby swamp where, as he put it, "a pack of hounds [were] rushing by in full panic pursuit," but as the sound died down, "we saw nothing of deer, or fox, or nigger, hounds, or huntsmen." He had with him a bull terrier named Judy acquired in Texas, who was aggressive enough to intimidate wild boars. Farmers he met in northern Alabama believed that Jude, as Olmsted called her, had great potential as what they called "a Nigger dog." One of them who owned slaves wanted to keep the dog on the promise that he would breed him and send Olmsted some of the puppies. Another man used Jude to teach a lesson to a group of black children. Throwing the animal a piece of bread, which was quickly eaten, the man told the child that Jude "could just snap a nigger's head off, if one was to run off," the same way that a human would cut off a chicken's head with an axe.[25]

Instilling fear was often a part of the capture itself. According to one man, professionals usually called off the dogs when the animals caught up with their prey, unless the runaway offered resistance, in which case "they'll let 'em tear him a spell," partly as a lesson to the other slaves. A Methodist minister told a story about a runaway who was discovered hiding high up in a tall cottonwood tree, nearly out of sight. When the hunter shouted for the slave to climb down, there was no answer, so the white man took an axe and began to cut the tree. When the job was about half done, the fugitive said he would come down if the hunter promised that he would keep the dogs away. The request was denied because the slave had made the capture difficult, and the chopping continued. When the tree was about to fall, the fugitive jumped to the ground, and the dogs attacked him. "He fought them hard and got a hold of one by the ear; that made them fiercer, and they tore at him until the hunter was afraid they'd kill him and stopped them."[26]

Olmsted could defend the use of force to maintain discipline among an unpaid and what he considered an uncivilized workforce, but the callous disregard for the lives of African Americans bothered him. "What we call the sacredness of human life, together with a great range of kindred instincts, scarcely attaches at all, with most white men, to the slaves." He came to believe they only regretted the death of a runaway because of its economic consequences. One case in point came from a conversation he had on a steamboat going from Mobile to New Orleans with a young man whose escaped slave had died. The owner was migrating to Texas from Alabama and had taken an adult male with him to sell along the way or on arrival. The two rode a steamboat from Montgomery to Mobile, but the slave got away there and hid on another steamboat going back up the river. Learning what had happened, the owner sent telegraph messages to the captain of the boat, who found the runaway but then failed to take care of him: "They just put him in irons; likely enough he didn't get much to eat, or have anything to cover himself, and he took cold, and got sick—got pneumonia." After enduring similar conditions in the Montgomery jail, he died. His master lamented only one aspect of what had happened: "Twas a dead loss of eight hundred dollars, right out of picket." Near Jackson, Mississippi, Fred overheard a man talking familiarly with several slaves in a hotel. The fellow described himself as soft-hearted, using as evidence the fact that while some people "were mighty quick to shoot a nigger," and that while he always carried pistols with him, he had never shot any of his enslaved people and did not think he ever would "long as they behaved themselves." Another person near Natchez discussed the civic responsibility of whites with respect to runaways by giving the example of a man who caught a runaway but did not put him in jail because there was "a fever raging there." The slave escaped but was re-caught, yet the owner was angry that the fugitive had not been lodged with the sick inmates, saying that it was the captor's duty to put a captured runaway in jail regardless of the circumstances and "leave the rest to Providence."[27]

Olmsted also wrote about an aspect of slave control that southerners seemed to take for granted, the active role played by the white population, including those who owned no bondspeople. Slave codes gave slave owners nearly unlimited power over their human property and the masters used it to restrict their activity while at home or away, and the loosely organized, mounted slave patrols that policed the rural South at night enforced the web of control with on-the-spot punishments, but Olmsted believed it was ordinary citizens who made the system work. "The security of the whites is in much less degree dependent on the action of the patrols than on the constant, habitual, and instinctive surveillance and authority of all white people over all black." He had seen "a gentleman, with no commission or special authority oblige negroes to show their passports [permission slips written by their owners, generally known as passes], simply because he did not recognize them as belonging to any of his neighbors." On another occasion, the journalist witnessed a twelve-year-old girl stop an elderly black man on the road, "demand to know where he was going and by what authority," and make him turn back when she did not like the answer, enforcing the order with a threat to have him whipped. She probably could have done it since the authority of white people over the enslaved had few limits beyond the rights of their owners. Olmsted quoted a Knoxville, Tennessee, paper that defended the burning of a black man in part because it was not done by a mob but rather "one thousand citizens," who were "cool, calm, and deliberate."[28]

Olmsted seldom thought about why the enslaved people of the South took unauthorized leave, and when he did, it was the owners that he was concerned about not the workers. "The interruption and disarrangement of operations of labor, occasioned by slaves 'running away,' frequently causes great inconvenience and loss to those who employ them." The most common explanations for flight were the desire to get out of work, avoid punishment, or protest ill treatment. Also "it is said to often occur when no immediate motive can be guessed for it—when the slave has been well-treated, well fed, and not overworked; and when he will be sure to suffer hardship for it, and be sure to suffer severe punishment for it on his return." The journalist thought that in these latter cases the cause was probably "the natural instinct of freedom in a man," a noble-sounding sentiment that he promptly discounted by claiming that it was also common to "domesticated beasts and birds."

Olmsted also cited, perhaps only half-seriously, Dr. Samuel Cartwright, a widely respected southern physician on the faculty of the University of Louisiana, who believed that escape and flight were the symptoms of a disease peculiar to the African race that he named drapetomania, which could be cured either by improving the living and working conditions of slaves or by whipping them. Cartwright also claimed that absenteeism and many other labor problems of southern slave owners was caused by another disease he called Disaesthesia Ethiopia or, in layman's terms, "Obtuse Sensibility of the Body, the symptoms of which are generally described as 'rascality.'" It causes them to "break, waste, and destroy everything they handle—abuse horses and cattle, burn or rend their own clothing, and steal others to replace what they have destroyed. They wander about at night and keep in a half nodding state by day. They slight their work—cut up corn, cane, cotton, and tobacco when hoeing it, as if for pure mischief." All these activities, historians have come to call not "rascality" but "day to day resistance to slavery." A third disease identified by Cartwright was Nostalgia, "the yearning for Home." Neither he nor Olmsted thought of it as a cause of the escape and flight of enslaved people, but, as we shall see, it was a very important factor.[29]

Olmsted never referred to the Underground Railroad by name and had little to say about fugitives who attempted to escape to the North. There is no reason to believe he had an aversion to these topics, rather the omission reflects the fact that he spent little time in Maryland, Virginia, and Kentucky, the southern border states from which most flights to the North originated, particularly those by land. On his way back from Texas, however, the journalist met a man somewhere between Woodville and Natchez who was thinking about moving to that state but worried that "negro property isn't very secure there." If slaves were not contented, "the road would always be open to Mexico." But then he opined that if runaways did reach Mexico, they would come back because their lives as free persons would be so much worse than they had been as slaves. The man did not wait for Olmsted to respond, which was his loss, because Fred had just learned a lot on that subject.[30]

The horseback tour of Texas was a family outing designed to improve John Olmsted's health rather than provide information on the South, but it turned out to accomplish nothing for the former and a great deal for the latter. The introduction to *A Journey Through Texas* claimed that "the notes on slavery in the volume are incidental," but nonetheless there were a lot of them. In Natchitoches, Louisiana, before crossing into the Lone Star State, the brothers amused themselves by reading the "queer advertisements of runaway negroes in French in the local newspaper." African American fugitives were part of the dangers the Olmsted brothers lightheartedly associated with sleeping around campfires: "who knows what wild-cat, wolf, or vagabond nigger may be watching to spring upon you if you go further from the light?"[31]

Early in January 1854, they heard stories about runaways while wait-ing out one of the winter storms known as "northers" in a hotel in the small east Texas town of Caldwell. One fellow refugee from the weather told about a man he had known in Georgia who had a special method for dealing with runaways: "he would bind his knee over a log, and fasten him so he couldn't stir; then he'd take a pair of pincers and pull one of his toe-nails out by the roots." This was accompanied by a threat to pull out two toenails if the victim was caught a second time and four if there were a third incident. According to the storyteller, the owner never had to do it more than twice on any one slave. One fellow in the group was chasing a fugitive of his own. He had bought this "first rate nigger" in Mississippi for a very low price because he had run away on three occasions, but the enslaved man had always tried to get to Illinois, and the new owner felt that taking him to Texas would break that habit. Now he appeared to be on the way to Mexico, and the master had arranged to meet a slave catcher with dogs at this hotel, but it looked like the weather would keep him from coming. He asked everyone in the group to be on the lookout for the fugitive and warned them that he had taken a double-barreled shotgun with him. That brought up the question of whether he would use it to prevent capture, and the answer was affirmative: "He was as humble a nigger when he was at work as ever he had seen; but he was a right res-olute nigger—there was no man had more resolution." One of the party wondered if it might be possible to take the gun away by pretending that he wanted to look at it, but the owner thought the fugitive would not be tricked that easily. A discussion then ensued about the escapee's chances of making it all the way to Mexico. He would have to stop at night and might be given away by the fire if he attempted to cook game he had shot, but it was assumed that any black man or Mexican he met would help him out, and he could probably avoid being seen by any whites. Opinion was divided on whether it was worth continuing the chase.[32]

At the end of February near Indianola on Matagorda Bay, Fred and John ran into a small party of men hunting for a runaway who had escaped from someone called "the Judge." They told a tale worthy of the Wild West. The fugitive had been given a week off at Christmas and used it to make some money by hiring himself out. After that experience, he did not want to come back and became violent when threatened with a whipping if he didn't. He "cut the judge right bad. Like to have killed the judge. Cut his young master, too." The pursuers had been chasing the man for ten days and caught him once, but he kicked one of them while they were tying him up and got away when someone's pistol misfired. A desperate chase followed: "My dog got close to him once. If he'd grip'd him, we should have got him, but he had a dog himself, and just as my dog got within about a yard of him, his dog turned and fit [fought] my dog, and he hurt him so bad we couldn't get him to run him again. We run him close, though, I tell you. Run him out of his coat, and his boots, and a pistol he'd got. But 'twas getting towards dark, and he got into them bayous, and kept swimming from one side to nother." It seemed the fugitive might make it to Mexico where the chasers assumed he would soon realize how much better he had lived as an enslaved person in Texas than a free man in Mexico. Sometime later near the Rio Grande, the Olmsteds met several more slave hunters, these apparently looking for any fugitives who might be near the border. It was, they said, not a very profitable business: "It's more trouble to get the money, after you' jugged 'em, than it's worth."[33]

Early in April, the Olmsteds crossed the Rio Grande from Eagle Pass, Texas, to Piedras Negras, Mexico, and almost immediately Fred met two formerly enslaved men and had an extended conversation with one of them. He had been born in Virginia and brought south by a slave trader, sold there and taken to Texas, and escaped into Mexico about five years earlier. During that period, he had been treated well by the Mexican government, learned to speak fluent Spanish, joined the Catholic Church, and traveled throughout much of northern Mexico working as a personal servant and a mule driver. He would like to see Virginia again but was comfortable living where he was. He said many African American refugees had trouble adapting to life as free people living in a foreign country, but they were happy to be where they were. The government treated them well, the people were friendly, work was available, and while the wages were low, so was the cost of living. Olmsted's experiences over the next four or five days he was in Mexico and his conversations along the border seemed to validate these generalizations. Commenting to his readers on the conventional wisdom of whites in the southwest that runaways were miserable in Mexico, he gave a sarcastic response: "The escape from the wretchedness of freedom is certainly much easier to the negro in Mexico than has been his previous flight from slavery, yet I did not hear of a single case of his availing himself of this advantage."[34]

His experience on the Texas-Mexican border seems to have renewed the positive attitude toward victims of the Fugitive Slave Act that Fred had announced prior to his travels to the South. The *Journey Through Texas* contains a sympathetic statement about why enslaved people risked so much to escape. "The impulse must be a strong one, the tyranny extremely cruel, the irksomeness of slavery keenly irritating, or the longing for liberty much greater than is usually attributed to the African race, which induces a slave to attempt an escape to Mexico." The self-styled objective observer even set aside his racial prejudice and gave the risk-taking fugitive a significant tribute: "Brave negro! Say I. He faces all that is terrible to man for the chance of liberty, from hunger and thirst to every nasty form of four-footed and two-footed devil. I fear I should my-self suffer the last servile indignities before setting foot in such a net of concentrated torture."[35]

The apparent contradiction between Olmsted's praise for an enslaved person who sought to escape slavery altogether and his lack of sympathy for one who fled only for a few days can be explained by his value system. He believed in human freedom but also in hard work and efficiency. He instinctively took the side of escapees who sought to escape their bondage altogether but saw those who only wanted a few days off as shirkers who were bad for the system.

The focus of Frederick Law Olmsted's illustrious career began to change even as he was finishing up his work on the South. *A Journey in the Seaboard States* was published in January 1856, *A Journey Through Texas* in January 1857, the *Back Country* in 1860, and the *Cotton Kingdom* in 1861. Meanwhile, the author spent eight months in Europe, followed by several years as the editor of a literary magazine, and then in September 1857 he was chosen to manage the ongoing construction of the Central Park project in New York City, a job that would eventually involve the supervision of four thousand workers. In January 1858, he and the English-born architect Calvert Vaux began the design of a new plan for the park, which was accepted in April of that year, and Olmsted oversaw its implementation until June 1861. Determined to contribute to the winning of the Civil War, he then became general secretary of the Sanitary Commission, a privately funded agency that provided clothing, bedding, and other supplies for wounded soldiers, helped to transport them from the battlefields to hospitals, and encouraged the Union army to implement lifesaving sanitation practices that had been developed by the British during the Crimean War. When the war was over, he and Vaux formed a partnership to practice what they named "landscape architecture," designing Prospect Park in Brooklyn and then for the remainder of the nineteenth century similar projects in other major American cities.[36]

An echo of Olmsted's earlier experience in the South, unremarked upon as such by the man himself, came during the war in March 1863 when he was once again in the Lower Mississippi Valley, this time on a fact-finding mission for the Sanitary Commission while Ulysses S. Grant was preparing his final assault on Vicksburg. Landing at Lake Providence, Louisiana, Olmsted found two elderly black men sitting on cotton bales taken from a nearby plantation. Not surprisingly, the erstwhile journalist struck up a conversation with them. Their master had fled South, taking all the able-bodied slaves with him but leaving the superannuated ones. In addition, "deh was t[h]ree likely fellas, de did reckon wot was gwine to happen, and de did get off in the swamp and he doan git dem; not that time he doan."[37]

{ CHAPTER 2 }

Like Ants into a Pantry

IN *A JOURNEY THROUGH TEXAS*, Frederick Law Olmsted, or per-haps John Olmsted, who ghostwrote the book from his brother's notes, described the Mississippi River valley below the mouth of the Ohio River as "a great wilderness of unexplored fertility, into which a few men have crawled like ants into a pantry." The metaphor captures nicely the eco-nomic motivation and the avidity of the white men who wrested control of the region from the indigenous population, although the process was well past exploration and the region no longer a wilderness by the 1850s when the Olmsted brothers were there. The conquest of both the Native Americans and the environment had taken place in two quite separate stages, one in the colonial period of American history and the other in the antebellum years.[1]

During the 1720s a French toehold on the Gulf Coast expanded into a footprint along the Mississippi River from New Orleans to Natchez. France created a permanent population of Europeans and Africans, built the city of New Orleans, constructed a series of levees that allowed some control over the riverine environment, and learned to cultivate rice as a mainstay of their diet. Spain took over Louisiana after the French and Indian War and over the next four decades increased and diversified the population, midwifed the birth of an agricultural economy that remained largely unchanged down to the Civil War, and bequeathed to America a city that was vital to the commercial development of a large section of the country and possessed of a multicultural society that would have a significant influence on American culture.

Not until after the War of 1812 did their purchase of Louisiana have much impact on the region, but during the 1820s the Americans expelled the Choctaw and Chickasaw Nations from the State of Mississippi and over the next four decades turned the delta region from Vicksburg to Memphis into the central province of the Cotton Kingdom that stretched south to Baton Rouge where the Sugar Bowl began. While the colonial powers had relied on a workforce the first generation of which was born in Africa, antebellum settlers brought enslaved workers with them and purchased thousands of black people provided by the internal slave trade that brought them into the valley from the eastern coast and the border states. Underlaying the rapid growth in population and agricultural production was steamboat transportation, which allowed people to move freely up and down the rivers of the valley, ship their commodities to eastern markets, and buy manufactured goods at reasonable prices.

Between 1717 and 1721 the French commercial enterprise known as the Company of the Indies shipped as many as 7,000 settlers to Louisiana, and by 1726 about 4,000 of them were still alive and living along the Mississippi River as far north as Natchez, with outposts near the mouth of the Arkansas River and at Natchitoches on the Red River. Over the next five years the company imported 3,500 enslaved Africans, many of whom also soon died. During the latter part of the 1730s, however, the population stabilized and then began to grow through natural increase, so that by the 1760s there were 11,000 colonists in Louisiana, more than half of them people of color and a high percentage of them Creoles born in the New World.[2]

Black labor was vital to the success of the colony, but so also was African know-how. The slaves came with hunting and fishing skills that the Europeans lacked, and they had raised livestock and cultivated a variety of crops. Their experience in growing rice helped the French to make it the staple carbohydrate of lower Louisiana. Many knew how to handle boats, an important skill where both people and products traveled mainly by water. Africans felled cypress trees and operated the water mills that turned giant logs into lumber. They dug, and probably helped to design, the levees and sluices that allowed crops to be grown along the banks of the Mississippi and the bayous of the Atchafalaya Basin. By law the enslaved had Sundays off, and they used them to raise vegetables, chickens, and hogs for themselves and to sell in New Orleans. Urban blacks did domestic labor but also played important roles in the commercial life of the city. Masters who had no immediate need for their slaves made money by renting them out, usually allowing them to keep some of their wages.[3]

European pathogens introduced by the Hernando de Soto expedition and later European explorers and traders had greatly reduced the native population of the Lower Mississippi Valley, but there were still some 70,000 Indians living there in 1700. Corn, beans, venison, fish, and bear grease provided by the Indians were vital to the survival of the early French settlers and continued to be important parts of their diet long after the Europeans had learned to grow food of their own. Deerskins were a major export of Louisiana into the 1750s. The native Atakapas and Opelousas who lived in the western part of the colony smuggled horses and cattle into French Louisiana from Spanish Texas, and they became the basis for a lively herding industry. Symbiosis had its limits, however: warfare was not uncommon, and along with disease, alcohol, and a growing dependence on European technology it allowed the French to dominate the small tribes in the region, even as they traded with them. The powerful Natchez on the site of the eponymous modern city rebelled against French encroachments on their land, killing more than two hundred colonists and capturing their three hundred slaves during a surprise attack in November 1729, a disaster for the French that made Point Coupee the northern limit of their large-scale settlement. The Choctaw in southern Mississippi and the Chickasaw who lived north of them were large enough to be independent actors in the imperial struggles of the eighteenth century. War and disease weakened both tribes down to about 1750, but they made a gradual demographic comeback after that.[4]

French Louisiana was a difficult place to live for both its white and black inhabitants, and the settlers got little help from the mother country, which took control from the bankrupt Mississippi Company in 1731, but the colonists, both the French and the Africans who survived the early years were a tough people, and they created a viable society. Rice and fluvial engineering were perhaps their two most important contributions to later generations. By the time Spain received Louisiana in the 1760s, the banks of the Mississippi River were settled with farms and plantations from a few miles below New Orleans up to Baton Rouge, the land along them was divided in "long lots" that ranged from 28 yards up to 512 yards wide at the riverfront and extended up to several miles back into the swamps. They were protected by levees, usually three feet high, that were used for both flood control and irrigation. Indigo was a lucrative but capital-intensive export crop grown on irrigated land, tobacco was produced on higher ground and exported, but the sale of lumber brought the most money into the colony. New Orleans was the commercial center of the colony, and its merchants played an active role in the Atlantic economy.[5]

The French government valued Louisiana mostly because the Mississippi River was a gateway to Canada and was not upset about losing it at the end of the Seven Years' War. Nor was Spain excited about getting it, Madrid being mainly interested in using the place as a barrier between the rapidly expanding Anglo-American society in the east and their own colony of New Spain in the west. The Spanish government, however, did much to develop Louisiana. Recognizing the need to increase the population and aware that almost no one in Spain wanted to go there, they encouraged the immigration of non-Anglophones from elsewhere. Colonial governors provided land and financial aid for some 2,500 French refugees expelled from Acadia by Great Britain. The first wave of Cajuns arrived in the 1760s and settled on the Mississippi River in the Baton Rouge area, and later groups built small farms along La Fourche Bayou west of there. Between 1779 and 1785 an equal number of Spanish-speaking immigrants from the economically depressed Canary Islands arrived. Spain also reopened the foreign slave trade that the French had closed in the 1730s, and Louisiana planters responded with enthusiasm, buying more than 12,000 black people between 1763 and 1796. Most of these were born in Africa, although they arrived from the West Indies, and a high percentage appear to have been ethnically Kongo. The already cosmopolitan culture of Louisiana became more so in the 1790s when the slave rebellion in Saint-Domingue forced large numbers of whites and free blacks to flee, taking their enslaved workers with them when they could. Some 5,000 people came to Louisiana, divided equally among the three groups. In 1800, there were an estimated 45,000 people living in the colony, 55 percent of them enslaved. New Orleans contained about 8,000 people in 1803, about half of whom were African Americans, about half of them free people and half of them enslaved.[6]

The economic activity that brought great riches to the Lower Mississippi Valley in the antebellum period began to develop in Spanish Louisiana during the 1790s, and Americans played an important role in its development. US citizens who moved into the Natchez region grew upland cotton and removed its seeds with Eli Whitney's gin, and French planters who had lost the market for their tobacco began to do the same thing. During the same period, owners of the large plantations from Baton Rouge south began shifting into the sugar industry, responding to a new market opportunity created by the social upheaval in Saint-Dominique that devastated production there, and led by planters who had immigrated to Louisiana bringing with them black and white experts in the complex technology of that industry. The production of sugar in Louisiana would always be limited by a growing season that was shorter than in the West Indies, but by the Louisiana Purchase in 1803 about seventy-five plantations had a total output of five million pounds. Meanwhile the export of these commodities along with the constantly increasing number of flatboats that arrived daily filled with produce from the Ohio Valley continued to expand the commerce and population of New Orleans.[7]

Under the French the institution of slavery in Louisiana was governed by the *Code Noir* introduced in 1724, which treated enslaved people both as subjects of the Crown entitled to its protection and as a dangerous form of property. Masters were encouraged to "govern the said slaves as a good father of the family," and they were required to have them baptized and instructed in Catholicism and allowed to marry, provided that the owner approved of the prospective spouse. Married husbands and wives were not to be sold separately, and their children under the age of fourteen were not to be sold without their parents. Slaves had Sundays and church holidays off. Masters had to provide specific amounts and types of both food and clothing. They could manumit slaves if they wished, and free black people were supposed to have substantially the same rights as white citizens. Owners were forbidden to torture their bondspeople or maim them, and for corporal punishment allowed only "to have them chained and flogged with sticks or cords." Slaves also had a recourse against ill treatment: those that were not "fed, clothed and maintained" or subjected to "barbarous and inhuman treatment" could complain to the government, and their masters were subject to prosecution.

The paternalism expected from the owner, however, was more than balanced by the degree of control and the severity of punishment that the state reserved for itself, a legacy of the French experience in the West Indies. Slaves were not permitted to carry weapons, even large sticks, except if hunting and with the written permission of their masters. Those belonging to different masters were not to assemble for any reason and could be whipped, branded, or even put to death for doing so. Owners who allowed such gatherings to take place could be fined. Slaves were not to buy or sell goods, engage in business activity, even on behalf of their master, or own any property. A slave who stole livestock, produce, or various other commodities was subject to corporal punishment that could include branding with the *fleur-de-lis*. One who struck his master or a member of his or her family hard enough to cause a bruise or bleeding was to be executed, and violence against any free person might incur the same penalty.

Despite the provisions of the *Code Noir,* the treatment of slaves depended as much on circumstance and custom as it did on law. During the 1720s and 1730s as the French colonists struggled to create permanent settlements in lower Louisiana, the little evidence available suggests that they worked their slaves as hard as they could and punished them however they wished, but also allowed them any freedom that was consistent with economic progress. One of the most significant privileges was the opportunity to make money, which ignored the specific prohibition of that in the *Code Noir*. Enslaved people cultivated small plots of land, raised poultry and hogs, and could sell their produce if they wished. This had long been the practice in the West Indies, mainly because it relieved slave owners from some of the burden of feeding and clothing their workforce. Slaves could also hire themselves out to work on Sundays.[8]

In the 1740s when France halted the importation of African slaves, Louisiana masters realized that a more benevolent attitude toward their enslaved workers might be necessary to encourage a natural increase in their numbers. The frontier environment also gave leverage to the slaves, some of whom were armed and used along with friendly Indians in the militia forces that fought against the hostile Natchez and Chickasaw. Aware of their own importance, the blacks took advantage of the situation to expand activities that were clearly at odds with the code. In 1752, a French governor issued police regulations designed to control a situation that he felt was getting out of hand—the first of many such attempts that would continue for more than a century, all of them dealing with similar or related problems and none of them very effective. Slaves were traveling away from home without passes, selling goods without written permission, assembling for all sorts of purposes, sometimes with the approval of their owners, buying liquor and drinking in taverns, and acting in a manner toward whites that the governor deemed disrespectful, all these behaviors being particularly evident in and around New Orleans.[9]

In 1769, the Spanish colonial governor Alejandro O'Reilly replaced the *Code Noir* with the legal system that governed slavery in Spanish colonies, which, briefly put, placed more emphasis on the humanity of the enslaved than did the French one. The most important part of this for the history of Louisiana was the concept of *coartación*, which gave enslaved people the right to purchase their own freedom or have third parties do it for them. Coupled with improved economic conditions over the next three decades and local customs that allowed slaves to earn money in various ways, *coartición* altered the nature of society in New Orleans, where free people of color were 3 percent of the population in 1771 and 19 percent in 1805. In the latter year, one out of every three black people in the city was free.[10]

Louisiana slavery also lacked the intense racial quality of the English colonies. The *Code Noir* prohibited interracial marriages and forbade white men from keeping black concubines, but the former provision was sometimes ignored, and the latter appears to have had little effect. An analysis of public documents for Point Coupee Parish done by historian Gwendolyn Midlo Hall indicates that mixed-race sexual relations were common and that many female Indian, African, and Creole slaves were freed by their white lovers who also manumitted many of their mulatto children. Gradually a free black population appeared in the countryside.[11]

Despite alterations in the law, the practice of slavery seems to have changed very little when the source of its authority moved from Paris to Madrid. Still French slave owners, particularly the larger planters, believed that Spanish officials were being too lenient with the enslaved population. In 1777 members of the Cabildo, the New Orleans city council, drew up a new code that would have moved Louisiana back toward the more severe French model had the colonial governor not refused to go along. Not until the American takeover were Louisiana's Creole elite able to free themselves from what they saw as onerous restrictions on their ability to control the people they owned.[12]

French slaves often fled from their owners and seem to have been more successful than those in the English colonies. The long lots of the French that extended back from the rivers rather than along them meant that most plantations were bordered in the back by swamps, which rural fugitives could easily flee into and remain hidden close to a place where they could steal food or have it given them by family members and friends. Low-lying New Orleans was surrounded by swamps that provided the same opportunity to runaways. Many bondsmen were accustomed to hunting and sometimes having guns in their possession, and they found it relatively easy to live off the land, filled as it was with fish, fowl, and four-legged game. There was always a shortage of labor in Louisiana, and fugitives sometimes worked for employers who did not ask questions, something especially true in the lumber industry. Many escapees also ran to New Orleans where they could blend in with the large black population. City slaves and free blacks assisted runaways, often harboring them in their own living quarters. A few runaways fled up the Red River, attempting to reach sparsely settled northern New Spain. In the early years of the colony, Louisiana escapees took refuge with Indians, but as the tribes became more dependent on the colonial government, they returned the fugitives most of the time.[13]

The Gallic system for dealing with runaway slaves varied significantly from that in the English mainland colonies. Running away was not a crime in English law, and the American colonists treated it as a problem of labor management to be dealt with by the owners of slaves, actively assisted by the public once the fugitive was off their master's property. Local governments in this system were empowered to set up patrols, but they were made up of citizens rather than full-time law enforcement officials and were designed to serve the public more than the state.[14]

The French referred to runaway slaves as maroons, a word related to the Spanish *cimarrón* meaning wild. They called the activity itself *marronage* and distinguished between *petite marronage*, running away for a short time and for limited purposes, and *grand marronage,* attempts to achieve long-term or permanent freedom. Slave owners themselves usually dealt with the petite version, and the *Code Noir* gave them the privilege of searching for their missing property anywhere they wanted and using any means that they deemed appropriate. The prohibition on excessive punishment applied in this case, however, as it did in all other matters of discipline. Both whites and free blacks who sheltered runaways were subject to heavy fines and the latter could be re-enslaved. The government was also expected to search for, capture, and punish runaway slaves, a power that was used mainly for grand marronage. An escapee who was still missing a month after being reported (*dénoncé*) was subject to severe punishment: the first time having their ears cut off and being branded with the *fleur-de-lis* on one arm, the second having a hamstring cut and being branded on the other arm, and a third resulting in execution. In this, as in other situations where the government inflicted corpo-

42

ral punishment, owners were compensated if the victim was maimed or executed. The public was assigned very little role in dealing with runaway slaves they did not own. The New Orleans proclamation of 1753 did call upon white persons to stop any "Negro or slave" out on the streets of the city or public roads and to "inquire for his written pass." It warned, however, that citizens must not harm anyone they challenged: "The negro is subject only to the police regulations of the country and to the tribunal of his own master."[15]

The influence of the *Code Noir* was limited, especially provisions that restricted the power of slave owners, but it did have some effect. Some masters asked the government to capture their runaways. In 1739, Dame Francoise Ruellan reported that her servant Titus had run away "without cause," something that he had done several times before, and she wanted him "apprehended and punished as the ordinance directs." She may have said "without cause" since mistreatment was prohibited under the *Code Noir* and was often used by runaways to excuse their escapes. In 1747 Jacques Judice wanted help getting back Manuel, who had run away, been caught and chained to a wooden block in his cabin, and then ran away again, carrying the block with him.[16]

Pierre Garçon was clearly concerned that the government would take the *Code Noir* seriously when he made a public declaration that he had his slave Jeanneton imprisoned not only because she had run away for eight days but also because she threatened to say that she was pregnant with his children, a charge that could have resulted in her being taken away from him and one that he denied. Similarly, Bayou, who was captured at Point Coupee in 1748, probably had the *Code Noir* in mind when he said he fled from his masters in the Illinois Country because the man "made him work every day, even Sundays and feast days, gave him no food nor clothes, nor even the time to sleep during the night, and ill-treated him for nothing." The ploy, if that was what it was, may have worked because his only punishment seems to have been being sent back to the owner.[17]

Fugitives who lived in the wild sometimes ate beef even though stealing cattle was a capital offense under the *Code Noir*. In 1748 Jean Deslandes found one of his cows coming out of the woods with a rope around her neck and assumed that a runaway had tried to steal her, and several weeks later he discovered a group of fugitives armed with guns and hatchets at the back of his plantation smoking meat over a fire.

Deslandes put together a force made up of one Indian and ten of his slaves and dispersed them, wounding one in the process. Runaways were aware that it was better to be found guilty of stealing chickens rather than large animals. Francoise, captured in 1836, said he ran away from his master because he was going to be sold, but that he stayed at the back of the plantation living on food taken from slave cabins during the day and milk he got from cows out in the pasture, making a point of saying he had never stolen any bovines. Bobo, who was found near New Orleans in 1772, said he had been free for well over a year, most of which was spent in the woods and swamps where he hunted with a stolen gun, took provisions from area plantations, and sometimes slept in the cabins of friendly enslaved people. Jacob, who was with him, had been out six months. Both men denied stealing cattle.[18]

Francois Livet, a planter living on the river above New Orleans, reported his slave Pierrot to the Superior Council in 1736 after the man had been gone for nine months. Pierrot had just been captured and tied up by Raphael, a slave on a nearby plantation, whom he then talked into loosening the ropes so that he was able to escape. Now he was again in the woods and living on food stolen from Livet's plantation. Livet may have had a shaky title to Pierrot, however, because three days after he made his declaration a Monsieur Pierre wanted it recorded that he had also owned a slave named Pierrot who had run away four years earlier. If the two masters were looking for the same runaway, it should have been easy to determine whose property he was, since Pierre's Pierrot had Pierre's initials branded on his breast, probably from an earlier attempt to escape.[19]

Another seasoned runaway was the mixed-race Pierre Delapie, who fled from his owner in the summer of 1773 and not long after was hired by another planter who lived not far away. Not happy with that situation, Delapie talked three slaves into leaving with him, one of them a man named Vulcain who was hamstrung, probably because he had marooned twice before. The group, that also included two women, traveled in stolen boats to New Orleans and managed to sail to Cuba, where they probably met a dozen or so other successful fugitives from Louisiana.[20]

For the most part, public officials avoided the maiming or executing of runaways that would have lessened or ended their value, but in the 1760s, at the very end of French control over the colony, a zealous attorney general decided to make an example of twenty runaways being held in custody, each of whom had fled alone and been reported by their masters. At least eighteen suffered grievous bodily punishment—one was strangled to death, another was broken on the wheel (tied across the spokes and beaten until each bone in his body was fractured multiple times), two were hanged, five were flogged and branded, two were either flogged, branded, or hamstrung, and seven had both ears cut off and were branded. Spanish administrators may have been less harsh, but it is hard to know. In 1771 a group of five maroons were captured at Natchitoches, all of them originally from New Orleans and left at different times. Mariana gave most of the recorded testimony. She had left the city eight months earlier with another woman, a man, and a child. At Natchitoches, she met Louis, who had escaped several years earlier, and began to live at a maroon camp where they were joined by other runaways who left New Orleans after her. After their capture, all the maroons were taken back to the capital city where Mariana and four others were each given two hundred lashes. Louis had a long record of escapes and was sentenced to "the full rigor of the law . . . according to the custom of the country," probably a reference to the lingering effect of the *Code Noir*, which meant he would be executed.[21]

Running away and especially grand marronage became more common after Spain reopened the slave trade in the 1760s and African-born blacks flooded into Louisiana. In 1770 wealthy planters serving on the Cabildo proposed that a small unit of special policemen to be known as *cuadrilleros* be created for the sole purpose of chasing down runaway slaves, and that they be paid from the proceeds of a tax imposed on slave owners. Other than that, the system was based on the provisions of the *Code Noir*. Owners were to report runaways, who would then have thirty days to return without penalty; those caught after that would receive corporal punishment increasing in severity with repeated offenses—from ear cropping to ham-stringing to execution. The program was not accepted at that time, but three years later, at the urging of planters in the New Orleans area, the council tried again, this time in concert with Governor Luis de Unzaga y Amezaga, and a comprehensive plan was agreed upon at a meeting of the council, the governor, and some of the most prominent plantation owners held on August 25, 1773. All slaveholders were to be assessed based on the number of slaves they owned as determined by an annual census and the resulting fund used to pay for the capture of runaways and to reimburse owners whose slaves were wounded or killed in the process. Masters had to report runaways within five days of the escape, and the government was to publish the names of all known fugitives. Individuals who brought in runaways on the list were to be paid a graduated reward that increased the farther from New Orleans that the capture took place. Unzaga sent a copy of the plan to Madrid, but the Cabildo put the plan in effect immediately and created a small force of *caudrilleros* made up of free blacks, a group that those at the meeting had suggested would be the most effective slave catchers. Four years later the Crown formally approved the idea of slaveholders paying for the government to capture runaway slaves but required that the payments be voluntary rather than coerced through taxation, which led to a funding problem that was never solved. Nonetheless, the state-sponsored efforts to capture runaways continued even though finding the money to support the program was always a problem.[22]

Fugitivism again increased in the 1780s following the importation of African-born slaves. Runaways led by a man named St. Malo created a small settlement in a nearly inaccessible place in the Bas de Flueve region between New Orleans and the mouth of the Mississippi. The fugitives lived in symbiosis with the local plantation slaves, who sometimes chased cattle into the swamps where the maroons slaughtered them, and the two groups ate together. What the law viewed as an outlaw population numbered in the hundreds although far fewer were in the settlement at any one time. Most of them were Creoles, although African-born slaves were also involved, and at least a third of the entire group were women. The Miró government sent several expeditions against the rebels in 1783 that eventually destroyed the settlement and captured or killed more than one hundred maroons. On June 19, St. Milo was hanged along with three of his lieutenants in the Place d'Armes while a large portion of the New Orleans population watched. He immediately became a martyred hero to the African American population and is remembered as such today.[23]

Potentially more dangerous was an intended uprising at Point Coupee organized in the spring of 1795 that was influenced by the ideology of the French Revolution and the slave insurrection in Saint Dominique that had begun in 1791 and was later led by Toussaint L'Overture. A more immediate cause was the abolition of slavery by the French National Assembly in 1794, which led to the false belief among New World slaves that France had forced Spain to do the same thing and Louisiana planters were refusing to comply. Enslaved immigrants from Saint-Dominique doubtless played a role in raising the consciousness of Louisiana Creoles about these developments. A Belgian schoolteacher named Joseph Bouyavel and an American tailor named George Rosenberg, both antislavery partisans, are known to have been involved in this activity. Slave leaders included two *commanders* on the estate of Julien Poydras, Jean Baptiste and Antoine Sarrasin. The conspiracy was found, the conspirators were tried, and fifty-seven slaves and three whites were found guilty. Twenty-three of the rebels were executed and their heads displayed on posts along the Mississippi River between Point Coupee and New Orleans. The rest were whipped and sent out of the colony. Two of the white agitators were sentenced to forced labor in Cuba, and one was deported.[24]

The uprising of slaves that took place in Louisiana in 1811, eight years after the Louisiana Purchase, is correctly referred to as the largest American slave revolt, but it is better understood as the last slave revolt of colonial Louisiana, influenced almost certainly by the arrival between 1803 and 1809 of more than seven thousand slaves from the West Indies who were well aware that the enslaved people of Haiti had won the fight against their French masters. It took place on the German Coast above New Orleans, which by that time was dominated by Creole French grandees and a few American early arrivals, all of whom owned large plantations on which advanced machinery and factory-like labor organization were producing large amounts of sugar and selling at prices made possible by an American tariff on the commodity.

The revolt began on January 8, on the plantation of Manuel Andry, who owned eighty slaves, one of them a man named Charles who was the leader of the rebels. They stormed Andry's house in the middle of the night and killed his son, but the owner fought through a group of assailants and escaped across the river, where he immediately began rallying a force of planters, lower-status whites, and a few free blacks. Meanwhile, the rebels moved south toward New Orleans, killing one more planter along the way and gaining supporters who brought their total numbers to two hundred or three hundred men. News of this traveled rapidly, and planters living near New Orleans swarmed into the city, where Governor William C. C. Claiborne quickly blocked the Bayou Bridge by which the rebels might have entered the city. He also sent American general Wade Hampton with a small force of soldiers, sailors, and militiamen north to meet the threat. An artillery unit that was north of Andry's plantation on its way to Baton Rouge also turned around to box in the slaves. Wednesday night Hampton arrived at a plantation in St. Bernard Parish where the insurgents had stopped, but he delayed attacking until the following morning by which time they had retreated a few miles back up the river to a plantation owned by Bernard Bernoudy. While the slaves were moving into a defensive position, they were attacked by the men organized by Andry, a well-armed group of about eighty men, who had crossed the river. The ensuing fight was a bloody rout; not only were the slaves surprised by the sudden appearance of the whites, but also only about fifteen of them were armed with firearms, the rest carrying a variety of agricultural tools. By the end of a ten-day mop-up operation, 115 rebels were dead, captured, or missing. Almost all the captives were executed (often after being dismembered) and their heads put on poles along the river as a warning to the remaining slave population.

Manuel Andry later described the rebel slaves as "a horde of brig-ands," but he also noted that they began the fight with "colors displayed and full of arrogance." The first comment suggests they were outlaws, as their masters preferred to see them, but the second makes them sound like revolutionaries. Unfortunately, the contradiction is not easy to resolve since the evidence from post-battle interrogations is strangely silent on the question of motivation, and the white population seems to have pre-ferred thinking about the incident within the context of grand marronage rather than Haitian-style revolution.[25]

In 1806 Louisiana Territory adopted a Black Code that included elements of its colonial past. Many of the paternal provisions in *Code Noir* that were retained or expanded by the Spanish government were incorporated in the set of laws, making it distinctly different from those in all other southern states. All slaves except for personal servants and those associated with household management were guaranteed "the free enjoyment of Sundays" and were to be paid 50 cents if they did work, either for their owners or for others. Field hands were to have thirty min-utes for breakfast and two hours for a midday meal. They were guaranteed gardens for their personal use, or if those were not available to be com-pensated with extra clothing. Children under ten years of age could not be sold away from their mothers. Masters were also required to provide for sick workers and elderly ones.

A major change altered the system for dealing with runaway slaves to make it congruent in most respects with Anglo-American practice. No longer did the government have any direct responsibility for capturing fugitives, although justices of the peace could organize a posse to "disperse" groups of runaways, search for weapons and stolen goods, and arrest any involved in criminal activity. Owners were free to pursue and search for their missing runaways anywhere except in the private homes of white people, the exception a change from the past no doubt made to conform to the Fourth Amendment of the American Constitution. There was a clear expectation that the public responsibility for capturing runaways would be taken over by citizen volunteers. Individuals who captured fugitives belonging to other people could take them to a county jail where they would be paid $3 if the runaway was taken "on the highways" and $10 if caught "in the woods." The law specifically said that the money could be paid to slaves who captured other slaves, something not done in other parts of the South and that probably reflected the Louisiana past in which slave owners had used their bondsmen for slave hunting and militia duties. The captured runaways were to be put to hard labor and kept for up to two years. If not retrieved by their masters during that period, they were to be sold at public auction.[26]

Another way in which the colonial past lingered into the antebellum future of Louisiana was the legal principle known as redhibition, which was based on Spanish civil law that was itself derived from Roman antecedents. Redhibition was defined in the civil code of Louisiana as "the avoidance of sale because of a vice or defect in the thing sold" serious enough to make it "either absolutely useless, or its use so inconvenient" that the buyer would not have bought it if he had known of the problem. "Apparent defects," those that were easy to see, were not covered, nor were "latent defects" if the seller warned the buyer about them prior to the sale. The code gave no further guidance about what would make an inanimate object defective, but with both livestock and slaves it was more specific. Latent defects included "vices of body" and "vices of character." Vices of body were further divided into "absolute" and "relative." The mere presence of absolute vices was a basis for negating the sale. The absolute vices of body in horses and mules were "short wind," "glanders [an infectious disease]," and "founder [an inflammation of the foot]." For slaves they were leprosy, "madness," and epilepsy. In both cases, relative vices of body included any illness or physical defect serious enough to have prevented the sale had the buyer been aware of them.

The latent "vices of character" category only applied to slaves and it included being "addicted to theft" or "in the habit of running away." A slave could be said to be in the habit of running away if he "had absented himself from his master's house twice in several days or once for more than a month." To get his money back on the sale, a buyer had to prove that the "habit" had shown up both before and after the sale. An exception to this rule was provided if a slave ran away three days after the purchase, which was considered prima facie evidence that he or she was a chronic escapee. The right of redhibition existed only for one year, after which the warranty was void. In 1834 the Louisiana legislature changed the law to give buyers more protection when they purchased slaves that were brought to Louisiana from other states. If a slave had not been a resident of Louisiana for eight months at the time of sale, the three-day period in which a single act of running away was a cause for return was extended to two months—unless the slave had been subjected to "unusual punishments" during that period.[27]

The United States took control of Louisiana, in this case all the land drained by rivers flowing east into the Mississippi River, in a ceremony at New Orleans on December 20, 1803. The western side of the Lower Mississippi Valley was now open for American settlement. On the eastern side, however, the region north of Natchez was still occupied by large numbers of Native Americans who had to be removed before white settlers could move in. That process had begun with the Treaty of Fort Adams in 1801 by which the Choctaw Nation ceded western Mississippi north to the Yazoo River and ended with the Indian Removal Act of 1830, which forced 14,000 Choctaws and 5,000 Chickasaws to leave their homelands in Mississippi and move across the Mississippi River, through Arkansas, and into what became Indian Territory and later Oklahoma.[28]

International diplomacy and domestic imperialism opened the Lower Mississippi Valley to Americans, but it was the steamboat that allowed them to exploit its potential in a rapid and thorough manner. Prior to 1815 commerce on the Ohio and the Mississippi Rivers moved in much the same way as it had five thousand years earlier on the rivers of the Middle East. That began to change in 1811 when the steamboat *New Orleans* made a successful journey from Pittsburgh to its namesake city. In 1818 there were thirty steamboats operating in the Lower Mississippi Valley. In 1850 there were more than seven hundred steamboats, and together they made more than three thousand arrivals at New Orleans.

After departing the Crescent City, they could be in Natchez in less than a day, Louisville in five days, and Cincinnati in eight days. The official tonnage (carrying capacity) of the boats varied from under one hundred tons to well over five hundred tons. One of the larger boats might carry 60 first-class passengers in the cabin on its second deck and 120 others on the main deck below, where they shared the open air with livestock and freight. Deck passage was uncomfortable but cheap. In 1850 an Ohio River farmer who had arrived in New Orleans on a flatboat with his marketable produce could ride back to Louisville for $3.00. Small steamboats traveled up the White and the Ouachita Rivers in Arkansas and the Yalobusha River that fed into the Yazoo in Mississippi. The shifting currents of the sinuous rivers, and fallen trees in the water, especially the vertical ones known as sawyers, made river transportation dangerous. It was made more dangerous by the seemingly foolish but undeniably exciting interest in racing on the part of both passengers and crews. Together these things led to one out of every hundred trips ending in a navigation accident, a fire, or the bursting of a boiler, and the loss of many lives by drowning or scalding. Federal regulation that began in 1853 included inspection of boilers and licensing of captains and pilots, and they dramatically improved the situation. A byproduct of all steamboat transportation was a significant deforesting of riverbanks. The average steamboat consumed about thirty cords of wood a day, a total of roughly 34 million cords from 1811 to 1860, coming from 22 million trees that could have filled a six-hundred-square-mile forest.[29]

The United States government devoted a large amount of money and effort to improving navigation on the river system and achieved a considerable amount of success, largely owing to the efforts of Henry M. Shreve, a steamboat captain and inventor who was made superintendent of Western River Improvements in 1826. Shreve designed and built the *Heliopolis*, a double-hulled steamboat with an iron-plated beam across its prow and a steam-powered windlass. It removed embedded trees by first smashing into them to loosen their grip on the river bottom and then hauling them out of the water. Between 1830 and 1837, the *Heliopolis* and three other snagboats like it removed an estimated 6,700 snags from the Mississippi and its tributaries. Another spectacular success was the clearing of the 150-mile-long overgrown logjam known as the Great Raft on the Red River, accomplished under Shreve's direction. Clearing the river opened navigation to the newly founded and aptly named city of

Shreveport and allowed the Red River parishes of northern Louisiana and the counties of southwest Arkansas to become part of the cotton kingdom. From 1834, when three-fourths of the work was done, and three years later when the Panic of 1837 slowed western migration, immigrants bought 1.4 million acres in that region. The Louisiana portion had a population of 7,500 in 1830 and 48,000 in 1860.[30]

Steamboats quickly monopolized the transportation of large cargoes upstream on the Mississippi River system, driving out the keelboats that had been poled or pulled against the current at an average speed of fifteen miles a day. Flatboats, however, a decidedly low-tech type of watercraft, held their own throughout the antebellum period. The English novelist Charles Horton saw the latter in the early 1840s and wrote an artful description. "A flatboat is nothing more than a quadrangular floating box, . . . composed of rough-sawn planks, and provided with a rude kind of cabin, made sufficiently water-tight to float down the current to its destination, and no further." Contemporaries often called them arks, probably because of their cargoes—which included chickens, hogs, horses, and mules, as well as flour, corn, meat, lard, whiskey, and lumber, and sometimes slaves also on their way to be sold—and their size, which ranged from 12 to 20 feet wide and 20 to 150 feet long, and carrying capacity, that started at about thirty tons and went up to three hundred tons. Capable farmers could construct flatboats themselves, the crews were semiprofessionals from the neighborhood, and the building material was sold at the destination. They usually descended the river only at high-water periods in the fall and spring and required a month and a half to go from Pittsburgh to New Orleans but were an economic way to take nonperishable goods to market. Horton viewed them lined up along the New Orleans levee "as far as the eye could see" and close enough together so that "one may run along the floor formed by their flat-covered roofs as upon the deck of a ship." Together they formed a floating strip mall and farmer's market that allowed customers to come aboard the boat and buy from the producer.[31]

The effects of westward immigration made possible by Indian Removal and more efficient by the steamboat were already apparent in 1827, when the Austrian-born novelist Charles Sealsfield journeyed down the Mississippi River. He floated on a keelboat that was often passed by steamboats "dashing through the water with the noise of thunder and vomiting columns of smoke." Sealsfield described Memphis as "a small settlement on the Tennessee side. It was founded in 1819, incorporated in 1826, and had a newspaper in 1827. There were only 630 inhabitants in 1830, however, because the city was still overshadowed by Randolph, located on the Second Chickasaw Bluff fifty miles to the north. At the mouth of the St. Francis River, Helena, Arkansas, was built on "dwarfish round hills" twenty feet high that created one of the few places relatively safe from flooding on that stretch of the Mississippi. The village was attractive from a distance although "the cabin houses" looked cruder when seen up close. The author noted that Arkansas Territory had been separated from Missouri in 1819, that Little Rock was the capital, and aside from the "Volcanos" (presumably at Hot Springs) not much was known about it. Sealsfield was impressed with the Walnut Hills and the city of Vicksburg on top of them, which had been founded in 1819 and slowly grew as settlers moved into the region vacated by the Choctaw. It had become the county seat of Warren County in 1825, and Sealsfield counted fifty houses, three stores, and a few steamboats loading cotton at the landing.[32]

Beginning in the late 1820s and increasing rapidly between 1834 and 1837, settlers moved into the alluvial plain that stretched for two hundred miles from just north of Vicksburg to just south of Memphis and spread inland along the arc of the Yazoo River that was seventy miles from the Mississippi at its widest point. The region came to be called the Delta because of its soil, which was thought to be as fertile as that of Lower Egypt. Annually "washed by the Mississippi" and thickly covered with trees and other vegetation, it was difficult to clear and drain but richly repaid those who could afford to do those things. By 1840 there were nearly 11,000 people living there, 78 percent of them enslaved workers. Census data for 1860 is incomplete, but the population was about 50,000 and about 87 percent were black. Large plantations dominated the region, especially in Issaquena County where there were only 95 agricultural households, of whom 73 owned more than 20 slaves and 21 of these planters owned more than 100. Enslaved blacks outnumbered whites by more than 9 to 1 in the county. Cotton production averaged nearly nine bales for each fieldworker. Bolivar County was more typical than Issaquena, but there were still 142 planters among the 392 white families and 18 of them owned more than 100 slaves. Bolivar's slaves were 86 percent of the county's population, and the county produced over five bales of cotton per worker.[33]

Vicksburg merchants were major beneficiaries of Delta growth. By 1860 they were handling 250,000 bales a year, most of them coming from Deer Creek, which flowed through Bolivar and Issaquena Counties, and from the Sunflower and the Yazoo Rivers. Vicksburg also helped itself by promoting the Vicksburg and Jackson Railroad, which was completed in 1840 and brought considerable amounts of cotton from inland plantations to the Walnut Hills as well.[34]

Cotton production in the northern portion of the Delta was important to the growth of Memphis. Planters in Tunica County, at the north end of the Delta, and Desoto County in the rolling hills of Mississippi to the west found it easier to haul their cotton-filled wagons there rather than south to the upper parts of the Yazoo River system where steamboats were available to carry the product to Vicksburg. Memphis also benefited from the rapid growth of West Tennessee and the slower settlement of eastern Arkansas, which became the cotton frontier in the 1840s. The US government built a road from the Mississippi River opposite Memphis that connected it with Little Rock, and private interests built plank roads to the south and east. The population of the city grew from 1,200 in 1840 to nearly 9,000 in 1850 and over 22,000 in 1860. Between 1830 and 1860 the number of cotton bales handled by Memphian merchants rose from 35,000 to 398,000, in the latter year more than 1.5 times those in Vicksburg and 8 times those in Natchez.

Memphis also developed a commercial and manufacturing sector that gave it a character closer to that of Louisville than those of the smaller cities of the lower valley. Major General Edmund Pendleton Gaines, who commanded the American Army in the west, was a major booster of the local economy and largely responsible for convincing the government to locate a navy yard in Memphis, which stimulated economic growth for a few years before it closed. A public school system began to operate in 1841 and a professional police force later in the decade, both signs of the civic progress that had occurred in Louisville fifteen years earlier. The *Memphis Appeal*, founded in 1841, was little different from the other two newspapers in the city for a few years, but then it began to report local news and put out a daily edition along with a weekly version that eventually had five thousand subscribers, most of them in the surrounding countryside. By 1850 Memphis had telegraph service with regional cities, and steamboats were providing packet boat services to New Orleans, Louisville, and Cincinnati. In 1851, a cotton mill went into operation. Business elements within the city worked hard to secure railroad transportation and received their final reward when the Charleston to Memphis Railroad was completed in 1857. By the Civil War, manufacturing was an important element of the economy, and foreign-born whites, mostly Irish workers and German retailers, outnumbered the enslaved portion of the population.[35]

Memphis was also a major player in the internal slave trade. An anti-slave traveler wrote in 1852 that "the most conspicuous object [there] was a brick building, with a very large sign, bearing this disgusting inscription: —'Bolton Dickens and Co. Slave-dealers.'" A few years later Nathan Bedford Forrest was not only the dominant trader in Memphis but also one of the largest in the South, selling around one thousand slaves a year. The English traveler Charles Mackay was on a steamboat that picked up people who may have been part of Forrest's stock-in-trade. Mackay memorialized the event in a few lines of a long poem he wrote on the Mississippi Valley:

> We took on board a "cargo" of miserable men;
> A freight of human creatures, bartered, bought, and sold
> Like hogs or sheep or poultry, the living blood for gold.[36]

Across from Memphis, the Arkansas Delta stretched along the Mississippi River from just below the Missouri bootheel to just above the Arkansas-Louisiana state line and extended west to the Ozark Highlands north of the Arkansas River and the Ouachita River in the south. The northern part lacked the 210 frost-free days necessary for ideal cotton farming, but the soil throughout was as fertile as that across the river. The western side of the Mississippi lacked the elevated bluffs of Memphis, Vicksburg, and Natchez, and because of that Helena was the only Arkansas port of any significance.[37]

During the 1820s Arkansas Territory was settled by people from Kentucky and Tennessee, many of them coming down the Southwest Trail that crossed the territory diagonally from southeast Missouri to the Red River border with Texas. In the 1830s southerners began to push across the river from Mississippi and settle in the Arkansas Delta. Cotton production reached 65,000 bales there in 1850 and rose to 367,000 in 1860. The population of Phillips County doubled from 7,000 in 1850 to 15,000 in 1860, and the proportion of enslaved people rose from 37 percent to 60 percent. Chicot County, at the southeast corner of Arkansas, might be thought of as the Issaquena County of Arkansas: In 1860, 81 percent of its population were African Americans, and they did the physical labor that produced 41,000 bales of cotton. The soil in most of southern Arkansas is much less rich than in the Delta, but yeomen farmers and planters grew significant amounts of cotton in the bottomland of the Red and the Ouachita Rivers. Below Arkansas on the Louisiana side of the Mississippi, plantation agriculture had begun earlier. Rapides and Avoyelles Parishes, on the Red River below the Raft and Catahoula and Concordia Parishes to the east of them were suited for producing cotton.[38]

Natchez in the 1830s was in its glory, with 3,540 citizens living in six hundred houses that Sealsfield found "regular and elegant" in general, and "several of them with colonnades, exhibit throughout a high degree of wealth." The city had a courthouse, its own bank, and a branch of the Bank of the United States. Natchez continued to be one of the most opulent of southern cities over the next three decades, famed for the genteel style of the "nabobs" as the wealthy planters and merchants were called. It did not grow very much after 1830, however, and lost its political influence early in the Jacksonian period. The agricultural hinterland was confined to a narrow strip of alluvial lowland, all of which was under cultivation by the late 1830s when depression struck the cotton market. At that point, the city had a population of about 5,000 people, of which 40 percent were enslaved. During the prosperous 1850s Natchez grew to 6,600, 2,000 more people than Vicksburg; but equally with that city, as well as Helena, and Little Rock, largely devoid of the economic diversification that characterized Memphis. After leaving Natchez, Sealsfield continued down river to New Orleans, writing only a brief comment about Baton Rouge, a river town that suffered from its proximity to New Orleans, where residents went for most of their business needs. Fortunately for the growth of Baton Rouge, hostility toward the political power of New Orleans led rural state legislators to make it the capital of Louisiana in 1837, generating enough administrative and economic activity to bring its population to over 5,000 people by 1860.[39]

Below Point Coupee the climate is warm enough for the successful cultivation of sugarcane, and somewhere around Baton Rouge the Cotton Kingdom merged into the Sugar Bowl, which spread across the Louisiana Delta formed by the Atchafalaya River and Bayou Teche to the west and Bayou Lafourche to the south. Sugar production was a small but very profitable industry by the time that Louisiana became the property of the United States, and it attracted Americans who had access to the large amount of capital necessary to build and operate a sugar plantation, which cost twice as much per acre as a rice plantation and well over ten times as much as a cotton plantation. By the 1840s Louisiana was producing 200,000 barrels of sugar a year and continued at that level until the war. In 1850, 125,000 slaves were involved in their production. In 1860, about two-thirds of Louisiana sugar was produced by the largest five hundred planters who were less than 15 percent of those involved in the industry.

The Louisiana sugar industry stood out among American business enterprises both for its use of technology and its innovative system of labor management. Steam power began to replace horses and mules in sugar mills in the late 1820s and was standard on larger plantations by 1860. So was a vacuum process that used heat from the engines to dry the sugar at a lower temperature than direct fires, producing more sugar from the same amount of juice and a whiter, better-quality product. Burgasse, the dried husks of sugarcanes after the juice was squeezed out, was used as fuel, replacing the more expensive wood that had been used. The cutting, hauling, and processing of sugarcane had to be done in a six-to-eight-week period during the late fall and early winter that involved intensive, often round-the-clock, physical labor. To get the work done, planters sometimes organized the workers into shifts, and they routinely rewarded them with money and extra privileges. The complexity of production also required sophisticated skills that gave slaves an opportunity to earn extra money and achieve a small degree of upward mobility.[40]

New Orleans had a population of about 8,000 in 1804 when it became part of the United States, and it grew rapidly after that, reaching 17,000 in the Census of 1810. In 1820, the beginning of the antebellum period, the Crescent City was home to 41,000 people, making it the fifth largest city in the United States. By 1840 New Orleans was officially the third largest city, its population of 102,193 exactly 20 people fewer than Baltimore, the second-place metropolis. The Census of 1840, however, marked the zenith of its position in the urban hierarchy. New Orleans contained 174,000 people in 1860, but it had fallen to sixth place. New York City, the largest city in the country throughout the period, outnumbered New Orleans two to one in 1820 and 1840 but five to one in 1860.[41]

The rapid rise of New Orleans among the nation's cities was based entirely on commerce flowing down what J. D. B. De Bow called "the most magnificent channel of nature's own digging." Exports from New Orleans in 1835 were valued at $54 million as compared to $30 million from New York, slightly more than 20 percent of its 327,000 bales of cotton going to the North and almost all of the rest to Europe. Imports were much less significant to the economy of the Crescent City, but most of the clothing and other manufactured goods consumed in the Lower Mississippi Valley came from the Ohio Valley downriver to New Orleans before being shipped to retailers upstream.

New Orleans reached the zenith of its national economic prominence in 1840, just as it did with respect to population. The amount of commerce handled by the city's merchants would continue to grow until the Civil War, but it represented a diminishing share of the agricultural production of the Upper Mississippi and Ohio valleys. The Erie Canal that was finished in 1825 drew agricultural commodities from the Great Lakes region back to the East. More important, the transportation revolution that had put steamboats on the Mississippi River after the War of 1812 began to transform land travel only two decades later. A short line railroad connected the Ohio River to the Great Lakes in 1848, the Baltimore and Ohio Railroad reached Cincinnati in 1857, and Chicago, which was home to 4,500 people in 1840, had a population of 100,000 in 1860 and was the center of east-west railroad traffic that carried much of the goods that had once gone south. New Orleans was left with a reduced geographic hinterland, but fortunately for the city's merchants that region produced more and more commodities. Arkansas, Tennessee, Mississippi, and Louisiana added 4 million acres to their cotton fields in the 1850s, and New Orleans shipped 2.2 million bales of cotton in 1860, more than twice the annual amount in the mid-1840s.[42]

As the city grew, its racial and ethnic makeup changed dramatically. In 1810 white people were just a little over one-third of the population, in 1820 they were not far short of one-half, and in 1860 they were 85 percent. Even though their percentage of the city's population decreased, black people increased in numbers down to 1840, but after that they became fewer and fewer. There were only about 14,500 slaves in the city in 1850, 450 less than in 1820. The free black community included 11,000 people in 1860, more than in 1820, but much less than in 1840. European immigration was the driving force behind the population change. In 1850, the first years for which data is available, there were 48,600 foreign-born people living in New Orleans, nearly half of the white population, among them were 20,000 immigrants from Ireland and 11,000 from Germany. The Irish outnumbered the enslaved; Germans were more numerous than free blacks.[43]

The immigrants took work away from both slaves and free black people, but other causes also affected their decline in numbers. The sectional crisis increased hostility toward free blacks throughout the South, and while that was less true in New Orleans, it still discouraged some of them from coming to the city or remaining there. A decrease in slave ownership occurred in many southern cities in the last decades of the antebellum period, and it may have been related to the problem of controlling bonded labor in an urban environment. The major factor, however, appears to have been an increased demand for slaves in the countryside caused by rising cotton prices, which made selling slaves to work in cotton fields more financially attractive than leasing in the city.[44]

While traveling through Kentucky on his way from Cincinnati to Louisville, Charles Sealsfield stopped for breakfast one morning at a small planation near New Castle, Kentucky. As he ate, three horsemen rode by:

> Two of the party had each a negro slave running before him, secured by a rope fastened to an iron collar. A tremendous horsewhip reminded them at intervals to quicken their pace. The bloody backs and necks of these wretches, bespoke a too frequent application of the last. A third negro had, however, the hardest lot. The rope of his collar was fastened to the saddle string of the third horseman, and the miserable creature had thus no alternative left, but to keep an equal pace with the trotting horse, or to be dragged through ditches, thorns, and [woods]. His feet and legs, all covered with blood, exhibited a dreadful spectacle.

The captured slaves had run away two days before, Sealsfield learned, "dreading transportation to Mississippi or Louisiana."[45]

Fifteen years later Abraham Lincoln saw a group of ten or twelve black men who had been "sold down the river" and were being transported on a steamboat. Writing to a friend, he reflected on their fate: "Separated from the scenes of their childhood, their friends, their fathers and mothers, and brothers and sisters, and many of them from their wives and children . . . [they were going to a place] where the lash of the master is proverbially more ruthless and unrelenting than any other." They were obviously flight risks: "A small iron clevis was around the left wrist of each, and this was fastened to the main chain by a shorter one at a convenient distance from the others; so that the negroes were strung together precisely like so many fish upon a trot-line." Nonetheless, the captives "were the most cheerful and apparently happy creatures on board." Lincoln saw their behavior as evidence of God's grace in providing people with the strength to endure hardship. A less theologically minded observer might have related it to male bonding, masculine pride, and indomitable spirit.[46]

In September 1834, George W. Featherstonhaugh (pronounced Fanshaw), an English-born geologist working for the United States government, saw what he called "a singular spectacle" near the New River in southwestern Virginia.

> It was a camp of negro slave-drivers, just packing up to start; they had about three hundred slaves with them, who had bivouacked the preceding night in chains in the woods. The female slaves were, some of them, sitting on logs of wood, whilst others were standing, and a great many little black children were warming themselves at the fires of the bivouac. In front of them all, and prepared for the march, stood, in double files, about two hundred male slaves, manacled and chained to each other.

These people, as Featherstonhaugh learned later, were on their way to Natchez. They belonged to the firm of Franklin and Armfield, one of the largest companies in the slave-trading business, which had its headquarters in Alexandria, Virginia. One of its principles, John Armfield, was leading the New River party. Featherstonhaugh referred to the group as a coffle, a term derived from the Arab word *qāfila*, meaning caravan. He knew it from a book by Mungo Park, an English explorer who had visited the Niger River Basin at the end of the eighteenth century and seen slave traders taking captives from there to the Atlantic Coast.[47]

Slavery did not bother George Featherstonhaugh, mainly because he took a condescending view of African American character and ability: "The poor negro slave is naturally a cheerful, laughing animal, . . . if he is well fed and kindly treated, is seldom melancholy; for his thoughts have not been taught to stray to the future." Nor was the Englishman against the slave trade, explaining to his readers, correctly, that the declining fertility of Chesapeake soil brought about by centuries of farming meant there was a surplus labor force in that region and the expansion of agriculture in the southwest created a demand for workers. From his own moral perspective, small farmers in Virginia could not be blamed for selling a slave or two to make ends meet, nor planters for taking the opportunity to rid themselves of a few troublesome bondsmen. Still the scene at New River "revolted" him because it broke up families, "tearing, without an instant's notice, the husband from the wife, and the children from their parents; sending the one to the sugar plantations of Louisiana, another to the cotton-lands of Arkansas, and the rest to Texas." For that, he blamed the white men he saw at New River, "who were tolerably well dressed, and had broad brimmed white hats on, with black crape round them, [and] were standing near [their captives], laughing and smoking cigars." These were the culprits, "sordid, illiterate, and vulgar slave-drivers" who took advantage of the situation and sometimes got rich in the business. For Featherstonhaugh, they "have nothing whatever in common with the gentlemen of the Southern states."[48]

These ideas about virtuous planters and nefarious traders were widely shared at the time. Harriet Beecher Stowe gave them classic expression in the first pages of *Uncle Tom's Cabin* when she introduced the slave trader Haley, "a short, thick-set man, with coarse, commonplace features, and that swaggering air of pretension which marks a low man who is trying to elbow his way upward in the world." He "was much overdressed, in a gaudy vest of many colors, a blue neckerchief, bedropped gayly with yellow spots, and arranged with a flaunting tie"; his "large and coarse" hands were "bedecked with rings"; "he wore a heavy gold watch chain . . . which in the ardor of conversation he was in the habit of flourishing and jingling," and his speech was short on grammar and long on profanity. Mr. Shelby, the Kentucky planter, on the other hand, "had the appearance of a gentleman," a social type that Stowe apparently felt was so familiar that it required no further description. Haley showed himself to be motivated only by money and have little concern for the welfare of the slaves, while Shelby was a self-described "humane man," who appreciated and respected the honest, capable, and loyal slave Tom as both a Christian and the patriarch of a large family. He also had considerable affection for the cute and precocious four- or five-year-old Harry, the son of Eliza, who famously would flee for freedom lest he be sold away from her. Shelby, however, was in debt and agreed to the sale of both. For Stowe, Shelby is a weak but decent man, while Haley is a villainous one.[49]

Attitudes like those of Featherstonhaugh and Stowe are part of what historian Michael Tadman has called "the myth of the reluctant master." For some owners, the selling of slaves may have been an occasional and regrettable necessity, but for most it was a profitable side line, often referred to as "Negro Speculation." Eastern planters who sold human property to slave traders earned on average 15 percent as much doing that as they did by marketing their agricultural products. Few, if any, owners bred their slaves for the sole purpose of selling the offspring, but almost all of them encouraged child-rearing and were disappointed when it did not happen. One prominent planter lamented his failure: I have taken more pains to raise young negroes and nurse all . . . I have read, consulted with everyone and spared no exertion—but all in vein. The hand of fate appears to interpose and forbid prosperity to me." Nor were the exporters the only masters interested in the fecundity of their servants. Mississippi Valley purchasers valued slave women for their fertility and were happy to sell the children they produced. Mississippi Valley slave markets also sold slaves in the same callous manner that slave traders bought them. An enslaved person sold in Virginia and sold again in Natchez might be sold two or three times during their lives, each time with little regard to any personal relationships that might be dissolved in the process.[50]

The domestic slave trade took away 10 percent of the slave population in the older portions of the South from friends and family and brought them to places where most of them worked under more difficult conditions than before and were punished more harshly. They suffered in many ways, some of them subtler than others. Take John, for example. In 1844 the Supreme Court of Louisiana approved a lower court decision allowing John Rist to get back from John Hagan money he had paid for John in January 1839. John had proven to be "a great runaway and a great drunkard and thief" and to suffer from "bodily maladies," both defects that warranted his return under the doctrine of redhibition. Witnesses for Rist said John had run away four or five times during the year after he had been purchased, once for ten days and another for two weeks; and two different doctors swore that he suffered from a gastric problem that made it impossible to work. Neighbors called him "a trifling no account runaway negro," who was "in the woods all the time when he was not sick," and the medical men agreed that because of the illness he was "perfectly useless on a farm."

This John was a very different man from the one who had been brought up in Hanover County, North Carolina, from where Doyle O'Hanlon gave a deposition saying that he had known John for ten years as "a strong able and well-conditioned negro for hard labour on land or water," and that he was responsible enough that O'Hanlon had made him the foreman of a small steamboat. O'Hanlon had sold him in June 1838 to a man named McDonald in Charleston who had rented him out for four months before shipping him to New Orleans. During that period John was a driver for a livery stable owner who deposed that the slave never ran away or was drunk and was not sick. "He was a stout hearty fellow." A co-worker said John was "esteemed" by the boss.[51]

What happened to John between October 1838 when he left Charleston and January 1839 when John Rist bought him, we do not know, and he may well have contracted an illness before the sale. After that he might have been severely mistreated by Risk. Or perhaps John nursed a long-standing hatred of slavery that would have resulted in the same behavior in South Carolina as it did in Louisiana. One senses, however, that it was not a medical problem, physical cruelty, or a sense of moral outrage, that changed him, but rather that the slave trade had robbed him of the self-worth that derives from doing useful work in a skillful manner and of the respect of others that comes from with it. Instead, his new owner wanted only hard physical labor of a repetitive sort and unquestioning obedience

❊ CHAPTER 3 ❊

I Had Rather a Negro Do Anything Else Than Runaway

THE STATE OF MISSISSIPPI defined a runaway slave as one absent without permission "from his usual place of residence, or from the service of his owner or employer," which was the way the term was understood throughout the South. The most common type of this absenteeism was what an Arkansas statute called "strolling about from one house or plantation to another," which was done by both men and women who stole away at night to visit friends, lovers, or spouses or to attend clandestine meetings, dances, parties, or religious services. A more serious problem for white society was described by the Territorial Assembly of Louisiana in 1804: "Many times slaves run away and lie hid and lurking in swamps, woods and other obscure places, killing hogs and committing other injuries to the inhabitants." Known as "lying out," the practice of staying away from home for a few days or weeks continued throughout the antebellum period.[1]

Fugitives sometimes remained not far from their home but with no intention of returning, living as maroons who stole food and supplies, built dwelling places, sometimes earned money by hiring themselves out, and even planted crops to sustain an existence independent of white people. They were often willing to resist being captured, and they sometimes had the weapons to do so effectively. The same ties of family and affection that caused some people to risk whipping in order to spend an evening with people they cared about, motivated others to attempt trips back to places they had once lived. In the Lower Mississippi Valley, a significant number of enslaved people ran away hoping to return to their former homes in eastern slave states. Over time, as more and more unwilling immigrants grew familiar with their new homes, and then were sold to other places in the valley, escapees fled back to where they had recently been. Rural slaves also fled to cities, where they could hide among a community of free blacks and relatively unsupervised slaves and enjoy the benefits of urban living. Then there were freedom-seekers who wanted to live in a place where there was no slavery. For residents of the Lower Mississippi Valley, Mexico was a possible choice. Not only had the Mexican government abolished slavery, but an unfriendly relationship with the United States meant it was unwilling to assist Yankee slaveholders in getting their property back. Getting to the North was a long and difficult journey by land, but the steamboat made escape by water a viable option.

Unlike the French and Spanish, white Americans viewed running away as disobedience rather than as crime. The masters of fugitives were responsible for getting them back, but states and local governments provided them with assistance. Neighborhood patrols organized under state law but staffed by local civilians helped to control the comings and goings of slaves, including those who were lying out. State laws also empowered citizens to take suspected runaway slaves into custody and deliver them to county jails, collecting a fee for the capture and a reimbursement for their travel expenses. Sheriffs were required to advertise the prisoners, turn them over to owners who came to get them, and sell those who were unclaimed. Underlying the legal structure was a widely shared belief on the part of white people that they had a common interest in seeing that the enslaved population stayed where their owners wanted them to be.[2]

On January 20, 1853, less than a month before the first of Frederick Law Olmsted's "Letters from the South" appeared in the *New York Times*, the front page of the newspaper was given over to an article titled "The Kidnapping," which detailed the remarkable story of Solomon Northup, a free black man from Saratoga, New York, who had just arrived back in Washington, DC, after serving twelve years as a slave in the Red River region of central Louisiana. In the spring of 1841, at the age of thirty-three, Northup had been lured to Washington by two men who then drugged him and sold him to a slave trader named William Burch, who shipped him to New Orleans. There he was sold to William Ford, who owned a small lumber mill near Bayou Boeuf in Rapides Parish, not far from Alexandria, sold again a year later to a carpenter named John Tibeats, who worked in the area, and shortly after sold a third time to Edwin Eppes, whose cotton plantation was close by on Bayou Boeuf in

Avoyelles Parish. Northup remained with Eppes until January 1853 when he was rescued by Henry B. Northup, a prominent attorney and politician from Saratoga, who was not a relative of Solomon's but had known him and his family. The *Times* article, apparently based on information used in a lawsuit instituted against Burch, also noted that Northup's experience was remarkably like that of the eponymous protagonist of Harriet Beecher Stowe's novel *Uncle Tom's Cabin*, who had lived in the same region while owned by her fictional villain Simon Legree.[3]

Five months after the *Times* article, *Twelve Years a Slave: Narrative of Solomon Northup, a Citizen of New York Kidnapped in Washington City in 1841 and Rescued in 1853, from a Cotton Plantation near the Red River, in Louisiana* was published, a richly detailed volume of more than three hundred pages. The rapid publication was made possible in part by the work of David Wilson of Whitehall, New York, the author of several books of fiction, who had been hired by Henry B. Northup. In a brief preface, Wilson referred to himself as "the editor," saying that the book was Solomon's history "as received from his lips," suggesting it was a verbatim transcription, but he also added that any "faults of style and expression that it might be found to contain" were owing to him, indicating that he had written the book rather than transcribed it. Wilson also pointed out that important aspects of the narrative had been documented, and he believed that it was a truthful account that gave an accurate view of slavery. He was right about the factual nature of the book, which is a tribute to Northup's memory and his determination to give an accurate account of what had happened to him. Sue Eakin and Joseph Logsdon, who edited a republication of *Twelve Years a Slave* in 1968, found evidence of many of the people, places, and events that are mentioned in the book, making it one of the most valuable sources on southern slavery that we have.[4]

An important part of *Twelve Years a Slave* is Northup's description of the friendships, shared backgrounds, and familial relationships that were common in slave quarters throughout the Lower Mississippi Valley and were the basis for black communities that recreated those that had existed prior to the slave trade. The plantation was their basic social unit, but neighborhood communities also included nearby plantations. William Ford, who purchased Northup in New Orleans, also bought Eliza, who had come from Washington in the same shipment of slaves, and Harry, who had joined them in Richmond. At Ford's plantation in the Pine

Woods, eighteen miles from Red River, they met Rose and Sally, both house servants who were also from Washington. Eliza and Sally talked about people and places that they knew from there, including Eliza's former owner, and the father of her children who had been sold away from her in New Orleans. Among Ford's other slaves was Sam, who had worked on a farm in Georgetown and was sent to Louisiana with Sally. He had heard of James H. Burch, the slave trader who had purchased Northup from his kidnappers. Walton was Sally's husband; John, Ford's sixteen-year-old cook, was her son; and Antony was a blacksmith from Kentucky.[5]

After a year or so, this group of friends was broken up because William Ford suffered a financial setback and was forced to sell eighteen slaves, among them Solomon, Harry, and Sam. John Tibeats, a carpenter, bought Northup and took him twenty-seven miles away to a plantation owned by William Ford's wife on Bayou Boeuf where he had been working. Eliza had been sent there earlier, and Solomon shared a cabin with her, along with a man named Lawson, his wife, Mary, and a fifth slave named Bristol. William Ford had been a benevolent master, but Tibeats was an uncouth and brutal one. One day he started to whip Northup for a small infraction, and Solomon fought back and was only saved from lynching by the intervention of Chapin the overseer. Later, while he was tied up in the afternoon sun, Rachel, the cook on that plantation, came out and gave him water. That evening after he was released, Eliza and Mary fed Solomon, and others of their co-workers gathered in the cabin to hear Rachel describe how he had beaten Tibeats in the fight and how the carpenter and several other white men had nearly hanged him but were stopped by the courageous action of the overseer, who had threatened them with pistols and then sent Lawson to bring William Ford. Northup again had a support group, even though most of their assistance was psychological.[6]

After a time, Tibeats sold Solomon to Edwin Eppes, who had recently bought a farm further south on Bayou Boeuf, where Northup toiled in the cotton fields for the next eight years. The small group of fellow workers at Eppes's place had been purchased as a group and brought from the East together. Abram was sixty years old when Solomon arrived. He had been born in Tennessee and at the age of forty sold to a trader who took him to South Carolina and sold him to James Buford, who was the sheriff of Williamsburg County in that state. Wiley had also been a slave of Buford's and managed the sheriff's ferry on the Black River. Phebe was Wiley's wife, whom "the kind master" Buford had purchased from a neighbor so the two could be together. With them were Bob and Henry, Phebe's children from a previous marriage, both now in their twenties. "Aunt Phebe" had been an excellent field hand but was now a house servant, a "sly old creature," Northup called her, who was very talkative unless Eppes or members of his family were around. Edward, apparently a child of Wiley and Phebe's, was thirteen when Northup first mentions him; not a good field hand, he took care of the Eppes children. Another of Buford's former slaves was the charming, attractive, and athletic Patsy, a young woman of twenty-three who was the object of Eppes's "lustful eye" and hated by his wife because of it. She suffered regular punishments and died after an especially severe whipping. During his years as a slave, Northup always missed his wife and family in New York, but these people along with his older friends owned by the Ford family did much to replace them. Once when Eppes had rented him out to help in the sugarcane harvest in St. Mary's Parish far to the south, Aunt Phebe sent word to Solomon about how Patsy was bearing up under their master's brutal treatment. On another occasion, he asked for and received permission to visit his old friends at Ford's even though it involved nearly a day's walk.[7]

Northup knew enslaved people who visited in the neighborhood without permission and some that escaped the daily work routine by lying out. One of them was a woman named Nelly, who had worked with Solomon clearing land at the Red River site. She hid for several nights in the corncrib at the Ford plantation, eating food supplied by the slaves until they decided it was too dangerous both for her and them. Northup himself gave food to a woman named Celeste, who built a hut on a dry spot in the swamp and lived there all summer. She returned home when the weather got colder and endured a severe whipping and time in the stocks as punishment. A group of males who were hiding out for an extended period robbed a cooked pig from Northup one evening when he was carrying it home.[8]

Slave neighborhoods were the locus of plots involving various types of anti-white activities. Most of these were minor things such as stealing food, but in October 1837, four years before Northup got there, at least six male slaves and three free black men were hanged in Rapides Parish, all of them said to be involved in planning an uprising designed to kill all the white people in the area. A slave named Lewis Cheney had warned his owner and was rewarded with his freedom and $500 to use in moving somewhere he would be safe from the wrath of the enslaved people he left behind. As Northup heard the story from the black community, Cheney had been the leader of the group and recruited the others before selling them out. The goal was not to kill their masters but to escape from them and flee to Mexico. The plan involved stealing food and mules and meeting at a rendezvous place "far within the depths of a swamp."[9]

Before Tibeats sold Northup to Eppes, he rented him to a man named Eldret, who was clearing land in a canebrake about thirty-seven miles from the Ford plantation. After a month of work, Eldret gave Solomon permission to return home for a visit but neglected to give him a pass. Tibeats, who happened to be at Eldret's place at the time, told Solomon of his danger. "You'd be taken and sent to jail . . . before you get halfway there." And then he wrote one: "Platt [Northup's slave name] has permission to go to Ford's plantation, on Boeuf Bayou and return by Tuesday." As Northup explained to the reader, any white man he met along the way could have stopped him, even whipped him if they wanted to. Lower-class whites were more apt to do it because "catching runaways is sometimes a money-making business," with the captor receiving a fee for turning the alleged fugitive over to the sheriff. A poor white "considers it a god-send to meet an unknown negro without a pass."[10]

The Bayou Boeuf neighborhood was patrolled at night by mounted men with dogs who were paid by the planters to capture and return slaves found away from home without passes. Nonetheless, people often went out without permission, particularly around the neighborhood where they were well known. Wiley, Phebe's husband, left home one evening without a pass to visit a friend, wound up staying away most of the night, and was caught by the patrol on the way home. Not only was he bitten by a dog during the arrest but he was also whipped before being taken home and then whipped again by Eppes.

Instead of convincing him to stay home, the punishment pushed Wiley into a more serious form of running away. He decided to leave for good and return to South Carolina where he had been happy as a ferry boat operator. Without telling Phebe or anyone else, he stockpiled a week's worth of food and fled into the swamp one night. Eppes quizzed and threatened the other slaves without learning anything and searched the area with dogs without finding any trace of his errant bondsman.

Three weeks later Wiley returned. He had gotten as far as the Red River, some twenty miles away, by traveling at night and hiding during the day, sometimes climbing trees for concealment, but was captured and taken to the jail in Alexandria. A friend of Eppes saw him there, paid the necessary fees, and provided a pass so he could go home. He told Wiley the note included a suggestion that he not be punished if he returned on his own. Whether that was true or not, Eppes gave him a severe beating.[11]

Solomon Northup was a rational man, but like many victims of severe punishment, he made one desperate, fear-driven attempt at escape that had no real chance of success. Again, it was caused by Tibeats, who in a fit of anger attacked him with an axe. Northup fought back successfully enough that the carpenter fled, but he returned forty-five minutes later, on horseback with two companions and eight dogs. Seeing them from a distance, Northup leaped over a fence and ran through the woods into a marsh. The dogs soon followed and as Wilson put it, "every howl was nearer and nearer. Each moment I expected they would spring upon my back—expected to feel their long teeth sinking into my back." The text indicates, however, that the dogs were too far back to see the fugitive and lost the scent when he reached deep water. Before long Northup reached Cocodrie Bayou and swam across, safe from the humans and canines chasing him but now in a deep and dark swamp where water moccasins and alligators frightened him just as much as had his pursuers. He kept going through the night, moving from hummock to hummock and striking the water with a stick to scare away the snakes and gators. Early in the morning he found himself on dry land and not far from William Ford's plantation. Seeing no other option, he went there and asked for help. Because he still held a mortgage on his former slave, Ford was again able to save him from the carpenter, who could have had Northup executed for striking him.[12]

There is no reason to doubt the essential facts of Northup's flight, but David Wilson may have made the swamp sound more terrifying than it was, if not to Northup then to enslaved people who were more familiar with the watery environment of the Lower Mississippi Valley. Ford supposedly told Northup that he "never knew of a slave escaping with his life from Bayou Boeuf." On the same day, however, the planter warned Tibeats that threatening slaves with violence was a self-defeating management practice that would "set them all running away. The swamps will be full of them." Later Northup himself says that although they were always captured eventually, "the woods and swamps are, nevertheless, continually filled with runaways." In addition, as we have seen, his friend Celeste had remained hidden in the swamp for an entire summer, living in a hut she constructed out of fallen tree limbs and palmetto leaves.[13]

Solomon made one attempt to flee by water. While he was working as a hired-out slave on a sugar plantation along Bayou Teche in southern Louisiana, he took the desperate chance of approaching the northern captain of a steamboat, explaining that he was a kidnapping victim, and asking for permission to hide on the boat when it went back to the free states. Luckily the man was sympathetic and did not expose him, but he claimed that the consequences to himself and the owner of the boat were simply too high to take the risk.[14]

Bennet H. Barrow owned and personally managed Highland, a large cotton plantation in West Feliciana Parish, Louisiana. He was a strict disciplinarian who often whipped slaves for not "doing their part," meaning, for example, they had not picked as much cotton as he thought they should have. For him, slacking off was bad, but absconding was worse: "I had rather a negro would do anything Else than runaway." Barrow was never able to eliminate absenteeism, but his determination to catch and punish runaways stopped most of them from leaving often or staying away for long. In a man named Ginny Jerry, however, he met his match.

On October 3, 1839, a particularly frustrating day for him, Barrow told a slave named Dennis that he intended to whip him and Dennis "put out." Barrow sent Jack, probably a trusted slave, after the escapee, promising him $50 if he caught him. The day after that Dennis's brother, Lewis, who had been lying out nearly a week, came back, and Barrow "gave him the worst Whipping I ever gave any young negro," convinced that it would teach him a lesson. Barrow was also building a jail, hoping it would provide a long-term solution to his runaway problem; and he planned to imprison Dennis and his like-minded brother from Saturday night to Monday morning on a regular basis.

Barrow blamed their mother, B. Lucy, for his problems with the sons; she was, he wrote, "the greatest rascal & smartest negro of her age I ever saw." The description is instructive. In English usage, a rascal was a member of the rabble, a commoner of the lowest class and characterized by dishonest and even rebellious behavior. In the American South, the term was usually applied to slaves and in 1851 Dr. Samuel Cartwright, as we have seen, blamed it on a medical condition he called Disaesthesia Ethiopia, which caused them to "slight their work," "wander about at night," and "[pay] no attention to the rights of property." Cartwright attributed this behavior to a "stupidness of mind" brought on by disease but Barrow blamed it on intelligence![15]

The biggest "rascal" on Barrow's plantation was Ginny Jerry (probably the name was originally Ginny's Jerry), or G. Jerry, as Barrow often wrote his name. Ginny Jerry caused Barrow many more problems than did B. Lucy's boys. Two years earlier, on October 1, 1837, Jerry had been off the plantation for a while when he was caught by Barrow's friend, Parnell, and brought home. Almost immediately he escaped again. Six weeks later, two men out hunting found Jerry's camp and one of them shot at him twice. Three days later, Barrow and Riddell, another friend, "set on the roads" at night hoping to catch Jerry. They did not see him, but a black man did go by on horseback and ignored their calls to halt until Riddell "put a load of small shot in his leg." Barrow's slave catcher Jack captured Jerry on April 1, 1838, six months after he had fled. According to Barrow, Jack "had to beat him very much—cut him with a club in 3 places very bad. On the head—and two cuts on the hand." Barrow thought Jerry had been doing well as a fugitive, "as perfect *a sheik as ever lived.*" Three weeks later, the master planned what seems an odd punishment for Ginny Jerry, making him wear women's clothes because he ran away "without the slightest cause." Over the next few years, Jerry continued to resist control, working as little as he could and running away several times. One day in October 1839, he claimed to be sick and then, as Barrow dryly put it, when the owner told the slave "to work it off," Jerry "concluded to woods it off." This was just three weeks before Barrow decided to build his jail, and G. Jerry was one of its first two inmates.[16]

On December 6, 1839, Barrow caught a fugitive belonging to a Captain Howells who said he had been living with Dennis. That night Barrow went to their camp, "through briers—cane &ct. rainy constant— dark as could be," and waited there from 8:00 until 1:00 in the morning, but Dennis never showed up. The camp itself was "very comfortable[,] Cooking utensils in abundance[,] meat &c." The next day Jack went after Dennis, taking Howells's slave with him, but Dennis spotted them fifty yards away and ran. Jack chased him to no avail, and Howells's runaway got away also. On the eleventh, Howells's cotton gin house burned down, and he blamed Dennis, but Barrow, who believed Howells was one of the cruelest masters in the area, thought he was probably trying to protect his own slaves from prosecution, which would cost the owner time and money, and perhaps even the slave. On the twenty-first, three of Barrow's black servants went after Dennis and found him, but according to Barrow, they "acted the rascal" and contrived to let him get away. Finally, on the twenty-third, an overseer in the neighborhood caught the fugitive and brought him to Barrow. Dennis, like Jerry, seems to have thrived during his period of lying out—he was "as fat as he can be." In another of his original punishments, Barrow determined to exhibit Dennis on Christmas Day in the slave quarter on a scaffold "with a red Flannel Cap on."[17]

After his escapes in the fall of 1839, Ginny Jerry stayed at home for nearly two years, but in the middle of August 1841 Barrow whipped him for inadequate cotton-picking, warning at the same time "if he ever dodged about from me again [I] would certainly shoot." The next day, Barrow was tipped off by another slave that Jerry was leaving. He found him in a bog in the bayou behind the slave quarters and shot him in the thigh. A week after that, Jerry ran off again, and Barrow wrote that he would shoot to kill him if he had the chance, or if not sell him. On September 22, he spent another miserable and fruitless night of slave hunting, waiting at G. Jerry's camp where he took refuge from the cold and rain in a hollow tree. A day later some neighbors caught the fugitive and brought him home.[18]

Barrow did not sell Jerry, although he doubtless punished him severely. In June 1842, when Jerry left again, however, the owner confided to his diary that he had not whipped the slave nor even talked to him for six months. Jerry was gone for another three weeks. In November of the same year, he was put in the stocks for some reason, but one of the other slaves let him out and he was gone again. Four days later, Barrow was out fox hunting, and his dogs picked up Jerry's scent and chased him for a while without success. Not until May 1843 was he caught, having been gone six months and three days according to Barrow's careful calculation, and, as the owner disgustedly put it, "looks fat as can be."[19]

Ginny Jerry's last recorded escape occurred in June 1845 and ended badly for him. He had been part of a group of eight or ten slaves that had stolen several hogs and Barrow "ducked & gave them a good thrashing." The next day "Mr. Ginny Jerry" as the planter put it, "Felt insulted at his treatment & put out." Barrow claimed he would happily pay $100 to get a chance to shoot the fugitive. He did not get the opportunity and finally in early September hired "negro hunters" to get him. Their dogs soon found a trail and chased Jerry for about a mile when he took refuge in a tree. Barrow "made the dogs pull him out of the tree, Bit him very badly." He thought Jerry would not run away again for some time. Whether he was right, we do not know as the diary ends the following year.[20]

To Barrow, his owner, Ginny Jerry was a rascal, an incorrigible slave; to others he was a rebel fighting for freedom, and he may have seen himself that way as well. But he was not simply resisting slavery, he was also choosing a lifestyle that was dangerous but involved not only a degree of freedom but also of comfort. Barrow's statement that Jerry lived like "a sheik" while in the woods was certainly an exaggeration, but along with the later comment that he came home "fat as can be," it indicates that being a hunted fugitive had a positive side, especially when compared to life in the slave quarter. For Jerry, and probably Dennis as well, lying out was a choice rather than a reaction.

Bennet Barrow's hands-on management seems to have limited fugitivism to Ginny Jerry and a few other bold runaways, but other slave managers were less successful, particularly overseers whose authority depended on its being supported by the owner of the plantation. James K. Polk, the future president of the United States, was the owner or managing trustee of several plantations in western Tennessee and northern Mississippi on which workers took advantage of weak overseers. Polk lived with his extended family in Columbia, Tennessee, about forty miles south of Nashville, but after being elected to the US House of Representatives in 1825, he spent much of his time in Washington. As the eldest of nine children, he administered his father's estate, which included land in Fayette County near the town of Somerville, Tennessee, about thirty-five miles east of Memphis, on which the family began operating a small plantation around 1833. Polk kept up with what was going on there through monthly letters sent by the overseer, a man named Ephraim Beanland, and from reports sent by the congressman's brother-in-law, Dr. Silas M. Caldwell, who visited the place from time to time.[21]

Beanland ran the West Tennessee plantation for a year beginning in the fall of 1833 and never succeeded in keeping his enslaved workers from leaving. In December he wrote Pope that two of them had escaped on November 28. The plantation storehouse had been broken into, and the overseer was convinced that a man named Jack was responsible. Jack denied it, but Beanland thought he was a habitual liar and punished him anyway. Soon after, Jack and another man named Ben fled. Beanland believed that both men had gone back to Columbia and was afraid that they would be allowed to stay there, which would have serious consequences for him. "If they ain't [brought back] the rest will leave me also." One of the enslaved people had already run away, because A. O. Harris, another of Polk's brothers-in-law, wrote him that Ben had arrived back in Columbia along with a man named Jim. They claimed that Beanland had whipped Jack severely and rubbed salt on the wounds as he was doing it. Neither of them wanted to go back, and Ben absolutely refused, saying that Polk himself had promised to rent him out or sell him if he wanted to stay in Columbia. Harris was uncertain what to do, but finally convinced Jim to return to Somerville and hired Ben out to the local ironworks for $100 per year, telling Beanland to rent a West Tennessee slave and pay the same amount.

Dr. Caldwell, the other brother-in-law, was at the Fayette plantation early in January 1834 and wrote Polk about Jack, the other escapee, whose experience on the run was much more eventful than those of the other two. He had gone to Memphis where he met two white men who captured him and took him down the river in a skiff with them, apparently with the intention of going to Texas and selling him there. A man named Hughes came upon these three at a hiding place along the river about 150 miles below Memphis. He recognized the white men as thieves and took all three 80 miles back up the Mississippi River and lodged them in the Phillips County Jail in Helena. Then Hughes took a steamboat to Memphis and rode over to Somerville where he offered to bring Jack back for $140. Instead Beanland and another man accompanied Hughes back to Helena and picked up Jack themselves, paying Hughes $100 for his role in the capture.

With Jack back on the plantation, Beanland attempted to deal with what he saw as the cause of his problems, namely that the workers he punished now understood that they could flee back to Columbia and find refuge with members of the Polk family. He wrote James K. saying that Ben was "a great scoundrel" and because he had been "friended" in Columbia other slaves would also run off if Beanland punished them.

In a letter written to James Walker, a third brother-in-law, the overseer predicted that if Ben were not returned, he was sure that Jim would leave and so would another man, named Wally. Even Hardy, a trusted slave allowed to drive the wagon to Memphis by himself, had run away for a week. Beanland believed he had too many bosses and that they did not support his authority. He had to please both Caldwell and Harris, he wrote, and "if I donte please every negro on the place they rin away rite strate." Within days both Jim and Wally did leave. Polk recognized the validity of the overseer's argument and had his surrogates send both Jim and Ben back to Beanland. James Walker also wrote a letter that the overseer read to the workforce, saying that anyone who ran away in the future would be sold. Whether because of that or not, the slaves stayed on the plantation for a while.[22]

Late in March Beanland attempted to "correct" Jack for something, and the servant cursed him and ran off. Beanland followed and caught him, but Jack had a stick and broke it over the overseer's head, and Beanland stabbed him twice with a knife. Writing to Polk about the event, Beanland said a doctor had seen Jack and said the wounds were not serious, that Jack had been in chains since the event, and he claimed he would never work for the Polks again. Beanland was equally adamant: "I can worke him and I intend to do it." Six months later Jack was gone. Thinking he had headed for the Mississippi River again, Polk sent Beanland to Memphis to search for him there and in Arkansas. Luckily for the overseer, Jack was caught by someone else and taken. Beanland was not enthusiastic about getting "the olde scoundrel" back, partly because the neighboring planters thought the chronic runaway was setting a bad example for their slaves as well as Polk's.[23]

In October 1834 Polk sold the Fayette County plantation, and he and Dr. Caldwell bought eight hundred acres of land in Yalobusha County, Mississippi, near the river of the same name, and just east of the Delta. It was about two hundred miles from Columbia, Tennessee, which continued to be the home base for the Polk family and their relatives. In early 1835 Caldwell took about thirty-five enslaved men, women, and children to the Yalobusha place and in two and a half weeks built a house for the overseer and four cabins for the workers, as well as a kitchen, a smokehouse, and a stockyard. The new plantation was also stocked with tools, food, and cotton seed. Ephraim Beanland, who was good at producing corn and cotton despite his problems with the slaves, served as overseer there for about a year, but if he wrote any reports during 1835 they are not extant. In January 1836 Caldwell fired the overseer, claiming that he had "run off" three slaves that cost more than $50 to get back.[24]

For the next several years, the enslaved people on the Mississippi plantation seemed to have stayed there, at least most of the time. After John I. Garner took over as overseer in September 1839, they began to assert themselves once again. A man named Charles left early in November, for no reason according to Garner, although the overseer believed he had gone to Tennessee where his wife lived. A woman named Marener was in the habit of "strolling" about the neighborhood, and when Garner punished her for it, she took refuge with Albert F. McNeil, a cousin of the Polks who also lived in Yalobusha County. Charles came back on his own in December, but by the middle of January 1840, Addison was "in the woods." Meanwhile Dr. Caldwell, who now lived in Haywood County, Tennessee, was again protecting the family's slaves from a man who had been hired to manage them. Caldwell wrote Polk, who was about to become president of the United States, to tell him that "your boy Henry Carter . . . is runaway [and] his reason for doing so he says the Overseer threatened to shoot him he says For nothing." Not surprisingly, Garner explained the events differently. He claimed that Henry had been slacking off his work so much that the overseer attempted to punish him and Henry resisted. Garner said he told Charles to hold Henry but Charles wouldn't do it, and Henry managed to get away "into the swamp." When the overseer went after him, Gilbert, Charles, and Perry all ran the other way. Garner thought Henry might come back for some clothes that night, and he got some men to stand watch. Perry did come back for some reason and was shot in the legs with small pellets when he attempted to run away. He was now back at work, but the other three were gone.[25]

What became of Garner is unknown, but in January 1841 Isaac H. Dismukes took over the management of the Yalobusha plantation. Within six months, he was having problems that would have been very familiar to his predecessors. Sometime around the middle of June, Addison fled, and a month later, Dr. Caldwell reported that the slave was back with him in Haywood County, Tennessee. Again, a plantation manager had been abusive. "From the wounds that are on his neck and arms it appears the overseer intended to kill him and he is afraid to stay there." Caldwell hired Addison out and wrote to the president asking what he should do. Two weeks later, Mrs. Caldwell, the president's sister, wrote to his wife saying that her husband had gotten Gilbert out of the

Somerville jail and sent both him and Addison back to the plantation. "From all accounts," wrote Mrs. Caldwell, "the overseer drinks and manages badly." But she acknowledged that all the information came from the slaves and was thus, as she put it, "Negros news," meaning that it might not be true. Addison was not sent back, and Gilbert ran away two days after his arrival in Mississippi. The frustrated Dismukes complained that an immediate whipping would have prevented the flight, but that he had been told not to punish the slaves unless a neighbor, Major Bobit, was present. He had also heard that Gilbert had told the other slaves that Caldwell wanted to buy him. All the slaves "beleave Tennessee is a parridise" and want to go back there. He told Polk that only he, his employer, could stop the slaves from running away, "for you noe that you have had men hear of different ages and sises and they runaway from all." Had Addison been sent back, Gilbert would not have left. Probably because of this, Addison was sent back, but he fled once again.[26]

We know nothing about what happened on the Yalobusha plantation during the years in which James K. Polk was president of the United States except that the overseer was James A. Mairs, who replaced Dismukes in 1844. After Polk died in 1849, however, his widow, Sarah, became the owner and took an active role in the management. Mairs reported to her regularly in letters addressed "Dear Marm." In January 1851, he reported that some of the workers were "behaving badly" and at least a few were "in the woods." Gilbert, who had been on the plantation for fifteen years, was one of them and he was gone for at least two months, and another man named Pompey was out for a month. In 1853, Joe absconded, taking Bill Nevels with him, but he came back six days later because Bill was sick. Other slaves fled from time to time, but a man named Harbert developed into the chief culprit. He escaped in January 1856 and was captured in Memphis. He left again in February, and Mairs learned that he had gotten a pass from someone and ridden the train at least part of the way to Memphis where he planned to get on a boat, perhaps to go north. Again, however, he was captured and brought home. In one of the last letters extant, Mairs wrote that Harbert had left again in September, taking three other slaves with him. In a report that suggested little had changed since 1835, the overseer informed Mrs. Polk that the runaway apparently hoped she would sell him to someone in Memphis. "He likes to be in a sity."[27]

≈

Escaped slaves who lay out in hidden places not far from where they lived usually returned home within a few weeks, but often they attempted to stay away much longer, and sometimes indefinitely. This was particularly true in the southern part of the valley where the dense swamps provided good cover and marronage had a long history. In 1854 a French newspaper reported that there were significant numbers of "nègres maroons" along the German Coast above New Orleans, living in rude cabins they had built in the swamps behind the plantations and subsisting in part on cattle that they stole and butchered. English language newspapers rarely used the term maroon, but they wrote about the same problem. Early in January 1856 three white men brought six slaves into the town of Plaquemine, located in Iberville Parish, south of Baton Rouge, whom they had captured in "the woods" where the fugitives had been living for over two years. The local newspaper was irate about the situation. "These runaway slaves kill your cattle. In the cold and piercing days of winter, they do not remain all night in the dark, dreary swamp. No; they visit the quarters of your servants in your own yard . . . There is scarcely a night in the week that your poultry yard is not inspected by some black rascal."[28]

Maroon communities included women as well as men and sometimes children. One female runaway who returned to her New Orleans owner in 1827 said she had been living within eight miles of the city in an area between the Gentilly Road and Lake Pontchartrain known as "the trembling prairies," specifically on a tract of dry land located deep in the swamp and surrounded by watery quicksand that prevented access except by a circuitous and well-hidden route. Some fifty or sixty runaways had been living there in permanent homes, cultivating corn, sweet potatoes, and vegetables and raising hogs and chickens. No doubt they also fished and hunted. The *New Orleans Mercantile Advisor* claimed that they also left often "to pillage by night in the environs of the city."[29]

Early in 1841 a father and son out hunting in St. Martin Parish, southeast of Lafayette, came upon a runaway slave named John, who had escaped from a local planter two years earlier. John shot at them but the gun misfired, and then he grappled with the son until the father shot John in the neck from a few inches away and killed him. A newspaper report claimed the maroon "had been implicated in the Lafayette Insurrection" (of which we will say more later) and been shot on an earlier occasion. He had a horse, and his cabin contained "plenty of provisions." In 1843 men in Assumption Parish found a group of runaways living "on a raised raft in the middle of a swamp" behind a plantation. They captured two of them and "dispersed" the rest. "The suburbs of Natchez are said to be infested with a large number of runaways," read the lead sentence in a July 1845 *Picayune* story about "an old and valuable family servant" who was stabbed to death when he tried to stop "a runaway committing depredation upon the property of his proprietor."[30]

Maroons often stole food. In the city of Carrollton, next to New Orleans, a resident came home to find "the entire contents of his larder eaten or carried off," presumably "the work of some runaway negro infesting the neighboring swamp." The homeowner set "an axe trap," the technical details of which the paper did not explain. According to the account, the following Sunday night, the burglar returned and the trap was sprung, and while the intruder was not harmed, "it scared him so badly he made for the swamp, leaving a stolen side of bacon on the fence."[31]

There is also evidence of marronage in the Mississippi Delta. In Fayette County, southwest of Memphis, a planter named Cole reported being approached by a black man while he was out riding in one of his fields. Cole thought the man might have a message for him, and indeed he did. He announced that he was a runaway, that he was armed with "a splendid brace of pistols and a bowie-knife," and he wanted to see Cole so that he could pay him for the food that Cole's slaves had been providing him for the last several weeks. He also showed a large amount of money, claiming it came from robbing houses in Memphis. Cole asked about two of his own slaves that had run off. The runaway said that they were with him but causing him so much trouble that he was willing to turn them in. Cole and he then arranged to meet the following day when the runaway-thief would take the planter to his missing slaves. Instead of going alone as he had promised, Cole took his overseer and another man with him, both armed with shotguns, and they succeeded in surrounding the runaway, who quietly surrendered and turned over his weapons. He said he was tired of living the way he was, having done it for five years, and would be happy to return to his former master in Alabama. Then he offered to take Cole to a deserted cabin where the planter's slaves were staying, and all four of the men went there. The runaway suggested he go in first to put the others off their guard and then the whites could come in and take them. After waiting a few minutes, Cole and his compatriots entered the building only to find the runaway had gone out a back window and ridden off on one of their horses.[32]

In the summer of 1856, four escaped slaves along with an Irishman were found in a cave about four miles from Helena. The Irishman fled into the river and was either picked up by a passing boat or drowned. The blacks, all of whom were from the immediate neighborhood, were arrested. The cave was fitted out for at least semipermanent occupation, albeit heavy on the alcohol: the inventory (perhaps exaggerated) included one thousand pounds of bacon and pork, a barrel of crackers, a barrel of bourbon, a barrel of "Deans whiskey," and ten dozen bottles of ale. In addition to that there were cooking utensils and "good comfortable beds."[33]

Bennet Barrow's diary does not mention any escapees who might be trying to go back to a place where they had once lived, but Polk's slaves fled from northern Mississippi and returned to their former homes in Tennessee, and Northup's friend Wiley tried to go all the way home to South Carolina. Many other slave owners thought their fugitives were headed to some place where they had previously lived. In the first decade after the War of 1812, some runaways attempted to go home along the route of the Natchez Trace that connected the Mississippi River town with Nashville. In September 1818, William Sugg, a subagent at the Choctaw Agency near what three years later would be Jackson, the new capital of the state, placed an ad in the *Mississippi State Gazette*, published at Natchez, announcing that "a black negro" named Harry "was brought to the Agency House on the 16th of that month." Harry was about twenty years old, five feet, six inches in height, and "diseased" in some way he did not specify. The runaway claimed that his owner was Caddie Byon, a Frenchman, who lived along Bayou Lafourche southwest of New Orleans. Sugg wanted Byon to come to the agency, pay the charges associated with the capture and imprisonment of Harry, and take the slave home. Two years later, John Forsyth, who lived near Natchez, was willing to pay the very large sum of $100 for his mulatto slave Ned, whom Forsyth described succinctly as "aged 35 to 40 years, stout built, light black, bow legged, thick lips and [having an] ugly face." Forsyth had recently purchased Ned and "supposed he will endeavor to get back to Kentucky, as he has been heard to express wishes to that effect." James Daswell, who lived in Washington County, three miles east of the Mississippi River, stated that Solomon and Abraham, who had run away from him, were attempting to get to Alabama.[34]

Other homesick runaways tried to get back to the southeast. In July 1836, an unnamed "Negro Man" owned by Martin Miller of Fayetteville, Arkansas, and apparently rented out to Zenus Pratt of Pope County, fled from the home of David War, in Spadra, the county seat of Johnson County, Arkansas, apparently while Pratt was visiting there. Pratt offered a $50 reward for the return of the man who "was brought from Georgia, and is probably making his way back to that State." In 1850, twenty-four-year-old Anthony and fifteen-year-old Sam escaped from their owner in Bienville Parish in Louisiana, and were thought to be on their way back to Decatur, Georgia, from where they had been brought slightly over a year ago. This was probably not Anthony's first escape since he could not "fully straighten his right hand" owing to old gunshot wounds in his arm and shoulder. In 1857, B. B. Mitchell of Memphis bought Bent, who was twenty-two years old, five feet, six inches tall and "rather chunky built," "likely" and intelligent, and had both a mustache and a beard, from Nathan Bedford Forrest, the leading slave trader in that city, who had brought Bent from Charleston, South Carolina. Bent had only been in Memphis for about four months, and Mitchell thought he would attempt to make his way back to South Carolina. That same year G. B. Thomas, who lived on Bayou Boeuf, thought that his slave, Simon, a house carpenter, might try to return to South Carolina where he was raised, although it was more likely that he would head for New Orleans.[35]

One man did make it from Mississippi to South Carolina only to meet a tragic end. He was six feet tall, stout, in his late thirties, had a long beard, and was nearly naked when he was found on Edisto Island. Men from the neighborhood had pursued him along a creek in a swamp. Even though armed only with a knife and club and hit with bird shot, he refused to surrender until receiving a mortal wound. He "appeared to have been runaway a long time." Before dying he said his name was Sam and that he was originally from South Carolina where he had been owned by many masters.[36]

Although some unwilling immigrants continued to flee to the East, others were attracted to new neighborhoods created by slaves in the Mississippi Valley from which they had been sold away. According to his owner, Pennington Tucker of Natchez, Phill, a thirty-year-old slender man with a "yellow complexion," had once been stolen and taken to Arkansas where he was sold, either in Little Rock or in Davidsonville, in the northeast part of the state. Phill must have formed a relationship with someone in Arkansas because he had several times escaped from Tucker and attempted to return there. The multiple escape attempts probably explain why Phill was branded with an S on one cheek and a C on the other and had "notches or slits on both ears." He was also wearing an iron on his neck and another on one leg when he fled. Tucker offered a $10 reward if Phill was captured in Mississippi and $20 if he were taken in Arkansas Territory. That same year, another runaway anxious to get to Arkansas was captured and turned over to the circuit court of Independence County, where Batesville was the county seat. Henry, had been owned by Asa McFelch of that county but sold to M. Foche, who lived twenty-five miles north of New Orleans. Apparently northern Arkansas had some attraction for Henry, perhaps because of friends in the area or maybe because enslaved people lived better there than in the sugar-producing region of Louisiana.[37]

H. F. Wade of Tchoupitoulas Street in New Orleans advertised in the New Orleans *Daily Picayune* for Robert, who called himself Sam and had fled on July 13, 1841. Wade had purchased Robert in Little Rock, and he had no doubt Robert would try to return there. Two young enslaved men, Noah, who was fifteen and copper colored, and Lige, a "dark mulatto" who was fourteen, both fled from T. B. Dillard of Pontotoc County, Mississippi, in April 1860. Dillard had bought them a few weeks earlier in St. Louis and presumed they would try to get back to that city, passing through Memphis on the way. Phillip Trammel thought that Tom, who escaped from Trammel's Lafayette County, Arkansas, plantation, would try to get back to the vicinity of Little Rock where he had grown up. Luke, a "tolerable" blacksmith, left his owner's home fifteen miles south of Little Rock in June 1826, thought to be headed for the "Sheb[b]oleth Lead Mines, in Missouri, where he formerly lived and to which place he appeared to be attached."[38]

In 1822 Louisiana officials in New Orleans received startling news from St. Martinville in the Atakapas region: "The good people of this place are all on the alert. The freedom and equality granted to the blacks by the Mexican constitution have set the slaves from this neighborhood on the wings for that country." Most of them had not gotten far. "A group of twenty-five had gone, fourteen were caught on the Grand Prairie. Four were arrested in this place as they were absconding with their master's horses." Key members of the group were privileged slaves. The supposed leader, who was still at large, was the "son of Mr. Neuville Declosest." Another, who was caught leaving with a horse and gun belonging to his owner, was well educated and clever: "The Rascal asked if by the common-law they had a right to do so— He was formerly a servant of Judge Porre's & I suppose, thought that he had picked up law enough while dusting his master's law book to shield him from harm in case of detection." A third, "called on Mr. Robin to borrow his horse, to go in search, as he pretended, of his master's horses and away the fellow went full speed, but fortunately the horse fell and he was arrested."[39]

Slavery in New Spain had been on the decline since the middle of the seventeenth century when the gold and silver was long gone, the Indian population had begun to increase, and interbreeding had weakened the importance of racial distinctions. By the time that Mexico became independent in 1820 there were only an estimated three thousand enslaved people in the country, and the ideology of independence was strongly in favor of citizenship for all. The Plan of Iguala promulgated in February 1821 guaranteed all inhabitants freedom and equality. The Constitution of 1824 did not address the issue of slavery, but a presidential decree of 1829 officially abolished that institution everywhere except in Coahuila where American immigrants were permitted to keep those they already owned. Despite that concession, the Mexican legislature refused to ratify a commercial treaty with the United States until a provision for the extradition of runaway slaves was removed. Opposition to helping American slaveholders get their black fugitives back hardened after the Texas Revolution, was reinforced by the Mexican War, and continued to the Civil War.

Life was not easy for the freedom-seekers who did reach Mexico. Those near the border were in danger of being kidnapped by American slave catchers, who found it easy to enter Mexico and return safely, with or without their quarry. Finding jobs and starting new lives was not easy for the refugees and gaining Mexican citizenship was difficult for males. The government treated them like visitors from other countries, classifying them as aliens but allowing them to become citizens of Mexico if they could prove they were citizens of some other country, but that was impossible for the former slaves. Integration in Mexican society was another path to citizenship and could be achieved in various ways, becoming Catholic helped and so also did a letter of recommendation from the local government where you lived. In this case, women benefited from their secondary legal status in Mexico as in most countries. They were not eligible for citizenship in Mexico, but their freedom and other basic rights were protected by the government.[40]

After Texas became independent, newspapers there began to carry advertisements from Louisiana slave masters who believed their escaped laborers were on their way to Mexico. While Solomon Northup was working in Edwin Eppes's cotton fields, Henry, a twenty-five-year-old mixed-race carpenter who spoke French, fled from his Cajun owner on Bayou Boeuf and got to Fayette County, located between Houston and San Antonio, before being captured. In 1841 the *Red-Lander* newspaper in St. Augustine, Texas, carried an advertisement for Anthony, a Creole man who spoke only a little English, and another man, both of whom had run away from Madame Cloutier, a widow living in Natchitoches. Anthony was following in the footsteps of at least a few Africans who had fled from their French owners in and around that colonial town nearly a century earlier. James, who claimed to be owned by a man in New Orleans, was committed to the Sabine County Jail in Texas in September 1841. Given that Sabine County is on the Louisiana-Texas border southwest of Natchitoches, James may have gone up the Red River to that city before striking out for Texas and presumably Mexico. In 1846 Peter, owned by a sugar planter also on Bayou Boeuf, was caught and jailed in Houston. Jim and Abram left their home fifteen miles south of Baton Rouge in June 1850 and five months later reached the vicinity of Austin, Texas, where Jim was captured. Doshy Wallace, "a very light mulatto" who had straight hair and was "fine spoken," and her fifteen-year-old daughter Elizabeth were imprisoned in Fannin County, having fled from Jesse Paxton, who lived in Washington Parish, Louisiana. In 1859 the *Trinity Advocate* published in Palestine, Texas, reported under the heading "Not Quite so Fast" that a "light yellow" colored man had walked into the town with a "carpet sack on his arm" and when questioned by several suspicious citizens said that he was a Mexican, but after being caught making several inconsistent statements finally admitted that he was a runaway from Louisiana on his way to Mexico.[41]

After Henry Shreve cleared the Great Raft on the Red River, the region above it developed into a northwest extension of the Cotton Kingdom. Shreveport, incorporated in 1839, became an important city, Bossier Parish on the east side of the Red River and Caddo Parish on the west side were carved out of Natchitoches Parish, and across the state line in Arkansas, Lafayette and Hempstead Counties flourished. Soon freedom-seeking slaves living in the region began to flee toward Mexico. In 1841 Harry, a "good looking" man in his mid-twenties, fled from T. Bossier in Caddo Parish and was captured later "on the San Antonio Road" but escaped. Bossier placed an ad for him in two Austin, Texas, papers. In 1848 Thomas Dagley, the sheriff of Fannin County, advertised that Tom, described only as "dark" and "heavy set," had been brought to him by a justice of the peace after being found "riding a pacing horse." Tom claimed to be free, but William H. Gill had told the sheriff that he had once owned Tom, whose real name was Shade or Shadrack, and sold him to a man in Shreveport. Levi, who escaped from Hempstead County, Arkansas, probably in 1850, had the hard luck to be captured on the San Antonio-Laredo Road only thirty miles north of the Rio Grande. In 1856 a carpenter named Joe belonging to Mr. Johnson, who lived on the Red River below Shreveport, was captured in Dewitt County, more than halfway to Mexico.[42]

Despite the difficulties of living in Mexico, getting there was the main problem. Three slaves from Mississippi met a horrible fate. Early in the spring of 1850 scouts for a wagon train traveling from El Paso to San Antonio found two escaped slaves from Holly Springs, Mississippi, on the West Texas plain near the Pecos River, some two hundred miles north of the Rio Grande. Henry and Melinda had been traveling for more than a year with a companion named Morgan and had obviously lost their way, being closer to El Paso than to the Rio Grande when found. They had been out of food for some time. After boiling pieces of oxen hide and then going without any nourishment at all for three days, they had discussed drawing lots and having the loser commit suicide so that he or she could be eaten by their companions. Morgan and Henry quarreled over the plan one night, and Morgan threatened Henry, who resolved the issue by cutting Morgan's throat after he had gone to sleep. When found, Henry and Melinda were cooking his flesh. A Texas newspaper editor made no negative comments about the runaways or their cannibalism but simply noted he had heard of people having to "devour each other to save themselves from starvation at sea but never before on land."[43]

Arkansas was a crossroads for runaway slaves. Some black escapees appear to have been attracted to Arkansas Territory for the same reason that a variety of disreputable white people went there: it was a sparsely populated place where the hand of the law was relatively light. One of these was Jesse, "five feet two inches high, square made, black complexion," who fled from Joseph Cotton of Lawrence County, Tennessee, about fifty miles east of Memphis, in May 1828. A month later, Jesse was captured in Greenock, in Crittenden County, across the Mississippi River from Memphis, but escaped from the jail. Ten months later, Cotton heard that Jesse had left with a companion who was later shot near Little Rock and that he himself had been captured somewhere along the Arkansas River fifty miles west of that city. John, who was in the Pulaski County Jail in 1842, told the sheriff that his master had brought him from Virginia to Nashville. In 1856 two men in the same place who were captured together said they had come from Sparta, Georgia, but probably they also had escaped from a slave trader who had brought them further west.[44]

Indian Removal caused escaped slaves to travel through Arkansas going both west and east. Slaveholding was part of what made the Cherokee, Choctaw, Chickasaw, Creek, and Seminole "civilized tribes," and the black people they took with them to Indian Territory were followed by some who escaped from their owners in order to be with unwilling immigrants, just as being there led others to flee in order to get back to their old homes. Many Cherokees had already moved to eastern Arkansas before the War of 1812, and after the New Madrid Earthquake at the end of 1811, they left the lower St. Francis River valley and settled along the Arkansas River near the modern city of Dardanelle. In 1821 Austin, a thirty-five-year-old man who had "lived a considerable time in the old Cherokee nation," escaped from a new owner, who lived near the mouth of the Arkansas River and thought the fugitive would go to the Cherokees, either in Tennessee or in Arkansas. Similarly, after Celia, "a large, likely woman, inclined to be fat," who was being held as security for a debt owed by her owner, broke out of the Pulaski County Jail, Isaac Watkins, the jailer, assumed she would try to return to Walter Weber, a chief of the western Cherokees whose property she once had been. Ben, who broke out of the St. Francis County Jail in 1833, was assumed to be following his wife, who had been sold to a man living with the Choctaws and taken her west with him. William Hall, on the other hand, who lived at the Choctaw Agency in Arkansas, assumed that the twenty-nine-year-old Spencer, who was six feet tall and had "tolerable long whiskers," would try to get back to Sumpter County, Alabama, following the same route through Memphis they traveled less than a year ago when Hall had bought him. Two mixed-race brothers in their late twenties, Colin and David, tried to use Indian Removal as a way to migrate away from their owner: they set off down the Tennessee River from Tuscumbia, Alabama, dressed as Indians, "their disguise so complete that it would be difficult to detect them, unless their hair is examined, and their hands, which are harder than those of Indians." They even could speak a little Chickasaw.[45]

Escapees to and from Indian country often went on horseback. Simon had been raised in Chambers County, Alabama, and brought west by a Creek woman named Winey, who apparently sold him to B. L. E. Bonneville, who lived near Fort Gibson, in what is now Muskogee County, Oklahoma. Simon was last seen riding toward Little Rock on a "light cream colored mare on his way back to Alabama." Joe, who left Aberdeen, Mississippi, on a bay horse, was thought to be on his way to Arkansas. Billy, Washington, Harwell, and Will were all mounted on horses nice enough for Pierre Juzan, their owner, to describe them each in detail. Juzan thought the runaways were on their way to Lauderdale, Mississippi. They also took a rifle, a shotgun, and plenty of food for the trip. One suspects that Harry, who escaped from a Creek chief in April 1834, might have taken a horse if he had wanted one. The Creek Agency was on the Verdigris River, however, and he went off in a canoe with ten beaver traps, a rifle, and an axe.[46]

Ephraim, also known as Eaf, did not migrate with the Indians and did not stay with them long. Ne-ta-ki-jah, a Choctaw chief, bought him in Little Rock while on his way west and sold him to Joseph A. Doak, who owned a trading Post in Indian Territory. After Eaf ran away, Doak described him as about twenty-seven years old, five feet, five inches tall, well built, and reasonably good looking, "very talkative, fond of drinking and gambling." The fugitive was seen in Little Rock a month or so after that, and later was captured on the Saline River thirty miles to the south. He escaped again and was caught and brought back to Little Rock. Doak then sold him to Samuel M. Rutherford of that town, and Ephraim escaped immediately. Rutherford offered a reward of $100 for Eaf, perhaps in recognition that getting him back would be a difficult job.[47]

≈

In December 1860, a private citizen living in Derby, Indiana, arrested a runaway slave who, as a local newspaper put it, "was making his way to the Dominion of her Majesty Queen Victoria." The fugitive was named Dick and he had started out near Jackson in East Feliciana Parish, about seven hundred miles to the south in August and about four months later crossed the Ohio River near Stephensport, Kentucky. He was taken up not too far north of there, perhaps because he assumed he was safe having reached a free state and unaware that the white people in southern Indiana had strong southern sympathies. Dick's captor took him back to Kentucky, so he could be jailed in a slaveholding state.[48]

A few escapees from the Lower Mississippi Valley did make it to the North. Several of them made the pages of the *Portage County Democrat* published in Ravenna, Ohio, near Cleveland, where runaways often crossed Lake Erie to the Canadian city of Chatham, In February 1855, the paper reported on heavier-than-normal traffic on the Underground Railroad. Seven "lots" of runaways had passed through the Ravenna "terminus," all the fugitives from Kentucky except for "two middle aged, stout, men who had come on foot from Louisiana, sleeping by day, and following the north star by night."[49]

Many owners thought that their missing workers were on their way north. Jerry, owned by Ransom Moore of Fort Smith, Arkansas, was a good candidate for a successful escape. In his mid- to late thirties, he was older than many runaways and had some gray hair on his head and probably also in his "tolerably large whiskers," but he was "slim and well made," and "a very likely, cunning, and artful fellow," who also had a fondness for both drinking and gambling. Jerry had grown up near Georgetown, Kentucky, before being brought to Arkansas around 1825, so he knew something about the geography between there and the North. Sampson Gray, who lived near Little Rock, was Jerry's first owner in Arkansas, and it was he who sold the slave to Moore. Sometime around April 1830, Moore sent Jerry to Little Rock with a pass that authorized him to hire himself out to someone there, probably to do the carpentry work at which he had some skill. After Jerry escaped, Moore assumed he had procured "a forged pass or perhaps forged free papers, and will endeavor to pass himself as a freeman . . . [and] most probably make for a free state." Even before the owner could get his ad in the *Arkansas Gazette,* Jerry had been seen in Conway County to the north of Little Rock.[50]

One of the Natchez "nabobs," Samuel Scott, who owned Stamply Hill Plantation in Jefferson County, Mississippi, thought that Harry, a thirty-year-old man who fled at the end of February 1847, was trying to get to a free state. Harry had a "little stoppage in his speech, and a down-cast look when spoken to," but he may have had a feisty temper as a portion of his right ear had been bitten off, and he was a chronic runaway. Scott was sure that if jailed the runaway would give false names for himself and his master as he had done on earlier occasions, which indicates that Harry would rather be sold to a stranger than returned to his owner, an uncommon sentiment among fugitives. He had been gone four months when Scott's ad appeared in the *Mississippi Free Trader*. The planter wanted it reprinted in the *Louisville Journal*, and he offered a $100 reward if Harry were captured in a free state, as opposed to $25 if he were taken in the South.[51]

James K. Polk's bondswoman Marener, who irritated her overseer by frequently leaving home to travel about the neighborhood was not atypical. Husbands and romantically inclined young men went out at night more than did the objects of their interest, but many women also absented themselves after dark.[52]

The slaves of John B. Nevitt were probably truant more often than most because his plantation was on the edge of Natchez. On March 13, 1831, Nevitt gave Milly and Betts passes to go into the city during the day, and they stayed out until eight that night. Nevitt resolved to stop giving passes, and a week later Betts ran away with Delly. Seven days after that, Betts came home and Nevitt decided not to punish her lest it discourage Delly from coming in. On April 8, Delly was discovered hiding in a barn with a man named Albert, and Nevitt had them both whipped. In June, Milly ran away.[53]

Women also attempted long-distance escapes. Females were half the adult black population in the Lower Mississippi Valley, but they made up only 8 percent of the runaways in newspaper advertisement, outside of New Orleans where they were much more numerous. Fewer women escaped because they were the primary caregivers for their children. They were also less familiar with the world beyond the neighborhood, since it was usually male slaves who went on errands into town, traveled with their masters on business trips, and were rented out to work on other farms and plantations. On the other hand, they seem to have been able to hide effectively in small cities. Charles Rapley of Little Rock felt the need to advertise in the local paper for Isabella, who was seventeen or eighteen years old and "nearly white," who had been missing two weeks, but he believed was still "lurking somewhere in the vicinity of this city." William Jones of Memphis, which had a few thousand more people, thought that Martha was still "lurking about this place" even though she had been gone for three months. Melinda, who was twenty-two, "tolerably large," and "dark copper" in color, left the Saline County, Arkansas, plantation of Asher Bagley after he died, and was thought to be in the vicinity of Pine Bluff, a small community on the Arkansas River in neighboring Jefferson County.[54]

While most enslaved women stayed home with their children, Flora left Natchez in 1828 to find hers. She was in her late thirties, "yellowish" in color, had excellent teeth, and according to the advertisement "disposed to be insolent in her manners." It was believed that she had a pass and would pretend to be a free person. She had "children in some part of this state, and will, most certainly, use her exertions to get to them." Another fugitive woman was Matilda, who had been working for John A. Terrill of Natchez for several years "peddling goods" when she left in 1825 with $150 of his merchandise. Terrill was convinced that the mixed-race young woman would try to pass as an Indian and make her way to freedom in Mexico.[55]

Women runaways were often captured and languished in jail just as men did. Among them was Lucy, who was committed in June 1828 to the Adams County Jail in Natchez. She was owned by a man in Franklin County, which bordered Adams on the west. Maria, who was in the Adams County Jail in early 1829, was "somewhat marked with a whip." The jail in Chicot County was the ending point for many unsuccessful escapes that began in lower Louisiana. Among them was Jane, a twenty-year-old, five feet tall, black woman, who was wearing "an old striped calico dress" when committed. She had been purchased in Baron County, Kentucky, by a slave trader who carried her to New Orleans where she was sold to a resident of that city. Lydia, who was imprisoned in Vicksburg in 1835, had come west from Jackson and claimed to have "been out three months." In the same jail a few months later was Betsy, who belonged to the estate of the deceased Osborn Ford of Franklin County and had been hired out to a man living along the Mississippi River twenty-six miles below Natchez. Harriet, who was also incarcerated in the Warren County Jail that year, had come from Hinds County, perhaps having traveled from Jackson to Vicksburg in the hope of escaping on a steamboat. Matilda, also from Hinds County, was there too, probably having traveled with Harriet. Mary, in the same jail a month later had come from the same place. Emaline, a twenty-one-year-old woman, and her one-year-old daughter Virginia Elizabeth fled from William Coopwood of Fayette County, Tennessee, and ended up in the Shelby County Jail in Memphis.[56]

Women sometimes ran away with their husbands. Peter and Susan, who had recently been purchased from an owner in the small town of Batesville in the Ozark foothills and taken to Arkansas Post in the Delta region, fled from the latter place apparently to return to the former. They were caught once but escaped again. The flight of Maria and her husband, Ned, illustrates some of the drama and complexity of an enslaved family. They left their owner in Saline County, Arkansas, in June 1840, taking a two-month-old baby with them. Owner Thomas C. Steen thought they had been "run by a white man," meaning stolen, but there must have been more to the story. Maria and Ned were both described as black, but their child was multiracial, "rather yellow in appearance." Ned also had an unhealed bullet wound in his thigh.[57]

An unnamed woman who lived in East Feliciana Parish showed remarkable loyalty when she ran off with her husband, Dave. He had left the night before after shooting his master while the man was eating dinner. The wife was only sixteen or seventeen, and the local newspaper said she was subject to fits, not very intelligent, and "very easy alarmed by the sight of a whip." If found away from her husband, it was thought she would provide information about his whereabouts, presumably through some means of torture. Another Louisiana woman not named in the advertisement absconded with an unnamed man and headed for Natchez. There is no evidence they were married, but she must have cared about him, because he had "a scar on the foot, just above the heel, done intentionally [to himself] to prevent his walking so that he might not be sold in North Carolina." The brutal evidence of how much he wanted to stay in the East would have made it very hard for him and his companion to get away.[58]

John, about thirty-five years old, and Polly, a house servant ten years his junior, were a married couple living in Virginia when their owner sold them to a slave trader, who took them to the New Orleans market. There they were purchased by different men and escaped rather than be separated. They were together when captured and taken to the Chicot

County Jail in November 1844. After more than a year in which neither of their new owners responded to advertisements indicating where they were, both were scheduled to be sold on February 2, 1846, no doubt hoping to be purchased by the same person.[59]

A different kind of relationship was revealed in an advertisement in the *Arkansas Gazette* in 1837 stating that a white man named Richard Carter was headed to Arkansas from Jackson County, Tennessee, four hundred miles to the east, and carrying with him a "light bright yellow color" seventeen-year-old woman named Jemima, who was four or five months pregnant. Richard Carter was well-enough known to Dale Carter, who posted the ad, for him to give a detailed description and warn that he was carrying a rifle, two pistols, and a knife, and the enslaved woman was owned by Permelia Carter. Dale and Permilia claimed that Richard had stolen Jemima and intended to sell her, but it seems just as likely that the two fugitives had eloped carrying their unborn child with them.[60]

Similarly, a mixed-race young woman named Grace with long, straight, black hair left a plantation on Lake Washington in Washington County, Mississippi, with the overseer there, a man named Paul A. Guire, who was ten years older than she was. Henry Knox, her owner and his employer, claimed the two had been having sexual intercourse for about three months before they went off together. Knox referred to Guire as a thief and emphasized the significance of his action by going out of his way to state that his parents, who lived in the area, were respectable people. Not only did he offer a reward of $200 for Guire and $100 for Grace, but his neighbors had pitched in another $300 for anybody who brought the overseer back. There was no suggestion that he intended to sell the slave, rather it was thought he was taking her either to Texas or a northern state.[61]

Often when women went off with their husbands there were others in the group. Ann, who was in her early twenties and described as "shrewd, sensible, bold and impudent in her address," and her close friend Bridget, who was about ten years older and "stout built," left Petit Gulf, Mississippi, in the fall of 1825. They were with Henry, Ann's husband, and John, both of whom were Ann's age and mixed race. John was from Cuba and could speak Spanish. It was thought that the group would stay together and go down the river to New Orleans. Randal, a blacksmith in his mid-twenties who could read and write, and his wife, Maria, a few years younger, left Robert Liles's plantation in Mississippi along with another women and two men. They crossed the Mississippi near Point Chicot carrying four guns among them, probably intending to escape into the same swampy Arkansas Delta that served as a hiding place for white criminals. Moriah, who was about twenty-five, short, and "thick set," and "yellow complected" escaped from a Chicot County plantation along with her husband, Joe, who was in his early thirties, about five feet, nine inches tall, and black, and another man. The runaways were caught and jailed in Union County just west of Chicot County.[62]

Twenty-one-year-old Winey left an owner in Monroe Parish, along with her husband, Robert, an ox driver. They went with Jack, who made shoes, played the violin, was described as "much of a villain," and was thought to be trying to get to Texas. Charlotte, who was seventeen, ran off with Sam and several other men. Jacob Reider of Little Rock, did not know where they were going but wanted them back from wherever it was. He offered a calibrated reward: $10 for each of them if captured in the township, $20 in the county, $30 in some other part of Arkansas, $50 in another slave state, and $100 if captured in a free state. Among a large group of runaways advertised by the sheriff of Carroll Parish, Louisiana, in May 1835 was Cressy Ann, a twenty-one-year-old mixed-race woman belonging to Robert H. Bowmar of "prairie Jefferson" in Ouachita Parish, who had her child Mary Jane with her. Two men also owned by Bowmar were in the group, and another two owned by someone else in the parish. One of the men was later shot in the thigh and captured. Sabra, a black woman, "tall and spare," and about thirty years old, accompanied her husband, Simon, and five other men who escaped from a plantation on Milliken's Bend, across the river from Vicksburg in 1839. Their owner, an absentee planter named William H. Edington, believed the group had crossed the river into Mississippi and was attempting to reach a free state. Some of them had tried to do that a few years earlier, only to be caught at Lake Washington, fifty miles to the north.[63]

CHAPTER 4

De Boat Am in De River

MUSIC WAS A central part of the black culture that developed in the antebellum South, most of it spiritual in nature, expressing the deep Christian religiosity that was a major source of psychological and emotional support for the enslaved. Secular protest music was a dangerous form of artistic expression, but there was some of that as well, including the following lines that arose in the Lower Mississippi Valley.

> I's gwine from the cotton fields, I's gwine from de cane,
> I's gwine from the o'l log hut dat stan's down the lane;
> De boat am in de River, dat comes to take me off,
> An' I's gwine to join the exodus and strike out fo' de no'f.[1]

Solomon Northup took a big risk when he asked a steamboat captain to help him escape and get to the North, but it might have had a big payoff: the travel time was only a few days, in many ways it was less dangerous than going by land, and it was often possible to get assistance from the many slaves and free blacks who worked on the vessels. The captain's decision to say no, however, was also reasonable: runaways on steamboats were usually found out, one way or another, and when that happened the captain could be sued or prosecuted. For enslaved people living in New Orleans, or able to get there, another option was to get on a sailing ship going to a northern port, to Mexico, or to Liverpool or Le Havre. By the 1850s there were also steamships on the coastal routes. The river system also made it easier for enslaved people living in the valley to travel to other places in the region where they might have friends or family.[2]

Steamboats were the most efficient form of water transportation, but many fugitives also floated away from their owners on flatboats. Lattuce, an enslaved carpenter in Natchez, gathered up his tools and other belongings in October 1824, got aboard a flatboat loaded with hogs, and headed for New Orleans with four or five dollars in his pocket. His owner described Lattuce as "obedient and pleasant when sober" but "much given to intoxication," and thought that he would attempt to pass himself off as a free man. About the time Lattuce left the city, Ben arrived in the Adams County Jail in Natchez, having left Arkansas Territory six weeks earlier hoping to float to New Orleans on a raft. Anderson, who had fled from his owner in Fayette County, Kentucky, on a flatboat going down the Ohio River was in the same place.[3]

In January 1825, George, a twenty-eight-year-old man "of light Negro colour," left Concordia Parish, across the river from Natchez, in a large oaken skiff. His master thought he might try to get to New Orleans and find a steamboat that would take him upriver to Kentucky from where he recently had been brought. He described the slave as "something of a madman when drunk" but otherwise "perfectly satisfied with his situation." Obviously, this man, like many other slave owners, had a hard time understanding why his servant would want to leave him. Francis B. Bouis, who lived six miles above the Point Coupee church, believed that three of his workers might have been "decoyed away by some boat's crew" when they went missing in February 1825 and asked people along the river to watch for them. One of them was Molly, whose smallest toe on each foot had been cut off, probably because she had previously attempted to escape by land.[4]

A young black couple, Jim and Hannah, had been traveling with their master many months from Washington, DC, on the way to Louisiana and were floating down the Mississippi River on a flatboat when the ungainly craft struck a tree stuck in the river bottom and protruding from the water. The boat capsized; their child was lost in the water along with some other people; and the last they saw of their master "he was hanging on to the sawyer that wrecked them." The two slaves managed to hang on to a part of the boat and float to safety, but sometime afterward they were captured and placed in the Claiborne County Jail.[5]

George and Thomas were on the final leg of a trip from South Carolina to Louisiana when they escaped from a flatboat only to be captured and jailed in Concordia Parish. In 1848 a coal boat found a runaway slave named Charles in a skiff at Horseshoe Cutoff on the Mississippi River near Memphis and took him to New Orleans. Charles said his owner lived in Davidsonville County, Tennessee, where Nashville is located, which means he may have floated down the Cumberland River to Paducah, Kentucky, and then on down the Ohio and the Mississippi before his capture.[6]

Dick fled from New Orleans and was thought to be headed for Natchez, so he probably left on a steamboat, but his chances of freedom were improved by his earlier experience as a barber shaving people on flatboats. He was sixteen, small for his age, and, according to his owner, "has all the airs of a barber when so employed, with his comb case under his arm and a comb in his hair, which he is very fond of putting up and dressing." He "has an insolent air and is quarrelsome and impudent." He also had a very nice wardrobe, since he took with him "five or six shirts and pantaloons" and also "a good blue cloth coat, a pair of wide black crepe pantaloons [pants], and a black silk roundabout [short-waist jacket]." He spoke English and some French. Most steamboats had barbers on board who operated their own small business, so Dick may have become an entrepreneur.[7]

A runaway named Tom escaped by taking advantage of both old and new watercraft technology. Along with Brun and John, he stole a skiff, left the plantation owned by Shapley Owen in Carroll Parish, and got to Island 95 near Vicksburg. There they were captured by a white man named Gershen Brown, who put the three escapees to work rather than taking them to the sheriff. Two months later, Brown let Tom leave in a small boat that carried him to New Orleans. Not long after, Brown became aware that Shapley was coming to get the slaves, and he let Brun and John leave. They were later captured in Vicksburg. Meanwhile, Tom had somehow gotten on a steamboat and traveled to Cairo, Illinois, from where he managed to get to Pittsburgh and presumably freedom. Owen sued Brown for his self-interested harboring of the three escapees and the steamboat *Niagara* for carrying Tom away without Owen's permission. He won compensation for both his temporary loss of labor and his permanent loss of property.[8]

One enslaved man may have used steamboat transportation to free himself from Bennett Barrow's tight control. In June 1831, the planter put an ad in the *Woodville Republican* for Giles, a tall, thin man black in complexion. He was "a good field hand, cook, accustomed to the water, a good house servant, &c. &c." Barrow was sure that Giles was trying to get away for good and would try to get aboard a steamboat and make his way to the North. "He is a negro of good sense and much ingenuity; and there are few better qualified to make their escape than he is." Anxious to get the man back and aware it might be hard to do, Barrow offered a $100 reward.[9]

More so than escapes by land, those on water, and especially in steamboats, required immediate action by the owners of the fugitives. Thus on Monday, July 24, 1837, William Johnson noted in his diary that he had been "writing and Flying Around as Buisy as you please." Johnson was a free black barber and businessman in Natchez who owned at least four slaves and had just learned that one of them, a man named Walker, had run away on a steamboat. Johnson quickly wrote a description of Walker and gave it to a Mr. Birk, who was leaving on another boat and promised to give it to the sheriff in Louisville, Kentucky. He also sent an advertisement to the *Natchez Courier*, asking that it be published in the daily for a week and in the weekly edition until further notice. Johnson's ad described Walker as about forty, six feet tall, thin and muscular, having a full head of hair and a beard, and being "very black." He usually smiled when spoken to, showing healthy teeth that were white despite his regular use of chewing tobacco. He leaned to the side when walking and stooped a little. "His feet is pretty Large." He was said to be a Baptist. Walker had been brought to Natchez by a slave-trading firm, sold there, but then returned by the new owner. Johnson bought him at auction "as an unsound Slave," paying the very low price of $55. What was wrong with Walker is not clear. Johnson at first thought he was mentally challenged but later seemed to value him highly.

Two weeks after Walker left, Johnson wrote his sister that the slave had been stolen by someone staying at the landing known as Under the Hill, and he never expected to see him again. A few weeks after that he heard Walker was in jail in Paducah, but eventually learned the captive was someone else. In December, a professional slave catcher visited Johnson's barbershop asking what he would pay to have Walker captured and brought home. Johnson offered $50 and expenses, but the man laughed and said it would cost $300 and expenses. The next day, Johnson upped the offer to a flat $300 for Walker's return. He also offered to sell the slave for $300 "just as he stood," meaning the buyer would get the title but still had to find and capture his purchase. Johnson thought he might have a deal, but that did not happen. Three weeks later, he posted an advertisement making the same offer to the public. Saying that Walker's wife was owned by a man in Bourbon County, Kentucky, and he might have gone there, Johnson offered a $200 reward if he was captured and brought back from that state. If the fugitive were found in the free state of Ohio, he would pay $300. And he would accept $300 "for the Chance of Him."[10]

Another valued escapee was Thomas Peters, who had been a "trusty servant" in the Natchez tavern owned by his master, Richard Terrell, from 1816 to 1828. He was a mixed-race man, dark in color, shorter than average, and in his early thirties. According to Terrell, he was a good cook, could do rough carpentry work, read, wrote "indifferently," and was "tolerably intelligent for a slave." This description probably under-estimated Peters's talents, because Terrell eventually hired Peters out as a steamboat steward, a highly responsible and well-paid position. He worked first on the *General Wayne* and then on the *Talma*. In May 1830, Peter left Natchez on the latter boat bound for Louisville and never returned. Terrell later learned his slave had been in Pittsburgh in June, and he became convinced that some "villain" had encouraged his escape and helped him get away.[11]

Despite what Richard Terrell thought, Thomas Peters may have needed little or no assistance. Enslaved people who worked on steam-boats made money in various ways and could go ashore when the boats were docked in southern cities. As a cook, Peters probably had more cash than other crewmen when he arrived at Louisville and found it relatively easy to lose himself in the city of 10,000 people, 2,500 of whom were enslaved. Finding passage across the Ohio River would have been more difficult, but he could have paid someone or perhaps gotten assistance from one of the several hundred free black people living there. That was in 1830; in 1850, fleeing slaves would find an even more positive envi-ronment. In that year, Louisville had a population of 20,000, including nearly 7,000 slaves and more than 700 free blacks.[12]

A very large number of enslaved people in the Lower Mississippi Valley shared at least some of the steamboat experience that allowed Peters to get away. In 1850, nearly 750 steamboats were in operation on the Mississippi and Ohio Rivers and their tributaries. An average vessel carried a crew of twenty-six, but large boats serving the big cities on the main rivers usually had at least forty crew members and many had more. A steamboat crew of forty would usually have eight officers—a captain, and several each of pilots, engineers, and mates, and a clerk. The cabin crew of about ten would be headed by the steward, who was usually white and often had an assistant, one or two cooks, two or three waiters, and two or three chambermaids. The number of deckhands would be roughly equal to that of the cabin crew, and they would include a few who handled the boat itself, roustabouts whose main duty was to load and unload cargo, and firemen who carried wood on board but spent most of their time feeding it into the boiler furnaces. The cabin crew worked longer hours than the deck crew, but they enjoyed better food and accommodations. Firemen did intense physical labor in stifling and sometimes searing heat, a job so difficult that they worked in four-hour shifts.[13]

Historian Thomas C. Buchanan's careful study of steamboats docked at St. Louis in 1850 found that 18 percent of the crew members were African American, 12 percent enslaved and 6 percent free. Those figures, however, reflect river commerce coming from Illinois and Iowa with all-white crews. Above Cincinnati on the Ohio River, the crews were also almost entirely white. On the lower portion of the Ohio and the Mississippi south of Cairo there were many black crewmembers, and below Natchez there were few whites other than the officers. By the 1850s, perhaps 3,000 slaves and 1,000 free blacks living in the Lower Mississippi Valley worked on steamboats each year. Moreover, most of them were young men who left those jobs after a few years and were replaced by others like them, so many more thousands of potential runaways had steamboat experience.

Steamboat work was hard, but it had many advantages over picking cotton. Stewards and first cooks often made $50 a month. Firemen earned $35, the other deckhands $30, and waiters $20. Usually these regular wages were collected by the owners, but they sometimes gave a small portion to the workers, especially those who were particularly valuable. In addition, cabin workers sometimes got tips from the passengers, although these were usually given only to free blacks. All enslaved workers did get to keep money they were paid for working on Sundays, and that was sometimes $1 per day. Like their white fellow workers, black crew members, slave and free, were allowed to carry small items on and off the boats that they bought in one port and sold in another, a significant source of income for them.

"Been all a-roun' the whole roun' world" were words to a song that Mississippi Valley steamboat workers sang, and the exaggeration was pardonable. New Orleans was one of the largest cities in the United States and the most exotic. Natchez, Vicksburg, Memphis, even Little Rock, and especially Louisville, were all exciting places when compared with the rural South and being familiar with them was something of which a person could be proud. Just like their white counterparts, the enslaved boatmen drank, gambled, and enjoyed romantic relationships as well as sexual liaisons. In addition, they had a chance to enjoy African American culture and build networks of friends and acquaintances in all the river ports.[14]

Hiring slaves out to work on steamboats was profitable for their masters, but it weakened their control over their servants and gave them a worldliness that was subversive to their authority. John Scott was one of many talented and ambitious slaves who took advantage of that. He was brought to New Orleans sometime in 1837 and must have had a history of running away because Mathew F. Maher, who bought him, waived the right of redhibition. Maher was looking for a drayman, but Scott wanted to work on a steamboat, and the new owner "could not get much work out of him" until he agreed. Maher leased Scott to the steamboat *Crusader* on which he worked as a cook—an excellent position, but then, he "was a likely smart Intelligent negro," whom one of his supervisors thought was as valuable as any slave he ever saw. When that job came to an end, Maher got him another one, but Scott "immediately disappeared" and was later found on the sailing ship *B. Morgan* at the Balise (at the mouth of the Mississippi and the last place that vessels stopped before entering the Gulf of Mexico). He was brought back to New Orleans and jailed. Maher must have thought that Scott would run away again because he sold him for the bargain price of $400 to Samuel McMaster, who bought him while still in jail and waived any guarantee against running away.

For the next two years Scott worked on a succession of steamboats, usually making his own arrangements for employment. Theophilus P. Minor, master of the *Nashville*, hired him as a cook at $25 per month after requiring that McMaster come in person and give his permission. Scott was only on the boat for about a month because he hurt his foot on a fishing line. McMaster then arranged for him to work on the *Dewitt Clinton*, again for $25 a month, out of which he allowed him to keep money for shoes. A free colored man who worked that vessel testified to Scott's independent manner: he "seemed to have no master, he acted as he pleased." When Scott asked for a job on the *Jubilee*, Captain Richard

Grooms said he "was afraid to hire a colored man, with[out] taking some precautions to be sure of his Masters consent." Again, McMaster came in person and gave his approval. Later Grooms said that Scott "was a good Cook and acquitted himself to my entire Satisfaction." He was chief cook on the *Lady of the Lake*, and McMaster allowed him to keep enough money to buy his own clothes. "A small boy was carrying his trunk," when he left that boat for another job. This time he was the second steward on the *Louisiana*, but that was not good enough for John Scott, because he left that boat in Louisville and was never heard from again.[15]

Slave owners were aware of the threat posed by the work experience of their servants. Bill, sometimes known as Will, was owned by John C. Morris at Montgomery's Point, at the mouth of the White River when he ran away. He had been the steward on a steamboat that regularly went up the Arkansas to Little Rock, and Morris thought he had probably left to become a steward or waiter on another boat. Thomas Thorn of Little Rock advertised for thirty-five-year-old Ben in both that city and Memphis. He had owned the slave for about six months and before that Ben had worked as a steamboat fireman. He believed that Ben had left on a boat and was going to Tennessee to visit his wife. Henry Borrough of Mount Ida, Arkansas, near the headwaters of the Ouachita River, was willing to pay $200 for Anderson, who was about twenty-seven, copper colored, and had a pleasant personality. Anderson had been "hiring out on the river" after running away from Borrough but was captured and put in the Johnson County Jail. Like many country lockups, it was not a very secure facility. Despite being "fastened to the floor in the upper room by a log chair," Anderson escaped. Borrough thought a white man had helped him and was willing to pay a $300 reward if he were arrested.[16]

Tom had been working for Mr. Mattocks, who was operating a steamboat on the Mississippi River when he escaped from the vessel at Natchez. He headed inland, perhaps toward the Natchez Trace but was captured in Amite County. Madam Wooten of St. Francisville was probably right that her servant Bill had acquired free papers before he left on the *Splendid* bound for Louisville. "Genteel in his address," "plausible in his discourse," and experienced as a waiter, Bill may well have gotten a job on the cabin crew. Billy, who was thought to be hiding in Vicksburg waiting to get on a steamboat, had done the same thing the previous year when he was only seventeen and reached Florence, Alabama. He had worked on several boats and was considered a good deckhand.

E. M. Ford of Somerville, Tennessee, noted that his "negro man" Paschael, had "done some service on flat and steamboats" and would probably try to get work on one of the latter, perhaps to get to Nashville where he had once lived. Ford ended his ad with a warning that was relatively common: "Owners of boats and others are cautioned against employing or in any way harboring this fellow, as the severity of the new law will not in such case prevent its enforcement."[17]

Black steamboat crewmembers sometimes aided other fugitives who wanted to escape. The New Orleans *Daily Picayune* was convinced this happened often: "Colored stewards, or cooks, or hands on boats use their cunning and the means peculiar to their positions to conceal slaves on board boats till they reach safe places for landing." And they did. In 1850, a slave named Lewis was punished "for having inveigled and secreted a runaway named Sam" on the steamer *Rainbow*. A chambermaid on the steamboat *Illinois* helped a woman belonging to Madame Artincer of Bourbon Street to escape, although the runaway was arrested in St. Louis. The same year, Patrick was arrested in New Orleans for assisting Mary to get aboard a steamboat. In 1854 "a little negro girl," believed to have been "run off" from New Orleans by the pastry cook of the *R. H. Winslow*, was taken off that vessel in Louisville.[18]

White people also assisted runaways. On an April afternoon in 1850, a man calling himself James Anderson came to the steamboat *Yorktown*, commanded by Thomas J. Haldeman, which was due to depart for Cincinnati that evening, and booked passage for a slave woman, saying he was sending her to his wife who was staying in that city. The clerk, a Mr. Washington, warned him of the danger of letting an enslaved person go to a northern city, but Anderson accepted responsibility, saying she had grown up as part of his family and was a trusted servant. He paid $10 for the passage, and the woman was allowed to ride in the ladies' cabin on the second deck. The following morning, however, Henry Parish of New Orleans visited Haldeman's agents in the city, Marsh & Ranlett, claiming that he was missing a slave and had learned she had left on the *Yorktown*. A letter was sent to Haldeman via the steamship *Bell Key*, which passed the *Yorktown* before it reached Nashville, and the fugitive was taken off there and returned to her owner.[19]

Forged passes were also widely used by those who planned to escape bondage on steamboats. In 1841 the sheriff of East Feliciana Parish had an experience that illustrates their widespread use. He had been in Paducah and returned home on the *Nautilus*. Early in the trip, he was angered by the behavior of a free black fireman on the boat, who, as the sheriff put it, was "insolent to a white man." He contacted Captain Smith, master of the vessel, who asked for the deckhand's papers, and it turned out the proof of freedom was dated 1804, at least a decade before the black man was born. Captain Smith quickly took the imposter into custody and began to check the papers of the remaining blacks on board, an investigation that revealed that three more of them were fugitive slaves. What happened to the fireman is not clear, but two of the runaways were jailed in Memphis and the third escaped only by jumping in the river. Recounting this story, the *Jackson Herald* praised the captain for taking prompt action once he became aware of the situation. The editor went on to encourage southern gentlemen who traveled on steamboats to call for the scrutiny of freedom papers and the passes carried by African American members of the crew. He believed that "hundreds" of slaves working on the boats carried forged passes and that many had no papers at all.[20]

Slave owners sometimes let trusted slaves travel on steamboats to do things for them and provided them with passes, which created an opportunity for fugitives to carry false permission slips. The *Picayune* printed an example of such a pass: "To all to whom it may concern—The bearer of this, my colored boy Henry, has my free permission to travel up the river to Cincinnati by any of the steamboats, and at the end of 30 days to return to me in town. [Signed] Benj. Eaton, Orleans St., New Orleans, Aug. 28, 1845." The person carrying this forged document might have been caught, or at least suspected, because few owners would send an enslaved person to Cincinnati, a city notorious for its abolitionist sympathies. Defending a captain who had lost a rented slave when his steamer was docked in Cincinnati, a witness in the negligence case brought against him declared that, "it is a matter of almost absolute impossibility to prevent them from being run off" in that place, a statement that would have been equally correct if he had said "running off" as well as "being run off."[21]

One runaway left with multiple items of forged paperwork that included a pass and free papers as well as "sundry drafts, checks, etc." Not only did the man escape, but the owner was later forced to pay the bill for his passage. Eight enslaved men were arrested in New Orleans in 1849, each of them carrying a pass written by the same person in Louisville. Because of different dates on the documents, the New Orleans police judged the men to be escapees. They had access to steamboats as part of their work, which involved carrying meat on board to be used in the boat's kitchen.[22]

Being able to pass for white was helpful for any enslaved person who wanted to escape the South and particularly effective when combined with the advantages of steamboat transportation. Norbon, who was only fifteen years old, was described by his Kentucky owners as a "bright mulatto," who "could be taken for white." The young man had been seen somewhere on the Ohio River, perhaps on his way to Natchez or New Orleans. James M. Wall of Milliken's Bend, in Carroll Parish, wanted steamboat captains to be on the lookout for William, who had sandy-colored hair and gray eyes and was "nearly white" but could not pass a close inspection. When interviewed at his home in the Canadian province of Ontario, Williamson Pease said that his mother was described as a mulatto while they lived as slaves in Tennessee, and he had been told his father was a white man. Once on a steamboat being taken to New Orleans, he was approached by a white man who told him he could escape: "You're as white as my daughter there, . . . all you've got to do when we get to a landing is to take your clothes and walk." Pease did not explain how he got to Canada, but it is a safe assumption that he had taken the man's advice.[23]

In 1852 a man calling himself Henry Smith got on the *Western World* in New Orleans and rode almost to Memphis before being revealed not only as an African American but also as a runaway slave named Robert. Cabin passengers were shocked because the fugitive had mixed easily with them and eaten regularly at the captain's table. Well dressed, well spoken, and well mannered, Robert had darkish skin that may have made his dinner companions think he was of Spanish descent, until a sharp-eyed steward exposed him to the captain. His owner sued the steamship company for damages because it had allowed a slave to take passage without his master's approval and a jury agreed and awarded them. A divided supreme court overturned the decision however, the majority being heavily influenced by the passengers' acceptance of Robert and sympathetic to the problems such cases caused for steamboat officers, whose duties made it impossible for them "to scrutinize minutely the hair, skin, and complexion of everyone on board."[24]

Women as well as men attempted to escape by steamboat. Peggy was "delicate and small," worked for a New Orleans milliner, and had four dresses, "one of them silk," as well as what the Adams County jailer said were "many other articles of clothing too tedious to enumerate." In 1831 Zabett, a small, slender twenty-five-year-old black woman who had hidden on the steamer *Brandywine* while it was in port in New Orleans, was dropped off at the Chicot County Jail. She claimed to have been born near Culpepper Court House in Virginia and owned by the Wallace family, who took her first to Louisville and then New Orleans. She also said Arthur Wallace had freed her, but she had no papers to prove it. Diana, who claimed to be a free woman but was being held in the Tipton County Jail, said she had been a cook on "Capt. Ewen's boat." In July 1849, "a Negro woman" was arrested who claimed she had been hidden by a chambermaid on the steamboat *Illinois*.[25]

A few children also attempted steamboat escapes. Eleven-year-old Harry, who was four feet, five inches tall and claimed to belong to Mrs. Phillips in New Orleans, was dropped off from the steamboat *James Monroe* at Cypress Bend in Chicot County and taken to jail. An unnamed sixteen-year-old boy of "yellow complexion, who belonged to Mr. Johnson of Vicksburg," was dropped off in Helena by the steamboat *Lexington* in May 1838. After Charles, a mixed-race, intelligent, and talkative boy twelve or thirteen years old was gone from Louisville for two months, his owner decided he had probably taken a steamboat either to Natchez or St. Louis.[26]

A fifteen-year-old girl named Adele was captured at the mouth of the Mississippi. Her story allowed the editors of the *Picayune* to elaborate on one of their favorite complaints about New Orleans society. Adele had been assisted by "one of those free colored loafers—too many of whom are permitted to remain in our city." That man, Alfred Pattis, had supposedly "enticed" her away from her owner, "a Mr. Faisons of St. Philip Street," and hidden her in "one of those dens of rascality," a free-colored boardinghouse owned by a Jesse Fowler, all the while disguised as a boy. Then Adele avoided capture with the assistance of the cook of the barque *Eleanor*, probably as part of the cabin crew, only to be discovered by the ship's mate at the Southwest Pass and transferred to a vessel on its way back up the river to New Orleans. Not until after the *Eleanor* had gone on her way, did authorities learn of the role its cook had played in the attempted escape, and officials there sent a boat after the ship her to bring him back. Pettis had left New Orleans before Adele and was on his way to Baltimore.[27]

An enslaved family, father, mother, and two children, were captured despite being equipped with free papers "well calculated to deceive any person except those well acquainted with the handwriting of the notaries" that were supposed to have produced them. They came close to escaping on a steamboat but were done in by another technological marvel of the pre–Civil War era. Their New Orleans master sent a telegraphic message to the Balize that reached their boat just before it sent off from there to Panama.[28]

Williamson Pease, the light-skinned man who took a steamboat north and eventually reached Canada, was not the only Lower Mississippi Valley fugitive to do that. Benjamin Drew, who interviewed Pease, also recorded the experiences of John Warren, who was then living in London, Ontario, one hundred miles northeast of Detroit, Michigan. Warren was born in Tennessee and taken to Marshall County in northern Mississippi when he was twelve. Having learned the rudiments of reading and writing as a pre-teen in the company of white children in Tennessee and then practiced surreptitiously while in Mississippi, he was able to write three passes for himself when he decided to escape in 1854. One gave him permission to travel to Memphis, the second allowed him to work there for the rest of the year, and a third said he could hire himself out on a steamboat and travel outside the state of Tennessee. Using these, he got to Memphis safely and worked in the city for only three days before getting a job on a boat going to Jacksonport, Arkansas, and back. A second steamboat took him to Cincinnati, where he jumped ship and contacted abolitionists who got him on an Underground Railroad line that took him beyond the reach of the Fugitive Slave Law.[29]

In 1816 Louisiana passed a law making it a crime for the master or commander of any ship or watercraft to "receive" on board or "conceal" once on board a slave without the owner's permission and to assist them to escape. A person convicted under the law was required to pay all expenses incurred by the owner and serve three to seven years in prison at hard labor. Moreover, if a slave were found on board a vessel without the owner's permission, the presumption was that the intent was to assist him in escaping and the accused was responsible for proving otherwise. The law and its provisions were well known to slave owners, and they relied on them. Along with civil legislation related to reimbursement for loss of property and a variety of damages, it resulted in much litigation and quite a few cases that were decided by the Louisiana Supreme Court. The trial records and court decisions provide a great deal of evidence of how the law operated, how enslaved people tried to escape by boat, and what happened to those fugitives.[30]

John Scott, whose escape from the *Louisiana* was discussed earlier, was the cause of one such suit. His owner, Samuel McMaster, filed a petition in the Parish and City Court of New Orleans alleging that N. Beckwith, the master of the steamboat *Louisiana*, either by "influence and persuasion or culpable neglect," allowed Scott on board the steamboat and carried him to Louisville, without McMaster's "knowledge or consent." Since then Scott had been "concealed & kept from the service of your petitioner." McMaster wanted Beckwith to pay him $1,500 to cover the loss of Scott and damages associated with it. He also claimed that Beckwith was about to leave the state and asked that he be required to post bail for that amount. Moreover although this was a civil suit for damages only, its language suggested that the captain was guilty of a crime for which he could be imprisoned. For his part, Captain Beckwith claimed that McMaster was "in the habit of permitting the slave Scott . . . to hire himself & act as his own master" and thus the loss was his own fault. In addition, the captain argued that Scott was a "habitual runaway and of no Value to anyone."

The New Orleans court that heard the case decided that Beckwith was at fault but awarded McMaster only $800 rather than the $1,500 he wanted. The owner had claimed his slave was worth $1,100, but he was only given the $400 that he paid for Scott and the $400 in damages that he requested. On appeal, the Louisiana Supreme Court was even less generous, denying him the damages because he knew Scott was a runaway and should have been prepared for the consequences. No doubt to protect Beckwith from criminal charges, it also declared that while the captain was at fault and liable for the cost of the slave, he was an honest and honorable man who had not knowingly aided Scott to escape.[31]

The trial record of one steamboat escape reads like a mystery story, one in which the plot is never fully revealed. On January 10, 1837, the steamer *Henry Clay* under the command of Captain John A. Holton left New Orleans bound for Louisville. A few days later it was forced to stop because low water on the Ohio River made it impossible to cross a sandbar at the mouth of the Cumberland River. The *Henry Clay* joined several other steamboats, including the *Daniel Webster* and the *Rocky Mountain*, all of which were moored close together along the Kentucky bank of the river and had gangplanks connecting them to each other and to the shore. That night another boat arrived, the *Wave*, which was smaller than the others and had a shallower draft that would allow it to cross the bar the next morning and continue up the Ohio River.

According to the later testimony of Captain Spalding, who commanded the *Wave*, Captain Holton asked him to take some of the *Henry Clay*'s passengers and four members of its crew with him to Louisville. The crewmen were all free blacks he said, three cabin boys and a waiter, and Holton wanted Spalding to put them to work if possible. Spalding took all four of the men, and because he needed a steward hired one of them, Jim Thornton, whom he had seen on the *Henry Clay* being "very active" in waiting on the big table in the main cabin, to do that job. The pilot of the *Wave* also testified to seeing Thornton on the *Henry Clay*, and while carrying luggage from that boat to the *Wave*. He described Thornton as a copper colored, "well proportioned" man, about five feet, ten inches tall, whose "hair was combed away from his face."

With its new passengers and crew members on board, the *Wave* steamed up the Ohio River and soon came upon the steamboat *Tuscarora*, which had run aground. Again the smaller boat took on passengers. Among them was Henry F. Peterson, who had been in Vicksburg and was on his way to Wheeling, West Virginia, from where he would continue on to Baltimore. Immediately on boarding the *Wave*, Peterson saw Jim Thornton and recognized him as an enslaved man named Shadrach whom he had known in Baltimore. In fact, Shadrach had belonged to Peterson's close friend, H. H. Slatter. Peterson had been with Slatter when he purchased the slave, who was at that time in jail, had seen him many times after that, and had accompanied Slatter to Alexandria where the owner put Shadrach and several slaves on a brig and sent them to his brother in New Orleans. Peterson explained all this to Captain Spalding and asked him to arrest the man calling himself Thornton, but Spalding refused, saying that since the captain of the *Henry Clay* had asked him to take Thornton on board, it was Holton's responsibility if he was not who he claimed to be.

The *Wave* continued its journey, but ninety miles below Louisville, it was forced to stop because the river had iced over. That was at night, and in the morning the passengers were unloaded, leaving them to find whatever transportation they could. Shadrach, alias Thornton, and his three fellow crew members from the *Henry Clay* must have left very early, because when Henry Peterson got off, they were nowhere to be found. The alleged runaway was never captured, although later one of the passengers from the *Tuscarora* claimed to have seen him in Louisville.

Captain Spalding of the *Wave* was right about Captain Holton of the *Henry Clay* being responsible if the free black Jim Thornton turned out to be the slave Shadrach. Holton was in a great deal of trouble. Slatter sued him for $1,600, the value of the slave Shadrach, whom he claimed had been carried out of Louisiana without Slatter's knowledge. No one appears to have disputed that Jim Thornton was Shadrach or that Slatter owned him, but Holton denied the slave was either a passenger on his boat or a member of the crew. He claimed the fugitive must have come up the river on one of the other boats that were tied up next to his and then come on board just before the passengers and crew members transferred to the *Wave*. The first mate of the *Henry Clay*, who was Holton's brother, testified that it was his job "to see what persons were on board and in particular if there were any runaway negroes among them." He claimed that deck passengers were frequently "mustered" for that purpose, and he was certain that the slave Shadrach was not there. The judge found the defense argument unconvincing and ordered Holton to pay Slatter. He did not believe, however, that the captain acted with intent and neither did the Louisiana Supreme Court, who heard the case on appeal: the "good character and excellent reputation" of the captain "entirely acquits him of any improper motives." Even Peterson, the man who had recognized Shadrach, and who had been on the *Henry Clay* during earlier trips, said he had no reasons to doubt the captain's "watchfulness, carefulness or honesty as master of the boat."

This absolution of Holton is curious, since it leaves unexplained how Shadrach managed to serve on the cabin crew of the *Henry Clay* without either the mate or the captain knowing that he was there. But then he was a remarkable man, able to get aboard the *Henry Clay*, somehow to be transferred to the *Wave*, brazen it out when confronted by Peterson, and get away even after being exposed.[32]

A case that arose a few years later was simpler with respect to the facts but more complex relative to the law. At around eight p.m. on or about June 24, 1840, the steam-powered towboat *Tiger* pulled away from the wharf at New Orleans and began taking the ship *St. Mary* to the mouth of the Mississippi River from where it would set sail for New York City. Early the following morning eighteen to twenty miles from their destination, Captain Junius Beebe of the *Tiger* was on the quarterdeck of the *St. Mary* having a cup of coffee with Captain R. W. Foster, commander of that vessel, who was also giving orders to his crew. Abruptly Foster asked a nearby sailor who he was. The man said he was the second cook. Foster said, "No, you're not, I have never seen you before." The sailor went on to explain that his name was Tom and that he was a free black man. The captain then demanded to see his papers, and Tom said he did not have any. He had come to New Orleans from New York on the ship *Orleans* and soon after arriving had become sick and was taken to the hospital where somehow the papers were lost. Foster declared that he was going to send him back to New Orleans as a suspected runaway as he was legally bound to do. Tom begged him not to and said the cook could vouch for him, and the cook did, claiming to have known Tom in Liverpool, England, and visited him and his family at their home at number 12 Mulberry Street. The captain was either convinced that the two men were lying or at least unwilling to take the risk that they were not. At the Balise, he transferred Tom into Beebe's custody to be taken back to New Orleans and had the captain deliver a note to the mayor explaining the situation.

The captain's judgment was confirmed on the towboat ride back to New Orleans when Tom confessed that his true name was Tom Taylor, and he had escaped from his owner in that city. Further information on the runaway was quickly found in an advertisement published in the *Daily Picayune* a month earlier. Thomas B. Winston, of No. 7 Front Levee, described a slave named Tom Taylor who had run away the previous Saturday night. He was a "dark freckled mulatto," somewhere between twenty-six and thirty years old and five feet, ten inches tall, who "looks rather dull in countenance." He had a rupture severe enough that he might have been wearing a truss when he left. Tom may have looked dull, but his life certainly was not. Winston's wife, Margaret, had bought him in Natchez in April 1839 but did not purchase his wife who also lived there. Within a month of being taken to New Orleans, Tom ran away, and the Winstons had to retrieve him from the Natchez jail. He left again in August but was found in New Orleans. On a third attempt in October, he got as far as Baton Rouge.

Mrs. Winston had purchased Tom for $800 and received a full guarantee against the vices and maladies associated with redhibition. She could have returned him after the first or second escape. Probably she kept him because Tom, who worked as a waiter, was a good source of income. She also attempted to profit from his last escape. When Captain

Beebe asked for a reward for returning Tom, Mrs. Winston told him to ask the owners of the *St. Mary* for it. She also spurned Captain Foster's attempt to reimburse her $10 for services performed by Tom while he was on the ship. Instead, in April 1841 she filed a civil suit against Foster and the owners of the *St. Mary* asking for $1,700. That included $800 for Tom, $400 for damages, and the $500 fine, which under a recently passed law was due the owner of a slave found aboard a vessel leaving the state without his owner having given permission for him to be there.

The money for Tom was only included in case he was not released from jail and returned to her. The damages were based on the interesting claim that Tom's value had been diminished because he had "discovered that the way to escape from the State was so easy." The fine was the central issue in the case. Winston also asked that the *St. Mary* be taken into custody and held as security for the future payment of the fine and damages. That was done, and the ship was held for two days until the owners put up a $600 bond. In June, the district court judge reached his decision. Because the evidence indicated that the first cook had connived to aid the escape, he ruled that Winston was due the fine money of $500 along with interest from the time the suit was initiated and any costs associated with the case. Captain Foster and the owners promptly appealed the judgment. One year later the Louisiana Supreme Court overturned the district court decision. It ruled that the fine related to cases in which owners found their slaves on the boat. In this case the captain discovered the runaway and promptly turned him over to the proper authorities. The first cook did seem to have assisted Tom, and the captain and owners were responsible for his actions, but this too was obviated by action of the captain. They were not liable for the fine and Mrs. Winston was forced to pay the expenses.

Tom, of course, was the big loser in these proceedings. No doubt he would have laughed at Winston's claim that it was easy for a slave to escape from Louisiana. The Winstons lost some money, but they did get their slave back after the district court decision, and it is doubtful his fourth escape diminished his value any more than had the first three. No doubt the Winstons were unhappy about paying the costs incurred by Tom's incarceration, which lasted nearly a year. At 18 ¾ cents a day, it came to $71.78, to which was added $5.25 for clothing. On the bright side for them, the total was reduced by $30.94 that the prisoner had earned on the city chain gang.[33]

In an 1841 case a steamboat captain was found culpable despite what appeared to be his best intentions to follow the law. The enslaved man Prince, a house servant and cart driver in New Orleans, went on board the steamboat *New York* carrying luggage, calling himself Ned, and saying that he was a free man who just arrived on a steamer from Cincinnati and was looking for work on a boat going upriver. The boat's engineer hired him on the spot, ignoring the captain's orders not to take on any crewmen without checking their papers. Prince's ruse was not discovered until the boat was in the Ohio River, but the captain immediately put him in irons and transferred him to a vessel going back down the river. Somehow Prince again escaped and was never found. His owner sued and was awarded $1,500 for the value of the enslaved man and $200 that had been spent trying to find him. The court ruled that the captain was responsible for the actions of his engineer.

The Louisiana Supreme Court found for boat captains about as often as they awarded money to slave owners, influenced not only by the reputation of the captains but how they dealt with each situation. In a case decided in 1833, the justices found for the captain of the *Hercules* who had failed to discover two fugitives brought on the ship by a white man who claimed to be their owner. The actual owner of the slaves argued that the captain was negligent in not getting his permission or filing a description of the slaves. The court ruled, however, that the 1816 law did not require descriptions of slaves brought on board by their owner, and the captain had no way of knowing his passenger was not the owner.[34]

In 1849 the court reversed the decision of a lower court that had favored the slave owner. Captain Botts left New Orleans heading up river in the afternoon and by evening found an enslaved man who was hiding on board the boat. Botts kept going through the night and then delivered the slave in Baton Rouge. The man's owner argued that Botts should have put the slave off immediately. The court decided, however, that the captain had acted prudently by not stopping after dark at someplace where he might have had to search to find an officer of the law and instead waiting until he reached an urban area where legal officials and a jail would be readily available. The decision may also have been influenced by Captain Botts's reputation. In 1840 as captain of the steamship *Architect* he had a runaway aboard when he left New Orleans but only discovered him after the boat had landed in Louisville and the man had gone ashore. Botts followed the fugitive to Baltimore, captured him, and sent him home on a coastal sailing vessel.[35]

{ CHAPTER 5 }

The Urban Runaway

LITTLE ROCK, THE CAPITAL of Arkansas, which had a population of fewer than four thousand people in 1860, and New Orleans, Queen City of the South, which was more than forty times as large, were at opposite ends of the urban spectrum in most respects, but the peculiar institution of the South functioned similarly in each place, and markedly differently than it did in the countryside. And the same was true of Natchez, Vicksburg, Baton Rouge, and Memphis, in fact all southern cities.

Urban slaves were less closely supervised than those on farms and plantations and enjoyed more social and economic opportunity. A majority were household servants and among those were many who performed duties such as shopping and running other errands that gave them limited but significant decision-making powers, daily interaction with white people on a not entirely subservient basis, and a certain amount of control over their own time. Many others were hired out to do various types of labor, both skilled and unskilled, and sometimes allowed to find their own jobs. Urban slaves usually had money in their pockets and found lots of ways to spend it. Collectively they formed semiautonomous subcultures with their own churches and social activities. These things made urban living more attractive for enslaved people than life on plantations and farms, making cities a magnet for runaways from the countryside.

Despite their advantages, urban slaves led difficult lives. Domestic servants worked long hours and did not have Sundays off. Enslaved people who enjoyed more freedom were still subject to their masters' wills when the owners chose to assert them. Whippings were not uncommon, and police officials were usually willing to administer them for a small fee. Thus unhappy, freedom-seeking slaves fled from the cities even as rural runaways struggled to get into them. Urban slaves also ran away, or more accurately walked away, from their owners but remained in the same city, where their dark skins acted as camouflage within the large African American populations that also provided them aid and comfort.

Advertisements subscribed by urban slave owners often suggested that the missing slave was "lurking about" just as those by planters thought theirs might be "lying out."

In 1859, a Little Rock newspaper warned that "runaways are hid in the vicinity and are in the city every night." "Negroes traverse the streets at all hours of the night." There were about three thousand white people living in the city and they owned about eight hundred black people. Many of the enslaved worked in the nearby countryside but were often in town. Collectively they formed a community that included a high percentage of families, a web of social relationships, and a loose social structure based on occupation and access to the white power structure. By 1850 there was a black Methodist church that had over two hundred members and taught reading, writing, and arithmetic in its Sunday school. Many slaves dressed as well as most whites and some of them significantly better. The city attempted to regulate black behavior through a series of ordinances that were enacted in 1826 and strengthened occasionally down to the Civil War, but day-to-day enforcement was left to a police force consisting of one constable. Meanwhile, enslaved people met together during their free time, purchased liquor when they wanted it, and some of them carried knives and even pistols. Self-assertiveness on the part of slaves was encouraged by masters who were unwilling or unable to discipline their servants, in part because they depended on them too much.[1]

In 1840 Matilda Fulton wrote from Little Rock to her husband, US senator William Fulton, who was in Washington, from Rosewood, the small plantation where the family lived, that she and the children had driven into Little Rock on Sunday and that "our man Joseph got so drunk he could not drive me home." Joseph may have developed his drinking habit sometime earlier when he worked at the Anthony House, a hotel in the town. Matilda gave him a lecture and no longer allowed him to drive her. He "joined the temperance," but she was not optimistic that it would stop him from drinking. Eventually Joseph ran away. Manuel also caused problems for Fulton. He had a wife in Little Rock and was unhappy staying at Rosewood. On one occasion, after he had been gone more than a week, the mistress said of her slave, "I suppose he will come home in the morning [but] indeed he is his own man." Workplace responsibility had led to personal freedom, as it often did. Despite this leniency, Matilda

Fulton was a strong woman who ran the family plantation when her husband was away and did it effectively. Her approach to management, which does not appear to have involved much corporal punishment, may have contributed to a lack of discipline, but the urban environment was an important factor.[2]

Most Little Rock owners whose servants went missing probably advertised them on posters or not at all, but once or twice a month the *Arkansas Gazette* or another local paper carried an ad for an absconded worker. Many of these were for slaves thought to be trying to get far away, usually by fleeing west to Indian Territory. William Woodruff, who owned the *Arkansas Gazette* and could do it for nothing, advertized for four different runaways. Henry, who fled in 1836, was "a shrewd, sensible fellow" who could "invent a plausible story" to avoid being taken, and if he was, should be put in irons lest he get away again. Five years later, John left, probably with three other men living not far away. Woodruff thought they might be trying to get to the North. Moses left in 1844. According to the editor, he was "a notorious liar, and quite boisterous when intoxicated." There was a good chance he was "lurking around this vicinity." In 1857, when Tom was gone, Woodruff was certain he was "lurking about Little Rock."[3]

The situation in Baton Rouge was similar. The city had a slave patrol that was seldom in operation, a curfew system dependent on the sound of a bell that was seldom rung, and laws against slaves drinking, gambling, or holding Sunday dances, none of which were well enforced. Stealing by slaves—that is, appropriating part of what they had helped to produce—was common enough that a standard joke, told apparently by both blacks and whites, involved one servant asking another the price of his new hat, and the second man responding that he did not know since the clerk was not there when he got it. At least one slave was reported to have a charge account at a local drinking establishment. Sunday frolics by slaves and free blacks were often associated with gambling and fighting. Runaways, either from inside or outside the town, were a regular part of the urban milieu. The most egregious example was one who took up housekeeping in the belfry of the Methodist church. In 1857 during a discussion of additional construction funds for the Deaf and Dumb Asylum in Baton Rouge, a state legislator told his colleagues that during the previous winter runaways often took refuge under an unfinished section and their campfires had endangered the building.[4]

The relationship between William Johnson, the free black barber and businessman in Natchez, and his slave Steven illustrates the type of running away that was common in southern cities. When he started keeping a diary in 1835, Johnson seems to have had four or five slaves, one of whom was Steven. He is first mentioned as being hired out to "Messrs Neibert & Gemmell." Things must have been going well, because a month later Johnson wrote that he "took Steven into my shop to work at the trade," meaning he would be taught to be a barber. Six days later, however, Steven went out at night without permission and was whipped by the volunteer patrol that policed Natchez. Johnson whipped him the next morning, beginning a pattern that continued for the next eight years. Steven was a valuable servant, assessed at $800 for county tax purposes, but one day in September 1836 Johnson realized that he had not received any wages from him, despite the fact that he was again hired out, his haircutting career apparently over. Under a whipping, Steven admitted that he had kept all the money he had received. A month later, he ran away, apparently to attend a camp meeting, and a man named Earl Clapp, who may have been employing him, had the slave "stretched Out" and gave him what Johnson called "a genteel whiping for me." In March of 1838 Johnson sounded both discouraged and defeated when he noted that Steven had run away the previous evening for the second time in a week, adding that "only God knows where he has gone to." "If I should have the Good Luck to Get Him again I will be very apt to Hurt his Feelings." After that, however, either Steven stayed at home or Johnson gave up worrying about him for there are no references for more than a year.[5]

Then in January 1840, alcohol became an issue. Johnson wrote that Steven had gotten drunk "as usual" and then run away. In the cryptic sentence that follows, the master seems more concerned than angry. "I hope that I will be able to put Him in a Safe place yet if I dont mind." Over the next few years, Steven continued to run away for short periods every few months almost always in alcohol-related incidents. In October 1840, Johnson's friend, the free black man Robert McCary, found Steven very drunk on top of a wagon somewhere and brought him home. Johnson put him on the Natchez chain gang that was used to punish enslaved people, most of them runaways, by making them work on city public works projects. One morning in March 1841, he woke up to find that Steven had gotten out the previous night and had been arrested by the guard—a professional police force that had taken over from the volunteer patrol. He had him "flogged" before he picked him up. A month later, he had to pay $5 to a man who had captured Steven and brought him home. When the slave ran away a month later, Johnson went out to the Forks of the Road, a major slave trading venue just outside Natchez, to see about selling Steven but could not find a deal he liked. September 12, 1841, was a busy day for Steven. He had been rented out to haul wood in a swamp near Natchez but came back to the city and stole a watch from someone. Johnson found out about both things, had Steven whipped, and then took him back to work.[6]

Despite his frequent escapes and the corporal punishment that almost always followed, Steven does not seem to have put up much resistance to capture, most of the time being brought home by some friend of Johnson's or one of his several free black employees. Indeed, Johnson does not always seem to have taken Steven's absences very seriously. "I came very near Cetching Steven tonight. He was in the Stable adjo[i]ning to mine but he Jumped up and ran into the weeds somewhere." In September 1843, however, Steven became violent when two of Johnson's men brought him home, fighting with them, breaking a window in the shop, and biting an Italian man who was renting space from Johnson. He was taken to the guardhouse for the night, and Johnson gave him thirty-nine lashes the following day. On the way home, Steven continued to resist, and Johnson and his crew locked him in a corncrib. The barber resolved to "send him to New Orleans," presumably to be sold, but did not immediately follow through.[7]

In December 1843, three months after the fight scene, and following another drinking binge, Johnson decided to sell Steven for $600: "He must go for he will drink." It was not hard to find a buyer, and the deal was made. Johnson, however, was not happy at the outcome. The reason for the sale, he wrote, was "Liquor, Liquor." "Poor Fellow. God Bless Him." "There are many worse fellows than Steven is." The following day, December 31, 1843, Johnson was sad, "many tears was in my eyes," because of selling Steven. On New Year's Day, the slave master took his property down to the ferry and received the $600 payment. He sent Steven off with a parting gift of one set of suspenders, one pair of socks, and two cigars. Doubtless William Johnson's status as a racially mixed, free black man affected his feelings for Steven. Few white masters would have cried after selling a chronically disobedient slave or have given him gifts, but Johnson's relationship with his servant, a mixture of violence, benevolence, and even friendship, was not extremely different from some other urban slave owners. John B. Nevitt, one of the rich Natchez nabobs who lived near the city, also found that his slaves took advantage of their proximity to the city.[8]

A man named Jerry, who belonged to Nevitt, spent much of 1831 escaping from his owner's control so that he could visit his wife, who lived on a plantation owned by William J. Minor across the Mississippi River near the town of Concordia (now Vidalia) in Louisiana. On January 13, Jerry was driving a wagon that somehow slipped into a bayou, drowning one of its two horses. Despite that, ten days later Nevitt gave him a pass to visit his wife, and Jerry returned just before dawn the following day. On February 4, Jerry "ranaway" in the morning, but he returned the following day, and Nevitt "forgave" him. On the twelfth, Nevitt gave Jerry another pass to see his wife. On the twentieth he ran away again and was gone for a week, again at Minor's plantation, but this time endured a whipping on his return. On March 27, Jerry and a man named Reuben were given passes to visit their wives along with $11 "for work done," probably after being hired out to someone. High wind on the Mississippi River prevented them from getting back in time to start work the next day, but they arrived by noon. On May 2, Jerry went to see his wife without a pass and was given "a light flogging" on his return. He got a pass to visit on June 12. The next time Nevitt mentioned Jerry was in October, and this time it was based on news that the overseer on Minor's plantation had shot him. The next day, however, Jerry returned with a note from that man saying that he had indeed shot at Jerry but had missed. This time, Nevitt gave his slave "a severe whipping."

Other Nevitt workers also braved punishment by defying the restraints imposed by their owner. On March 4, Bill, Reuben, Betts, and Milly all got passes allowing them to go into Natchez. The two men came back drunk, and the women stayed out until eight, longer than was allowed. Nevitt resolved not to give any more passes, but six days later he allowed Bill to visit his wife. The next night, the "negroes were unruly in the quarter," and Betts ran away with a woman named Delly. Betts was gone for six days but returned on her own, and Nevitt decided not to whip her because it might discourage Delly from coming back. After more than a week, Delly was found in a neighbor's straw barn with another of Nevitt's slaves, a man named Albert, and the master gave them both "severe" whippings. Albert was not deterred. He was flogged in February after running away even though he had come back the following day, but he must have left again and been gone longer because he was captured in late March and held in the Natchez jail. Nevitt paid $3.00 in fees to have him released and then gave a blacksmith $1.50 for installing an iron collar around his neck. Despite the iron and having his hands tied behind his back; on the way home, Albert escaped into one of the wooded ravines along the river known as punch bowls. He was gone for another nine days before being found hiding out with Delly. Reuben also had a wife on the Minor plantation in Louisiana and went over there sometimes with Jerry. On May 2, he returned home after a five- or six-week absence, and Nevitt put an "Iron" on his leg and kept it there for five weeks. On September 25, Reuben got another pass "to go over the river." Milly, who had stayed out too late with Betts back in March, ran away in June, although for how long we do not know. Bill, who had gotten drunk in Natchez with Reuben, was sent to Natchez for supplies on April 26 and took a few gallons of molasses for himself. Nevitt whipped him, put him in jail, and then sold him to a neighbor for $600.[9]

Plantations required that some workers have special skills, blacksmiths being the best example, but cities offered many more opportunities for talented people, and slaves took advantage of them. One such was Harry, who was probably born in Jamaica, spoke both French and English, and was still a teenager when he arrived in Louisiana via Charleston. Robert J. Nelson bought Harry early in 1824 and took him home to St. Francisville. Nelson needed someone to work in his fields, but Harry did not want that job and immediately ran away. He was soon captured but escaped again, this time reaching Woodville before being caught. Nelson then took him to Natchez to sell but could not find a buyer, perhaps because Harry ran away while there and was gone for two or three days. Back at home, Nelson traded the recalcitrant slave to a trader named Lloyd, who sold him to Ananias Dunbar, who also lived in St. Francisville. Dunbar kept Harry for a year or so and then sold him to his neighbor Andrew Skillman.

Dunbar and Skillman both came to regret their purchases, but they had no reason to blame Nelson, who warned both of them what might happen. Even when he sold Harry to the trader Lloyd, Nelson had told him that Harry might make a good body servant "but would not suit for a field hand." Later Nelson and Dunbar lived in the same boardinghouse, and Dunbar told Nelson that he was very happy with Harry, and that he planned to educate him and put him to work in his store. Nelson said Harry "was rascal enough without an education," adding that when he had owned him, not only did the young man run away, but he usually stole something to take with him, once a pair of pants and on another occasion several vests. He thought it unwise to put him in a business situation that required trust. He agreed, however, that Harry had potential, saying he would not have sold him for less than $1,000 if the slave had been willing "to stay with him." He suggested Dunbar use him in a domestic capacity, specifically as a cook.

Dunbar ignored the warning and went ahead with his own plan, which seems to have worked well until February 1826, when Harry was caught stealing clothes from the store, or at least colluding with other slaves who carried out the actual thefts. He ran away to avoid punishment but was soon caught and brought to Dunbar's home in chains—which were immediately secured to a bedpost. While the very angry master was preparing to whip his clerk, his neighbor Andrew Skillman arrived on the scene and offered to buy Harry. According to witnesses, Dunbar warned Skillman that Harry was "a rogue," "a rascal," and a runaway, and that because of that he would sell him for $600, but Skillman must take him at his own risk. Skillman asked Harry if he would stay with him, and when the slave said yes, he made the deal with Dunbar. Apparently Harry's recent behavior had not greatly damaged his reputation, because someone else soon offered to pay more money for him than Skillman had, and Dunbar attempted to get him back by offering Skillman the most expensive beaver hat in his store.

Skillman was pleased with his purchase, and even told Robert Nelson that he did not blame Harry for stealing from the store, saying any slave would do the same. Nelson again warned the new owner about Harry, saying he was not only a runaway but "one of the highest rascals in the country," although he was a "fine pastry chef." Skillman did put Harry to work "in the house." Whether he did any baking is not known, but he took Skillman's children back and forth to school in a carriage, and did errands for his master, often going into St. Francisville on his own and usually riding a horse when he did.

After three months at Skillman's, Harry ran away, taking three other slaves with him. It was on a Sunday, the day the enslaved had off and received their weekly food allowance, and there was "a negro dance in the country." Not until Monday morning did anyone notice that the four were gone and had taken all their clothes with them. A prolonged search of the riverfront, a nearby swamp, and the city of St. Francisville yielded no clues. Skillman waited a few weeks and then placed an advertisement for them in New Orleans, Louisville, and Cincinnati, offering $400 for the group if they were captured out of state and $50 for each one if caught individually.[10]

Most urban runaways were like the ones discussed above; they wanted as much freedom as they could get but did not use violence to take it. Some, however, did. One was Sol, the "African Bandit of Natchez," whose capture in June 1848 made for excellent copy in the *Mississippi Free Trader*.

> He was found in the house of a colored man, named Green, from which he ran pursued by the officers. In getting over a fence he fired a pistol and came almost within a hair's breadth of hitting officer Benbrook. He gained entrance to the house of Mr. Purnell, ran into the parlor, [and] bolted and barricaded the doors. He exploded the cap of another pistol at the breast of Capt. Dillon of the City Guard, intending to have shot him through the door panell. Green, who had harbored him, was commanded to break in the panell with an axe, when the officers brought him within range of their double-barrelled guns. He even then, with the hair triggers drawn upon him, for a time refused to surrender, demanding that the officers should disarm before him, or at the same instant of time. He was finally captured, with some wounds and will now have to await his trial for life.

Sol, short for Solomon, had once belonged to a citizen of Natchez but was sold several times, the last to someone in northern Mississippi from where he had escaped several years before the above events. He had returned to the city, living as a maroon along a bayou several miles from town and, according to the paper, coming into Natchez daily and using the house of a free black man as his headquarters. "In the double character of preacher and conjurer, he had acquired quite an ascendancy over the negro people with whom he became acquainted" in Natchez. At the same time, he "reigned as chief bandit over the runaways and outlaws" at his hiding place in the country. An interest in women had been his downfall. He proposed marriage to one slave who refused him and then "abducted" another named Charlotte, who lived with him for a while but was later captured. She provided the information that led to Sol's capture. A week after being taken, Sol broke out of the Adams County Jail along with four other runaways. The newspaper at that point referred to him as being "of African hue and a heart still blacker," and hoped he would be captured before he started an insurrection like Nat Turner had in Virginia. Still, the paper noted that there were those "who expressed much sympathy that the bandit was so harshly dealt with before."[11]

After struggling during the 1820s and 1830s, Memphis grew rapidly in the last two decades of the antebellum era and developed a dynamic economy. During the 1840s, problems relating to urban growth became significant enough that the Tennessee legislature passed a new incorporation act that made the existing town of South Memphis part of Memphis and gave the new city council expanded powers of government. By 1850 the population was 8,841 and ten years later it was 22,623, making the Bluff City the sixth largest urban area in the South. The number of enslaved Memphians increased from 2,360 to 3,684 in the same period, but they dropped from 27 percent of the city's population to 16 percent as European immigrants arrived in the city. On the eve of the Civil War, there were nearly 7,000 people in Memphis born outside the United States, almost 32 percent of the population. The Irish formed a larger group than the African Americans. By 1860 the city was shipping more cotton per capita than New Orleans, had a strong manufacturing sector, had hosted two regional conferences on economic growth, and was linked by railroad with Charleston, South Carolina. The Memphis City Council in 1857 praised the "system of railroads and the mechanical skill and industry of our people" and boasted of its agricultural hinterland. Were a political unit created by merging West Tennessee with northern Mississippi and making Memphis its capital, it boasted, the result would be "the finest State in the Union."[12]

Even as they became a smaller portion of the city's population, enslaved people increasingly challenged the control of their owners and of the city. In November 1849, the *Memphis Daily Eagle* published an editorial titled "Negroes in the City" to address complaints the paper had heard from many citizens about the behavior of black people, both enslaved and free. A major issue, the editor thought, was that "an extraordinary number of slaves are permitted to hire their own time," which he claimed lessened their value as property, presumably because it made them harder to control. It also "debauches the slave himself," which the paper related to another major concern, namely that "liquor and other articles are freely sold to slaves." These things were not only bad for owners and their servants, the editor opined, they were a threat to slavery itself: a bondsman with this much economic and social freedom was a "strolling agent of discontent, disorder and immorality, among our slave population."The *Daily Eagle* also complained about the growing number of free blacks in the city. Although there does not seem to have been more than a hundred of them, the paper thought they should be removed. They were "immoral, unproductive, slothful, and injurious to property" and set a bad example. In fact, the two groups socialized together "at negro resorts [that] abound in different quarters of the city."[13]

Fugitivism was common in Memphis. As early as 1841, there were regularly eight or ten runaway slaves in its jail. That year the city sought permission from the Tennessee legislature to lease them to a private company that would create a chain gang to work on its streets. On February 2, 1849, the city council received a report that free black sailors on the steamboat *E. W. Stevens* had been "recruiting" slaves in the city for passage to free states. Women were often able to get free and hide in the growing city. Martha, a seventeen-year-old woman who took all her clothing when she ran away from her master in the middle of February 1838, had been gone for at least six months when the man finally decided to put an ad in the paper offering a $25 reward to anyone who could find her. Amanda had been gone more than three months, when her owner informed the public that "she was lurking about Memphis when heard of last."In 1857 John F. Sale claimed that the ten-year-old "Mulatto Girl" that he had rented out to Julius Holst had either run away or been stolen.[14]

In March 1850, a newly strengthened city council passed the city's first comprehensive ordinance dealing with its black population. Titled "Free Negroes and Slaves," the measure was an attempt to control both groups. Free blacks living in Memphis were required to register with the city, as were visitors who intended to remain more than forty-eight hours. Neither was to allow a slave to visit them after dark or on Sunday without a written pass from their owner. Enslaved people who lived outside the city were forbidden to remain after dark without a pass, and those living in the city required permission to be out after nine p.m.—a reduction of one hour from a previous curfew of ten p.m. Slaves, free blacks, or groups including both, could not assemble in public places without the approval of the mayor and under the supervision of a white person. A stern rule against allowing slaves to hire themselves out or, as the ordinance put it, "to act as a free person of color," included a fine for owners who allowed their servants that privilege. Another measure made it illegal for an enslaved person to rent living quarters within the city even if his owner was willing to let him do it.[15]

The police force responsible for enforcing the new ordinance was slowly strengthened since its creation in 1839. It started with a night watch made up of two men, each paid $400 annually and allowed to supplement their income by arresting runaway slaves and collecting the same $5.00 that the State of Tennessee paid anyone who performed that service. One officer was to be on duty each night from 10 p.m. until morning. He could call on citizens for help in enforcing the law, and they were subject to a $10 fine if they refused. The following year, an additional watchman was hired, and the force was upgraded at intervals until 1857. In that year, the city created a sophisticated police department with a command-and-control structure and full-time officers, all with detailed descriptions of their powers and responsibilities. In 1860 patrolmen began to receive $10 per month to equip themselves with dark blue uniforms with yellow stripes on the pant legs, dark blue caps trimmed with leather, and leather belts with sheaths for fourteen-inch hickory batons with wrist straps.[16]

As part of its professionalization, in October 1858 the Memphis police department began to keep a "Station House Register" listing the names of people arrested, the crimes of which they were accused and the arresting officers, and with space for additional comments. An analysis of the entries in calendar year 1859 provides insight into the nature of crime in the city and the degree to which the enslaved population was part of it. The police arrested 2,000 people that year, 87 percent of whom were white. Nearly half of them were charged with drunkenness, and most of those with disorderly conduct as well. Another 10 percent of the incarcerated whites were listed as vagrants. Stealing of one sort or another was common and so was fighting. From the beginning of record keeping until the summer of 1859, when someone called a halt to the practice, officers identified the foreign-born by place of nativity, which revealed that fully three-fourths of the white people arrested for excessive drinking were from Ireland.[17]

Tennessee law required urban police officials to distinguish between runaway slaves owned by residents of the city and those that had come in from out of town. A local slave "found going at large without a pass and without being able to give a reasonable account of himself" was not to be treated as a runaway but instead detained "in some same place, but not the county jail." The police then posted a notice so that owners could pick up their servants after paying a charge of one dollar. It was a good deal for urban slaveholders, who otherwise would have been liable to pay the regular "taker-up" fee, as the law referred to it, to whomever had brought the slave in as well as whatever jail costs were involved.[18]

A total of 264 slaves were arrested by the Memphis police in 1859, 22 a month distributed rather evenly throughout the year. They represented 13 percent of the arrested people, slightly less than their 16 percent share of the city's population. The charges indicate that Bluff City slaves engaged in the same sort of conduct as those in the smaller cities of the Lower Mississippi Valley, that is drunkenness, fighting, stealing, and gambling. The largest category was infractions involving passes. Of the 116 people in this category, 3 had forged passes, 1 had a pass that was "no good," and the rest had no passes at all. Some of the last were listed as out after curfew, the others were put down as "no pass," but none were listed as runaways. Doubtless some of the enslaved out without passes had no intention of returning home, but there is no way of knowing how many. In addition, there were 27 slaves who were listed as runaways and were presumably fugitives from outside the city.[19]

Joseph Holt Ingraham was twenty-one years old and had grown up in Maine and attended one year at Yale College before he arrived in New Orleans in 1831. After an extended stay in the city, he moved to Natchez where he married a planter's daughter and took up permanent residence. In 1835, he began a lifelong career as a writer with the publication of *The Southwest by a Yankee*, a two-volume account of his experience in the Lower Mississippi Valley. Despite the New England upbringing highlighted in the title of his book, and unlike Frederick Law Olmsted two decades later, Ingraham found little to criticize about the region, and presented a positive view of slavery. He was a gifted writer, however, who left us a vivid description of the Crescent City in the 1830s as it began its rise to national prominence.[20]

Ingraham was struck by the multiculturalism of what he called "the only 'foreign city' in the United States," where in the Place D'Armes, now Jackson Square, he found "not only natives of the well-known European and Asiatic countries . . . but occasionally Persians, Turks, Lascars, Maltese, [and] Indian sailors from South America and the Islands of the sea." Omnipresent in this mixture was the black working class. Along Levee Street where boats were loaded and unloaded, "horse-drays were trundling rapidly by, sometimes four abreast, racing to different parts of the Levee for their loads—and upon each was mounted a ragged negro, . . . standing upright and unsupported." On the early morning streets "black women, with huge baskets of rusks, rolls and other appurtenances of the breakfast table were crying, in loud shrill French, their 'stock in trade,' followed by milk-criers, and butter-criers and criers of everything but tears: for they all seemed as merry as the morning, saluting each other gayly as they met . . . and shooting their rude shafts of African wit at each other with much vivacity and humor." The city market was a long single-story building built of brick and stucco with columns on the front and a hall running its full length on either side of which were stalls where vendors sold fruit, vegetables, meat, and fish. It was filled with "a dense mass of negroes, and mulattoes, and non-descripts of every shade . . . all balancing their baskets skillfully on their heads." He "did not see one white person to fifty blacks," and remarked on an important aspect of the domestic economy: "It appears that servants do all the marketing."[21]

There was also much evidence of the city's new prosperity and growth. The French-owned shops on Rue de St. Pierre "were occupied by retailers of fancy wares, vintners, segar manufacturers, dried fruit sellers" and sixteen of them sold claret and Madeira. On Chartres, "the most fashionable, as well as greatest business street in the city," there were "cafes, confectioners, fancy stores, millineries, parfumier's, &c. &c." Crossing Canal Street, he came into the newer part of the city, the American section then known as Faubourg St. Marie: "The buildings were loftier and more modern, . . . the signs over the doors bore English names" and nearly all the businesses were "retail and wholesale dry goods dealers, jewelers, booksellers, &c., from the northern states." Canal Street itself was half again as wide as Broadway in New York City and when the trees lining either side reached maturity, Ingraham thought it would be "the finest mall in the United States, rivaled only by New Orleans's own

Esplanade," a long promenade that paralleled the old canal connecting the city with Lake Pontchartrain via Bayou St. John. On later outings with friends, Ingraham enjoyed the French cafés popularly known as coffee houses, particularly the upscale ones with large rooms decorated with artwork in which white gentlemen sipped drinks, smoked thin cigars, and played dominoes.[22]

Eight years of unparalleled economic expansion later, an Englishman with much broader experience than Ingraham's rode into New Orleans on the railroad that connected Lake Pontchartrain with the city. James Silk Buckingham had gone to sea at a very early age, was imprisoned by the French during the Napoleonic Wars when he was eleven years old, sailed around much of the world, and then ran a newspaper in Calcutta. Back in England he published *Travels in Assyria, Media and Persia* in 1829, edited several unsuccessful literary magazines, and served in Parliament from 1832 until 1837 where he was associated with a variety of reforms including the abolition of press gangs, the elimination of tariffs on grain, and the construction of urban parks and libraries. In 1842 after more than three years of travel in the United States, he wrote a two-volume work titled *The Slave States of America*.[23]

On his arrival in the Crescent City, Buckingham was immediately impressed by the Mississippi River waterfront and the four-mile-long levee that was six feet high and one hundred feet wide at its top. On the riverside, vessels were anchored three- and four-deep, sailing ships in front of the American sector, steamboats opposite the Vieux Carré, and bateaux and rafts below it; collectively they were a spectacle unequaled by any other port where he had been. Throughout the large open area between the levee and the city, goods were loaded and unloaded, passengers embarked and disembarked, an estimated 1,500 flat-bed, horse-drawn drays moved rapidly back and forth, and all manner of goods were bought and sold. It "was the most animated and bustling" part of the city. Less exciting but also remarkable were the five city markets: the Poydras, the Washington, the St. Mary's, the Meat Market, and the Vegetable Market; all of them long, roofed, and well-ventilated buildings usually set in public squares and notable for their cleanliness and good order.[24]

Buckingham was in New Orleans as part of a nationwide speaking tour and had enough money to enjoy its new luxury accommodations and attractions, which he described in detail for his English readers. The St. Charles Hotel, also known as the American Exchange Hotel, stretched along one hundred yards of St. Charles Street within easy walking distance of the quay. Among the salient points of his lengthy description was the total cost of land, construction, and furnishings that ran to $750,000, a gentlemen's dining room that could seat five hundred, and a ladies' dining room with room for two hundred that was also open to families. The building itself, inside and out, was not only the "largest and handsomest in the United States," but in his experience the entire world. There were public baths in hotels and other places around the city; the most impressive of them was the Arcade Baths, completed in 1838 at a cost of $120,000, whose 9,000 square feet encompassed not only twenty-four bathing areas but also a coffee room, shop, billiard hall, ballroom, and forty-two rooms for overnight guests. Another wonder of the decade was the St. Charles theater built in 1835, among whose lavish furnishings was an English-built chandelier that was thirty-six feet around and contained 23,000 "cut glass drops." Commenting on the gaiety of New Orleans high society, Buckingham noted that "in addition to the theatrical amusements, operas, ballets, concerts, and balls, which continue without intermission during the winter season," there were frequent masquerades. On Saturday nights, party-goers often attended the theater until midnight and a masquerade until morning. As he remarked dryly, "a New Orleans' Sabbath is, therefore, very different from a New England one."[25]

Buckingham had less to say about the urban improvements of the 1830s that served the larger public, mentioning only that much of the city was lighted by the Gas Works that had begun operation in 1834, although the French Quarter continued to use oil lamps hung on ropes in the center of the streets. He might have written about the Water Works completed in 1835 that pumped water from the Mississippi River into an elevated brick reservoir where it was allowed to "settle" and then, with its mud removed, pumped through cast-iron pipes to most parts of the city. In the circumspect opinion of *Norman's New Orleans,* the product was "capable of being made fit for all domestic purposes," but citizens of the city were still drinking rainwater. In addition to the Pontchartrain Railroad, there was the New Orleans and Carrollton Railroad that carried people back and forth from the metropolis to its first bedroom community. The New Orleans Press also completed in 1835 was turning ginned cotton into bales, over 250,000 of them a year by the 1840s; and the United States Branch Mint, finished about the same time, was producing gold and silver coinage.[26]

The modernization of New Orleans in the 1830s owed much to the release of energy allowed by a reorganization of the city that occurred in 1836. Hoping to ameliorate the long-standing animosity between the Creole French population and the Americans who had arrived after 1803, the Louisiana legislature divided New Orleans into three semiautonomous entities: a First Municipality, that encompassed the old city that was dominated by the French; the Second Municipality, north of Canal Street where most of the Americans lived; and a Third Municipality below the First that was home to many of the newly arrived immigrants from Europe. Each of these had its own city council and a recorder who exercised both executive and judicial authority. The mayor of New Orleans was left with little power except for control of the citywide police force that was created at the same time. This highly ineffective form of city government had the positive result of allowing the Americans to take control of their own affairs, and they used that freedom to invest in projects long hampered by the Creoles, who resented the pushiness of the English-speaking newcomers. In 1852 the city was reunited, and the mayor and a city council were once again in charge of the whole. The municipalities lapsed into voting districts, although each of them retained a recorder's court to deal with local crime. At the same time the city of Lafayette, which had been in Jefferson Parish, became part of New Orleans and was incorporated into the American sector that had been the Second Municipality and was now the First District. The French Quarter that had been the First Municipality became the Second District, and the Third Municipality became the Third District.[27]

Unlike Ingraham, Buckingham was an opponent of slavery who believed the United States would never get "the respect and esteem of mankind" until it abolished the institution. The Englishman also did not share the New Englander's view that the enslaved population was "merry as the morning." Instead he noted that the newspapers regularly carried advertisements for runaway slaves and that this "desertion" showed that they were not happy with their situation.

Buckingham was also impressed by how much the owners of slaves depended on them. "The love of ease," he said, that characterized the Creole population had strongly influenced the Anglo-Americans to the extent that slave owners in both groups delegated much more responsibility over household management to their bound African Americans than the English did to their free white ones. One result was that domestic servants took the opportunity to appropriate small amounts of money for themselves as they bought and sold things on behalf of their owners. Many masters also relied on the income they made leasing their slaves, which gave the workers a degree of power that they used to negotiate for the freedom to live away from their owners. Buckingham did not say so, but it was the power of slaves not the benevolence of their masters that underlay the social and cultural freedom expressed in the music making and dancing that took place in Congo Square and in a myriad of other ways. Buckingham agreed with the white people he met that the situation of enslaved people in New Orleans was better than any place else in the South and thought that their food, clothing, and workload were superior to those of "Irish peasants and English hand-loomers." Nonetheless, he pointed out to his readers that the masters feared their servants would rise against them.[28]

Unnoticed by tourists like Ingraham and Buckingham, and probably most of its inhabitants, New Orleans in the 1830s was also undergoing the beginnings of a major demographic change. In September 1843, the *Picayune* called New Orleans a kaleidoscope of nations, offering as evidence that in the Third Ward of the Second Municipality use of the German language was so common that "the very pigs grunt in that language," and the area around Girod Street was filled with Irishmen "speaking with as graceful a brogue as if you stood on the banks of the Shannon or at the lakes of Killarney." The impact of European immigration was reflected in a drop in the proportion of African Americans in the city's population, who were 50 percent in 1820, 42 percent in 1840, but only 14 percent in 1860. In a city of 175,000 people the year Abraham Lincoln was elected, there were only 14,000 slaves and 11,000 free blacks. Included among the 160,000 white people were 66,000 who were born outside the United States, a third of whom were from Ireland and nearly that many from Germany. The impact of the change on the city's labor force was apparent early in the 1850s when Frederick Law Olmsted observed that "the majority of the cartmen, hackney-coach men, porters, railroad hands, public waiters, and common labourers, as well as skilled mechanics, appear to be white men."[29]

Although their numbers diminished, African Americans were a powerful force in New Orleans throughout the antebellum period. In 1830, James

Stuart, an Englishman staying at the Planters and Merchants Hotel, noted that all the waiters were slaves, hired from their owners and paid $20 to $25 a month in addition to room and board. They slept on the floor in the hallways, and the clerk told him that "no evening passed on which he had not to give some of them stripes." It was an unpleasant task for him, so much so that he sometimes sent the victims to the city prison and had the whipping done by the jailers. Many masters and mistresses, he told the Englishman, did the same thing with their domestic servants. They were given a note indicating the number of lashes to be inflicted and required to bring one home stating that it had been done—a receipt as it were. The owners could choose whether the whipping took place with the victims flat on the ground or with their hands and feet tied to posts. Stuart told his readers that "in passing the prison in the morning, the cries of the poor creatures are dreadful."[30]

Not surprisingly, there were many deserters from the New Orleans army of enslaved people even as it grew progressively smaller over the years. In 1850 the city's many newspapers contained 475 separate advertisements for missing slaves. A large majority, in fact nearly 8 out of 10, of the runaway advertisements in New Orleans were placed by residents of the city and pertained to their own slaves. Some of those were thought to have left the city, but the great majority appear to have remained there. As late as 1859 slave owners believed New Orleans to be "one of the safest of hiding places for runaway slaves." Even though it dropped from having nearly 43,000 members in 1840 to less than 24,000 in 1860, the black community was able to give assistance to fugitives. Free black people could provide them a place to stay, and so could the many hired-out slaves with monthly passes who lived on their own. Masters told the editors of the *Picayune* "that without going more than a few squares from the residence of their masters, [many escapees] found security in the lodging places furnished by those who live under the protection of passes, for months." The newspaper particularly deplored the practice of allowing rented slaves to find their own jobs, creating what it called a "species of *quasi* freedom" that had "severed the ties that had bound master and slave." "They have been permitted to hire their own time and with the nominal protection of their masters, though with none of their oversight, to engage in business on their own account, to live according to the suggestion of their own fancy . . . provided only the monthly wages are regularly gained." The practice had also "created a feeling of discontent and longing for more freedom on the part of those servants who, while kept in the family of their masters, have opportunities of intercourse with those who hire their time."[31]

Given that they could find assistance and even room and board a few blocks from where they lived, New Orleans escapees, even more than those in other cities deserve to be called walkaways. This ease of flight helps to explain several differences between the demography of the runaway population in New Orleans and that in the rest of the Lower Mississippi Valley. Nearly one in three escapees in the Crescent City was a woman as compared to about one in ten elsewhere. The New Orleans figure exaggerates the propensity of New Orleans women to abscond, however, because the ratio of women to men in the city's slave population was significantly higher than any place else. Females made up 59 percent of the enslaved population of the city as compared to about 50 percent everywhere else, and in the population age fourteen and above they were 66 percent. Had there been an equal number of adult male and female slaves in New Orleans, the women would have been only 25 percent of those advertised, one in four rather than one in three, but still two and a half times as many as elsewhere. The old and young were also more likely to escape in New Orleans than elsewhere. In the rest of the Lower Mississippi Valley, and indeed the entire South, at least 70 percent of advertised fugitives were young adults between the ages of fifteen and twenty-nine, but in New Orleans that group was only 52 percent. Children fourteen years old and under were a full 10 percent of Crescent City fugitives and only 2 percent elsewhere. Adults over fifty were 5 percent in the big city and 1 percent elsewhere. Physical strength and endurance were not very important if you were not going very far and could spend the night indoors.[32]

New Orleans runaway advertisements document the continuing role of enslaved people in the commercial life of the city. Twenty-year-old mulatto Lucy, for example, was "well known in the city," having worked in her owner's "Soda, Pie, and Cake shop," which may have been one of the many small retail establishments on Royal Street from where she made her escape. George Anderson was also "well acquainted and well-known": He had apparently learned to deal with horses while working in a livery stable, gone on to drive a cab, and most recently was operating a milk wagon for Citizens' Dairy. Gus was a carpenter. Ellis was a plasterer. Betsy did cooking and washing. Dennis was a cooper. Ben Nash was "well known on the Levee as a steamboat man." Susan was a hairdresser. Ben "had long been employed in the ferry business of this city." Philina was a "superior hairdresser and seamstress." Oscar Dunn was "an apprentice to the plastering trade." Isaac was "something of a carpenter." George Allen Blackson had "sold bread for several years at the lower end of Poydras market." John Cunningham, who ran away in February, "pretends to be good cook" but was obviously not content in that position, having escaped three months earlier only to be arrested and imprisoned along with a white man "for stealing cotton on the Levee." The "griff negro boy" Isom Bondy, who was six feet tall, "thick made," and forty-five years old, may have resented his menial and physically demanding job as a dockworker since he was "very intelligent" and liked to use "high-flown language." Bald in front, he sometimes wore a wig that his owner thought looked like "Indian hair."[33]

Escapees were often able to stay at large even though they were spotted from time to time. Dan, a short black man who had worked as a drayman, was well known in the city and after leaving his master had "been seen about the grog shops near the corner of Customhouse and Levee Streets." Morris Butler, a thirty-year-old "light griffe" with "an intelligent eye," worked at white-washing and plastering when enslaved but on his own was visible "strolling around negro grog shops and gambling houses." In February 1848, George A. Botts offered a $50 reward for Brazile, who was an active participant in the unique social life of New Orleans. He was from Charleston, twenty-one years old, a mulatto, "rather slender," and had a "Roman nose" and was a "genteel person." He had run away six months earlier and was seen several times "dressed in women's clothes" and on other occasions "in genteel male attire." He also attended balls in the city on a regular basis.[34]

Advertisements illustrated the dangers that slave owners took when they hired out their slaves and especially when they also gave them the freedom to find their own employment. Sarah, for example, left the home of T. C. Twichell on September 6, 1848, "with a pass from her mistress to look for a place to work" and was still gone a week later, despite having "been frequently seen in the upper part of the Second Municipality." James Noe's advertisement for the slender black man, forty-five-year-old Calip, indicates his lack of control over him. Noe had arranged for Calip to have a "medal" from the city that gave him the privilege of hiring himself out but claimed he had become "to[o] lazy to work." Calip had been absent for a week or so, lurking about the city and last seen "near the Old Meat market" and no longer working but using the medal to keep from being taken up as a runaway. Bill's ad read like a resume. He "has been a cook for many years, has been on different steamboats with Capt. Andrews, has likewise been cook on boats of the Alabama river, has been cook for M[adame] Andrews, in Poydras street, also [Madame] Proctor, in Royal street, and for the last two years in a private family in Lafayette [then a town adjacent to New Orleans] from where he left on the above date [May 23, 1848] in the forenoon." Dan had gone into business for himself. He had been employed as a whitewasher in the First and Second Districts for several years and was continuing in that line of work "in the rear of the city."[35]

Slavery in New Orleans was regulated by the Black Code of 1806 and by city ordinances. Many of the enslaved benefited from Section 1 of the code, which required owners to give them Sundays off or pay them fifty cents for working, but that provision did not apply to personal servants, of which New Orleans had many. Section 30, which set up the pass system, had a major impact on the Crescent City, and probably not in a way the legislature intended. Slaves were required to have passes when outside of the plantation or the city where they lived—which in 1840, for example, confined those of New Orleans to an urban area containing about 100,000 people. Other state laws dealing with slavery applied to New Orleans, but the web of control was largely based on city ordinances.[36]

In 1856 Henry J. Leovy was tasked by the city council to produce a digest of old and new ordinances and later complained that he had to use old newspapers to find the details of some, as well as categorize the 3,300 that had been passed in the previous four years. His finished product, done speedily and skillfully one should add, contained a heading titled "Slaves and Free Persons of Color," all twenty-one provisions of which were passed January 7, 1857, but almost certainly represented regulations that existed through most of the previous half century. Couched for the most part in terms of prohibitions and punishments, the list suggests the types of things the enslaved population would do if the ordinances would not be enforced, which the evidence suggests they were not. Under the threat of "twenty-five lashes" for disturbing the peace, slaves were forbidden "to quarrel, yell, curse or sing obscene songs" or to "gamble in the streets, roads or other places, or on the levee." The same penalty applied "for any slave who shall abuse or insult a free person" or carry "a cane or stick" unless "blind or infirm." Owners of "cabarets, grog-shops, groceries, or coffee-houses" could be fined and lose their licenses if they allowed whites, free colored people, and slaves to play "cards, dominoes, or other games" together. A requirement that a slave have a pass from his or her owner to live outside his master's home, ride on public conveyances, buy or sell things, buy liquor for himself, and stay out after curfew, makes it clear that those things could be done with a pass, which many of them had, either real or forged, and which were seldom checked anyway. The city's police were specifically assigned duties with respect to some of these, arresting whites, free colored people, and slaves who were playing cards together, for example, and they had a general responsibility to enforce all of them. They were not, however, required to arrest runaway slaves. The city had only one ordinance on that subject, and it dealt with a narrow but very important issue. The city provided a $10 reward for "any person" who would "arrest" a runaway slave on board a steamboat, sailing vessel, or flatboat and bring the captive to a city jail.[37]

The antebellum police department of New Orleans had evolved to meet the rapidly growing demands of urban growth and by 1860 was professional by the standards of the time. In 1805 when the city received a municipal charter from the Territory of Orleans, it immediately created a police force, known officially as the Civil Guard and less formally as the "gens d'Armes," whose primary purpose was to assuage the ever-present white fear of a black insurrection. Well-armed, mounted, and on the streets at regular intervals during the day and night, it was a paid, urban version of the volunteer slave patrols that operated in rural areas, and its regular duties included enforcing the evening curfew, arresting runaways, and dealing with any other suspicious activity on the part of the enslaved population. Over time as the city grew, its citizens became less fearful of a slave uprising and more concerned with day-to-day violence, crime, and the enforcement of city ordinances. In the mid-1830s, the Crescent City increased the number of its policemen, took away most of their arms, and made them walk regular beats. After city government was again centralized in the 1850s, they began to wear blue coats with brass buttons and stiff, up-turned, military-like collars. Officially they carried wooden batons, handcuffs, and "rattles" used to call for help. In violation of city regulations, most of them also carried concealed handguns to deal with criminals, who since the 1840s were similarly armed and responsible for an annual murder rate of 30 per 100,000, as compared, for example, with Philadelphia where it was 3.4 per 100,000.[38]

The New Orleans policemen were not required to chase runaway slaves, but they arrested a few almost every day. Their authority was based on the right of any white to stop and examine any slave not accompanied by his owner, and they did it for the same reasons the civilians did, public spirit and financial benefit. As the *Picayune* once explained: "Police authorities contend it is no part of their regular duties to hunt after runaway negroes, which are mere property . . . and that if they do ferret them out, it must be done outside of their regular business, and with a view to liberal consideration." The "liberal consideration" they wanted, and were accustomed to receiving, was compensation by the owner. How else to explain, as a newspaperman reported wryly, that the policeman's wallet recovered from the thief who had stolen it in December 1843 had no money in it but did contain "a pen and ink etching of a burglar, a warrant for the arrest of a man charged with assault and battery, and an advertisement offering a reward for a runaway slave." Or the action of a Second Municipality policeman who was referred for possible disciplinary action in June 1850 after he left his post to search for a runaway in nearby Lafayette.[39]

According to the paper, most of the owners were happy to pay the police for these special services, but at least a few were not. A positive example involved a man whose slave had been gone for a long while, and apparently was no longer advertised. He asked what sort of reward would be appropriate and when $50 was suggested wrote a check for $125. The opposite approach was taken by an owner from Mississippi who asked for police help and promised "a liberal reward," but then returned home before the fugitive was found and refused to pay anything when he was. In response, the department chose not to release the captive to a local agent of the owner but instead forced him to make a special trip to New Orleans to pick him up in person.[40]

Even when rewards were not involved, the "taking up" of suspected runaways could be good for a municipal budget. In 1856 a cow in Lafayette, which had become the Fourth District of New Orleans four years earlier, wandered out an open gate and crossed the boundary line into Carrollton, which was then in Jefferson Parish. An enslaved man belonging to the cow's owner pursued the animal and was arrested and taken to jail by a Carrollton policeman, over the objections of a white bystander who was familiar with the slave and his owner and explained the situation. The owner himself went immediately to the station and retrieved his bondsman but only after paying $3 for the arrest, $2 for transportation to jail, $2 for commitment and release, and $2 for jail fees, the last including "board" although the slave got nothing to eat. The cow, which was valued at $60, was never found. In an article titled "Overdoing Things," the *Picayune* complained of people who encouraged horses, mules, cows, and goats to stray into the urban limits of New Orleans so they could collect a 50 cents reward from the city pound and claimed that something similar was happening to human property. "Negroes sent out on errands are frequently arrested when there are not the slightest grounds for supposing them to be fugitives from service, and positive losses and annoyances to their owners are the result." An example was the recent arrest of a slave by a police officer despite the fact the man had a pass from his owner that was countersigned by the mayor of the city and was sleeping in the house for which he had been given permission. He was in jail for two nights.[41]

Private individuals sometimes tried to make money from fugitivism. John Otto Green was a free colored man who was well known and respected in the city and acted as a police informant, making small amounts of money for providing information about the whereabouts of stolen property and runaway slaves. One day he asked a policeman named Evans if a mulatto slave named Sandy had absconded from a Mister Wade. Evans explained that not only was Sandy gone but Wade had offered him $5.00 to get the fugitive back. Green, who was probably aware of both these things, offered to turn Sandy over to the officer if he would pay him $3.00 that Green had spent feeding him. Evans paid the money, got Sandy back, and immediately arrested the informant for harboring a slave. After the griffe slave Daniel escaped from his owner David Fellows of 35 Rampart Street, a man calling himself Joseph Populus came to Fellows saying that had learned Daniel was in the hands of an abolitionist society run by a free colored preacher who planned to assist the runaway in getting to the North. Populus offered to get Daniel back for $75. Fellows agreed, paid the money, and got a receipt for it, but never saw Daniel or Populus again.[42]

Arrest reports produced by the unified police department of New Orleans beginning in 1852 make possible a macroscopic view of runaway slaves in the context of urban crime. During the twelve months that began in November 1853 and ended in October 1854, 22,854 arrests were processed of which 1,307 were enslaved people who had deserted from their owners, or at least were thought to have done so. On average, New Orleans locked up three or four accused runaways every day. There is no evidence as to how many were brought in by private citizens and how many by policemen. The runaway arrests were 5.7 percent of the total number of arrests, as compared, for example, with public intoxication, which was the cause of 21.5 percent (intoxication and disturbing the peace was a separate charge that made up 4.4 percent of the total). On the other hand, that was only one drunk for every twenty-six people in the free population of New Orleans, and there was one arrest of a runaway slave for every twelve slaves in the city. Women were 15.7 percent of all those detained for causes other than being runaway slaves, but 24.4 of the runaways were female—well below the percentage of women in runaway slave advertisements.[43]

Municipal crimes in New Orleans were dealt with in the recorder's courts, one of which was in each municipality after 1835 and in each district after 1852, and *Daily Picayune* reporters wrote about their activities on a regular basis, focusing heavily on anecdotal information delivered in a jocular fashion designed to appeal to a wide audience. Despite the large number of local runaways that were arrested, there is little evidence that the police or the public considered them an important threat either to the property interests of slaveholders or to the safety of the white public. In 1849, a reporter wrote that overnight cases in Recorder Baldwin's court were of a very "uninteresting character," few in number and for "trivial offences": five were for vagrancy, two for drunkenness, and three for being runaway slaves. On New Year's Day 1851, "there were a large number of arrests . . . in the Second Municipality, but they were mostly runaway or fractious negroes, and men who were too much elated with seeing the new year in with proper libations." Toward the end of 1851, a reporter joked that either the police of the Third Municipality were not doing their job, or the people had become more virtuous because the arrest records for the week showed only "the apprehension of a runaway negro, or the locking up of a man to allow him to become sober." Quite the opposite might have been said of Recorder Seuzeneau's court as reported on March 22, 1854, when three men accused of violent crimes were processed "and there were also several sailors who had deserted their ships, drunken men, lewd women, and runaway negroes" who were locked up.[44]

Many alleged runaway slaves were arrested for minor thefts. Simeon, who had escaped from Mr. Torrey and stolen a pair of shoes belonging to Mr. Soule, was arrested and ordered to receive twenty-five lashes. Another slave who was accused of fighting was sentenced to the same punishment but could avoid it by paying a $5.00 fine, the money apparently coming from his owner, Mr. Batson. Jack, who had no pass and was suspected of being a runaway, was arrested for having stolen a box of cigars. Ben was arrested for stealing several items of clothing. Jules, who was arrested as a runaway, also had "a lot of clothing" with him that was believed to have been stolen. Thomas Emerson was captured with a washing tub. Paul, who belonged to a Mr. Regan and was believed to be a runaway, was arrested on Lafayette Street for being drunk and having with him a horse thought to be stolen.[45]

The New Orleans walkaways were often assisted by friends, most of them probably members of what were known in the city as its "free colored" people, the men of which were abbreviated in public documents as f.c.m. and the women as f.c.w. Enslaved people living on their own, however, also helped other slaves to become free or remain free, and occasionally white people did the same. Quite a few advertisements included a sentence reminding readers that "harboring" runaways was against the law. An ad for Dan, who drove a dray in the city, offered $30 for his capture and provided that "the above reward will be paid for his apprehension and security in any jail in this city, with the conviction of any person or persons who have been harboring or employing him." Another owner warned operators of boardinghouses and steamboats against harboring his missing washerwoman. Thomas Askew offered a $100 reward for anyone harboring Dennis, who worked as a cooper. Making barrels was a high-skill job that probably made Dennis especially valuable, and Askew may have thought that the person who assisted Dennis hoped to profit from the crime. Whatever the case, six months later Dennis was still missing. John B. Byrne thought that his mulatto slave Robert, "who was well known in the city," was probably being harbored by Robert's wife, who had once belonged to Byrne. Byrne was determined to get Robert back. He offered a $25 reward to any person who could provide evidence leading to the arrest of any white man or free colored person who had assisted the slave and warned ship captains from hiring him "under the severest penalty of the law." Elizabeth was a fourteen- or fifteen-year-old girl under five feet tall and had a scar on her cheek and "hard hands" caused by severe frostbite. Her owner believed she had been "decoyed off" and offered a $50 reward for the arrest of the person who did it.[46]

Many escapes seem to have involved movement from one part of the city to another. For example, an advertisement in June 1841 sought information about an eighteen-year-old griffe named Peter who had "absconded" from his owner's home in Lafayette eight months earlier and was thought to be living in the Third Municipality at the lower end of the city. A month later, the "negress" Louisa, who left Bayonne Street in the city, was thought to be "concealed" somewhere in Lafayette, where she had been found after an earlier escape. An ad for Daphne noted that her husband was owned by "the Draining Company" and suggested she would "most likely be found some where among that Company's slaves," presumably living with them rather than working with them.[47]

The responsibility that some New Orleans owners gave to their slaves and they put to their own advantage is illustrated in an event that occurred in July 1851. J. R. Shaw gave Spencer, his "confidential" slave, $4,000 to deposit in the Louisiana State Bank. Despite his favored status, having been "permitted many indulgences and received much favor," Spencer did not make the deposit and instead mailed the money to Boston. He was not seen again until a week later when found in the home of a free colored man named Sandy Hawkins. Spencer confessed, and Shaw sent a telegraph to the Boston police, who intercepted the cash at the Boston post office. Spencer also incriminated a white man named James Dyson. Since a slave could not testify against a white man, the district attorney dismissed charges against Hawkins, and he testified that Dyson had gotten him to hide Spencer and paid for the man's room and board. Other witnesses claimed Dyson had "tampered" with Spencer before the theft, which led to charges that he had both harbored Spencer and stolen him, but he was only convicted on the first offense.[48]

Despite the widespread belief among slave owners that their missing bondspeople were receiving assistance, there were few arrests for harboring and still fewer convictions, only forty-three from November 1, 1853, to October 31, 1854. This may have been because daily interactions among whites, slaves, and free blacks were so common, and slaves had so much freedom, it was difficult to prove that a free person knew that a slave was a runaway or even enslaved. In August 1851, Richard Keenan hired an enslaved man named James to work as a cook in his restaurant, the Tremont House. In March 1852, James Blane, James's owner, went to the Tremont House with a policeman and found him working there along with evidence that he was sleeping on the premises. Blane accused Keenan of harboring the slave. Keenan responded that he had thought

James was free to hire himself out, and the fact that he had made no attempt to conceal the slave was evidence that he did not think he was a runaway. Not only was Keenan acquitted, but the *Picayune*'s brief account of the case suggests that his mistake was quite common and not very serious: "If it were only to prevent trouble and annoyance to themselves[,] persons should be cautious not to employ slaves without the permission of their owners." But then there was Leopold Bordenheim, who rented a room to an enslaved woman who lived there for a month before she was found by her owner, who then accused Bordenheim of having harbored her. He claimed that he did not know she was a runaway or that there were laws about renting to slaves and was let off with a $10 fine.[49]

Not surprisingly, many fugitives resisted being caught. One who made the news was Hal, who was purchased in Mobile in early 1843 and brought to New Orleans on the steamboat *Swan*, from which he promptly escaped. He found a job working in one boardinghouse, calling himself Claiborne, and in another one using the name George, in both cases claiming that he was owned by a man who allowed him to hire himself out and providing forged receipts for his monthly wages from the fictitious masters. When the police came to arrest him, Hal jumped over a railing, fled through a nearby house, and got several blocks away before being caught.[50]

Violent responses to attempted arrests were not uncommon. In July 1859 a free black man named Echo prevented the arrest of a runaway woman on the Gentilly Ridge by threatening a police officer with a double-barreled shotgun. On Saturday, when two men went to arrest a runaway black man at the corner of Love and Music Streets in the Third Municipality, "he stabbed them both dangerously, one of them it is thought mortally, and escaped." In 1840, Henry Nichols was near the New Basin Canal when he recognized Celeston as a runaway slave belonging to a Mr. Barclay. Nichols attempted to arrest him, and Celeston made a swipe at his throat with a razor, cutting him on the shoulder. Celeston was captured and charged with attacking a white man, which under the Black Code was punishable by execution. In November 1840, about 8:00 in the evening, three police officers from the Second Municipality went out to arrest a mixed-race man named Jeff who had passed for free, but they had been informed was a runaway slave. They found him on the levee taking part in a congo dance with about thirty other black people, but when they attempted to make an arrest, "the whole of his coloured companions assailed the officers with bricks and other missiles and rescued him. Some of the policemen got pretty seriously injured." The paper called for "the most rigorous punishment" of any of the participants who could be identified. Several days later another group of three officers found Jeff in a cabaret and captured him after a severe struggle. He was, said the paper, "an athletic, powerful man."[51]

In March 1845, a homeowner, who was not identified either by race or legal status, fired a "fowling piece" in the face of a Mr. Schexneydre, who was pursuing a runaway and was now expected to lose one of his eyes. In 1836 a white man hunting in the woods behind the city claimed to have been attacked by a runaway who "threw him and bit his arms and hand." The hunter broke free and shot his assailant dead. There was apparently some doubt about this account because the case went to trial, but the jury accepted the claim of self-defense. Some private citizens made a business out of capturing runaways, which could be a dangerous occupation. In December 1843, a dead man was found in the streets of New Orleans who had been stabbed many times, including once in the lungs and once in the heart. "His employment was the pursuit of runaway negroes, by some of whom it was conjectured he was killed." The violence associated with fugitivism in the city did not pose an important threat to the white public, but maroons living in the wilds close to New Orleans sometimes did.[52]

Henry C. Castellanos, who was born in New Orleans in 1827 and spent much of his life there, remembered that in his youth "Marais street was then deemed the border land lying between terra firma and the 'trembling prairie,' an impenetrable morass, beyond which none but experienced hunters for fugitives ventured to enter." Runaway slaves built homes made of willow branches thatched with palm leaves in the most inaccessible parts of this area and attempted to live in them on a semipermanent basis, always in danger of being taken by the slave catchers who used bloodhounds to find them.

As Castellanos explained it to his readers, "even when not pursued, these outlaws were compelled to emerge at night from their solitary haunts in quest of nourishment. Hence it was that New Orleans, despite the efforts of an inadequate police force, became the scene of nocturnal thefts and assassinations. With the spoils and money thus obtained, a 'cabaret' was always ready to supply the hunted-down outcast with powder, shot, whisky and such other articles as were required for his most pressing wants."[53]

In 1822, planters from the Tchoupitoulas area on the western edge of the city offered a $300 reward to anyone who could find the location of "a collection of runaway slaves, who have been joined by some of Mr. Lebreton's negroes" and take them to it. Twelve years later the *Louisiana Advertiser* wrote about "a band of runaway negroes in the Cypress Swamp in the rear of the city" that had been "committing depredations," including the plundering of a house along the new canal. A group of unarmed laborers working there had gone after the maroons but returned when fired upon. In 1846, twelve "gentlemen" from the Second and Third Municipalities went hunting for another gang in the faubourg Washington. They found a camp with some fifteen men and women and fired on them, killing one man and one woman and wounding two other women. Two years later, the *Picayune* reported that a Charles Cammeyer, "well known in this city for ferreting out and discovering the haunts of runaway negroes," had found a camp where eight fugitives were living and captured five of them, the other three having gone to New Orleans for provisions. The men had been making a living cutting wood "for some white man."[54]

The most famous maroon was Bras Coupee, best known in the largely fictional account contained in George Washington Cable's novel *The Grandissimes,* published in 1880. In real life Bras Coupee was an enslaved man named Squire, the personal servant and "huntsman" of General William du Buys, who, according to Castellanos, was a loyal supporter of slavery, but "who petted and completely spoiled the fellow." Despite his comparatively favorable situation, Squire repeatedly ran away, winning the name Bras Coupee after defying "a patrol of white planters," one of whom then shot him in the arm. He was taken to a hospital where the arm was amputated, and he was placed under guard while he recovered. Squire contracted dysentery and was thought to be so weak that the guard was removed, and the invalid promptly escaped through a window. For the next three years he lived in the swamps, leading a group of runaways much feared by the white people of the city, among whom the name Bras Coupee, as remembered by Castellanos, "became a familiar word, pronounced in hushed and subdued tones to frighten children."

In April 1837, two members of the City Guard were hunting rabbits in the back swamp when one heard a weapon misfire, turned and saw a black man twelve feet away, and shot at him, inflicting what he believed was a mortal wound. The next day, however, when a group of men came to retrieve the body all they found was a trail of blood. Three months later a Spanish civilian named Garcia claimed he was out fishing when he also heard a misfire. He charged at a black man who was reloading, and beat him to death with an iron pike he carried to moor his pirogue. The details of the event were later disputed, but the man Garcia killed was Bras Coupee. He brought the body back to New Orleans where the mayor had it put on display outside his office. Thousands of residents, black and white, turned out to view the corpse "with its crushed and mangled head."[55]

❊{ CHAPTER 6 }❊

Stealing Slaves to Sell or Save

RUNAWAY SLAVES HAVE sometimes been described as stealing themselves, a characterization that is literally true but in the American South not legally so. Enslaved people could be prosecuted for stealing other forms of property, but fleeing was treated as a form of disobedience rather than a criminal act, and dealing with it was the owner's responsibility not the government's. For the benefit of slaveholders and the public, state and local governments provided institutional support in the form of civilian slave patrols, reimbursements and rewards for people who captured fugitives, facilities for their incarceration, and advertisements to assist their owners in finding them.[1]

The taking of someone's slaves by someone other than themselves was a crime, and it was treated the same way whether the perpetrator intended to sell the stolen people or help them to escape. The stealing itself could be done as a form of robbery, with a gun pointed at the owner, for example, but that was almost never the case. Instead, the targets were lured away by promises of freedom and made complicit in an act that for them was much like running away, and one they hoped would have the same result. The Louisiana Supreme Court described the most common method succinctly: "The slave is induced to run away under the promise of liberty in a free state, whilst the real object of the criminal is to induce him to leave so that he may sell him."[2]

In the 1820s and 1830s, during the early frontier stage of western Tennessee, northern Mississippi, and all of Arkansas, slave stealing was often a sideline of outlaws who also rustled cattle, passed counterfeit money, and engaged in robbery and burglary. Throughout the entire antebellum period stealing slaves for profit was also practiced as what we might call white-collar crime by well-dressed and well-spoken individuals who were, or could appear to be, part of the southern middle class of planters and businessmen. Persons involved in legal disputes over slaves sometimes stole the property under litigation.

"Friends of the fugitive," as they have been called, helped slaves escape from bondage in the Lower Mississippi Valley as they did elsewhere in the South. Slaves sometimes, and probably often, helped other slaves, although they also sometimes helped to catch them. Local whites also played a role. Most important were free blacks, both because they were apt to be sympathetic to the cause and because they were often in position to provide significant aid. Public opinion, and sometimes individual owners, also blamed northern abolitionists for stealing their slaves, but that was seldom the case.[3]

Southern law was complicated by what has been called the "double character" of slaves as both property and persons. They could be bought, sold, and inherited but also punished for stealing things, setting barns on fire, killing people, and a host of other "crimes." The Arkansas Supreme Court once explained why it thought enslavement was compatible with legal responsibility on the part of the enslaved: "Though inferior in mental and moral endowments to the white race, and occupying a subordinate position, in the order of Providence, yet they are rational beings." Another opinion by the same court required slaves to disobey their masters if ordered to do something illegal: "In all things lawful, the slave is absolutely to obey his master. But a higher power than his master—*the law of the land*—forbids him to commit crime."[4]

The Louisiana law on slave stealing, which was passed in 1819 and remained in effect until the Civil War, stated that any person who should "inveigle, steal, or carry away" someone else's slave or "should aid such slave in running away" would be sentenced to a prison term of from two to twenty years hard labor.[5] Arkansas law was more typical of other states. It made a clear distinction between encouraging slaves to run away and stealing them. "Slave stealing" was a form of larceny and treated as a particularly serious one. The taking of most personal property was punishable by a prison term of one to five years, the stealing of a horse or mule made the guilty party liable for five to fifteen years, and the theft of a slave upped the possible jail time from five to twenty-one years. What Louisiana called inveigling a slave was a separate crime in Arkansas called "enticing away." A person who "shall induce" a slave "to abscond" from his owner "by means of promises of freedom or arguments, or shall aid or abet said escape" was guilty of a misdemeanor punishable by one to five years in prison. Arkansas not only attempted to prevent "enticing away" by punishing those who committed the crime, it also tried to forestall its commission. If a private citizen told a justice of the peace under oath that he believed someone was about to persuade a slave to run away, the justice was required to issue a warrant for the arrest of the suspected person and could require the payment of a bond up to $1,000 to guarantee his "good behavior" and appearance in circuit court.

States also criminalized separate acts that were often part of the process of helping slaves to escape and evade capture. Tennessee, for example, made forging passes, harboring slaves, or enticing them away punishable by three to ten years imprisonment. In Louisiana, the harboring law also prohibited removing iron chains or collars, but the penalty was only a fine of $200 to $1,000 or imprisonment from three to twelve months. This comparatively mild punishment may have been related to the situation in New Orleans where, as we have seen, the relative freedom enjoyed by the enslaved population made it easy for whites to hire runaways unintentionally.[6]

While the Louisiana statute of 1819 did not make persuading a slave to escape a separate crime from stealing him or her, the courts sometimes made that distinction. In 1858, the Louisiana Supreme Court took up the case of two men, Thompson and Baer, who were both charged with two counts under that law: the first was inveigling and stealing a slave named John from the New Orleans Gaslight Company and the second was helping John to escape. Thompson was convicted on the first count but found innocent on the second, and Baer judged to be innocent of the first but guilty on the second. Baer than appealed, arguing that the convictions were incompatible: If John ran away, he could not have been stolen, and if stolen, he could not be a runaway. The supreme court disagreed: "Two persons may agree to steal a slave, one may operate upon his mind and induce him to leave the service of his master and to accompany the other who intends to sell him. The first has then, in the sense of the statute, aided the slave in running away, the second has stolen him."[7]

Runaway slave advertisements suggest slave stealing was a common crime in the 1820s and 1830s. In 1820 Griffin Gayden, who owned a plantation near Liberty in Amite County, Mississippi, was adamant that Sophy, who was twenty-seven, short, dark-skinned, and shy, had been stolen and would probably be taken up the Natchez Trace toward Tennessee. He offered rewards of $50 for the thief and $10 for the slave. That same year, a mixed-race woman named Octavia, who was sixteen and had been recently purchased from an owner in Kentucky, left her new owner in Natchez. He thought someone might have "seduced her away," meaning with the promise of freedom. In 1825 Francis B. Bouis, who lived near Point Coupee, believed his three enslaved people, Toby, his wife Maley, and another woman named Eliza, had been "decoyed off," meaning encouraged to leave by a slave or former slave, in this case one or more individuals in a steamboat crew. In 1828 a Natchez owner named Peter Paul offered to pay $100 for the capture and conviction of William Carmichael, whom he thought "conveyed away" an enslaved family consisting of Bill, who was in his mid-forties and could play the fiddle, Mary, his wife, who was twenty-eight, and their four-year-old daughter Lucy.[8]

If the accused slave-stealer Carson Cooper was typical of criminals who did that sort of work, they were a rough lot. Cooper was a tall, well-built man, with blue eyes and a sandy-colored, unkempt beard, and whose dark complexion became red when he was agitated, which was much of the time. He walked with a swagger, talked loudly, behaved in a boisterous manner, and when drunk was "much disposed to dwell on scenes of bloodshed, in which he appears to have been from his own statement, a prominent actor." N. S. Webb of Pinckneyville, Mississippi, claimed that Cooper stole two slaves from him and then took them south to St. Francisville. There the thief turned them over to his nephew and accomplice, Narsworth Hunter, and provided a false bill of sale. Both men had been arrested for this crime but escaped from jail. They were thought to be still in the area, perhaps accompanied by Narsworth's brother Joseph, who was believed to have assisted Cooper in the commission of a murder. Joseph was similar in character to his uncle: He "talks loud and swears much, and for a youth of 18 to 20 years of age, is most astonishingly proficient in villainy." One of the Hunter brothers may have come to a very unhappy end. William Johnson, the Natchez barber, heard in November 1826 that a man with that last name was taken out of the Woodville jail by five or six people, shot three times, and "hung from a tree."[9]

Slaves were stolen throughout the Lower Mississippi Valley, but the crime was especially prevalent on its northwestern frontier. George Featherstonhaugh claimed Arkansas attracted frontier desperadoes because of the "very gentle and tolerant state of public opinion which prevailed there in regard to such fundamental points as religion, morals, and property." Sarcasm aside, the point was valid. Geography was part of the problem. The territory's eastern border on the Mississippi River was lined by a nearly impenetrable swamp that stretched many miles inland and made a useful refuge for outlaws; on the south, Arkansas bordered the Red River region of northern Louisiana, which was still in its frontier state; and the land west of Arkansas was unpromising enough that Andrew Jackson was willing to give it to the Indians.[10]

If he had been in Arkansas a year or two later than he was, Featherstonhaugh would doubtless have remarked on the strange case of Nixon Curry. In 1822 Curry was convicted of slave stealing in Iredell County, North Carolina, but he escaped from jail and killed a member of a posse that tried to catch him. Now wanted for both larceny and murder, he made his way to Arkansas and began to call himself John Hill. He settled among the Cherokee living along the Arkansas River near modern Russellville but later moved to the White River region of eastern Arkansas. There he married, had at least one child, and gained enough respect among his neighbors to be elected to the Territorial Assembly in 1833 and 1835. In 1836, however, a group of settlers from North Carolina crossing the St. Francis River at Strong's Ferry saw Hill and recognized him as the outlaw they knew as Nixon Curry. The lawmaker was arrested and placed in the St. Francis County Jail, but he broke out with the assistance of some friends. The sheriff offered a $300 reward to anyone who captured Curry but also made it seem that locking him up would be a loss to the public: "He is a gambler and drunkard, plays the fiddle, and is fond of joking, and makes a great many shrewd remarks—is good company, and a pretty smart man." Small wonder that Curry was able to remain free for five years more, living in western Arkansas before being killed by his son-in-law in a bar fight.[11]

Arkansas's popularity with slave stealers was well known. In 1822, a Baton Rouge slave owner advertised in the *Arkansas Gazette* for his servant Abraham whom he thought would probably try to get to Natchez, if he had left on his own, but he might have been stolen, in which case it was probable that he would be taken up the Red River "to Ouachita." The following year, another ad in the same paper suggested that James, who was missing from Scott County, Kentucky, had been "persuaded away by a worthless white man . . . fond of drink, and a blacksmith . . . who has been to Arkansas and will probably return there." In the summer of 1835, a young enslaved man named William told his new owner in Fayette, Mississippi, that he had been stolen from his previous home in eastern Tennessee and taken on a roundabout journey through Arkansas before he arrived in Natchez.[12]

In September 1835 George Penn was looking for Hannah, a forty-year-old black woman who he claimed had "a sulky appearance" and "bushy hair." She had fled from him wearing a "blue domestic frock" and carrying other clothes in the company of six other slaves. Four of the latter had been captured in Arkansas and two had drowned. One of them said they were "under the guidance" of Anson Moody, who had "enticed them away." Penn knew Moody as a slave stealer who had been given one hundred lashes and branded in Brownsville, Mississippi, for that crime. Moody may have been trying to aid the slaves, however, because Penn said the captives had been taken in Arkansas on their way to a free state and Hannah was believed to be continuing in that direction.[13]

The Trail of Tears that motivated some slaves to escape also provided opportunities for slave stealers. In October 1831, the *Arkansas Gazette* carried an ad for a black man and wife along with their two children, all of whom spoke Chickasaw, and had escaped from the Chickasaw Nation in Mississippi a year earlier. The Indian agent there believed they "had been run" by white men. In December 1831 Shadrack and Isham went missing from their home near Huntsville, Alabama, and a year later their owner Richard Haughton thought they "were stolen by some white villain or villains," taken to Mississippi and sold to the Choctaws (or "traded for cattle"), and "possibly may be taken to the Arkansas, with the Emigrating Indians." After Willis and Stephen ran away from Howell Ross, who lived near the falls of the Coosa River in Autauga County, Alabama, on January 1, 1832, he heard they were trying to reach either the Creeks or the Cherokees living west of the Mississippi, and he claimed to have "good reason" to think they had been run off by "some white villain or Indian."[14]

Outlaw gangs were also active in Arkansas. In 1828 one group of frontier criminals was operating on the upper reaches of the Ouachita River near Blakelytown, which became Arkadelphia in 1839. Under the heading "Another Murder," William Woodruff, editor of the *Arkansas Gazette*, voiced his outrage over a murder committed there in October of that year. A man named Elijah Bartlett had been shot and killed one evening while sitting at home. The murderer was thought to be a member of a gang of horse thieves who were among a group of "outlaws and fugitives from justice" who inhabited the region. Noting that the civil law, presumably meaning the sheriff and justices of the peace in Clark County, had been ineffective in dealing with the criminals, Woodruff advocated the use of "Lynch's Law," which was understood at that time to include not only hanging but also any other impromptu physical punishment administered by vigilantes. While he did not support that method as a rule, the editor thought "a small group of resolute men, under a prudent and experienced leader" might be needed in this situation.[15]

In the middle of June 1834, citizens from the Tennessee town of Covington, located fifty miles north of Memphis, carried out a large vigilante action against outlaws who made their home in the Mississippi swamp on the Arkansas side of the river that was locally known as The Morass. One week after the operation, Francis S. Latham began publishing the *Randolph Recorder* in the eponymous community located on the river itself a few miles west of Covington and provided the readers of its first issue with a detailed account of what happened. The villains according to Latham were among the robbers who inhabited nearly one hundred miles of the Arkansas Delta, emerging from there to steal "horses, negroes, cattle, and every species of property" and then returning to "their marshy skulking places," and when pursued secreted themselves "in the almost impervious canebrakes." Most recently a group of them had stolen the whiskey and flour cargo from a Kentucky flatboat that had run aground on a sandbar about ten miles below Randolph.

The campaign against the outlaws began when about thirty citizens from Randolph went to "Shawnee village," twenty-five miles down the river, and without resistance captured eight or ten prisoners and burned some of their cabins. The following day, forty or fifty "gloriously armed" men from Covington loaded themselves on a flatboat along with blankets and a week's supply of food and carried out an extended search in the same area. That sweep resulted in the arrest of about fifteen more criminals, some of whom had been involved in the flatboat robbery, "some known to be rogues of deep dye," and others "refugees from justice." All were brought before justices of the peace who sent seven to jail. Some of the remainder were let go, but four or five others, who everyone agreed were "villains" despite the lack of immediate evidence, were taken back to Arkansas where they were tied to posts and whipped before being released. A sheriff from St. Louis came down to Randolph to pick up one of the captured men, a well-known counterfeiter named Colonel

Stephen W. Foreman, who had recently escaped from jail there. Editor Latham graciously thanked a captain who used his steamboat to assist in the operation and another who had ferried some of the vigilantes back from Memphis, noting also that they had been "generously and hospitably entertained" while in that city.[16]

Three months after the vigilante action at Randolph, word reached Latham that some other counterfeiters and thieves had been captured in Gallatin, a city on the Grand River in northwest Missouri. Two of them had been released after providing information about the activities of more than twenty of their associates, which included making counterfeit money somewhere north of Randolph and taking it into Arkansas near the Crittenden County town of Greenock. They also stole slaves. As the abbreviated newspaper account put it, the confessions indicated that "Garrison has taken Beanford's negro into the Mississippi, to cross at St. Helena, then to his father's, opposite the head of the Island on White River; also he thinks that Garrison carried Magee's negro to Mobile, because G. said he got a check between Mobile and New Orleans, and got the money in New Orleans." Cryptic as this is to modern readers, it supported Latham's conclusion that the named men were "links in a long chain of [robbers and counterfeiters] that stretched from New-Madrid (Mo.) down the Mississippi."[17]

In March 1835 William Woodruff issued another warning in the *Arkansas Gazette* about outlaws, focusing this time on a group operating in Pulaski County, where Little Rock was located, and farther down the Arkansas River in Jefferson County. This gang, he claimed, "make a regular business of kidnapping negroes and stealing horses, and running them off to the lower country and selling them." The editor believed that this group was part of a larger network of "agents throughout the country." Again, he called on responsible private citizens to take action against them, arguing that when civil government was unable to deal with crime, the law of nature allowed responsible citizens "to take the lash in their own hands, and public opinion will sustain them in its prudent exercise." Vigilantism, however, could be a dangerous business, as Woodruff learned within three weeks. A Mr. A. C. W. Kille was shot and killed near the White River in eastern Arkansas by a man hiding in a canebrake. Witnesses had a glimpse of the murderer but not enough to identify him; Woodruff, however, was certain he was one of two men who had threatened citizens of Little Rock, including Kille, after they had administered Lynch's Law to other members of their outlaw gang.[18]

As if to mock Woodruff, the night of the same day he announced Kille's murder six men with blackened faces entered the Pulaski County Jail, threatened to kill the one guard on duty unless he gave them keys to the cells, and freed three prisoners. One of the prisoners was Fielding G. Secrest, who was in his early twenties but already, in Woodruff's words, a "quite notorious and hardened villain" who was accused of stealing horses and slaves; another was Morgan Williams, an accused murderer who walked with a crutch; and the third was Hiram, the slave of a local man who put him in jail "for safe keeping." After exiting the jail, Williams had apparently stolen a horse in Little Rock, then taken a better one ten miles from town, and later was seen on the Ouachita River in the southern part of the territory. Secrest and Hiram also stole horses and headed toward the Mississippi River, where the editor believed the white man was "now safely entrenched among his confederates in some of the almost impenetrable swamps of White River." He thought the gang had members scattered throughout Arkansas. The current wave of crime was worse than anything experienced in his previous fifteen years in the territory, and he was convinced that the courts and juries of the established legal system were incapable or unwilling to deal with it. He called for "a company of resolute woodsmen, inured to hardship, and familiar with the unerring use of the rifle" to search the swamps, caves, and other hiding places of the bandits, and no longer satisfied with the whippings, or even the hangings, associated with normal vigilante justice, he wanted them "hunted down like wild beasts and the carcasses left as food for the buzzards."[19]

It was probably Woodruff's column that led editor Latham in Randolph to report that the people of Arkansas were discussing a large-scale outlaw hunt like the one the Tennesseans had carried out the previous summer. He seemed skeptical, however, noting that the counterfeiter Colonel Foreman had escaped from the St. Louis jail again and suggesting that he was "now probably amusing the citizens of Little Rock with his exploits in manufacturing Uncle Sam's money for them." Two months later, an angry Latham was openly critical of Arkansas. In May 1835, another flatboat from Kentucky was forced to land at the same place on the Arkansas shore where the one had been robbed of its contents a year earlier. By coincidence, or perhaps by design, a group of locals held a drinking party nearby, and it became wild enough that one of them was murdered by some of the other revelers. Then, while the captain of the flatboat was sleeping on its deck, someone drilled holes in the bottom of the boat, and he woke up to find the craft sinking and willing hands removing its fifty-five barrels of tobacco. The next day a group of men including the local sheriff forced him to sell the cargo at less than half its market value. News of this spread quickly, and the owners of the boat came to Randolph, where local citizens helped them get back most of the tobacco before it could be shipped away. Seeing this whole episode as another example of the "robberies and cold-blooded murders that almost daily occur in this region," Latham voiced exasperation at his neighbors across the river:

> What a picture for civilized community? Is there no fault in the police of Arkansas? . . . We are aware of it being a wild uninviting portion of the territory, remote from executive control. But this is not reason why [a posse or vigilante group] should not ferret out and bring to condign punishment those whose hands are raised against the property and lives of every honest man. We even hear of threats made by them to burn our town for the part our citizens took a year ago.[20]

The criminal activity centered in eastern Arkansas set the stage for *A History of the Detection, Conviction, Life and Designs of John A. Murel, the Great Western Land Pirate,* which was published in Cincinnati in March 1835 and quickly reprinted in Athens, Tennessee. The title page said the book was written by Augustus Q. Walton, but that was a pseudonym used by Virgil Stewart, who played a leading role in the story that it told. John A.'s last name was actually Murrell not Murel. He was born in Virginia and moved with his parents to Williams County, Tennessee, where he grew up with four sisters and three brothers, of whom all the males became involved in illegal activities including disturbing the peace, stealing horses and slaves, and counterfeiting. In 1823 at the age of seventeen, John was charged with horse stealing. He fled to avoid a trial date, was caught and arrested, broke out of jail, was captured again, tried and convicted in 1826, and served twelve months in prison. A few years later he was living as a landless farmer, along with his wife, at least one child, and other members of the Murrell extended family, near the small town of Denmark, which was just south of Jackson, Tennessee, and about fifty miles east of Randolph.

The Great Western Land Pirate opened in August 1833 when a planter named Long living near the Murrells discovered that three of his slaves

were missing. A few days later one of them was captured by Long's overseer when the fugitive returned to pick up some clothes, and he confessed
that along with the other two he had been staying near the Murrell
homestead and all of them were being fed by John. Long gathered some
men, went to the place, and captured Murrell when he showed up with
a basketful of food. Murrell's story was that he was merely keeping the
runaways from leaving until he could inform Long of where they were.
Neither Long nor anyone else believed that, but a jury convicted Murrell
of harboring rather than stealing because there was no way to prove the
more serious charge. When Murrell was unable to pay the fine, however,
the judge gave him the unknown-to-law but perhaps appropriate sentence of serving Long without pay for five years. Murrell appealed and
was still free nine months later, when on January 18, 1834, John Henning,
a Methodist minister, found two of his slaves missing and concluded that
Murrell had stolen them, or perhaps arranged for someone else to do it.[21]

A week later the parson learned that Murrell intended to leave on a
trip, deduced he was going to pick up the stolen property, and convinced
a young man named Virgil Stewart, recently arrived in the neighborhood,
to follow him and prove the hypothesis. Stewart met Murrell a few miles
outside Denmark and spontaneously assumed a disguise as Adam Hues,
a man out looking for a strayed horse. He and Murrell started riding
side by side and remained together for six days, crossing into Arkansas
and then returning to Denmark. Along the way Stewart, alias Hues,
gained Murrell's confidence, and the outlaw attempted to recruit him as
a partner in crime by bragging about his own career, a saga that included
details about stealing slaves, robbing travelers, and murdering members
of both groups. The most spectacular part was Murrell's claim to be the
leader of an organization known as the Mystic Clan, which contained
one thousand men spread across the South who were planning to foment
a slave insurrection in the coming December so that they could rob banks
throughout the region during the ensuing chaos. The two men ended
their journey back at Denmark on February 2, where they were met by
Henning, who had been tipped off by Stewart and had Murrell arrested
on the spot. The following July, Stewart was the star witness against
Murrell at his trial in Jackson, Tennessee, which ended with the defendant found guilty of slave stealing and sent to prison for ten years.

Murrell's account of the Mystic Clan and its planned slave insurrection was as historian Joshua D. Rothman has put it, "incredible at best,
preposterous at worst, and downright weird either way." There is also

nothing in Murrell's documented history or his local reputation that suggests he had anything like the vision, talent, or leadership ability necessary to organize and carry out what would have been the most spectacular criminal event in American history. Murrell, however, did steal slaves, and what he had to say about that constituted something like a tutorial on the business, although one that exaggerated his own success working in the field. It was based on three real-world examples and buttressed by a legal argument that seemed to make the crime a particularly attractive form of felonious larceny.[22]

Murrell first discussed his involvement with an enslaved man named Sam who had been owned by someone in the Denmark neighborhood and then sold to a man named Eason who lived in Florence, Alabama. Murrell claimed to have come upon Sam by accident while traveling in that area. After renewing their acquaintance, he asked the slave how he liked his new master. "He is Hell," said Sam. Murrell then suggested he escape and come back to Denmark, offering to take care of him if he did. Not long after, Sam did that, and Murrell hid him until Eason posted an advertisement looking for his runaway. Then he turned the fugitive over to one of the other Murrell brothers and a man named Forsythe, who took Sam south through Mississippi and eventually into Texas, selling him several times along the way, after each of which Sam escaped and the three moved on. Murrell claimed the white men were paid $2,800 in total, $1,400 in cash, $700 of "ready-made clothing," and a bill of credit from Thomas Hudnel of Madison County, Mississippi.[23]

The second example was a show-and-tell dealing with enticement. Murrell and Stewart met an elderly black man named Clitto along the way who was getting ready to carry a bag of corn a half mile to a mill. Murrell told the man his master must be a hard man to send him on the errand in such cold weather. When the slave agreed, Murrell asked if he would like to be free and have the money to buy whatever he wanted. Clitto said he would, and Murrell made an offer: "I will steal you, and carry you off, and sell you four or five times: and give you half of the money, and then leave you in a free State." Clitto agreed, and Murrell sealed the deal by offering the slave a drink of whiskey—making sure to drink after the black man had taken his swig, a technique designed to win his trust. Before Murrell and Stewart rode on, the outlaw said he would send a confederate who would fire a pistol as a signal for Clitto to escape and take three or four "boys" with him, a promise he had no intention of keeping.[24]

For his last lesson, the outlaw told a long story involving a slave in Tipton County, Tennessee, who was enticed away by a confederate who carried his victim down the Mississippi River to Natchez in a skiff and kept him there until Murrell arrived. He took the fugitive aboard a steamboat bound for New Orleans, but Murrell was recognized on the trip by someone who warned the boat captain that he was a known thief and the slave was probably a runaway. The captain took the slave into custody, but Murrell somehow contrived to remain free and continue to New Orleans where he went to the mayor of the city and claimed that he owned the slave and the captain had taken him illegally. Friends confirmed the story, Murrell got the slave back, and the captain had to pay a fine. Murrell then sold the man in the city for $800; he escaped from his new owner and was taken to a parish up the river from New Orleans by Murrell, who was now pretending to be a Methodist minister and using the slave as a personal servant. Next, Murrell sold his black confederate to a man named Higginbotham for $700, and he again escaped and was this time taken to Arkansas where he was sold a third time. Murrell helped the slave escape one more time and then turned him over to another friend who murdered the man and threw his body in the river.

The disposal of dead bodies in water was a signature technique of Murrell's. Recounting the killing of one stolen slave he allegedly told Stewart, "I took out his entrails and sunk him in a creek"; and in another case, he "ripped open his belly and tumbled him into a stream." Murrell also killed several white travelers to get their horses, one of the bodies getting the now-familiar treatment: "I ripped open his belly and took out his entrails and sunk him in a creek."[25]

Murrell's argument with respect to the legality of stealing slaves hinged on the runaway advertisement and the offer of a reward it usually contained. He claimed it was "a commission to take the property into possession," and if the person who had the runaway "chooses to make a breach of the trust which the advertisement confides in him: and instead of carrying the negro to the owner, he converts him to his own use—this is not stealing, and the owner can only have redress in a civil action for the amount of his property." This was a novel idea that if accepted in court would have undermined a system that had been used by American slaveholders for two centuries. The idea that a public statement of ownership would weaken a person's claim to his property is strange on its face, and may explain why Murrell's theory seems never to have been tested. However, a dozen years after *The Great Western Land Pirate* came out, and perhaps because of it, an ambitious defense attorney argued something similar.

The case of *Morehead and Bryant v. The State*, decided by the Supreme Court of Tennessee in 1848, involved a series of events that began in June 1847 when the enslaved man Albert ran away from his owner, John P. Tagart, who lived in Hardeman County and was also its prosecuting attorney. Tagart published an advertisement for his missing servant, and in August two men, Morehead and Bryant, were arrested and charged with stealing him. They confessed to having harbored him near the city of LaGrange in Fayette County for several weeks, after which Bryant "run said slave to Mississippi" and sold him to someone in Pontotoc County. The buyer, however, failed to raise the necessary money, so Bryant brought Albert back and gave him to Williams, another partner, who was to take him someplace else to sell. Meanwhile, however, a posse led by Tagart captured Morehead and threatened to hang him unless he confessed to the crime and told them where to find Bryant—both of which he did. Taken into custody, Bryant also confessed.

Unable to dispute the facts, Morehead and Bryant's attorney challenged the law, claiming that his clients did not steal Albert but simply found him, and therefore he now belonged to them. The case was tried in a circuit court that rejected this argument, but the outlaws appealed to the supreme court, which may have taken the case to more firmly squelch what was a dangerous idea in a slaveholding state. Patiently, it explained that there was a distinction between inanimate property such as "a jewel, watch, or pocket book," which when lost "returns to the common stock of things" and belongs to whomever finds it, and living things such as livestock and slaves that can leave on their own. In the case of a horse, an individual case might require some judgment (depending in part, it suggested, on where the animal was found), but "it would be most absurd to apply [the 'lost' concept] to a rational, intelligent being . . . that may voluntarily form and carry into effect the purpose of throwing off his allegiance to his master and may transport himself beyond his reach." In the latter case, even if the owner lost "actual possession," he retained "constructive possession."[26]

Despite his jailhouse-lawyer legal knowledge, Murrell was an experienced criminal with a specialty in the stealing of slaves, and much of the narrative related to that activity was supported by a series of documents collected by Stewart after the book came out. Parson Henning confirmed everything the book said about him and his lost slaves. Four separate individuals supported *The Great Western Land Pirate*'s version of what had happened on the way to the Mississippi River and on the eastern side where Stewart and Murrell stayed for a few days, and that the two men had indeed crossed into Arkansas where Stewart said he had met members of the Mystic Clan. Thomas Hudnold, one of the largest slave owners in Madison County, Mississippi, backed up the story about the slave Sam, saying he had purchased a man by that name from Thomas Eason of Alabama and that the slave had been stolen three days later. John B. Higginbotham, who lived in East Feliciana Parish, verified that he had bought a slave from Murrell who also went missing, supporting Murrell's story about what had happened after leaving New Orleans. The most significant evidence had come in June 1835, when John Henning's son found his father's slaves in Avoyelles Parish, Louisiana, and they reported being decoyed off by promises of freedom, held in a "wilderness," and sold multiple times. Further support for that came from a D. O. Williams, who had lost three slaves in December 1833. He originally thought they had escaped by steamboat with the assistance of abolitionists, but said evidence obtained by the Randolph vigilantes from the Arkansas outlaws captured after the flatboat robbery in the summer of 1835 led him to a fruitless search through the Atakapas region of Louisiana. After he learned that Henning had gotten his missing slaves back, Williams retrieved his own from Avoyelles Parish also.[27]

Not all this evidence is necessarily valid but given the amount of it and what we know from other sources, it is reasonable to assume that Murrell did much of what he claimed to have done in the three examples that he gave. Outlaws did entice slaves away from their owners as Murrell claimed, although he mentions no failures and many prospective victims probably passed up the opportunity. The ease and speed with which he as a stranger recruited Clitto was something that probably did not happen often if indeed Stewart was telling the truth. Murrell also made it seem routine to steal a slave, sell him, and then help him to escape from the new owner, and repeat the selling and escaping process a few more times. A few years after *The Great Western Land Pirate* came out, another outlaw, as we shall see, bragged about doing the same thing, but there is little objective evidence that it was at all common. Murrell's adventure with the slave from Tipton County on their travels to New Orleans and back also seems embellished at the very least. Still, Murrell's basic modus operandi was the one commonly used by slave stealers. It was necessary that stolen slaves be taken far away from where they lived, and important that a local thief not leave home at the same time as the slave when missing. As a result, there was often more than one person involved in the various acts of stealing, harboring, moving, and selling.

Virgil Stewart first told his story at Murrell's trial, and it did not go over well. Not only did the defense claim Stewart had lied, but also that he had been one of Murrell's confederates before turning against him, something that many people in the area believed even before the trial and of which frontier ethics disapproved. From a legal standpoint, there was the problem that no hard evidence existed that proved Stewart's accusations; he himself collected the supporting documents well after the trial. The jury was at first deadlocked, and then under pressure from the judge, convicted the outlaw only of stealing Henning's slaves.[28]

When *The Great Western Land Pirate* came out a year after Murrell's conviction, a widely reprinted editorial in the Jackson, Tennessee, *Truth Teller and Western Tennessee Sentinel*, gave Stewart credit for telling the truth but thought that Murrell had told him lies "too incredible in themselves to [be] believed," adding that the book was badly written, and that the author (whom he assumed was Augustus Q. Walton) had sensationalized the content to sell more copies. Although Henning's slaves were found in Louisiana not long after the book came out, which convinced some people that Stewart's account was correct, both John Murrell and Virgil Stewart might have been forgotten had it not been for an event that occurred a year later.[29]

In June 1835, the planters of Madison County, Mississippi, came to believe their slaves intended to revolt and to prevent it executed eight white men and an unknown but considerably larger number of slaves suspected to be involved in the plot. Most of the evidence came from confessions extracted by torturing black people and threatening white people with execution, and the details were related to suggestions provided by the interrogators, some of which were inspired by the Mystic Clan and seemed to confirm its truth. A lengthy article from the *Lynchburg Virginian*, whose editor had disbelieved the original story but was convinced by what happened in Mississippi, was picked up in newspapers around the country, including the *Arkansas Gazette*, whose editor, William Woodruff, had agreed with the *Truth Teller*'s debunking of the tale a few months earlier.[30]

Slave owners in the Mississippi Valley believed that associates of Murrell continued to operate long after their alleged leader was sent to prison. In June 1837, John C. Morris of Montgomery's Point at the mouth of the White River in Arkansas advertised for a man named Bill, who had been "taken off by one of Murel's men" three years earlier. In 1839 J. W. Netherland of McMinn County in eastern Tennessee was looking for seventeen-year-old Lewis, who he thought might have been taken by "Murelites" who had been in that county a few months before attempting to steal slaves. In March 1852, two men named Clary and Bickerstaff broke out of jail in Ripley, Mississippi, along with a runaway slave who was also there. The two whites stole horses and saddles several miles from Ripley and were last seen headed west, believed to be on their way to Helena. Letters found with the men earlier made authorities confident that they were guilty of stealing horses and slaves and various other crimes and had confederates along a route from Mississippi to Texas. "So far as roguery is concerned, they almost equal the celebrated John A. Murrell."[31]

Six years after the publication of *The Great Western Land Pirate*, a lengthy pamphlet titled *Trials and Confessions of Madison Henderson, alias Blanchard, Alfred Amos Warrick, James W. Seward, and Charles Brown* gave the Mississippi Valley another account of slave stealing, this time providing evidence that people not only did it for profit but sometimes to assist slaves to escape to the North. The four men, usually known as the Madison Henderson gang, committed what the *St. Louis Republican* called "a complication of crimes in a single transaction" unique in the recent history of the city. On April 17, they entered a bank after business hours, killed one teller who slept in the office and another who happened to visit him, and after failing to break open the safe set the building on fire to destroy evidence of their crime. All the perpetrators were black, Henderson a slave and the rest free men. They were active criminals who had worked on steamboats at one time or another and lived at various places in the Lower Mississippi Valley. After the crime, they left the city separately, but a confederate gave away the plot in return for immunity, and the four were captured and returned to St. Louis. After a highly publicized trial, they were hanged on July 9, 1841. During the five weeks between their trial and their hanging, they were interviewed separately by Adam B. Chambers, publisher of the *Missouri Republican*, who wrote down what he called their confessions and published the collection along with related court documents in a short book he managed to print just in time to hawk it to the crowd who watched the men die. As Chambers recorded their life stories, Madison Henderson had a long history of decoying off slaves in order to sell them and Charles Brown had made money helping others escape to the North.[32]

According to Chambers account of his conversations with him, Madison Henderson was born in Virginia to mixed-race slave parents and sold when he was about fourteen to a slave trader named Blakey, who was associated with men that later formed the well-known slave-trading firm of Ballard, Franklin, and Company. While being taken to New Orleans on a steamboat, Henderson impressed one of that group, who purchased him for a personal servant and soon started him on a life of crime. Henderson accompanied his master on trips to northern Virginia, Washington, DC, Baltimore, and Charleston where they acquired slaves to sell in the markets at New Orleans, Natchez, and Vicksburg. Henderson assisted in the acquisition process in several ways. One of them was legal and probably appreciated by the owners of the slaves: "If the negroes whom we wished to purchase, were unwilling to be sold, it was my duty to overcome their objections, and by false tales of what my master would do for them, or the purposes for which they were wanted, induce them to agree to be sold." More often, however, he encouraged slaves to run away and assisted them in doing so: "The most important part of my duty was to coax off, and harbor negroes: in other words, to aid in stealing them." Henderson told enslaved people that the slave trader he worked with was from Philadelphia, was opposed to slavery, and would take them to Canada. The trader would then buy several slaves, others would escape on their own, and Henderson would hide them until they could be safely moved. Eventually the entire group would be sold. The scheme was particularly effective because the possibility of being sold and taken to the Mississippi Valley often did result in slaves running away, which made it less likely that owners would think that the runaways had been stolen.

Henderson provided Chambers with details about some of their activities. For example, they stole four slaves from a man named Brockman living in Baltimore: "My master and myself represented to them, that we would convey them off to a free state and make them free;

that he would propose to purchase two, to give them an excuse for run-ning away, through fear of being sold for the south . . . On the appointed night, I took my master's horses and the four negroes, carried them to a house, some distance in the country, as directed, and then delivered them to a man, who hid them away, whilst I returned and was with my master before daylight." They also stole from a wealthy planter named Baxter who lived outside Fredericksburg. Henderson and his owner stayed with the Baxter family for several weeks, during which the white man often went riding with Baxter's daughters, and both he and Henderson both "cohabitated" with several "yellow girls" who were house servants living in the basement. The master participated in the stealing of these two, carrying them away at night in his coach and then returning to the plan-tation before dawn.[33]

After a year or so of this activity, the master and slave team became worried it was becoming too dangerous and changed their strategy. The slave trader began to tout the virtues of his personal servant and sell him to others from whom Henderson would then escape. One victim of this scheme was Henry Clay, then Speaker of the House of Representatives. According to Henderson, he and his master stayed at the same boarding-house with Clay in Washington, and the two white men became friends, so much so that the trader joined Clay at a dinner with President James Monroe in the White House, during which Henderson stood behind the chair of his master. Clay was impressed with Henderson and bought him from his owner. Then the slave escaped and went off with his confederate.[34]

After more than three years of this activity, sometime around 1824, Henderson's master and partner in crime sold him to Samuel B. Blanchard of New Orleans, giving the slave the $900 selling price, on which the slave "lived a merry life for nearly a year." In fact, he did very well for the next fifteen years, working in Blanchard's New Orleans store and financing an expensive lifestyle involving fancy clothes and multiple women through various criminal activities. His close associates included James S. Buel, a young clerk who also worked for Blanchard, and James's father, a convicted counterfeiter, who had come to New Orleans after his release from a New York state prison. The gang drew heavily on the elder Buel's experience and his technical skill in forging bills of sale and altering checks. James did much of the planning and took the lead in executing the nighttime burglary of commercial establishments that became their specialty.[35]

Henderson was a junior partner but an active and skilled participant, and he played a key role when the gang began to steal slaves.

> The first negro we got I took from the door of one of the negro trader's establishments below the rail road. After talking to him a short time and promising to take him to a free state he consented to go. We put a new suit of clothes on him, slipped him on to the rail road car [that connected New Orleans to Lake Pontchartrain], just as the cars were leaving . . . [There we] put him on a vessel and took him to Mobile, where he was put up the next day at auction and sold.

One of their target populations was slaves working on the chain gangs of the city: "In New Orleans a great many persons, and especially the French, when their negroes run away or are suspected of stealing or other misconduct put an iron collar on them and with this on they work about the streets." These people were usually happy to run off but assisting them was so dangerous that the gang gave it up. In fact Madison was also once lured into a trap when he went to meet with a perspective victim and was slightly wounded by shotgun pellets as he made his escape.[36]

In the summer of 1840, Samuel Blanchard went to Boston on business and sent Henderson to St. Louis, where he was placed under the control of a man named Shaw but had permission to hire himself out. Blanchard came back from the east in September and would have brought Henderson back to New Orleans, but the Buels were arrested that month after a Dr. Barnes reported the theft of his "[silver] plate and professional instruments" and his enslaved servant confessed to assisting in the burglary. Without admitting that he was a member of their gang, Henderson told Blanchard that he knew them and might be arrested as a suspect, and the master allowed him to stay in St. Louis. By this time, he was working with the men who accompanied him on the disastrous attempt to steal money from the Petus Bank. Edward Ennis, a free black man, was part of the gang, and it was he who planned the job and convinced the others that it was necessary to begin it by killing the clerk. Why Henderson agreed to this reckless plan and to committing the murder himself is a mystery. After the participants left town, Ennis talked to a friend about what had happened, word got to the police, and the mastermind confessed in return for immunity—and eventually collected some reward money for his part in solving the crime.

The "confessions" made by the gang members were taken down after their convictions and were given in the face of certain execution. They were not made in the hope of leniency but did give the convicted men an opportunity to create a legacy for themselves. Historian Thomas F. Reilly has made a careful study of Madison Henderson's account of his life and career and been able to identify the John Brackman who owned Madison's parents and the slave trader Blakey, find evidence that the young slave was shipped to New Orleans, and learn that at least a few other individuals named in the document were real people. Perhaps tellingly, there seems to be no evidence of the planter Baxter or his 150-slave plantation. Nor was Reilly able to identify Henderson's slave-trader master, although he demonstrates that it could have been Isaac Franklin, who became the leading figure in the highly successful Armfield & Franklin firm. Additional support for Henderson's account comes from a newspaper account reporting the arrest of the Buels.[37]

While there is no evidence that Madison fabricated parts of his story, he almost certainly did. It is very hard to believe that a businessman well enough known to get an invitation to the White House would be able to get away with regularly stealing slaves from his customers over a period of three years, or that he would even want to try given the penalties involved. Many white southerners had no qualms about having sex with enslaved women, but doing so secretly with someone else's servants in whose house you were staying as a guest and in the company of your own male servant who was similarly involved, was reckless in the extreme. To say nothing of stealing the women immediately after. And would Henry Clay have never learned that his missing slave Madison Henderson was once again traveling with the man from whom Clay had purchased him? It is much easier to believe that Henderson exaggerated his experience to build up his reputation, much like Mississippi riverboat men who wanted to be thought of as "half horse, half alligator."

Historian Thomas C. Buchanan has suggested that Madison Henderson and his compatriots identified with the concept of rascality. As we have seen, white people called black people rascals if they thought them dishonest, unreliable, or simply hard to manage; but African Americans saw rascality as rebellion against an unjust system and something of which a man could be proud. Black rascals were "badmen," brave but also cruel, lovers as well as fighters, winners rather than losers, and stoic in the face of the capture and punishment that was made inevitable by the overwhelming power of their white enemies. For the members of the Madison Henderson gang, being remembered as notorious "badmen" was a positive thing.[38]

Madison Henderson's accomplice Charles Brown was also involved in what southern law called the stealing of slaves, but his specialty was what most northerners thought of as saving them, although he did it for money. Brown was born of free black parents in South Carolina and lived in Charleston until about 1831. At the age of fifteen or sixteen he moved to New Orleans and spent the decade before his death in the cities of the Mississippi Valley, working mostly as a waiter and engaging in various criminal activities and sometimes helping enslaved people to escape to the North on steamboats. He told Chambers that he grew interested in antislavery while living in Charleston and became involved with the movement in Cincinnati and in northern Ohio where he attended Oberlin College for a few months. At an American Anti-Slavery Society in Oberlin, he was recruited as an agent and assigned the task of helping slaves escape from the lower valley, for which he was paid $30 per month at first and later $50. He also said the Ohio Anti-Slavery Society provided him with blank certificates of freedom to be used by slaves in their attempts to escape and claimed that local Ohio chapters had copies of various county seals that they used to provide forged documents to support claims of freedom that might be challenged in southern courts.[39]

Brown said he had helped about eighty slaves to escape from New Orleans and sixteen from Vicksburg and gave the names of thirty he could recall. He gave details for some of the escapes.

> I took a mulatto woman named Frances belonging to a milliner living on Canal street [in New Orleans]. Mr. McMasters, the broker, boarded with her. Sometime previous her husband, who belonged to Mr. McMasters, had run away from his master in New York city and gone to Canada. He wrote back to some of his acquaintances to send him his wife Frances, and they applied to me to aid her. I supplied her with free papers and took her on board the Chester and accompanied her as far as Vicksburgh. I instructed her to come to St. Louis to the charge of a white man who would send her round to me at Cincinnati. Instead of obeying my directions and coming to Cincinnati, she remained in St. Louis and I subsequently had to come after her.

Another story must have shocked his readers. It began:

I had been absent at Cincinnati, and when I returned a colored man came to me and informed me that a Dutchman (his name I can't pronounce) who owned his wife Polly, was about to remove to Texas and carry her there. I furnished Polly and another girl named Mary with free papers, and a negro man called London, sometimes London Moss, who belonged to a black man named David Drake, residing about a square below St. Mary's Market. I took the three on board the steamboat Gen. Harrison and left for Cincinnati.

And then:

On the way up, the boy London appeared so much dejected and borne down with the idea of running away that I began to fear he would expose me. He had not over half sense. One night, about 20 miles below the mouth of the Ohio, about 3 o'clock he had been talking about the dangers, &c. of running away, and seemed to regret it so much that I determined to get rid of him. He was standing near the guard of the boat, I believe in the act of drawing up water, when I gave him a little shove and he went into the river. I never saw him afterwards. I believe he went under the wheel and arose no more.[40]

Brown's autobiography as told to Adam Chambers, and as it appeared in the printed *Trials and Confessions*, was seriously compromised by another account that came out a day or two after the execution. Reverend Bullard of St. Louis's First Presbyterian Church announced that he had talked with Brown several days earlier, and in the face of looming eternal damnation the condemned man had recanted much of his earlier account. According to Bullard, who made sure to say that he himself was no abolitionist, Brown admitted that he had not been hired by the American Anti-Slavery Society or received from them any blank documents for the use of runaway slaves. The slave escapes "were all of his own scheme," and there were many fewer of them than he had claimed. In fact, he now said he had personally assisted only seven slaves (including the examples above), about ninety less than in the original confession. The rest of those he named were rescued by other people. Editor Chambers published Bullard's statement in the *Missouri Republican* but defended his own account, writing that the specific nature of the accused man's story, which had included an accurate and detailed description of how the abolitionist organization was organized in the Ohio River border states, gave it a strong claim to accuracy. A pseudonymous writer, on the other hand, ridiculed both versions of the story and asserted that no reasonable person would believe either one.[41]

The trial in St. Louis was of enough interest in New Orleans that the *Daily Picayune* sent a special correspondent to cover it and commented several times on the contents of Chambers, *Trials and Confessions*. The paper had little interest in the two accomplices who were not associated with the Crescent City, but it gave a summary of the "monstrous villainies" carried out by Madison Henderson. The editor's main concern, however, was Charles Brown's revelations about the American Anti-Slavery Society and "the ease and facility with which slaves are enticed away by these black-hearted abolition emissaries." It was, the paper urged, "time for the adoption of precautionary measures that will fully reach the evil." After Reverend Bullard's revelations, the editors granted that there was probably some exaggeration involved in Brown's original confession but remained convinced that northern abolitionists were behind the escapes that did occur. That, of course, was a comforting interpretation for the white people of New Orleans, bolstering their belief, as the paper put it a week later, that "the slaves of the South were the happiest class of beings in existence" and had to be duped into running away.[42]

From a modern perspective, the amended version of Brown's story makes much more sense than the original. We know that friends of individual slaves, both in the North and the South, sometimes provided financial assistance to runaways, but there is no evidence that the AASS, or any other abolitionist organization, maintained a staff of people who assisted runaways before they crossed into the North or that they made available forged documents to be used in the process. It is also very unlikely that Brown, or anyone else, could have arranged nearly one hundred escapes. That he assisted a few people is probably true. He was able to read and write and seems to have had the knowledge, skill, and daring necessary to do the type of things that he claimed to have done, perhaps charging a considerable fee for his services. Why Brown would make up the story about the Ohio Anti-Slavery Society is a mystery, but he clearly was familiar with the group and may have developed some sort of a grudge against it. The exaggerated version of his initial confession is perfectly consistent with that of Madison Henderson's and likely also done so that Brown could leave the world with an enhanced reputation for rascality.

Whatever their truth, the revelations generated opposition to the employment of African Americans on steamboats. Public meetings in

Natchez and across the river in Concordia Parish called for an end to the practice. The *Mississippi Free Trader* went further, calling upon southerners "to rid the country of both the free negro and 'free slave' population," the latter an obvious reference to Madison Henderson and others like him whose masters exercised little control over their activities. Removing the first group and controlling the second would "guard against the rascalities of the hired agents of northern incendiaries." The New Orleans *Picayune* could not have agreed more. The editors considered it "abundantly proven that the free negroes employed upon the steamboats, and those prowling about the cities of the South, form a dangerous body of incendiaries." Admitting that many of these people were well behaved, honest, and hardworking, it asserted that "a large portion of them are fomenters of disturbance, and not a few are actively engaged in instigating and assisting slaves to escape."[43]

Three years later the *Picayune* issued another warning about free Negroes, this one stimulated by reports of New Orleans owners who had lost some of their most valued servants. There were free blacks in the city, wrote the editor, whose goal was "to entice away our laboring population, and to assist in concealing and harboring them here, and then facilitating their flight to Ohio—which is our Canada." In addition, runaways were often assisted by "colored stewards, or cooks, or hands on boats [who] use their cunning and the means particular to their positions to conceal slaves on board till they reach safe places for landing."[44]

Outlaw bands such as those that occupied the Arkansas Morass in the 1820s and 1830s were no longer present in the 1840s and 1850s, but the stealing of slaves continued to be common. Late in 1848, William Banton, who also used the last names Bennet and Angel, sold a man named Jim to J. W. Patrick in Alexandria, Louisiana, for $400 in cash and three horses valued at $325. Not long after, Patrick took Jim with him to New Orleans where he stayed at the Tremont House. Jim absconded from there, taking with him $800 belonging to his new owner. A week later, Patrick saw Jim at the race track in Carrollton, captured him, and took him to the jail on Barrone Street in New Orleans. Police there recognized Jim as a local runaway, and he was claimed by Thomas C. Jenkins of that city. Banton, who was then in New Orleans, was arrested both for stealing and selling stolen property. He had done something similar in Memphis, was also arrested, and fled from there while his case was under appeal. Banton was no frontier outlaw, although young and handsome as no doubt many of them also were, but also described as "genteel." Indeed, the crime reporter's description of him could have been a letter of recommendation: He is a "well-informed man, with a good address and in every way calculated to succeed in any of his undertakings."[45]

In one of the most celebrated escapes of the time, the enslaved man Henry Box Brown earned his name by having himself sealed in a wooden box and shipped from Virginia to Philadelphia. Brown came up with the idea on his own, but the concept was used for nefarious purposes a few years earlier by Mississippi River slave thieves. A husband and wife team and one associate stole an unnamed woman from someone in Alexandria, Louisiana, and shipped her "very carefully packed in a box" to New Orleans where in some unspecified manner the plot was foiled, and the three thieves and their victim were lodged in jail.[46]

In 1848, diligent police work by Captain Winter of the Second Municipality in New Orleans resulted in the capture of a slave stealer named Jefferson Cash, who was using the name William Johnson. Cash had sold a slave to a Negro trader in the Third Municipality, and the man had escaped the next day. He was captured by police shortly after and had with him a pass signed by Cash. Under questioning by Captain Winter, he said Cash had stolen him from his owner in Grundy County, Tennessee, and brought him to New Orleans. Stealing two horses along the way. Winter found the thief, who was carrying papers showing that his real name was Cash rather than Johnson and admitted that he planned to sell the stolen man.[47]

In 1858 another slave stealer named George Johnson was arrested at a plantation near Bayou Vidal in Tensas Parish. Johnson was accused of providing passes for four slaves, whom he intended to send to St. Louis or New Orleans where they would be captured and sold by men working with him. Somehow the plot was discovered, and Johnson was captured by a posse who found him in his home with two of the men who thought they had been rescued. The captors had a rope around his neck preparing to hang him when one of them persuaded the others to turn him over to the sheriff instead. The other two intended victims were arrested in Vicksburg, probably waiting for a steamboat that would take them where Johnson wanted them to go.[48]

≈

As Charles Brown's illicit career suggests, slave stealing designed to help bondspeople reach the North usually involved steamboat transportation. A specific example involved a girl being held in Paducah, Kentucky, who had been furnished with free papers signed by three men living in Little Rock. She claimed to be owned by Edward Tolbert of Shelby County, Tennessee, and to have accompanied a Mrs. Thomas on a trip to Hot Springs, from where she escaped and went to Little Rock where she got the help and left on a steamboat. The newspaper that carried the story believed she belonged to someone in Arkansas.[49]

While their motive is not clear, two free black men were convicted of stealing a slave from a New Orleans owner, one was given a three-year term in the penitentiary and the other five years. In 1842 Jordon Jainer was charged with inveigling two slaves away from the firm of Sidle and Stewart Swan, saying they were his slaves and took them on board a boat. A Captain Harper "got wind" of what was happening, took passage on the same boat, and arrested Jainer before it reached Carrollton. The officer may have waited for the group to get aboard to prove the slaves were being stolen, but by doing so he also pocketed the $10 that was paid by the city to any policeman who arrested a runaway on a boat.[50]

Also in 1842, the *Feliciana Whig* contained a more factual account of what appears to have been the attempted rescue of a slave. A man named Williams had been in Clinton, Louisiana, for a few days and then left with a slave named Joe, whom he promised to take to Cincinnati, Ohio. The two traveled together on a steamboat to the mouth of the Tennessee River, where Williams, now calling himself Wilson, got off, leaving Joe with two passengers who were to take him to Cincinnati. One of the passengers suspected that Joe was a runaway, however, and had him arrested in Louisville. When the article was written, Joe was back in the hands of his owner.[51]

The abolitionist Calvin Fairbank claimed to have rescued a young man from Arkansas, by disguising him as a local planter and traveling from there to Cincinnati by steamboat. William Minnis had been a slave living near Lexington, Kentucky, when his master died leaving a will that freed his slaves. Unscrupulous relatives suppressed that information, however, and sold Minnis to a trader that resold him to a man named Brennan living in Little Rock. Minnis was known to white people in both Lexington and Cincinnati who asked Fairbank to try to get him back and provided $250 to fund the effort. Fairbank went to Little Rock, and after a month of discrete searching found out quite by accident that Minnis was working in the hotel where he was staying. With the help of a Creole French barber and a New England schoolteacher, he disguised the eighteen-year-old, light-skinned Minnis in a wig, mustache, and beard, whitened his face with flour, and provided him with appropriate clothing and an expensive cane. The plan was to take him north on a steamboat by passing him off as a planter name Young who lived near his owner Brennan. Fairbank and Minnis boarded a steamboat at dusk bound for Memphis, only to find that Brennan himself was on the boat, but the owner walked by his slave and nodded to him thinking he was Young. At Memphis where they changed boats for the trip to Cincinnati, the slave trader who had sold Minnis came on board for a short time and chatted with Fairbank while Minnis strolled around the deck. After that the trip to Cincinnati was uneventful, and Minnis went from there to Canada. Later he moved to California and eventually he served in the Union army.

The Minnis story is fascinating, but Fairbank seems to have misremembered at least some of the details, including the name of the man he rescued. The only source for the episode is Fairbank's autobiography, which was published in 1890, when the abolitionist was seventy-four years old, had no money, and was being cared for by a friend. The accuracy issue is related to a famous episode in Underground Railroad history that occurred after the Little Rock rescue in which Fairbank and a woman named Delia Webster helped an enslaved man named Lewis Hayden and his family escape from Lexington, Kentucky, after which the two abolitionists were found out and imprisoned in that state. Delia Webster was a New England schoolteacher like the one Fairbank said helped him in Little Rock. Hayden, like Minnis, worked in a hotel; this one was called the Brennan House, the same name as Minnis's owner, and flour was used to make Hayden look fair skinned. While Fairbank was in prison one of his fellow inmates was an enslaved man named John Minnis. Calvin Fairbank was a true hero of the antislavery movement who spent many years in prison for helping enslaved people get out of the South, and the Minnis rescue may have happened exactly as the portrayed. It is more likely, however, that three decades later he conflated some of the details of that event with the later rescue of the Hayden family.[52]

In 1855 the *Picayune* warned that railroads were being used to circumvent the careful surveillance of steamboats carried on by the New Orleans police. "White men who infest this city," abolitionists presumably, were encouraging slaves to steal by promising to use the proceeds to assist them in reaching the North. The escapees were leaving on the Opelousas or the Great Northern railroads or by some other means of ground transportation and then heading for the Mississippi River where at someplace convenient "they await the coming of an up-river boat, which is hailed and on which they embark, the white scoundrel representing the Negro to be his slave." On reaching a port city on the north side of the Ohio River, "the negro is told he is free and thus the robbery of the slave owner is accomplished." The paper suggested that railroad agents and steamboat captains should carefully question any white man coming on board with one or two slaves.[53]

While the *Picayune* worried about slaves being stolen out of New Orleans, many stolen slaves were brought into the city. In January 1841 policemen arrested three men in a coffeehouse on the levee who had with them a slave woman named Julia, who said she belonged to a Mr. Wazorthy of St. Louis. In the summer of 1842, Officer Finn arrested two men he thought were runaways from Pass Christian and along with them William H. Nicholls, who claimed to be a free colored person, but whom Finn thought was also a runaway. He was also convinced that all of them were staying at a house on Barracks Street where other runaways were living.[54]

Peter, owned by Armond Troxlair of St. Charles Parish, was "forcibly taken," not enticed or even "run off." City police learned about his whereabouts and visited the home of William Morton on Jackson Street with a warrant to search the premises. After breaking into a locked back room, they found Peter bound to a chair. He said he had been captured by two men who took him in a skiff to New Orleans and then to Morton's. They intended to move him to Texas and sell him there. Officers waited at the house and arrested John Davis, whom Peter identified as one of the men. A newspaper reporter at recorder's court appears to have believed Peter's "straight 'up and down'" version of the events, but slaves were prohibited from testifying against white persons. Davis claimed that he had not stolen Peter but gotten him in a trade from a man in Natchez, and that while he had given Morton a bill of sale for Peter, he had not received any money from him, and thus the sale was not consummated. Morton's lawyer admitted that the circumstantial evidence against his client was strong, but claimed there was no proof that he was involved in the case in any way.[55]

In 1846 Bill C. Curtis, described as a "notorious character," was arrested in the Second Municipality for stealing a slave named Phyllis owned by Kasiah Perkins, a free woman of color in St. Louis. Bill was bringing Phyllis to New Orleans pretending to be her master, "but from some misconduct while on board," the captain put him off the boat at Natchez and kept Phyllis on board as a suspected runaway, with the intention of taking her to St. Louis on the return trip. Curtis showed up in the Crescent City with a bill of sale, but authorities thought it was a forgery and arrested him. The court sent a message to St. Louis explaining the circumstances and sent Bill to the workhouse as a vagrant until they heard back.[56]

Slaves were often stolen, or alleged to have been stolen, in circumstances where the legality of ownership was in doubt because of an unpaid debt or a dispute over an inheritance. For example, A. S. Bailey of La Grange, Tennessee, claimed that W. L. Moon and Ephraim Jackson had "smuggled off" eight Negroes that were under "execution," that is, liable for seizure in payment for a debt or back taxes. Two women, Tilly and Nanny, along with Nanny's six children had been taken away in a wagon that had crossed the Mississippi near Randolph. Bailey thought they were being taken to the Red River where they would be sold. W. B. Washington of nearby Sommerville might have been describing a runaway slave when he advertised in the *Memphis Appeal* in 1857 for James Tidwell, a white man "about 60 years old, heavy built, fond of talking and pleasing in manner," whom he claimed had "run or caused to run off" Ann, a sixteen-year-old black woman, whom he had earlier deeded to Washington as security for a debt.[57]

Roswell Beebe, a prominent Little Rock businessman and civic leader, was the victim of a major larceny. He and three others, including William Woodruff, had loaned money to James De Baum and his wife in the early fall of 1841 and received title to thirteen black people as security for repayment. The partners did not take physical possession of the human property, however, and about February 1843 a man working for the De Baums disappeared with all of them: Daniel and Eve and their two children, Littleton and Lucy and their three children, and Edmund and Emiline along with their two. After several months, the creditors put the entire group up for sale at an auction and Beebe bought the right to recover them. He advertised them as probably in Texas or on the way there and offered a $500 reward for anyone who could get them back and deliver them to his agents in Alexandria, Louisiana, or in New Orleans.[58]

The *New Orleans Picayune* found humor in a husband-and-wife dispute over slave ownership. When Adolphus Bryant arrived in New Orleans on a steamboat from St. Louis carrying two slaves with him, he was immediately arrested based on information that they were stolen. The complaint came from Bryant's wife, who said that the African Americans were "her particular property," meaning that she had inherited them, in this case from a previous husband's estate, prior to marrying Adolphus. Bryant's argument was that "what was hers was his," and that he had a right to sell the men in New Orleans where he could get the most money for them. The newspaper saw the dispute as "a family affair" but suggested in a jocular fashion that "the gray mare, however, may turn out the better horse."[59] The dispute became more serious a week later when Mrs. Bryant arrived in New Orleans and pressed the stealing charge against Adolphus and his brother William, whom she thought was also involved. Both were remanded to prison to await trial. The paper criticized the wife for making her husband out to be a felon because he exercised a right to property that "virtually, though not perhaps legally," belonged to him. In a final display of the male chauvinism common to the time, the paper again made light of the situation: "Oh Adolphus, Adolphus, . . . why did'st thou ever marry a 'vidder.'"[60]

Uncomplicated embezzlement was another way the slaves could be stolen. An example occurred in 1830 when slave traders Mark Brown and James Wiles entrusted James Loflin to take three slaves recently purchased in Virginia to Augusta, Georgia, and instead he took them to Louisiana or Mississippi with the intention of selling them in one of those places.[61]

Readers may have noticed that criminal justice in the Lower Mississippi Valley was hampered by jail escapes. Runaways sometimes escaped from jail, and thieves did so more often, probably because they were more apt to have outside help. In any case, breakouts were common. John Murrell escaped and stayed at large for several weeks before the trial in which he was finally convicted and sent to the penitentiary, and all four members of the Madison Henderson gang also broke out, although they only got four blocks before being captured. In many cases, escapes were related to shabby construction, but sometimes that was not the case. In 1852, five men—one man accused of stealing slaves, another locked up for assault and battery, and three runaway slaves—all broke out of a very well-built structure.

[They] effected it through the floor of the jail, which was built upon a stone wall four feet high, two feet of the wall being under the ground, and two feet above it.—Upon the wall were laid square logs, covered over with sheet iron and thick white oak planks which constituted the floor of the jail. Through this they bored and otherwise made an opening sufficient to admit their decent to [the] cavity below, when [where] they removed a stone of the wall and made good their escape.[62]

One light-hearted criminal seemed not to take the incarceration thing very seriously. During the night of September 27, 1847, a man named Powers accused of stealing slaves in Augusta, escaped from a Louisiana parish jail along with several other prisoners and left a note for his jailors.

> Gentlemen:
> Business compels me to leave the Parish of Alexandria parish jail this night; but I cannot help returning my sincere thanks to Mr. M. Stafford, Mr. T. Fearel and Mr. Reed, for their hospitality while in jail.
> Yours when you get me again.
> James Powers[63]

Finally, it is important to note that almost all the contemporary comment on slave stealing assumed that it was white men who tricked black people into going off with them. Doubtless that was often the case, but sometimes it was the slave who did the manipulating. He or she may have allowed themselves to be "inveigled" away in the belief that they could escape from the thief who had helped them get away. Or perhaps the whole thing was the enslaved person's idea, as it seems to have been in the following example. In 1859, as the *Bayou Sara Ledger* explained to its readers, George W. Thompson was arrested "for having run off from Point Coupee" an enslaved man named Johnson. Working together they stole a load of wood and sold it to the steamboat *New Uncle Sam*, having agreed to use the money to pay for passage to the North with Johnson accompanying Thompson as his slave. Johnson got hold of a skiff that they used to cross the river into Mississippi and then, either by water or by land, they traveled south to Woodville. There Thompson "took the largest portion of the proceeds" from Johnson and abandoned him. As a runaway slave, there was not much Johnson could do about that, but he soon came up with an alternative plan. Along with another enslaved man, he stole a skiff or used the old one and they made their way downriver to

New Orleans. There Johnson spent some of his money on new clothes, stayed in the city a few days, and then booked passage on a steamer going north. He must have been discovered as a runaway, however, and dropped off at Bayou Sara, where he told the whole story. A policeman from that town went looking for Thompson and found him "in one of those vile dens of infamy, at the upper end of St. Francisville." Drawing a lesson from the event, the *Bayou Sara Ledger* editor warned slaveholders to be careful because there were a lot of men like Thompson on the river. He should have advised them to watch out for slaves like Johnson, who seems to have used the white man Thompson for his own purposes.[64]

❦ CHAPTER 7 ❧

Each One Is Made a Policeman

VIOLENCE, OR AT LEAST the threat of violence, becomes an important part of labor management when workers have no meaningful financial incentive to work and are not fired if they refused to do so. Slave drivers in the American South used vicious whippings to make the victims work harder and to punish them for acts of disobedience. Scars from whipping, scars from branding, and other types of disfigurement and maiming are not common in runaway advertisements, but show up often enough to indicate that they were a credible threat. No enslaved person was safe from these punishments, but those who escaped and were caught appear to have suffered the most. As a visitor to the Natchez area once explained, "the law for a runaway when he is caught, is the lash, severely laid on . . . if he ever leaves the plantation without a pass, he is whipped by the first overseer that finds him, and then sent home and whipped again."[1]

Fugitive slaves were also the victims of physical abuse administered by people who did not own them. "Each one is made a police officer," is the way a Louisiana defense attorney described the section of the state's Black Code that allowed whites to stop, question, and arrest African Americans they suspected of being runaways or guilty of something else, including being disrespectful to them. Similar laws existed in other states, and they were the legal basis for the slave patrols made up of citizen volunteers who policed the roads at night looking for slaves who were, as the common phrase put it, "strolling about." Frederick Law Olmsted was probably correct, however, when he wrote that the off-plantation control of slaves depended on "the constant, habitual, and instinctive surveillance and authority of all white people over all black." Some citizens hunted runaway slaves for money, but many others arrested them out of what they saw as civic responsibility. In addition to recognizing a shared interest in supporting the system of racial oppression, slave owners and non-slaveholders alike were fearful of slave revolts and supported whatever degree of violence appeared to be necessary to keep them from happening. What was in effect the deputization of all white adults encouraged them to carry weapons and be ready to use them.

The violence between whites and blacks was not always one sided, however. Enslaved people sometimes attacked their owners out of frustration and rage, and fugitives sometimes resisted capture using weapons they had taken with them or stolen while on the run. The determination of white people to control black people, and the determination of black people to resist it, created a culture of violence in the Lower Mississippi Valley that continued for a century after the end of slavery.

A substantial body of evidence about the treatment of runaway slaves was presented in *American Slavery As It Is*, published in 1839 by the abolitionist Theodore Dwight Weld. It presented only the worst side of slavery but documented it effectively. Weld's wife, Angelina Grimké, and her sister Sarah, did the research, a large portion of it in southern newspapers of which the women claimed to have read more than 20,000 issues. One section of the book dealt specifically with permanent physical damage using evidence from runaway advertisements. Under the heading "Floggings," were twenty-five examples of people described using various forms of the phrase "numerous scars of the whip." Eight of them came from the Lower Mississippi Valley, including Mr. H. Varillat of No. 23 Girod Street in New Orleans, who was missing Jupiter, who had "a fresh mark of a cowskin on one of his cheeks." A second category included "Brandings, Maimings, Gun-shot Wounds, &c." This included ninety-four entries, twenty-five from the Lower Mississippi Valley. Among the latter were Mary, who had scars from a musket ball; another Mary, branded with an A in two places on her face; Anthony, who had had an ear cut off; and Josiah, who was scarred with a whip, branded with the letters J.M., and missing an ear, either cut off or bitten off.[2]

While "whipping marks" is a precise category and all of it resulted from punishment, the second list contained a variety of physical damage including missing teeth, knife wounds, burns, and assorted scars that might have come from accidents related to cooking and heating with open fires, the on-the-job use of sugarcane knives, and other accidents endemic to agricultural labor. Male slaves also fought with each other, just as white men did, and inflicted physical damage in the process. Only about 3 percent of Lower Mississippi Valley runaways were described as having permanent physical damage that definitely can be assigned to owner brutality, but the real amount is certainly higher.[3]

Moreover, advertisements for escaped slaves understate the level of slave master punishment because they leave out all the times that it worked. First time fugitives would not be scarred or mutilated until after they were captured, and it is probable that the punishment convinced many of them not to do it again, in which case there would be no newspaper record of whipping scars or missing toes. The same thing would apply in the case of multiple escapes. For example, in the story told by Olmsted a slave master cut off a toe each time one of his enslaved people ran off and said they always stopped after losing the second digit. In that case, there would not be a runaway advertisement describing any of them as missing two toes. Three missing toes may have been in the future for a captured fugitive of whom an Adams County jailor in 1827 noted that "two toes of his left foot have been cut off." More evidence of brutality comes from the interviews with ex-slaves done by the WPA which are filled with references to cat-o'-nine-tail whips, cowhides, people staked out for whipping, whipping scars, and bloody whippings, most of them the result of escapes.

Slave patrols also meted out physical punishment to people out at night without passes. In Arkansas, patrols were what the supreme court called "a slumbering power, ready to be aroused and called into action" by a justice of the peace when asked to do so by at least three citizens of a township. They were needed in the court's opinion because "the elevation of the white race and the happiness of the slave, vitally depend on maintaining the ascendancy of one and the submission of the other." It also underlined the local and citizen-based nature of slave control: "Quell[ing] all ordinary disturbances . . . by and among their slaves . . . can be better and more appropriately done by those who are friends and neighbors, having a common interest to protect, and a common danger to guard against, than by strangers whose interference has not been invited."

The law itself allowed for up to three mounted companies, each consisting of a captain and five others, to operate in each township, patrolling the roads at least once every two weeks. They were to look for slaves "strolling about from one plantation to another" without passes as well as those participating in "illegal assemblies," and were empowered to punish guilty persons with up to twenty lashes. Arkansas patrols had no specific responsibilities for arresting runaway slaves, whom the state defined as those more than twenty miles from home, but certainly they did so whenever possible. Again, a measure of the system's effectiveness comes from the memories of the WPA interviewees who often spoke of the whippings inflicted on their parents for being out without passes and referred to a well-known song with the refrain "Run Nigger Run! The Pateroles will get you."[4]

Both Mississippi and Louisiana charged their patrols with the capture of fugitive slaves in addition to their other duties and specifically allowed them to collect the fees that other citizens would have received for the same service, which was probably also the practice in Arkansas. Louisiana organized its patrols in a few sentences, giving them the right to search the slave quarters on any plantation, to arrest disturbers of the peace, vagabonds, and "suspicious persons." The rest of patrol organization and regulations, the state left to the parish police juries that ran local government. Mississippi went to the other extreme, writing a detailed law that required company captains in its well-organized militia to select men to serve on slave patrols, which appear to have operated on a permanent basis. Mississippi, like Arkansas, gave a legal definition of runaway, making it any slave found eight miles from home without a pass or one that had "lain out" for more than two days. Patrollers in that state were also charged with killing any dogs that belonged to slaves. In Tennessee slave patrols were organized at the county level rather than by township as in Arkansas. They were empowered to search slave dwellings on anyone's farm or plantation and were specifically ordered to seize any guns or other weapons that were found.[5]

Slave owners sometimes felt that patrollers acted in ways that infringed on their own rights or damaged their property, but the courts were usually willing to give the policemen a great deal of discretion. The Arkansas case that led the court to discuss the system involved a patrol operating in Ouachita County in the early 1850s that stopped several slaves coming home from "a religious exercise" at which both blacks and whites had been assembled. When the detainees could not produce passes, they were tied up and whipped. The owner, a Mr. Henry, sued the patrollers, arguing both that his servants were "so bruised and hurt by the beating" that it was some time before they could be put back to work and that the patrol was out of its jurisdiction since the episode had occurred in Jefferson Township despite the patrol being from Marion Township. The patrollers claimed that they had been invited by some white people in Jefferson Parish to disperse an unlawful assembly. The court had some sympathy for Henry's position, noting that even though the Jefferson County patrol had never done any actual patrolling, the Marion group had no business operating outside its own jurisdiction whether they had been invited or not. In addition, there was "an implied license" in Arkansas for slaves being allowed to attend religious services on Sunday. Still, while it was understandable that he would be very upset by what had taken place, Henry had not shown any special damage caused by his servants missing work and was not entitled to any compensation. Justifying a strict application of this requirement, the jurists claimed that anything less would encourage slaves to be "insolent" to whites.[6]

A Louisiana patrol did do significant damage to the property of a Louisiana slaveholder in 1855. About 11 o'clock on the night of August 1, an enslaved man belonging to A. Duperrier rode into the outskirts of New Iberia and was hailed by patrollers who demanded he stop and surrender himself. He did stop briefly, but then he turned around and galloped away. Two patrollers fired at him with shotguns from thirty-five yards away, inflicting wounds from which the man died the next day. Duperrier sued for damages, explaining that his slave had "standing permission" to visit his wife who was owned by a woman residing in the town and claiming that the shooting was entirely unnecessary. The Louisiana Supreme Court, however, ruled the patrollers were protected by the law that gave freeholders the right to stop any slave suspected of being a runaway and allowed the use of firearms to stop them if necessary. The statute called for a shooter to avoid killing the slave, but the court ruled that the current case did not violate that rule. It also noted that "current disorders" in the area justified the patrol in exercising a rigorous enforcement of police regulations.[7]

The Louisiana court did side with an owner in one particularly egregious case of excessive force that took place in the parish of St. Mary in 1836. Sandy had permission to visit his wife and children regularly at the house of Manuel Delukie where they lived, which was not far from his own place of residence. One evening while he was there, three members of the slave patrol entered and asked to see Sandy's pass, which they then claimed was illegal and ordered him to submit to a whipping. Sandy broke away and fled to a back room. One patroller went after him and when told to stop by his captain responded that "no damned negro should run over him." Sandy ran into the backyard, pursued by two patrollers who shouted that they intended to kill him. The chase ended when he jumped into Bayou Teche and drowned, even though one of the pursuers found a pirogue and attempted to rescue him. Sandy's owner sued for the loss of his property, claiming he was a skilled mechanic and carpenter and worth $3,000. The parish jury awarded him $1,000—significant evidence that the patrol had gone beyond what the community saw as reasonable conduct.[8]

From the late seventeenth century on, white Americans in the South had the authority to police the enslaved population when its members were in public without their masters; and at some point, if not immediately, the privilege became a responsibility, or at least a moral imperative. As the Mississippi supreme court explained a century and a half later: the law "expressly confers the right, and *the policy of the country, makes it the duty* [emphasis added] of every citizen to arrest a runaway slave." In fact, many local fugitives and perhaps most of those farther from home were apprehended by civilians rather than patrols or other law enforcement officials. An Arkansas statute of 1838 is a good example of the laws that encouraged that activity. "Any person may apprehend a negro or mulatto being or suspected of being a runaway slave," and receive a payment of $15 plus 10 cents per mile for the expenses required to take the captive back to his owner or to some public place of imprisonment. Most captured runaways gave the name of the person from whom they had escaped, preferring a quick return to a master that they knew rather than a long stay in jail, followed by being sold to someone who might be worse. If the owner did collect his property, he was responsible for paying the costs associated with the capture, advertising, and incarceration of the runaway; if not, the public was reimbursed out of the money made when he or she was sold at auction.[9]

Throughout the antebellum period, the Louisiana law with respect to capturing runaways who belonged to someone else was based on Section 32 of the Black Code. A white person could stop and question any black person thought to be a slave and away from where they lived or worked. When warranted, they could "seize and correct the said slave." If the subject resisted, the interrogator could "make use of arms but, at all events avoiding the killing of said slave" unless "the said slave assault and strike" him. In practice, the slave usually did not have to put up much of a fight before the killing was justified. An 1821 supreme court decision absolved a killer based on testimony that the victim "was of a bad character," was suspected of having committed a felony, attempted to flee, and tried to seize a gun.[10]

While they gave both patrols and individuals a lot of leeway, none of these laws was an unrestricted license for hunting human beings. In the case discussed above in which the Mississippi supreme court announced that capturing absconded slaves was a citizen's duty, it emphasized the importance of self-defense. A man named Thompson had found a slave belonging to Mr. Young "prowling about his premises in the night-time," ordered the intruder to surrender, and shot him when he started to flee. When the man died, Young sued for the value of the property he had lost, and the jury sided with him even after it was shown that the victim was carrying a knife and a club. Ruling on Thompson's appeal, the court summed up the law. "If any person, in essaying to capture a runaway, shall meet with resistance, he may lawfully oppose force to force." He may even "slay the resistant, if the resistance offered" involved a threat of "great injury" or loss of life. At the same time, slaves were "both persons and property," and the law protected both the "safety of the slave" and the financial interests of the master. Thompson had not shown he was in any danger and thus "the shooting could not be justified by any principle of morality, of law, or of policy growing out of the institution of slavery."

Justice Pierre Adolphe Rost wrote a remarkable opinion for the Louisiana court in 1850 that also sided with a master whose servant was shot as a runaway. The jurist gave a detailed and sensitive account of how the slave had behaved. One night Thomas Lawes and another white man were on the shore of a river that ran by the plantation where they worked when two black men came by in a skiff. Lawes called them to come over, which they did, asked to see a pass, which they gave him, and ordered that they be tied up while he read it. At that point, one of the slaves, apparently overcome by fear, started to run but then stopped, and Lawes shot him anyway. Justice Rost described the event as follows:

> Lawes, after nine o'clock at night, in front of his plantation, dis-
> covered two of the plaintiff's slaves in a skiff upon the river, rowing
> up; hailed them; made them come ashore; demanded their passes;

received a paper from them; and when in the act of getting a light to read its contents, the slave William broke away and fled, when the defendant, calling upon him several times to stop without being obeyed, fired upon him . . . The two slaves had their permits. On the first summons, they landed their boat; came on shore; delivered their permits, and submitted to the defendant. No need was there of violence or fetters; they were submissive and confiding in their innocence and obedience to their master's commands: two strong white men stood by them, one of them provided with a loaded gun. But defendant must have them tied, and ordered it to be done; with what view, under the circumstances, could the poor negroes think? For purpose of chastisement they must have thought. So thought the boy William, and fearful, as the witness describes him, . . . his first impulse was to run. He had never deserved a whipping for the nine years he had belonged to his good master, the plaintiff; he will be whipped now. He went a few yards—a voice calls for him to stop; it is that of his fellow slave, who is being tied by the witness; he no doubt recognises this voice; his just fright abated; the thought suddenly occurs to him that by running he aggravates the probable consequences of their arrest; that this attempt to avoid defendant will be fruitless, and he stops; but at that moment is shot down dead. He is shot at the moment when he is turning [a]round to come back and submit to be tied.

Lawes testified that he thought his shotgun was loaded with birdshot, not knowing that someone else had reloaded one barrel with buckshot in the hope of killing a crane. The lower court was unmoved, and neither was Rost, who called the overseer's actions "useless, barbarous, unjustifiable violence."

Rost went on to document the prevailing attitude of Louisianans toward the white public's role in slave control. He noted that the jury "had to contend against the prejudices of many planters, about the necessity of extreme measures in the police of slaves and the right of any one to shoot down a slave who does not instantly submit." In deference to those prejudices, Rost included a portion of the brief submitted by Lawes's attorney, which claimed that a finding against his client would weaken Section 32 of the Black Code and leave a Louisiana freeholder unprotected "in his attempt to enforce the police regulation of slaves."

This act of the Legislature of 1806, has conferred upon freeholders extraordinary power over slaves. *Each one is made a police officer* [emphasis added], and every slave found absent from his dwelling, *prima facie*, a criminal. To keep slaves under proper subjection and discipline, such a law was necessary for the country, where there was no standing or salaried police. It has operated well, and kept the country free from riot and rebellion. But the moment the use of arms is taken out of the hands of the freeholder, in the arrest and examination of wandering slaves, the peace and safety of the public is at an end.[11]

The type of citizen action southerners expected is illustrated by a story written by the editor of the *Mississippi Free Trader* in the early fall of 1849. He had been traveling from Natchez to Fayetteville and stopped at a "hospitable mansion" along the way. While he was sitting with several other men on the gallery that evening, four African Americans came down the road. One of them stopped briefly to ask if he could buy bread, but the rest continued walking. Viewing this as suspicious, the group at the house organized a party of five men and two dogs and went after the walkers. When the pursuers got close to the black men, one of them turned and fired at them, killing one of the dogs, "a valuable animal." Chasing now in earnest, the whites captured the shooter and went after the others. Sometime later, one of the pursuers fired into bushes where he thought one of the blacks might be hiding, and the man came out and surrendered. Under questioning, doubtless of a coercive sort, he explained that all four had recently escaped from a plantation near Natchez. He himself was a preacher who had written passes for each of the fugitives, giving them permission to travel to Port Gibson. According to the author, the documents were badly written and contained enough misspellings that they probably would not have been accepted. Still he thought local slaveholders should investigate possible sources of literacy among the enslaved population, warning that there might be people around "hired by abolition incendiaries engaged in deep-laid schemes of revolt and murder."[12]

Another example involves three black men who stopped at James A. Hudson's farm not far from Pine Bluff in October 1851 and asked someone how to get to the city. Learning about this, Hudson decided that the travelers were looking for "a secure retreat where they might obtain water and lay by [the] next day," and along with two of his neighbors he went to the place they had been sent and set up an ambush. The fugitives soon came up, one carrying a double-barreled shotgun and another a double-bladed axe. Hudson fired, apparently without warning, killing one of them, and the other two fled. Within a day or two, another had been killed and the remaining two were in the Jefferson County Jail. All four had fled recently from Union Parish, Louisiana, on the border with Arkansas.[13]

Near Marksville, Louisiana, in 1850, "a young man shot a negro boy, supposed [thought] to be a runaway." The same year "some [white] boys" near Memphis killed a runaway they were trying to arrest. In 1851, a runaway in Union Parish was killed by "a lad . . . who, it is said, was justified in the act." The following year, in Ouachita Parish, a slave named Jim Deek, who had run away, taking a double-barreled shotgun with him, was pursued by "a party of citizens" and shot dead by one of them. In 1853, a man in Natchez followed a runaway to a cave and killed him. The cave appeared to be a "den for a nest of similar characters" and an inquest determined that the killing was justifiable homicide. That same year a runaway who fired at two men at New River in Ascension Parish was shot and killed.[14]

Many such reports of runaway killings included some indication that the white man or men acted in self-defense, a detail that sometimes may have been added to protect them from prosecution. A small article in the *Opelousas Courier* suggests a possible coverup. The first sentence said a group of men out hunting runaways had shot a slave who had been gone for six months and that he died of the wound. This was followed by the news that the hunters had captured several other fugitives. Then, almost as an afterthought, the article noted that "the first mentioned runaway had made an attack with a cane knife on the hunters."[15]

Hunting runaways sometimes also resulted in collateral damage. A Mr. Guedry was hiding along a roadside in the Iberville Parish waiting for a runaway when he saw someone at a distance and called for him to stop. Instead the person turned and ran, and Guedry fired at him, killing a white man named Castagnol who lived in the parish. In 1841 Gilbert Sloane of Bayou Boeuf "was in the act of putting a new cap on a pistol for the purpose of pursuing a runaway negro, when it accidentally exploded, lodging the contents in the face of his wife." The pistol ball "entered the upper lip, carrying away four of her teeth, and lodged, it is supposed in the spine of her neck." When the newspaper story was written, the woman was expected to recover but the projectile had not yet been removed. Then there was a story from Mississippi that the *Daily*

Picayune hoped was exaggerated: "Three children were returning to their home from school near Liberty, in Amite County. They were overtaken by a pack of dogs in pursuit of runaway negroes. The dogs fell on them, and, before assistance could be rendered, *killed and nearly devoured every one of them!*"[16]

One afternoon in January 1851, a black man entered the Memphis office of John K. Chester, who was the city recorder, and presented a document that purported to be a certificate of freedom signed by the clerk of Lincoln County, Tennessee. He wanted both Chester and the mayor of Memphis to countersign it so that he could get on a steamboat. Chester thought the paper was an obvious forgery, a judgment with which several other persons agreed, and without telling the man, he went off to find a policeman to arrest what he thought was a runaway slave. Unable to find one, he returned, and apparently having a change of heart, suggested that if the black man confessed his guilt and told them who he belonged to, Chester would see that he was returned to his owner rather than be locked up in the jail. In response, the man pulled out a pistol and shot Chester in the head, killing him. Bystanders quickly subdued the offender, a group of people gathered, Chester's seventeen-year-old son arrived, someone gave him a gun, and he shot the slave in the back three times. After that, the mortally wounded man was taken to jail, but an "immense" crowd forced law officials to turn over the keys. They got the killer out and "swung him up to the nearest tree." Newspaper accounts emphasized that Chester was a good public servant and extremely well liked. Given the nature of the crime, the editors believed the treatment of the killer was understandable.[17]

Chester's killer must have acted out of a burst of anger and frustration that was irrational with respect to his remaining free, something that was not uncommon among slaves, many of whom attacked their owners without any hope of escaping punishment. Many runaway slaves, however, fought back against would-be captors with a reasonable chance it would work to their advantage, and it sometimes did.

On April 14, 1828, Charles Carlson of East Feliciana Parish came home from the fields and found that "his gun" was missing. Also gone was Carlson's slave Dave, "a stout fellow," who was about six feet tall, missing a portion of the thumb and forefinger on one hand, and rolled his eyes when spoken to." Dave had not shown up for work that day but had come to Carlson's house later that morning. The slave owner was "alarmed" by these events but lay down on his bed for a while and then came to the table for his evening meal. During dinner, a shot through the window hit him in the head. He "died instantly, his brains being scattered over the table and against the wall."[18]

A decade later, John De Hart, a former steamboat captain who owned a plantation in St. Mary's Parish, was also shot through the head while eating dinner. A newspaper description of the wound was an extreme example of the cultural fascination with violence: "The load entered at the left eye, which blew off the whole of the forehead, passed on into the wall, and scattered a part of the brain and hair on it; the head fell over onto the table or floor, in which situation the Coroner and three or four citizens found it." A habitual runaway named Bill was suspected of the crime and fled a few days later. He was caught several weeks after and implicated others. Five men were brought to trial; one was found innocent, and Bill and three others were executed. According to the paper, they had conspired to kill De Hart because he had placed them under the control of a mulatto overseer.

A similar event occurred at Bayou des Glaises in Avoyelles Parish. James Burroughs, "an old resident of the parish," punished for some reason one of his favorite servants, a man named Lewis, who fled afterward but did not go far. Apparently thinking he would come back, Burroughs went looking for Lewis at the slave's cabin and was told he was in the plantation kitchen. Finding him there, the master attempted to grab him, but Lewis hit Burroughs in the side of the head and then beat him. After Lewis fled, his own young son who was at the scene gave the alarm, shouting that his father had killed his master. Mrs. Burroughs came immediately only to find what the *Marksville Villager* called "a mutilated and bloody corpse."[19]

Armed runaways often fought despite being outnumbered. In the late summer of 1840, a brief notice informed readers of the *Picayune* that a Mr. Hall "was dangerously wounded with an axe" when he tried to capture a runaway near Dr. Scott's plantation about five miles north of Baton Rouge. The slave was still at large at the time of publication and his identity not known. In September 1840, the *Yazoo City Register* reported that a Mr. Wilkes found one of his servants who had been hiding in the neighborhood for some time and was bringing him home when the man drew a knife and stabbed Wilkes several times. He managed to get his own knife out, and the two fought until each of them was disabled. Wilkes sustained "a large cut in the abdomen, which entered the intestine," and nearly died. The slave's injuries were not reported, but he survived to stand trial.[20]

A planter named Samuel S. Fox was riding in his field just north of Vicksburg in September 1841 when he came upon an African American with a gun. Fox sent a slave to get a weapon but continued after the runaway by himself. On his way back, the servant heard a shot and soon found his master "weltering in his own gore," having been hit by "a very heavy load of buckshot."[21]

In August of 1842, two runaways from the plantation of Robert Brushears in Franklin Parish, in northeast Louisiana, Ben and Rollin, put up a determined resistance to arrest. They were captured on Bayou Salle, and with their hands tied put into a boat that also contained three double-barreled shotguns and ammunition. B. L. Wilcox, who was taking them into town, untied their hands so that they could do the rowing, and they threw him over board, shot him in the head, and escaped after firing on several other men. An immediate pursuit was unsuccessful, but a few days later, they were seen in a swamp and Theodore Le Beauve and two others went out again, and according to their account sighted the two and chased them into a marsh where shots were exchanged. Le Beauve caught Rollin and went after Ben, who shot him in the thigh. Le Beauve continued to advance, and when he got close, the runaway raised his gun but Le Beauve fired first and killed him. By the time the *Picayune* heard the story, Le Beauve was recovering and Rollin was waiting to be executed.[22]

In July 1844, H. D. Wright, the overseer on "the home plantation" of Daniel Turnbull in East Feliciana Parish, learned that a runaway named Bill, who belonged to a Mrs. Cox in East Baton Rouge Parish, was hiding in one of the cabins in the Negro quarter. When found, Bill had a hatchet and attempted to resist, but Wright shot him in the stomach and he died shortly after. In February 1845, a New Orleans steamboat pilot was beaten to death with an oar by a runaway while attempting to take the man back to his owner in a skiff. Later that year, a Mr. John Lindsay, who was an overseer on a plantation near Woodville, Mississippi, was killed by a runaway. Lindsay had seen the man enter a house in the slave quarters and followed him, carrying a pistol. In the confrontation that followed, the slave knocked the overseer's arm up so that he shot into the ceiling and then stabbed him in the chest. In July 1848 an unnamed runaway in Bossier Parish, along the Red River in northwest Louisiana, killed a man named O'Brian with a club, dragged the body into the bushes, and made off with his horse and gun. A few days later the runaway gave a knife belonging to O'Brian to a slave at a nearby plantation in exchange for information on how to get to Shreveport. The slave informed his owner, and the runaway was shot while attempting to escape in a skiff.[23]

In 1853 the *Daily Picayune* gave the details of an event that took place at Port Hudson, up the river from Baton Rouge. Two men from the city learned that a suspected runaway was working on a flatboat moored a short distance below the town and went down in a skiff to apprehend him. They took him into custody and put him to work rowing back up the river, but he picked up a hatchet lying in the boat and wounded one of the captors "very seriously," after which the two struggled and fell into the river. The other white man helped both men back in the boat but finding the captive still hard to control they put him ashore. They went on to Port Hudson, collected arms and hunting dogs, and returned. The dogs picked up the trail of the fugitive and the pursuers found him atop a pile of driftwood in the river and now somehow armed with a club and a pistol. The rest of the story deserves to be told as it appeared in a local newspaper:

> He bade defiance to men and dogs—knocking the latter into the water with his club, and resolutely threatening to kill any man that approached him. Finding him obstinately determined not to surrender, one of his pursuers shot him. He fell at the third fire, and so determined was he not to be captured, that when an effort was made to rescue him from drowning he made battle with his club and sunk waving his weapon in angry defiance at his pursuers.[24]

There is no reason to believe that these events did not happen more or less as described, but the sudden and unexplained appearance of a pistol that quickly turned into a club was another detail probably added to boost the agument for self-defense.

Later that year, the *Mississippi Free Trader* wrote about a "Dreadful Tragedy." Two men found a runaway in a home in Natchez, and in the fight that followed, he stabbed and killed one of the men, was himself shot in the hand, escaped, and hid "about the mill." According to the paper, "soon after the mill went into operation in the morning, he was discovered by the hands when he jumped into some part of the machinery and was instantly torn to pieces." That may have been what happened, and a coroner's inquest reached a verdict that it was, but the fact that one was held suggests an alternative explanation about how the man wound up in the moving parts of the mill.[25]

In June 1850, a runaway arrived in Little Rock on a steamboat and proceeded on land toward Indian country. Near Clarksville, he stabbed a man named Underwood who attempted to capture him. Somewhere not far from Fort Smith he was arrested while riding a stolen horse. In 1853, the Louisiana legislature provided $500 in compensation to an overseer who was shot trying to apprehend two runaway slaves wanted for murder. In 1854, a resident of Plaquemines Parish named Emile Beenel was walking through the woods with his twelve-year-old son on their way to go fishing when they came upon a black man who immediately fled. Beenel chased and captured him, but another African American came on the scene, and the unarmed white man gave up his effort. Writing about the event, a correspondent of the *Picayune* lamented that "for some time our woods have been infested with a gang of runaways, but so far no attempt has been made by our inhabitants to arrest them." In 1857 the slave Miles, belonging to Mrs. Eliza Primell, of Morehouse Parish, was found guilty of having "grievously and willfully wounded and mutilated Mr. Jerome Bres, of this parish, who had arrested said slave while a runaway." Primell had bought Miles in New Orleans the previous March, and he had run away shortly after being taken to her plantation.

A newspaper story that white readers probably found particularly troubling appeared in the *Memphis Appeal* in August 1856. J. B. Jones, who lived in Middleton, a town close to the Mississippi border in Hardeman County, woke up to find a black man "in a perfectly nude state" and shot at him. Slightly wounded the intruder fled, was pursued by dogs and captured, escaped, and was caught again the following day. He turned out to be Wild Bill, a runaway "who had been in the woods for about 18 months." Bill confessed to having conspired with Jones's own slaves to murder him and his wife "and then rob the house and make their way to a free country."[26]

In 1858 an overseer named J. T. Mack was out riding on a plantation a few miles from Memphis and came upon an unknown black man whom he decided was a runaway and attempted to bring him in. Mack had a shotgun, but on the way back the captive drew a pistol and attempted to shoot him, but the weapon misfired. Each grasping the other's weapon, they struggled until another black man arrived carrying a rifle and Mack fled. He returned with the plantation owner, a Mr. Bowden, both armed and accompanied by dogs. Another confrontation occurred, and Bowden was shot and killed. One of the fugitives was captured later, but the other escaped.[27]

Newspapers in the valley also reported violence committed by maroons, who were especially active in the sugar parishes of lower Louisiana. In March 1842, "a gang of runaway negroes" was found "encamped on a raised raft in the middle of a swamp in Assumption Parish, at the rear of a plantation belonging to Mr. Jerro." Some were captured "and the rest dispersed." In June 1843 Mr. Valcour Bergeoise and two other men shot and captured an armed runaway named William six miles below Donaldsonville. William was one of "ten runaways who formerly resorted to Bayou Sec."[28]

In 1852, a jury in the town of Franklin in the parish of St. Mary found Solomon Smith guilty of "firing at, and wounding, with intent to kill" a man named Hungerford and sentenced him to be executed. Smith was said to be the "leader of a dangerous set of runaway rascals [who had] for months infested St. Mary parish and were ultimately tracked and captured by the means of hounds." The local newspaper opined that not only his "many evil deeds" but also his "determined and malicious spirit" and "threats and well known vindictiveness" made Smith a threat to the safety of the public and justified the death sentence.[29]

An apparently groundless scare occurred in 1853 in Shreveport, by then a bustling city. On October 15, a man named Gardiner, who lived on Douglas Island, opposite the city, brought his family into town along with the news that one of his slaves had warned that a group of "runaway negroes, headed by worthless white scoundrels," also on the island, intended to burn the city to the ground that evening. "Gentlemen" from Shreveport searched the island and found no trace of the alleged incendiaries.[30]

In September 1854, the citizens of Thibodaux, a town along Bayou Lafourche in Lafourche Parish, were delighted to learn of the capture of "Wild Henry," a runaway slave who had been "the terror of the neighborhood." A man of "great cunning and adroitness," Henry was feared by the slaves who thought he was a conjurer who could cause their death by "scattering a few grains of sand upon the ground" and catch bullets and shot fired at him. For several years he had been "levying contributions from all the adjacent plantations and even from the town of Thibodaux itself." He was armed with a shotgun, two pistols, and a butcher knife when taken after being badly wounded by gunfire. Having shot at and wounded pursuers in the past, it was thought he would be quickly tried and executed.[31]

At Baton Rouge about 8 o'clock on an August morning in 1855, Constable Cousinard found two black men at the city's wharf filling a boat with bushels of corn and bags of cornmeal. He ordered them to stand still and threatened to shoot if they didn't. One obeyed, but the other ran. Cousinard shot and wounded him in the side, but he kept going "over fences and bridges" and escaped. The captured man, whose name was not given, was owned by a man in West Baton Rouge and had been gone from him for two years. His accomplice was Fisher, also known as John, who had escaped from a plantation in the Bayou Grosse Tete area six years earlier. The *Baton Rouge Advocate* editor was convinced "they were well provided with powder and shot, and there is no doubt they have arms secreted in the Bruley [perhaps a burned-over wooded area], in West Baton Rouge, or in the rear of Messrs. Hicky and Conrad's plantation, at both of which places bands of runaways are known to be secreted."[32]

Six months later the Baton Rouge paper reprinted an editorial from the *Iberville Gazette* published in the nearby town of Plaquemine. Titled "Desperate Runaway Negroes Armed to the Teeth," it was based on the recent arrest of six runaway slaves who were found with "over two kegs of powder, besides guns, pistols, revolvers, cutlasses and knives." Some of the group had "been in the woods upwards of two years," and one of them admitted to having been responsible for buildings that were burned in Bayou Goula in Iberville Parish the previous winter. After providing these details, the Iberville editor vented about the general problem.

> These runaway slaves kill your cattle and murder and rob those they find hunting in the back woods. At least they would take your life should you come suddenly upon them or attempt to arrest one of their number single handed. In the cold and piercing days of winter, they do not remain all night in the dark, dreary swamp. No, they visit the quarters of your servants in your own yard, and tamper with them for food and clothes . . . There is scarcely a night in the week, that your poultry yard is not inspected by some black rascal. He does not steal because he is hungry—no, but he thirsts for whiskey, and he has become so accustomed to its use and to thieving,

that we almost believe he would steal, if he knew had to throw his plunder into the river.[33]

In 1859, another act of arson took place near Bayou Goula, where the buildings had been burned several years earlier. The sawmill owned by Mr. Breaux was set on fire, and while he and his slaves were trying to put out the blaze, his home was broken into and a trunk opened that contained some money and valuable papers. The "thief and incendiary" was seen by a black woman who gave an alarm, but he was gone before any help arrived. A neighbor on his way to assist also saw the man and attempted to arrest him but was not successful. The next day a group of neighbors with dogs found "a runaway negro camp" and chased the owner for several days but could not catch him. Breaux's loss was $6,000 and he had no insurance.[34]

Maroon violence was prevalent in Louisiana, but not limited to there. "The suburbs of Natchez are said to be infested with a large number of runaways," read the lead sentence in a *Picayune* story in July 1845 about "an old and valuable family servant" who attempted to stop one of them from burgling his master's home and died when the fugitive stabbed him in the heart. In 1856 a young man of about twenty named Joseph Powell and two "schoolboys" from the Stephens family were hunting in the woods between Bovina and the Big Black River, not far from Vicksburg, when they came upon a "runaway camp well stocked with provisions." One of the Stephens brothers had a shotgun with him, and Powell took that and sent the boy to get help. Soon after, one of the runaways appeared and Powell ordered him "to stand." He agreed to surrender and offered to have his hands tied and walked up to Powell to have it done. When close, he grabbed the shotgun, knocked Powell down, and fired at the brother who had remained. The pellets knocked off his hat and grazed his head, and he fled. Powell tried to get up, but the runaway hit him with his flintlock pistol and knocked him down again. At this point, the brother sent for assistance returned after hearing the shot; and he and Powell subdued the slave and apparently tied him up. Soon after two more black men came on the scene. One of them snapped a pistol at Powell, but it misfired, and somehow the whites took the blacks into custody and "marched them in." The *Vicksburg Whig* wrote up the story calling the capture a "daring and courageous feat." New Orleanians read it on the front page of the *Picayune*.[35]

≈

"The South's greatest nightmare was the fear of slave uprisings," wrote the historian John Hope Franklin, and he might have added that the enslaved people of the region suffered greatly because of it. The most fanciful portion of Virgil Stewart's book on John Murrell was what its subtitle called *a Plan of Exciting a Negro Rebellion*, but it appears to have been the major cause of the bloody reprisals associated with an alleged slave conspiracy that occurred in Madison County, Mississippi, only a few months after its publication.[36]

Madison is located on the east side of the Big Black River just east of the Delta and is covered by wind-blown loess soil in which cotton thrived. In 1830 there were slightly fewer than 5,000 people in the county, and 44 percent of them were black; by 1840, the total population had tripled, and enslaved people had increased to 74 percent. In the latter part of June 1835, a plantation mistress living at Beatie's Bluff overheard some of her house servants discussing something that under questioning they admitted was a planned uprising of slaves. The woman's son warned people at Livingston, a small community nine miles away, and on June 27 a meeting of citizens there agreed to activate the system of slave patrols and set up a committee to carry out an investigation of the threat. Meanwhile, planters at Beatie's Bluff had questioned more slaves, whipping them if they denied knowing about the plot. One confessed that slaves on local plantations intended to start an insurrection on July 4, killing their owners with axes and hoes, arming themselves with stolen guns, marching on Livingston and other nearby towns, and eventually attacking Natchez. He also claimed that whites were involved in the planning. When this news reached Livingston, a mass meeting of citizens established a Committee of Safety empowered to arrest people, try them, and whip or hang those judged to be guilty, following state laws "so far only as they should be applicable to the case in question." Two white men who had been named were tried, convicted, and hanged; one of them confessed in the hope of leniency and said he was a follower of John Murrell. Over the next two weeks, three more white men, including one planter, were executed, and another hanged himself in a jail cell. Five slaves were killed in Beatie's Bluff, seven in Livingston, and an unknown number tortured, and perhaps killed, by owners determined to learn details of the alleged plot.[37]

Reports of rebellious slaves and rumors of insurrections were much more common in southern Louisiana than the rest of the Lower Mississippi Valley, but wealthy and well-established cotton and sugar planters dealt with them in a calmer and more disciplined manner than the new settlers of Madison County. Nonetheless the total of whippings, related forms of torture, and executions suffered by the enslaved population was far greater than in the Delta. Moreover in Louisiana the threat of uprising was usually related to fugitivism and the reality that runaways and maroons did pose a danger to white population.

In 1829 Rachel O'Connor, mistress of Evergreen Plantation in West Feliciana Parish, noted in her diary that a female friend on a nearby plantation had been robbed by runaways, who had even entered her bedroom while she was asleep. A few days later several of the fugitives were discovered along with part of the stolen goods. Later a white man shot at members of the same group, and in retaliation, at least as the story went, the runaways captured one of his servants and "cut his legs and arms off and then pulled out his eyes, and left him to die." Another report claimed that a local planter led a force of one hundred men against the runaway band and killed eight or ten of them. She hoped that it was true.[38]

In October 1831, two months after the Nat Turner insurrection in Virginia, O'Connor heard from a very frightened friend that "all the Negroes on little Robert Barrow's plantation had armed themselves and claimed their liberty." A military force was put together but it "found the overseer and the Negroes very busy at gathering their crops, as peaceable as lambs." Still, the event kept the white community on alert: "Poor little Fan," a servant of O'Connor's, "was afraid to go after the geese without a pass." In January 1836 Rachel learned of a planned uprising that was to have taken place the previous Christmas at a place called Thompson's Creek but was foiled when a female slave informed on the plotters. Two slaves were hanged; several white men thought to be implicated made their escape. O'Connor also heard that two more Negroes would have been executed except that their wealthy owners had gotten them off to avoid losing their valuable property.[39]

On the first of September 1840, under the title "A Negro Revolt," the New Orleans *Picayune* announced that "abolitionist incendiaries are creeping among us like moles" and supported the claim with information that four hundred "happy and peaceful slaves" had launched "a furious revolt" in Lafayette Parish the previous week. The rebellion was quickly squelched and forty of the participants were in jail with twenty of them sentenced to be hanged. Four "white abolition rascals" were involved along with one "yellow fellow," known to be "a great scandal." The following day it announced that nine of the participants had already been executed.

Doubtless these reports were exaggerated, but something did happen in Lafayette Parish, even if it was only the murder of black people uninvolved in rebellion. Three weeks after the initial story, five alleged rebels were tried by "the parish judge and jury of free holders," and four of the accused were sentenced to hang. One of those beat the gallows by poisoning himself. A fifth participant received fifty lashes and was sentenced to "wear irons" and spend the night in stocks for two years. Several later events involving runaway slaves were also related to the insurgency. Early in 1841, a father and son were hunting on a small island near Prairie Maronne, twenty miles southeast of Lafayette, when they accidentally came upon John, a runaway who had been in the woods for two years and was said to be implicated in the insurrection a few months before. John attempted to shoot at the whites, but his gun misfired, and he and the son grappled until the father walked over, put his pistol against John's neck, and shot him dead. John had made at least a semi-independent lifestyle for himself that included "a good cabin, plenty of provisions, a gun, ammunition, and a horse." Four or five months later a "white scoundrel" entered the home of Cesaire Mouton of Lafayette Parish and threatened the owners with "a huge knife." Mouton grabbed a loaded shotgun and gained control of the situation. The intruder was "among the number of those who were severely lashed last summer on suspicion of being involved in the late insurrection." He told Mouton he was doing the bidding of Jean Louis, a slave who had belonged to the planter and was "one of the ringleaders" of the revolt. He had run away after that event and sworn to kill Mouton.[40]

Following these events in Lafayette Parish, newspaper readers in New Orleans learned of another putative rebellion, this time in West Feliciana Parish. On Thursday, July 22, 1841, Captain Laurent docked his steamship *Clipper No. 1* at New Orleans and told of a "contemplated insurrection," again involving the plantation of Robert J. Barrow, Rachel O'Conner's neighbor who was a relative of Bennet Barrow's. The previous Friday evening, Barrow's overseer had heard slaves discussing an uprising that was to take place on August 1. Under questioning (and probably torture) they provided details of a plot involving enslaved people from Bayou Sara north to Natchez who planned to sweep through a large portion of the state attacking all whites and operating under the rallying cry of "No Quarter." About forty slaves were quickly arrested in the Bayou Sara area along with a white carpenter on Barrow's estate. Other slaves fearful of being implicated fled to the woods and swamps. More blacks were taken into custody at Woodville, and all were housed in the jail at St. Francisville where they were guarded by militiamen and citizen volunteers. The patrol was also on the alert. The New Orleans *Courier* quoted a letter from West Feliciana asking for "a dozen of your best Bowie knives." This excitement did not last long, however. As the New Orleans *Picayune* put it, "the great insurrection in the neighborhood of Bayou Sara has turned out to be a humbug." The first slave to confess and implicate others declared that he was afraid of a whipping if he didn't, and the white man who also gave evidence turned out "not to have the sense to go in when it rains."[41]

Bennet H. Barrow's slaves may have been involved in the alleged insurrection, and in any case he played an active role in its suppression. Laconic diary notations provide a guide to his activities, although they give few specific details about the whipping that was the main tool of investigation and the killing that was a common form of punishment. On July 17, 1841, a letter from his brother Robert Ruffin Barrow, one of the largest sugar planters in Louisiana, warned Bennet about the possibility of an uprising on August 1. At least one slave on each of six nearby plantations were thought to be involved, and several of Bennett Barrow's workers were mentioned. He resolved to investigate his own servants as well as those in the neighborhood. Two days later he found an enslaved man named David Bonner on Judge Wade's plantation who was thought to have been a leader. Several of the bondsmen on his relative Robert H. Barrow's plantation were found to be "deeply concerned." Bennett went out that night to watch for blacks passing on the road and found "a good many runaways about." The next day he found Old Pete on Robert Ruffin's plantation to be "deeply concerned [involved]." On the twenty-fourth he visited more plantations in the neighborhood. Eventually he was satisfied that the situation was under control: "Negros all cleared. But will be tried by the Planters themselves."[42]

A year later there was a report of a planned insurrection in Concordia, Madison, and Carroll Parishes, where, as a St. Francisville paper put it, "there are now in the swamps of those parishes about three hundred runaway negroes, all of them armed." "Facts elicited on the examination" of fifteen or twenty suspected slaves indicate that the uprising was to happen about Christmas. In May 1844 St. Francisville "was put in commotion" by the news that a small group of runaways "had assembled in a thicket about three miles from our town and bid defiance to their pursuers." Daniel Turnbull, owner of Rosedown Plantation, came into the community looking for help and about twenty men, "ready for an emergency," returned to the place with him only to find that the fugitives had gone. That evening Turnbull caught two slaves who had escaped from him and a Mr. Fair caught another who had been with the group. Later "a large mulatto man, armed with three pistols and a tomahawk, was shot by Mr. Mayo Gray" near James R. Dupree's plantation, living only long enough to say that he belonged to W. H. Johnson, a large plantation owner in Mississippi.[43]

The following month, Bennet Barrow noted that "Mr. Turnbull's negroes are cutting up a great many shines—16 ran off & and have defied him—are well armed[,] killed two of his dogs while [they were] in pursuit of them." He blamed the problem on Turnbull having allowed them to listen to preachers for the last five years. Later that same year Barrow went into action when "nearly all" of Miss Swift's workers ran off, hoping to get her to fire the overseer. Again, Barrow thought this act of "pure impudence" was the result of religious education. He planned to "see them put to order" if his recent illness did not prevent him from doing it. Four days later two men from Mississippi arrived with "a pack of dogs," and Barrow went out with them. They captured a woman who was part of a group and tried to get her to reveal where its members were hiding. Apparently, she led them to the wrong place or places because they "fooled the day off to no purpose." Barrow took the captive home and tortured her, "tried the cold water on her ladyship" as he put it. The next day the party went out again, and the dogs found a trail that led into a swamp and followed it at such a pace that the men could not keep up, and by the time they got them back four hours later there was no trace of runaways. The hunt went on intermittently for another three weeks, and eventually three out of the five runaways were captured. The slave catchers from Mississippi went home on November 8, but four days later the remaining fugitives were taken in or near the small community of Laurel Hill. Barrow continued to help Miss Swift by going over to her plantation and whipping the runaways.[44]

Historian Sally E. Hadden, who has detailed the development and operation of slave patrols in Virginia and the Carolinas, emphasizes the significance of white people acting as a community police force and argues persuasively that the Ku Klux Klan of the Reconstruction era was a direct descendant of the patrol system and performed much the same role with respect to freedmen as the former organization had with slaves. The same thing was true of the Lower Mississippi Valley. Individuals interviewed by the WPA had much to say about both patrols and the KKK and sometimes mixed them up. Charlie Hinton of Pine Bluff said that "the Ku Klux used to run my daddy if they caught him without a pass," which was only done by the slave patrols. Henry Blake of Little Rock thought of the two groups as one: "That gang that got after you if you let the sun go down while you out—that's called the Pateroles. Some folks call 'em the Ku Klux."[45]

The antebellum public responsibility for controlling enslaved people away from home was also extended to free African Americans after the Civil War, and it lasted for another century. Southern whites continued to act as unpaid policemen willing to use violence in support of white supremacy. Whipping became much less common than it had been, but other forms of lynching violence continued to be a major part of race-ased social control.

In the antebellum period, a decade before a runaway slave shot John K. Chester in Memphis, across the river in Crittenden County, Arkansas, two enslaved men escaped from the plantation of Thomas E. Clark, and when Clark went after them, they attacked him and beat him to death. A group of local whites soon captured the men and "hung them up on the nearest tree as an example for other refractory negroes." Four decades after the Civil War, a black man hit a white man with whom he was drinking and playing cards in St. Charles, a small town on the White River in Arkansas County, which is four counties south of Crittenden County. When a police officer tried to arrest him, he broke away and fled, taking the lawman's gun with him. Over the next six days, the county sheriff and members of his posse shot six black men to death, and the white people of St. Charles broke five more out of jail and killed them. According to a Little Rock newspaper, the cause of the bloodshed was "Defiance by Negroes."[46]

{ CHAPTER 8 }

Federal Fugitives, the Kidnapper Captain, and Gruesome Stories

THE CONSTITUTION INCLUDED a provision dealing with the return of "persons held to service" in one state who had fled to another, and Congress passed a law in 1793 designed to implement it, but the spirit of the one and the provisions of the other were frequently violated by both sides. Northerners, both white and black, resisted southern attempts to reclaim escapees, and the Underground Railroad carried them to Canada. Southerners not only ignored the minimal restraints on their legitimate activity but also captured in the North and took home black people who were not runaway slaves. The bitter feelings, courtroom struggles, small-scale violence, and mob activity associated with these events has led historian Stanley Harrold to argue a "border war" began in the 1830s because people on both sides "had reason to believe they suffered from aggressive action against their way of life, interests, rights, and sovereignty." For him the fugitive slave issue was an important cause of the Civil War. Similarly, Manisha Sinha, author of a recent and monumental study of the abolitionist movement, emphasized the catalytic role of fugitivism. "Fugitive slaves voting with their feet inspired abolitionism rather than vice versa," she states, and adds that "individual acts of slave resistance became the stuff of politics."[1]

The lower South was somewhat insulated from these things because its citizens had little personal contact with those of the North, and its fugitives rarely made it to the sectional border, but the white citizens of Mississippi and Louisiana hated the Underground Railroad as much as did those of Kentucky, and no southern newspaper attacked the Fugitive Slave Act of 1850 more virulently than the *Mississippi Free Trader*. Slavery in the Mississippi Valley and the people who attempted to free themselves from it did play a role in heightening sectional tension. The enslaved of that region were especially important as victims of the internal slave trade, taken from their homes and families and sold down the river where they ended their days living and working under conditions that were much worse than those in their home states of Maryland, Virginia, or Kentucky. Louisiana was where the kidnapped free black man Solomon Northup spent his twelve years as a slave. And if the readers of *Uncle Tom's Cabin* were thrilled by Eliza's heroic crossing of the icy Ohio River, they were equally appalled when Tom died on a plantation located along the Red River in Louisiana, whipped to death by Simon Legree for refusing to give away the hiding place of the two female runaways, Cassie and Evangeline. A number of much less well-known Mississippi Valley escapees also became part of the great national debate over slavery.[2]

John C. Calhoun's famous speech against the Compromise of 1850, delivered to the Senate by James Mason, his colleague from Virginia, while its near-death author sat at his desk too weak to speak, demanded that the North "do her duty by causing the stipulations relative to fugitive slaves to be faithfully fulfilled." Calhoun's concern was legitimate; northern citizens and their state governments had done much to hinder the return of escaped slaves to their owners. But that southern apologist ignored the fact that southerners had also violated the law, most importantly by kidnapping free black people living in the North and enslaving them in the South. Some background is necessary to make this clear and show how it was important to the people of the Lower Mississippi Valley.[3]

The right of a slave owner to pursue and capture a runaway slave was based on the common-law doctrine of recaption, which allowed the owner of lost or stolen property to take it back as long as that was not done in a "riotous manner" or through a "breach of the peace," and it became important during the Confederation period when northern states began to abolish slavery. When Congress prohibited slavery in the territory north of the Ohio River, it was careful to add a provision to the Northwest Ordinance stating that a bondsperson who fled there could be "lawfully reclaimed." As part of their goal to create a strong national government, delegates to the Constitutional Convention required states to give "full faith and credit" to the legislative acts, judicial proceedings, and public records of each other and respect "the privileges and immunities" of their citizens. Among specific provisions relating to these general concepts was one dealing with the extradition of criminals: a person accused of a crime in one state who fled to another and whose return was requested by the governor was "to be delivered up." The debate over that brought up the related issue of slaves who fled from a state where slavery was lawful to one where it was not. Without significant opposition and with little discussion, a provision on slavery was added to the Constitution: "No Person held to Service or Labour in one State . . . escaping into another, shall, in Consequence of any Law or Regulation therein, be discharged from such Service or Labour, but shall be delivered up on Claim of the Party to whom such Service or Labour may be due." This "fugitive slave clause," as it came to be called, was hardly as important as the one that counted an enslaved person as three-fifths of a white person or even the one that prohibited the importation of foreign slaves after twenty years, but it would turn out to be, as historian Paul Finkleman has put it, the most "vexatious" section of the Constitution dealing with slavery. One problem was vagueness. Who was to deliver up these black escapees and how was it to be done? Another issue was that in the case of criminals the request for extradition was made by a governor acting on behalf of a state, while in the case of a slave it came from a self-interested private citizen. And, of course, the biggest problem was the growing opposition to slavery in the northern states.[4]

In 1780 Pennsylvania began the gradual abolition of slavery by declaring that children born to enslaved people after that year would have the status of servants rather than slaves and be free from any form of bondage when they reached the age of twenty-eight. To begin gathering the information necessary for implementing that provision, the law required that all owners of enslaved people register them with the government and ordered that any that were not registered would be set free. John Davis's owner neglected to do that and fearing the consequence leased him to someone living in Virginia. When the newly formed Pennsylvania Abolition Society heard about this maneuver, some of their members entered Virginia, rescued Davis and brought him back to Pennsylvania—an act that Virginians viewed as stealing a slave. The lessee then sent agents into Pennsylvania who did the same thing—which Pennsylvanians viewed as the kidnapping of a free man. Both states then looked for help from the federal government, and Congress responded with the Fugitive Slave Law of 1793. This affirmed the right of a slave owner or his agent to enter a state and seize a runaway but required the captive be taken to a state magistrate or a federal court and the captor prove "either by oral testimony or affidavit" that the person in custody was a slave and belonged to him. Following that, a warrant was issued allowing the fugitive to be taken out of the state where he was captured. Anyone who attempted to hinder the capture or rescue the captive was subject to a fine of $500.[5]

In the four decades that followed the passage of the Fugitive Slave Act of 1793, a prelude to the Civil War developed along the Mason-Dixon Line and the Ohio River. People living south of these boundaries grew angry as enslaved people fled to freedom and free blacks and antislavery whites helped them escape from southerners who crossed the border after them. Northerners resented the fact that legitimate slave catchers some- times ignored the common law prohibition of violence, and criminals took advantage of the 1793 law to kidnap free African Americans. From their perspective, the peace of their neighborhoods and police power of their state governments were being sacrificed to the property interests of their southern neighbors. As the antislavery movement grew stronger and morphed into abolitionism the fugitive slave clause became a part of the national controversy over slavery. In 1826 Pennsylvania attempted to deal with the kidnapping problem through a state law that eliminated the option for a slave catcher to take an alleged slave into custody without a warrant and required stronger proof of ownership. Two years later New York allowed attorneys for black captives to use writs of habeas corpus on behalf of their clients and in some cases extended alleged fugitives the privilege of a jury trial. Other northern states passed similar measures, all of them known as "personal liberty laws."[6]

While residents of the Lower Mississippi Valley were seldom involved in these conflicts, they supported the southern side, but in one interesting series of events a group of Mississippi planters and politi- cians worked with the mayor of Philadelphia to assist free black children who had been kidnapped from that city. It began in August 1825 when a planter in Rocky Springs, Mississippi, named John Hamilton convinced a justice of the peace to take into custody four young black people, three teenagers and one young woman, who were being offered for sale by a trader named Ebenezer Johnson but told Hamilton they had all been kidnapped in Philadelphia. Hamilton contacted Mayor Watson of that city, who was able to secure evidence to support the boys' claim, and Hamilton took them to Natchez and sent them by boat to New Orleans and then back to Pennsylvania. Johnson, it turned out, was part of the Cannon-Johnson Gang, notorious for kidnapping black children from Pennsylvania, New Jersey, and Maryland and selling them in the South.

Four months later a servant belonging to David Holmes, a US senator from Mississippi who was soon to take office as governor of that state, told him a story about a teenaged enslaved male named Peter Hook whose experience was similar to the people rescued by Hamilton. He was a free black living with his parents in Philadelphia in June 1825 when he was lured to the city's dock by a black man and kidnapped at knife point by a white man named Joseph Johnson. He was kept in chains for several nights while Johnson captured three more young blacks, and then the four were taken down the Delaware River to a home near the mouth of Delaware Bay where they were kept for a few months during which the gang brought in more victims including a young woman named Lydia Smith. Eventually the group, now numbering close to twenty people, most of them free black teenage boys, were taken by boat to Petersburg, Virginia, from where they traveled overland in a coffle into North Carolina and then across Georgia and Alabama into Mississippi. Lydia Smith was sold in Monticello in the southern part of the state, and Peter Hook along with three other boys his age was purchased by a Mr. Perryman of Holmesville in the same area.

Shortly after learning of Hook's experience, Holmes and his friend, Joseph E. Davis, Jefferson Davis's older brother, learned that Lydia Smith had showed up in the Natchez slave market, and they took her into custody and recorded her story. She had been born a slave in Delaware but had been promised her freedom when she reached the age of twenty-one. Her owner died well before that, however, and she was in danger of being sold south when the Pennsylvania Abolition Society found out about it and protected her in Philadelphia for five years. She returned to Delaware, however, was enslaved again, and eventually was kidnapped by a man who took her to Joseph Johnson's house where she joined Peter Hook and his fellow prisoners. Her account of the kidnappers and the journey across the South was similar to Hook's.

Holmes and Davis wrote Mayor Watson of Philadelphia, saying that "public justice" and the "cause of humanity" required something to be done about this and that they were aware of the "benevolent feelings of Philadelphians." They asked the mayor to find witnesses who could testify to the truthfulness of Hook's account and that of Lydia Smith.

With information supporting the freedom of all the victims, the two men thought they could be found and rescued. Watson found out that both the kidnapped children at Rocky Springs and those in the group including Hook and Smith were taken by the Cannon-Johnson gang and police authorities were looking for them. He asked the people of Philadelphia for information about the children Hook had mentioned and sent a note to Duncan Walker, a prominent Natchez attorney, asking for his services in handling the documents and searching for the children. Watson offered to pay, but as the Natchez *Ariel* informed its readers, Walker was willing to do the work for free. Whether Peter Hook, Lydia Smith, or any of the others were found and saved, we do not know.[7]

Cooperation like that between civic leaders in Natchez and Philadelphia on behalf of black people was rare. An equally strange but much more characteristic series of events took place a decade later and led to a Louisiana woman becoming the plaintiff in a high-profile court case involving the Fugitive Slave Act of 1793 and the New York personal liberty law. Mary Martin, who lived in New Orleans, had bought Jack from a local slave trader in the spring of 1830, and the slave fled from her within a few weeks. At the time, a Spaniard who had a free black servant named Antonio Delestia was boarding at her house, and the two of them sailed for the Mexican city of Campeche. Martin suspected that Jack had gone with them and arranged for a search to be conducted there, which proved to be fruitless. Sometime after that Martin moved to New York City, apparently to be with her daughter, Agnes Lindsey, and in August 1833 she encountered Jack in that city. Following the provisions of the New York personal liberty law, she applied for a writ of habeas corpus from the recorder's court, gave a deposition explaining her version of the facts, and the man she said was Jack was taken into custody. He claimed to be the black servant Antonio Delestia, a free man born in the West Indies whose father was a Spaniard, and who had spoken nothing but Spanish until he was twenty. He had served in the Mexican navy and then immigrated to the United States where he lived in Philadelphia for nine months and then moved to New York and was currently "operating an oyster cellar under the Walnut Street Theatre." Unfortunately for Jack, he had claimed too much. Under examination in a courtroom he was unable either to speak or understand the Spanish language. He was allowed eight days to bring witnesses from Philadelphia to prove his case, but when they failed to appear, the court ruled in favor of Martin, and she was granted permission to take Jack back to Louisiana.

By the end of proceedings in the recorder's court, Jack's case had caught the attention of the nascent abolitionist movement in New York City, and one of its attorney's, Robert Sedgewick, filed a writ against Martin that won Jack a trial in the Superior Court of New York City. Sedgewick admitted that Jack was a slave but argued that Martin had become a citizen of New York and as a result could no longer own him or any other slave. The court rejected that argument, but Sedgewick appealed to the state supreme court. The justices there quickly disposed of the residency issue, declaring that there was no legal reason why a citizen of a free state could not own a slave in a slave state. The high court discussed the New York personal liberty law at length and declared it unconstitutional; ruling that the fugitive slave clause of the Constitution provided a legal basis for Congress to legislate on the issue, and once it had done so, no state had the right to do so. All Mary Martin or any other slave owner had to do to reclaim a runaway slave was to convince a magistrate that they owned the person in question.

The litigation was not over. The New York Constitution approved in 1777 had established a final appeals body known as the Court of Errors that was made up of high court judges and state senators, and it agreed to rule on the case. In July 1835, it issued what might be called a split decision. Isaac W. Bishop, an upstate senator, agreed with the supreme court and reinforced its attack on the New York law with a political argument: the issue not only involved the legal rights of states but also the "permanency of the government under which we live," and it arose only because of "zealous efforts for a premature and immediate abolition of slavery." Reuben H. Walworth, chancellor of New York State, took a different position but arrived at the same result with respect to Martin and Jack. He argued that the fugitive slave clause of the Constitution was self-enforcing, and Congress had no power to legislate on the issue, but that the police power of the states allowed them to determine the conditions on which it should be implemented. The Fugitive Slave Law of 1793 was unconstitutional, but the New York law was not. The recorder's court had followed the correct procedure and made the right decision: Mary Martin was free to take her slave back to New Orleans.

Jack's escape with Delestia's papers had won him a year of freedom, and Sedgewick's efforts had postponed his return to slavery by two years, but he spent the latter period in jail while the case was resolved. Despite Walworth's argument, the New York personal liberty law was weakened, but did not officially die for another seven years. Mary Martin was the winner but paid a price for her victory. Not until two years after finding her runaway slave was she able to get his services back, and between her legal fees and the cost of keeping him in prison, she must have been out a significant amount of money. To make up for this, her attorney asked the court for damages based on the loss of Jack's services during the two years when he was in jail. The obviously unsympathetic Court of Appeals considered awarding her 6 cents, and then discussed another motion to make it $60, and finally settled on $20, which they estimated to be the interest on her expenses.[8]

In 1842 the Supreme Court clarified the meaning of the Fugitive Slave Law of 1793 in *Prigg v. Pennsylvania*, a case involving circumstances similar to those that had resulted in the passage of the law. Edward Prigg captured a former Maryland slave named Margaret Morgan who was living as a free person in Pennsylvania and took her back to the woman who claimed to be her owner. Pennsylvania wanted to try Prigg on kidnapping charges, but Maryland refused to extradite him. This time the governors of both states contrived circumstances by which Prigg agreed to a trial that would find him guilty so the case could be appealed to the high court, which, it was hoped, would resolve the status of the law. Thomas C. Hambly, who presented the case for Pennsylvania, stated that there was no other issue "of more commanding import, of wider scope in its influence, or on which hung mightier results for the good or ill of this nation" than the right of southern owners to reclaim runaway slaves living in the North, linked as it was to the slavery question, which "has caused enthusiasm [excessive emotion] to throw its lighted torch into the temples of religion and the halls of science and learning," and was being debated not only in the courtroom but as well in the "village bar-room." Justice Joseph Story, who wrote the majority opinion for the court, said the same thing in less extravagant terms: resolving the fugitive slave issue "was vital to the peace and perpetuity of the Union itself."

Story believed in what has come to be called the historical-necessity theory, which claims that the Constitution could not have been approved without compromises on the issue of slavery and therefore its provisions relative to that subject, including the fugitive slave clause, had special importance. From that perspective, Story argued that the Act of 1793 was constitutional but not necessary. The right of a slave owner to take back his property guaranteed by the Constitution was not limited by anything else in it, including the prohibition against search and seizures, the right to trial by jury, and the need for due process of law. Pennsylvania's personal liberty law was unconstitutional, and so also were any other attempts by that state or any other to hinder the search for and capture of a slave.

After using most of a long opinion closing what from the southern point of view was a can of worms, in just a few sentences at the end of it Story opened another one. The 1793 law called upon state and local judicial officers to participate along with federal courts in examining ownership papers and issuing warrants that allowed owners to take their captives out of the state. Story found nothing in the Constitution that gave the federal government the right to order states to do those things. He ruled that they were free to cooperate in that manner but could not be required to do so. Northern states could not add to or detract from the provisions of the fugitive slave law, but neither did they have to assist in carrying them out. Chief Justice Roger B. Taney, a staunch defender of slavery, was upset by this dictum and wrote a forceful dissent on that aspect of the Story opinion, claiming that not only were states prohibited from hindering the operation of the law, but they were compelled to assist in its enforcement. As it turned out, Taney's concern was justified. A year after the Prigg decision, Massachusetts and Vermont passed laws prohibiting state officials from assisting in the capture and return of fugitive slaves. Within a few years Pennsylvania, Connecticut, New Hampshire, and Rhode Island had done the same.[9]

"Stigmatized as a slave-stealer at the South—branded as a kidnapper at the North—my situation is anything but enviable." Thus, did Captain James W. Hannum describe his circumstances in a plaintive letter to the New Orleans *Daily Picayune* written from Boston on September 11, 1846. In reality, no one in the Crescent City seems to have thought of him as a thief, but it was possible he would be sued by a slave owner for letting his runaway slave escape. In Boston, however, they did call him the "Kidnapper-Captain," and he was in real danger of being prosecuted on criminal charges. It was fair to say, as a sympathetic New England paper wrote, the captain was "caught between two fires."

Hannum was master of the brig *Ottoman*, which on or about August 17, 1846, had left New Orleans on its way to Boston. Seven days out, a runaway slave was found hidden in the cargo hold. The man's name was Joe, and he was well known to both the captain and the crew, having been on board regularly selling milk on behalf of his owner while the ship was docked in New Orleans. Mindful of the Louisiana law against harboring runaways, Hannum immediately began looking for a ship going the other way that could take Joe back to the Crescent City, but seeing none for the rest of the voyage, he sailed into Boston Harbor on September 7, carrying a runaway slave to what was arguably the anti-slavery capital of the United States.[10]

Boston was where William Lloyd Garrison had begun publishing the *Liberator* in 1831, the opening issue of which ridiculed moderation on the issue of slavery and demanded immediate abolition. In 1835 a mob drawn largely from the free black community of the city rescued two women runaways from a courtroom in which a slave catcher was about to receive legal authority to take them back to North Carolina. Nine months after the Prigg decision when legal action failed to save a local black man named George Latimer, the threat of another rescue by abolitionists made it impossible for the fugitive to be removed from the city and prompted the owner to sell him to a group of prominent citizens who set him free. When Massachusetts went on to pass a personal liberty law that prevented public officials from assisting slave catchers, the poet John Greenleaf Whittier exulted:

No slave-hunt in our borders,—no pirate on our Strand!
No fetters in the Bay State,—no slave upon our land.[11]

The Prigg decision protected the right of a slave owner or his representative to capture a runaway in Massachusetts, but Hannum was neither of these and had no standing under the Fugitive Slave Act. If Joe reached Massachusetts soil and the captain took him back to New Orleans against his will, Hannum was guilty of kidnapping under Bay State law and could be sent to prison for ten years.[12]

Determined to keep Joe off Massachusetts soil, the captain transferred him to a pilot boat and left him in the harbor while the *Ottoman* docked, and Hannum went to get advice from his employer, the merchant John H. Pearson. Pearson quickly decided that Joe had to be returned to New Orleans and arranged for another ship that belonged to him, the barque *Niagara*, to pick him up on her way out to sea. The captain, along with three friends and a boatman, sailed away from the city in a small craft, collected Joe from the pilot boat, and began to wait for the arrival of the *Niagara*. The weather turned bad, however, preventing ships from putting out to sea, and the Hannum group took shelter on Spectacle Island, four miles from Boston. The next day while Hannum and his friends were drinking in a local hotel, Joe got away, took their boat, and sailed to south Boston. Hannum commandeered another vessel and arrived there ten minutes after him. As Hannum later put it, "we took after him, through corn-fields and over fences, till finally, after a chase of two miles, I secured him just as he reached the bridge." Telling a group of onlookers that Joe had stolen his wallet, rather than that he was a runaway slave, the captain got his prisoner into a carriage, took him back to the boat, and sailed away. Realizing that the thief story would not hold up long and faced with more stormy weather, he sailed to an uninhabited island and hid with Joe among the rocks while his friends went to town to pick up supplies. They were recognized and pursued by angry Bostonians but got away and returned with a larger and faster sailing vessel, some crackers, and a bottle of gin. The *Niagara* arrived at two the following afternoon, but it was towed by a steamship filled with abolitionists looking for the captain and his captive. Hannum managed to get Joe on board the sailing vessel along with letters of explanation to people in New Orleans before allowing two police officers on the steamship to come aboard and escort him back to Boston.[13]

The Kidnapper-Captain had solved one of his problems, but the other had grown worse. On Wednesday night following Hannum's capture of Joe, a state supreme court justice issued a writ of habeas corpus for the captain and sent police officers to find him. The next morning after a fruitless search, a warrant was issued for his arrest on the charge of kidnapping. Faced with severe legal penalties and a hostile public, on September 16 Hannum wrote a letter to the *Boston Post* to explain "some of the particulars of the late slave case." Emphasizing the difficulties of his circumstances, he pointed out that he would face criminal charges in Louisiana if Joe was not returned and claimed that Joe's owner would also sue him for the loss. Unwilling to take all the blame, he pointed out that it was Pearson "(as I believe) with motives of the purest justice, who decided that [Joe] must go back." Hannum also said his friends had given Joe "presents in money and clothing" and that the runaway had "expressed his regret that he absconded from me—that he was willing to abide by me and return to his master." In addition, he professed to be opposed to slavery: None of his accusers "would be more rejoiced [than him] to see a slave set free, or the whole institution of slavery with its thousand curses, tumbled to the dust." In addition, he said he had written a letter to Joe's owners saying that in returning the slave, "I sacrifice feelings of humanity and private principles to the laws of the state [of Louisiana]."[14]

The kidnapping of Joe the runaway was the subject of what the *Boston Courier* called "A Great Meeting in Faneuil-Hall" on September 24. John Quincy Adams, former president of the United States, long-term member of the House of Representatives, and outspoken critic of that chamber's gag rule that prevented the reading of antislavery petitions, was the first speaker. Apologizing for his weak voice, he suggested that the audience was probably as surprised to see him there at his age as he was forty years earlier when the aged Elbridge Gerry, a signer of the Declaration of Independence, addressed a meeting in the same place held to protest the attack of the British warship *Leopard* on the American naval vessel *Chesapeake* and the subsequent removal of four sailors and their impressment into the British navy. Adams suggested that the present meeting was of similar significance, involving, as he put it, the issue of whether "this commonwealth is to maintain its independence as a state or not."

Following Adam's brief remarks, Dr. S. G. Howe, who acted as chair, summarized the kidnapping of Joe and asserted that "no person, except the owner of the runaway slave, or his agent, or a Marshal of the United States, had any right to touch him . . . and [that was why Hannum and Pearson had] hid their victim upon an island in our harbor, and forcibly detained him there." Perhaps reflecting the influence of Hannum's letter in the newspaper, he suggested that the captain "was more sinned against than sinning" and Pearson and his partners were the real culprits. Then, testing the limits of hyperbole, Howe claimed that he "would rather be a driven field slave on a Louisiana plantation, than roll in [the wealth of these merchants] and bear the burden of their consciences." Next he presented a series of resolutions for the meeting to approve. Included was a strong assertion of states' rights: The first duty of every government was to guarantee the personal liberty of every individual on its soil and no "foreign state or nation" had the right to restrict the rights or liberty of anyone on Massachusetts soil. Other resolutions declared that the people who cooperated in sending back the slave deserved "the stern reprobation of a community which has solemnly branded the slave trade as equivalent to piracy," called upon the owners of the *Niagara* to publicly disavow what they have done and make an effort to get the slave back, and suggested that a "committee of vigilance" be formed to protect anyone in the future who should be "in danger of abduction" from Massachusetts.

The next speaker was a Salem merchant named Stephen C. Phillips, who also placed most of the blame on Pearson and suggested that no Boston merchant "after such doings, could hold up his head and maintain his position in the community," a statement that caused "considerable noise and disturbance on the floor." Phillips was followed by the well-known antislavery orator Wendell Phillips, who felt the resolutions did not go far enough and pointed out that all Hannum needed was "a piece of paper" from Joe's owner making the captain his agent and the seizure of Joe would have been perfectly legal under the Fugitive Slave Act of 1793. For Phillips, the problem was the existence of slavery in the United States, and he called for the meeting to unite behind the abolitionist concept that "Law or no Law—Constitution or no Constitution—Humanity will be paramount." The like-minded transcendentalist Theodore Parker wanted the meeting to appoint a large committee that would make clear to all slaves that they could come to Massachusetts "for shelter and protection" and declared his belief that "when the laws of Massachusetts and the laws of the United States conflict with the laws of God then those of the divinity should rule." Finally, Charles Francis Adams, the son of John Quincy and a leader in the antislavery "Conscience" faction of the Whig Party, declared that the resolutions would have some effect and that he had not given up on the Republic.[15]

The controversy over the return of Joe did not end with the Faneuil Hall meeting. A week later, the New York City *Commercial Advertiser* supported Hannum's position that there were two sides to the story. The laws of slave states "are excessively rigid and severe upon all masters of vessels," and if the captain had not gotten the runaway back to Louisiana, "he might as well [have made] up his mind never to show his face again in New Orleans, on peril of ruinous fines and imprisonment." For the editor, this made Hannum's action as defensible as was Joe's: "If it is said that the slave had a natural right to escape from slavery, so we say the captain had a natural right to protect himself against the evils to which he was exposed by that escape." Furthermore, since the Faneuil Hall meeting did nothing to help Joe, "its only effect . . . can be to excite and sustain an exasperation of feeling between North and South, useless at best and very likely to be mischievous." By contrast, a Portland, Maine, newspaper articulated the antislavery sentiment in one pithy sentence: "Let no man become a kidnapper on Massachusetts soil for the sake of appeasing slaveholders in Louisiana." A letter writer to the *Boston Atlas* took a swipe at the Boston antislavery forces for not collecting funds to buy Joe out of bondage. John H. Pearson, the merchant for whom Hannum worked, wrote a letter to the *Boston Courier* saying that the strictness with which southern states enforced their laws against aiding runaways left him no option other than to send Joe back to New Orleans, and added a bold attack on those who would protect runaway slaves: "I consider that the free states have no right to succor the runaway slave, unless you trample the Constitution of the United States under your feet and make it a dead letter." The Charleston, South Carolina, *Southern Patriot* reprinted Pearson's letter, declaring, probably too optimistically, that because he was one of the richest merchants in Boston, "it would have its due effect on all in that section of the country, who, blinded by a fanatical zeal for what they term 'human rights' would trample on the Rights of the South without hesitation or scruple."

Meanwhile, Captain Hannum had revealed himself to be decidedly two-faced, one visage looking at Boston and the other New Orleans. On September 11, the day after he got Joe on the *Niagara* and was himself taken back to Boston to face legal proceedings, the captain had written to the *Daily Picayune* giving a detailed account of his efforts to get Joe back to his owner. This one was noticeably free of the sympathy for the runaway and the hostility toward slavery that figured prominently in his letter to the *Boston Post* a few days later. Instead he said, "bayonets glistened in all parts of the [steam] boat" that captured him in the *Niagara* incident, and "darkies were there of every hue" crying out, "Run him down," "Fire into him." Having failed to free the runaway, abolitionists were now attempting "to wreck their vengeance on your humble servant." Newspapers were calling him "the "kidnapper-captain." He asked the *Picayune* to print his account, so its readers would know that there were people in Boston (he and John H. Pearson, for example) who opposed the "abolitionists" whose "disgraceful proceedings" threatened to damage "the reputation of our beautiful city." On the twenty-second, probably influenced by the upcoming Faneuil Hall meeting, Hannum wrote a second letter to the New Orleans paper that was still more revealing of his feelings. He referred to "bloodhound abolitionists," wondered why there was such a fuss over "a vagabond drunken negro," and averred that justice had "emigrated to the South long ago," and it was to that section of the country he must look for help. The *Picayune* did print Hannum's letters, as he should have known it would, and when copies of the paper arrived in northern cities, the editor of the *Pennsylvania Freeman* published in Philadelphia called the first letter a "detestable example of cold-hearted atrocity," and the *Boston Courier* more charitably thought the second might be a forgery.[16]

Ultimately the tangible results of the "kidnapper-captain" episode were a victory for the pro-slavery side and did nothing for Joe. He was restored to his owner and no one purchased his freedom. Hannum was never arrested because of procedural issues that seem to have been grounded more in politics than in law. In New Orleans, about a month after Hannum sent Joe back to that city, the *Picayune* reported that Captain Long, master of the *New England*, found a runaway on board his vessel while sailing from New Orleans and promptly turned around and brought him back. Bostonians, however, could take some comfort in the outcome of an event that happened in New York while the Hannum episode was taking place in Boston. A runaway who was found on a ship coming north was freed by a judge who ruled that the sea captain had no legal authority to hold him; and after the man was arrested a second time, the same judge freed him again on the grounds that the Prigg ruling invalidated a New York State law that allowed the New York City Police to take part in his capture.[17]

One of the fugitives from the Lower Mississippi Valley reached safety in the North and taunted his former owner in a letter that became public. Albert Culbert of Boston wrote a letter to J. M. Davies at Hewett's Hotel in New Orleans in April 1847. Culbert said he had hidden on a steamboat nine months earlier but gave no further details about his trip to the North, no doubt unwilling to provide facts that might aid in the capture of future fugitives. He must have felt secure in Boston, however, because giving away his location made him vulnerable to slave catchers. He was now part of the "all colored" staff at "one of the best houses" in Boston, and the head waiter was writing the letter for him. He would be happy to serve Davies in the restaurant if he should visit the city. His health was not yet good, but it was improving under the conditions of liberty he now enjoyed. He hoped Davies would not blame anyone for helping him escape, because he had done it alone, and no one knew he was leaving. He was not worried about leaving his wife because there "are women enough here, and young ones at that." A Mr. Cumings had written Davies, apparently offering to bring Culbert to Cincinnati and return him, but Culbert said Davies should not bother going because it was a ploy by abolitionist friends to test his credentials: "They think me too bright to be a runaway." He had found many friends and had spoken at abolitionist meetings, including one attended by two thousand people. "You may judge my feelings—first to be free and then to be placed with gentlemen and ladies, upon the same footing and made to feel at home, enjoying all the blessings which it was designed by the great author of our being that all mankind should enjoy."

The *New Orleans Delta* printed Culbert's letter along with its own grim prediction about how things would turn out for him based on a commonly held Mississippi Valley view of how blacks were treated in the North:

> After a brief season of flattery, and exhibition at public meetings, he will be turned over to the cold, unfeeling charities of a heartless set of agitators . . . Having done everything to corrupt his morals [they will] turn him adrift, and recommend him, as an excellent "boot black," and avoid all recognition of him in public places. He will exist in honesty for a time, but, sooner or later, he will be "up before" the police, where, as to be black is conclusive of guilt, he will be "sent down" for six months, to break granite or pick oakum, having a solitary cell at night, in which to contrast his then condition with that of the nominal slavery, but real freedom, he lived in [when owned by Davies].[18]

Similarly irritating to southern whites was a story that appeared in the *Mississippi Free Trader* in 1842. It was written by a Natchez-area man who had been traveling by steamboat from that city to Cincinnati when he recognized a black man named Archy who had escaped from Mr. E. Peal of Natchez. He was able to have the escapee taken into custody, and Archy explained that he had been working as a steamboat steward and while ashore in St. Louis met a Mr. Fleming, whom he had known in New Orleans, and who now agreed to take him to Cincinnati for twenty-five dollars under the guise of being his slave. The writer and several other southerners attempted to capture Fleming and tie him up, but they were opposed by a larger number of "abolitionists" who were on the boat. In the scuffle, a man from Vicksburg was heard to say: "Oh God, for 10 Mississippians." Unable to have Fleming restrained, the author secured from the captain a promise to have him turned over to authorities in Louisville, but the boat went first to Cincinnati and Fleming was allowed to leave. The *Picayune* reprinted the story "to show slave owners the manner in which many of their negroes are carried off."[19]

A tale of the same genre gave a northern perspective on southern race relations. "A Scene on the Mississippi" was first published in the *Pittsburgh Saturday Visitor* and then reprinted in the *North Star*, the abolitionist paper published by Frederick Douglass. The writer, who called himself Traveller, said he took passage on a steamboat at New Orleans bound for Cincinnati and at the same time "a young man of noble appearance" booked a berth and came aboard with his wife. The couple said they were going to Indiana in the hope of buying a farm. The woman was nursing a child of about ten months, one of "the fairest and prettiest" the writer had ever seen, and she herself had "long black hair, deep blue eyes, and a delicate form." When the captain saw her, however, "he thought she had some nigger blood in her" and said she would have to travel on the deck rather than in a cabin. After some argument, the husband was reimbursed for higher fare, and the two went to the deck. The voyage began well, the passengers promenading on the passenger deck in fine weather, carrying on conversations, and watching other boats go by; but the happiness faded when they reached Natchez and the captain told authorities he thought there was a runaway aboard. The nursing mother was removed by police and put into jail until her husband could provide a certificate of marriage. The boat left, with passengers in tears, according to the narrator, who wrote that such events were common in the South yet their existence was ignored by people in the North despite their Christian values.[20]

A grisly story involving runaway slaves in northern Louisiana in the early 1840s became the subject of a battle between the *New York Tribune* and the *Mississippi Free Trader*. On May 11, 1842, the *Concordia Intelligencer*, located in Vidalia, directly across the Mississippi River from Natchez, published an account of a recent event involving three runaway slaves. Enoch was owned by Mr. B. Duran of Bayou de Glaize in Avoyelles Parish, who sold him to someone in New Orleans. He escaped and returned to Avoyelles where he convinced Joseph, who belonged to

Mr. Bennet, also of Bayou de Glaize, and a young woman from the same neighborhood to join him. Somehow obtaining weapons, they made their way north into Concordia Parish, where they killed a Mr. Harrington and forced his "very pretty" teenage daughter to come with them, later treating her in a "most brutal and revolting" manner. Then they killed another man, not identified, and went on to the home of a Mr. Todd, whom they also killed, and took his wife and daughter with them. A group of men from the neighborhood pursued the party for several days but could not find them. Sometime later, however, two men on a fishing trip found footprints in the mud and gathered a larger force that tracked the runaways to their hiding place. Joseph surrendered but Enoch escaped, although perhaps wounded by gunfire. Then, as the newspaper put it, "Joseph was taken out to the bank of the river, chained to a stake and *burned*." He claimed to be acting under the influence of Enoch, but also revealed that they intended to kill as many white people as possible and in fact the murder of a Mr. Boyden was planned for that very evening. The slave woman was jailed as a runaway, but there was much sympathy for her because she had treated the captured white women kindly and several times at the risk of her own life had saved them from being murdered. Enoch was still being hunted.[21]

On June 9, the *Daily Picayune* added details to the grisly story that came from a no-longer-extant account that appeared in the *Mississippi Free Trader*, based on information from "the Clerk of the steamer Sunflower." Some were minor and factual: Harrington's first name was Noah, Todd's was George, both lived along the Red River, and the slave woman was "a yellow girl named Margaret." Others formed a narrative: Enoch and Joseph had whipped Harrington's daughter with branches "until from torture she was compelled to yield to their hellish purposes," and when they threatened to kill the captives, Margaret "would throw herself on her knees and beg for their lives, saying if they shot them, the balls would have to pass through her body." The high point of the *Picayune* article was a lengthy section describing the burning of Joseph that was quoted directly from the *Mississippi Free Trader*:

> The boy was taken and chained to a tree immediately on the bank of the Mississippi, on what is called Union Point. Faggots were then collected and piled around him, to which he appeared to be quite indifferent. When the work was completed, he was asked what he had to say. He then warned all to take example by him and

asked the prayers of all around; he then called for a drink of water, which was handed to him; he drank it and said: "Now set fire—I am ready to go in peace!" The torches were lighted and placed in the pile which soon ignited. He watched unmoved the curling flame as it grew, until it began to entwine itself around and feed upon his body then he sent forth cries of agony painful to the ear, begging someone to blow his brains out, at the same time surging with almost super-human strength until the staple which was fastened to the tree (not being well secured), drew out and he leaped from the burning pile. At that moment the sharp ring of several rifles was heard—the body of the Negro fell a corpse on the ground. He was picked up by some two or three, and again thrown into the fire and consumed—not a vestige remaining to show that such a being had ever existed.[22]

The burning of Joseph was undoubtedly the most widely read paragraph ever printed by the *Mississippi Free Trader*. The *Picayune* story was the basis for articles in at least thirty-four other newspapers and probably many more. They included large cities in the North such as New York, Boston, and Philadelphia as well as small urban areas in that region such as Plainsville, Ohio; Jamestown, New York; Pittsfield, Massachusetts; New Bedford, Massachusetts; St. Johnsbury, Vermont; Gettysburg, Pennsylvania; and southern cities such as Alexandria, Virginia; Raleigh and Hillsborough, North Carolina; and Charleston, South Carolina. In most cases the *Picayune* account was reprinted more or less intact and with no additional comment; six papers published only a summary of the murder and kidnapping details, but only one, the *Philadelphia Inquirer*, abbreviated the description of Joseph's burning, judging that "some of the details are almost too difficult to print."[23]

About a quarter of the newspapers were critical of Joseph's lynching. The *Boston Post* seems to have been the first to run the short version, which introduced the burning scene with a comment critical of the vigilantes: "The captors were worse than the ignorant negro." Five other papers used that version of the story. The *Daily Atlas* of Boston voiced a similar view, saying it was not sure "which was the more revolting and disgusting," the actions of the runaways or the lynch mob. The *Republican and Emancipator* published in New York by abolitionists wrote that the killing of Joseph was "more horrible" than the murders committed by the runaways since African Americans even when innocent had no protection by the law while whites in similar situations had the benefit of trial and jury, which was not strictly true; Louisiana law gave slaves the privilege of a jury trial in such cases, it was simply ignored in this case. The *New York Tribune*, in its second year of existence under the editorship of founder Horace Greeley, and the *Evening Post* of the same city, both ran the *Picayune* article in full and without comment, but two other New York papers ended their stories with a paragraph noting that the editor of the *Mississippi Free Trader* had nothing critical to say about the vigilantes and added that "perhaps he thinks there was no great harm in torturing a criminal to death in the same manner that was used by the ecclesiastics of the Spanish Inquisition, and, no longer ago than within the last hundred years, by the law-givers and judges of England."[24]

William Lloyd Garrison's *Liberator* carried the whole story and also added what it called "the second act," which involved the capture and punishment of Enoch.

> The clerk of the steam-boat Highlander has informed the New Orleans Bulletin that while the boat was wooding [loading fuel for its boilers] a short distance below the mouth of Red River, those on board were invited to stop a short time and see another negro burned. They were informed that the fellow who was prepared for the exhibition was another of the gang recently mentioned as having committed enormities and fled to the swamp—one of whom was burnt, as recently published.[25]

A sequel to the 1842 newspaper controversy occurred twelve years later as sectional tensions heightened over the Kansas-Nebraska Act that threatened to bring slavery to the northern plains. On February 18, 1854, the *Mississippi Free Trader* published a letter from an unnamed correspondent in Somerville, New Jersey, that said the *New York Tribune* and other papers had published a story claiming that a slave had been burned at Union Point, Louisiana, and that four thousand slaves had been required to watch the event, adding that the information came from a story in the *Free Trader*. The Natchez paper printed the *Tribune's* article, which was the burning of Joseph article written by the *Free Trader's* editor in 1842 with a new introduction and conclusion added by the New York paper. It began by saying that a lynch mob had decided to burn at the stake "a negro who had the impudence to raise his hand against a white man," and ended with a claim that four thousand slaves were forced to watch the event and listen to speeches by "magistrates and ministers of religion" who warned them that they would suffer the same fate if they "were rebellious to their owners." In response, the *Free Trader* wrote that it had never published such a story, and the event had never happened. The *Tribune* story was "an entire fabrication" that showed how far northern fanatics were willing to go to slander the South.[26]

Despite its denial that the burning had occurred, the *Free Trader* began to look for evidence that it had and found some within ten days. Unable to locate newspaper accounts, including its own, the editor interviewed several older residents of the area who remembered the events, at least one of them having been at the burning and argued against it. A lengthy account published by the paper under the heading "Abolition Falsehood" gave details not published at the time, including the fact that the search for the runaways had gone on for more than a week, that Mrs. Todd had lit the fire that consumed Joseph, and that about thirty slaves were made to attend the burning. In the same issue, it also printed the 1842 article from the *Concordia Intelligencer,* which it received only after the type had been set on its own story. Despite these discoveries, the *Free Trader* was unapologetic about its attack on the *New York Tribune.* The northern paper's story was not "entirely" made up but was still "essentially" a "fabrication." Its faults were suggesting the event had taken place recently, that the cause of the execution was simply a threat to hit a white man instead of three murders and the rape of two women, and the exaggerated number of slaves who witnessed the event. Nor did the *Free Trader* apologize for the burning of the two runaways; instead, it asserted that "they who read the story will acknowledge in their hearts a perfect harmony between the crimes they perpetrated and the fate they met." The *Free Trader* also criticized the *Tribune* for giving "fanciful details of horror," ignoring or perhaps unaware that the original story was taken from its own pages.[27]

The *Free Trader's* initial denial generated a significant amount of controversy. The *Tribune* wrote, under the disingenuous "Correction," that it was very happy the burning story had turned out to be false. It claimed to have copied the story from a western paper that now appeared to have copied it from the *Anti-Slavery Standard,* the newspaper of the American Anti-Slavery Society. The New York paper seemed to have new information, however, because it asked to be "further assured" that no such article was in the *Free Trader's* issue for June 14, 1842. It then closed with a sarcastic comment on the larger subject, claiming that it had no wish to do an injustice to slavery "or add to the dark list of enormities which we are too often compelled to record as fruits of [that] institution."[28]

Other newspapers were quick to denounce what was thought to be the *Tribune's* error. The *Brooklyn Eagle* called it a "humbug," and *Newport Mercury* a "hoax." The *New York Journal of Commerce* happily referred to "the explosion of an abolitionist hoax," claiming the slave burning article "has had a tremendous run among the abolitionist journals, and caused as many bursts of indignation as Uncle Tom's Cabin" and that the *New York Tribune* had been "very ferocious about it." A sample of southern opinion came from the *Tri-Weekly Commercial* published in Wilmington, North Carolina, which quoted the *New Orleans Commercial Bulletin* as referring to abolitionist editors as "the most wicked of God's created beings," lacking both "shame" and "honor," and mentioning in particular the *New York Tribune* and the *Pittsburgh Gazette*. To this the *Gazette* responded with lengthy remarks that revealed the issues underlying sectional tension. "The attempt of the South to repeal the Missouri Compromise is mean, dishonest, and fraudulent, and only worthy of men who all their lives have been in the habit of wronging the unhappy slave." Slavery itself is "a foul blot upon the civilization of the 19th century, an unclean thing like the Plague and Leprosy, to be confined within its own borders, there to be hated, loathed and suffered to wear itself out and perish."[29]

Many newspapers printed the *Mississippi Free Trader* account that gave the details of what had happened in 1842, but few had much to say about it, probably because they agreed with the Natchez editor that Joseph and Enoch had gotten what they deserved. One outstanding exception to the tepid response was the *Washington Sentinel*, which printed a diatribe against the *New York Tribune*, calling it, among other things, a "dangerous, unscrupulous, and virulent enemy" to the Constitution and other national institutions, a "talented, but disorganizing and crazy journal," "thoroughly unsound and diseased." With respect to the punishment of the runaways the *Sentinel* eschewed racism, declaring: "Had they been white men, they would have merited greater torments," a statement that may have challenged the imagination of its readers.[30]

The hostility between the North and the South that led to the Civil War built up slowly throughout the aptly named antebellum period in what might be thought of as a drip, drip, drip series of events. In that sense, the Lower Mississippi Valley was one of the faucets.

POSTSCRIPT

AMONG THE ENSLAVED people discussed in the previous chapters, Solomon Northup is the only one whose name very many people would recognize. Mentioning a few of the others here serves the double purpose of giving a bit more life to their memory and underlining some of the important themes of the book.

William, who lived on Fashion plantation and drove Frederick Law Olmsted away in a carriage, had never run away and helps us to understand why other people didn't. As a trusted servant he lived well by the standards of slavery, he had made friends during his twenty years in Louisiana, and he had adapted by learning to speak French. His current home and environment were more familiar and probably more comfortable than the one from which a slave trader had taken him at age thirteen. He thought it would be nice to be a free man and believed he could be successful on his own, but he was not interested in leaving the South or even leaving Louisiana except to visit his mother. He did envy the enslaved people of New Orleans, who had more opportunities to make money than rural slaves and could enjoy the excitement of the city and the company of many other black people. William, like many others, most of them in worst circumstances, consciously or unconsciously, had decided that remaining where he was made more sense than risking the hardships and dangers involved in seeking freedom.

Northup's friend Wiley made a different choice. He had lived in South Carolina where Sheriff Buford had purchased his wife, Phebe, so they could be together, and given him the relatively pleasant job of operating a ferry on the Black River. Buford, or perhaps his heirs, sold both Wiley and Phebe, and they wound up on the Louisiana farm of the brutal Edwin Eppes, where Wiley became a field hand. When he went out without a pass one night, a slave patrol sicced their dog on him, whipped him, and took him home where Eppes whipped him again. Wiley had

had enough, and without telling Phebe, he stockpiled food and set out on foot for South Carolina, only to be caught after twenty miles.

Ginny Jerry never fled far from Bennet Barrow's West Feliciana cotton plantation, yet he waged a multiyear war against the owner's highly restrictive system of control. Jerry chose to woods-off, as Barrow put it, many times, staying out for varying periods that extended to six months and from which he returned looking healthy and well fed. Barrow was forced to spend a lot of time, including quite a few nights, trying to capture Jerry, and he finally had to hire a professional slave catcher, whose dogs did serious damage to their quarry when they finally tracked him down. Probably it was an attachment to family and friends that kept Jerry from striking out for someplace far away, but within the confines of the space he defined, he was a non-violent but very determined rebel.

Ben and Ephraim represent many enslaved people whose lives were disrupted by the Trail of Tears. Ben was captured in 1833 on the road from Memphis to Little Rock, having fled from the old Choctaw Nation in Mississippi to follow his wife who was being taken to the new one in the west. A decade later, Ephraim escaped from the Choctaw chief Ne-ta-ki-jah and fled east, getting to Little Rock and then a few miles south of there to the Saline River, where he was captured, escaped, and passed out of recorded history while still on the run.

Some husbands and wives fled together. Randal, a blacksmith on a Mississippi plantation, crossed the river and entered Chicot County, Arkansas, in 1836, along with his wife, Aaron, Maria, and Hiram, taking four guns with them, and doubtless intended to take advantage of the swampland, perhaps to go north, or south, or to take up a maroon-like lifestyle. A decade later John and Polly, victims of the slave trade who were sold together in Virginia, spent a year in the Chicot County Jail. They had escaped from New Orleans after being purchased by different owners and made their way upriver, probably by steamboat, but were captured somewhere along the way. The sheriff advertised his captives so that their owners could come and get them, but when that did not happen, they were put up for sale, their most realistic hope for future happiness being that someone would buy them both.

Slaves with vocational skills had better than average chances at making successful escapes, and it helped if the individual was also intelligent and audacious. John Scott was such a man. After being purchased in New Orleans, he asked to be hired out for work on a steamboat. His owner refused because Scott had a history of running away and gave him a job on land. Scott responded by malingering until he got what he wanted. He became a steamboat cook and after a time made an unsuccessful attempt to get away. That owner sold him, but a new one let him take another steamboat job, doubtless thinking that the high wages earned by cooks made it worthwhile risking the loss of a valuable property. If so, he lost the gamble. Scott absconded in Louisville, from where he probably made his way across the Ohio River and perhaps on to Canada.

The urban walkaways of New Orleans deserve to be remembered although the newspapers do not tell us much about any of them. Good representatives are Lucy, who worked in a pastry shop and was a favorite of her customers; Dan, a whitewasher who was hired out by his owner until he decided to go into business for himself; and George Anderson, who drove carriages and wagons and was working as a milkman when he left that job to pursue other opportunities.

Madison Henderson reminds us of the importance of slave stealing as a crime that preyed on freedom-seekers. Henderson is also an archetype of the black "bad man" cultural tradition immortalized, among other places, in the blues ballad "Stagolee" and in Easy Rawlins, the protagonist in many of Walter Mosley's novels.

White southerners thought of maroons as outlaws and some of them became notorious. One of these was Sol, whom a newspaper called "The African Bandit of Natchez." He was sold away from the city but came back and lived in the nearby wilds for two years with a small group of fugitive associates. Sol entered Natchez regularly to steal from the whites and socialize with the blacks, a villain to the one group and a charismatic hero to the other.

Ben and Rollin were two of the many fugitives who helped to create the southern culture of violence. They were captured but overcame a man taking them to jail in a boat, shot him using one of several guns that were in the vessel, and took refuge in a Louisiana swamp. Two days later, when found by a party of pursuers, Ben wounded one before being shot to death. Rollin was captured and executed. Even more than those two, the determination of runaways to resist capture is exemplified by the unnamed fugitive who drowned near Port Hudson because he refused to stop battling his pursuers long enough for them to rescue him.

A few fugitives from the Lower Mississippi Valley made it to the North. One was Albert Culbert, who taunted his former owner in a letter written from Boston. Another was Joe, whom the abolitionists of Boston could not save from the clutches of "The Kidnapper Captain." More valley escapees attempted to reach Mexico and some of them surely made it. Most flights to both places failed, but perhaps none so sadly as that of Henry, Melinda, and Morgan, who left Mississippi for Mexico, lost their way in Texas, and nearly starved to death until the first two murdered the last and cannibalized his body.

APPENDIX

LOWER MISSISSIPPI VALLEY
RUNAWAY SLAVE DATABASE

The anecdotal evidence in *Fugitivism* draws on a variety of newspaper runaway slave advertisements selected for their relevance to the Lower Mississippi Valley, but the quantitative analysis is based on a sample of advertisements from Memphis, Natchez, New Orleans, Little Rock, and Vicksburg designed to be representative of the geographical and chronological boundaries of the book. The advertisements include those placed by owners and those placed by jailors, but the New Orleans sample does not include any from jailors because the city police department did not advertise the runaways in its jails.

Table 1 gives the number of runaways in advertisements (not the number of advertisements) taken from each city and years from which they have been selected.

Table 2 breaks down the number of runaways between those advertised by owners who reported them missing and those advertised by jailors as having been captured.

Table 3 gives the number and percentage of runaways reported by owners as probably trying to get out of state, with their destinations given in groups of states.

Table 4 gives the number and percentage of runaways who gave information to jailors indicating the state from which they had fled, broken down between in-state and out-of-state origins.

Table 5 gives the number and percentage of runaways in five-year age categories based on information from both owners and jailors.

Table 6 gives the number and percentage of females and mixed-race people in all advertisements, broken down between those living in New Orleans and a group labeled "Elsewhere," which include those in New Orleans advertisements that have come from outside New Orleans Parish, which in this case and in the text is coterminous with the city.

TABLE 1

Lower Mississippi Valley Runaway Slave Database

CITIES	RUNAWAYS	YEARS
Memphis	262	1839–1860
Natchez	237	1820–1829, 1844–1853
New Orleans	428	1841, 1849, 1855
Little Rock	241	1835–1849
Vicksburg	228	1831–18835
Total	1396	

TABLE 2

Runaways by Owners and Advertisers

	NUMBER	PERCENT
Owners	949	68
Jailors	447	32
Total	1396	100

TABLE 3

Out of State Destinations Reported by Owners

PLACES	NUMBER	PERCENT
L. M. Valley	46	57
Free States	12	15
Slaves States	23	28
Total	81	100

TABLE 4
In-State and Out-of-State Origins
Reported by Jailers

PLACES	NUMBER	PERCENT
In-State	167	45
Out-of-State	203	55
Total	370	100

TABLE 5
Age of Runaway Slaves

AGE GROUP	NUMBER	PERCENT
Under 5	5	0
5 to 9	9	1
10 to 14	37	3
15 to 19	162	13
20 to 24	365	30
25 to 29	304	25
30 to 34	149	12
35 to 39	97	8
40 to 44	53	4
45 to 49	28	2
50 and Over	17	1
Total	1226	100

TABLE 6
Females and Mixed-Race Runaways: New Orleans and Elsewhere

		FEMALES	PERCENT	MIXED RACE	PERCENT
New Orleans	310	102	33	147	47
Elsewhere	1085	82	8	368	34
All	1395	184	13	515	37

NOTES

These notes use the following abbreviations to refer to sources of information:

AG: Arkansas Gazette
DP: Daily Picayune
HRSCL: Historical Records of the Supreme Court of Louisiana
MA: Memphis Appeal
MFT: Mississippi Free Trader
MSG: Mississippi State Gazette
VG: Vicksburg Gazette

INTRODUCTION

1. *Alexandria Gazette* (Alexandria, VA), Oct. 11, 1828.
2. John Hope Franklin and Loren Schweninger, *Runaway Slaves: Rebels on the Plantation* (New York: Oxford University Press, 1999); Larry Eugene Rivers, *Rebels and Runaways: Slave Resistance in Nineteenth-Century Florida* (Urbana: University of Illinois Press, 2012); David S. Cecelski, *The Waterman's Song: Slavery and Freedom in Maritime North Carolina* (Chapel Hill: University of North Carolina Press, 2001); Matthew J. Clavin, *Aiming for Pensacola: Fugitive Slaves on the Atlantic and Southern Frontier* (Cambridge, MA: Harvard University Press, 2015)
3. Stephanie M. H. Camp, *Closer to Freedom: Enslaved Women & Everyday Resistance in the Plantation South* (Chapel Hill: University of North Carolina Press, 2004), 5–7, 36–47, 68–76; Sergio A. Lussana, *My Brother Slaves: Friendship, Masculinity, and Resistance in the Antebellum South* (Lexington: University Press of Kentucky, 2016); Sylviane A. Diouf, *Slavery's Exiles: The Story of American Maroons* (New York: New York University Press, 2014).
4. Thomas C. Buchanan, *Black Life on the Mississippi: Slaves, Free Blacks, and the Western Steamboat World* (Chapel Hill: University of North Carolina Press, 2004); Christopher Morris, *The Big Muddy: An Environmental History of the Mississippi and Its Peoples from Hernando de Soto to Hurricane Katrina* (New York: Oxford University Press, 2012).
5. Among the many recent studies dealing with colonial Louisiana, Gwendolyn Midlo Hall, *Africans in Colonial Louisiana: The Development of Afro-Creole Culture in the Eighteenth Century* (Baton Rouge: Louisiana State University Press, 1992), and Gilbert C. Din, *Spaniards, Planters, and Slaves: The Spanish Regulation of Slavery in Louisiana, 1763–1803* (College Station: Texas A&M University Press, 1999), are most important for this work.

6. Walter Johnson, *Soul by Soul: Life Inside the Antebellum Slave Market* (Cambridge, MA: Harvard University Press, 1999); Walter Johnson, *River of Dark Dreams: Slavery and Empire in the Cotton Kingdom* (Cambridge, MA: Harvard University Press, 2013); Joshua D. Rothman, *Flush Times & Fever Dreams: A Story of Capitalism and Slavery in the Age of Jackson* (Athens: University of Georgia Press, 2012); Sven Beckert, *Empire of Cotton: A Global History* (New York: Random House, 2015), 108, 113; Richard Follett, *The Sugar Masters, Planters and Slaves in Louisiana's Cane World, 1820–1860* (Baton Rouge: Louisiana State University Press, 2005); Judith Kelleher Schafer, *Slavery, the Civil Law, and the Supreme Court of Louisiana* (Baton Rouge: Louisiana State University Press, 1997); Edward E. Baptist, *The Half Has Never Been Told: Slavery and the Making of American Capitalism* (New York: Basic Books, 2014).

7. Kenneth M. Stampp, *The Peculiar Institution: Slavery in the Ante-Bellum South* (New York: Random House, 1956), 110; Gerald W. Mullin, *Flight and Rebellion: Slave Resistance in Eighteenth-Century Virginia* (New York: Oxford University Press, 1972); Walter Johnson, "On Agency: A Ghost Story," in *The Problem of Freedom in the Age of Emancipation*, ed. Richard Follett, Eric Foner, and Walter Johnson (Baltimore: Johns Hopkins University Press, 2011), 8–21, quote on p. 8. For an excellent survey of slave agency, see Steven Hahn, *A Nation under Our Feet: Black Political Struggles in the Rural South from Slavery to the Great Migration* (Cambridge, MA: Harvard University Press, 2003), 16–61.

8. Richard C. Wade, *Slavery in the Cities: The South 1820–1860* (New York: Oxford University Press, 1964).

9. Thomas Ewing Dabney, *One Hundred Great Years: The Story of the Times-Picayune from its Founding to 1940* (Baton Rouge: Louisiana State University Press, 1944), 14–31; Tom Reilly, "The War Press of New Orleans: 1846–1848," *Journalism History* 13, nos. 3–4 (Autumn–Winter 1986): 87–88; Michael Schudson, *Discovering the News: A Social History of American Newspapers* (New York: Basic Books, 1978), 14–30.

CHAPTER 1

1. Frederick Law Olmsted, *A Journey to the Back Country* (New York: Mason Brothers, 1861), 30.

2. [Frederick Law Olmsted], *Walks and Talks of an American Farmer in England* (New York: G. P. Putnam, 1852). For a detailed account of this period of Olmsted's life, see the excellent biography by Laura Wood Roper, *FLO: A Biography of Frederick Law Olmsted* (Baltimore: Johns Hopkins University Press, 1973), 1–85; an authoritative summary is the introduction to Frederick Law Olmsted, *The Formative Years: 1822–1852*, vol. 1, *The Papers of Frederick Law Olmsted*, ed. Charles Capen McLaughlin (Baltimore: Johns Hopkins University Press, 1977), 3–12.

3. [Frederick Law Olmsted], "Notes from the Sea," *American Whig Review* 14 (Dec. 1851): 527.

4. Frederick Law Olmsted, *Slavery and the South, 1852–1857*, vol. 2, *The Papers of Frederick Law Olmsted*, ed. Charles E. Beveridge and Charles Capen McLoughlin (Baltimore: Johns Hopkins University Press), 11–12; Olmsted to Frederick Kingsbury, Oct. 17, 1852, *Papers*, vol. 2, 83; *Back Country*, vi; Roper, *FLO: A Biography*,

19, 40–43, 58–59, 83–85; White, "Connecticut Yankee," 10–13, 19–27, 30–36; Frederick Law Olmsted, *The Cotton Kingdom: A Traveller's Observations on Cotton and Slavery in the American Slave States, 1853–1861*, ed. and intro. Arthur M. Schlesinger (New York: Alfred A. Knopf, 1953), liii–lv.

5. Olmsted to Frederick Kingsbury, Oct. 17, 1852, *Papers*, vol. 2, 82.

6. Olmsted's itinerary has been painstakingly reconstructed by Charles E. Beveridge, see *Papers*, II, 467–71. For a narrative account of the journey, see Kenneth McFarland, "The Travels of Frederick Law Olmsted in the Antebellum South," *Magnolia* 20, no. 1 (Fall 2006): 3–10.

7. *Papers*, vol. 2, 471–82.

8. See Frederick Law Olmsted, *A Journey in the Seaboard Slave States, with Remarks on their Economy* (1856; repr., New York: Mason Brothers, 1861); Frederick Law Olmsted, *A Journey in the Back Country* (1856; repr., New York: Mason Brothers, 1861); Frederick Law Olmsted, *A Journey Through Texas; or, a Saddle-trip on the Southwestern Frontier* (New York: Dix, Edwards & Company, 1857); Frederick Law Olmsted, *The Cotton Kingdom : a Traveller's Observations on Cotton and Slavery in the American Slave States : based upon three former volumes of journeys and investigations by the same author* (New York: Mason Brothers, 1861). Newspaper articles not included in the books are reprinted in *Papers*, vol. 2. For which articles appeared in which volumes and on what pages, see Olmsted, *Papers*, vol. 2, 459–61; and for how material from the first three volumes was incorporated into *The Cotton Kingdom* and what new material added, see *Cotton Kingdom*, ed. Schlesinger, xxvii–xxxiii. Citations in this chapter come from the original editions except those from the *Cotton Kingdom*, which come from the authoritative Schlesinger edition, which includes both parts of the original two-volume publication.

9. *Seaboard States*, ix–x.

10. *Seaboard States*, ix–x, 537–38, *Cotton Kingdom*, 520.

11. *Back Country*, 396–97; *Seaboard States*, 520.

12. *Seaboard States*, 388, see also 18–19.

13. *Seaboard States*, 446.

14. *Cotton Kingdom*, 554–57.

15. *Seaboard States*, 96.

16. *Seaboard States*, 100–101.

17. *Seaboard States*, 160–61. On runaways in the Dismal Swamp, see Sylviane A. Diouf, *Slavery's Exiles: The Story of American Maroons* (New York: New York University Press, 2014), 218–38.

18. *Papers*, vol. 1, 10–11, 161–62, 163n11, 464, 469; *Seaboard States*, 435–36. On the origin and operation of the task system, see Philip D. Morgan, *Slave Counterpoint: Black Culture in the Eighteenth-Century Chesapeake & Lowcountry* (Chapel Hill: University of North Carolina Press, 1998), 179–87. On running away as a negotiation tactic, see Ulrich Bonnell Phillips, *American Negro Slavery: A Survey of the Supply, Employment of Negro Labor as Determined by the Plantation Regime* (1918; repr., Baton Rouge: Louisiana State University Press, 1966), 303–4; and Kenneth M. Stampp, *The Peculiar Institution: Slavery in the Ante-Bellum South* (New York: Random House, 1956), 113.

19. *Papers*, vol. 2, 213, 214, 470; *Seaboard States*, 656–63, 676.

20. *Seaboard States*, 678–84.

21. *Papers*, vol. 2, 222–23n2; "Calhoun, Meredith," *Dictionary of Louisiana Biography*, Louisiana Historical Society (lahistory.org, accessed July 6, 2015); Olmsted, *Back Country*, 73, 79, 81–82; "The South," no. 44, *New York Daily Times*, Nov. 21, 1853. On the gang system, see Morgan, *Slave Counterpoint*, 187–92. The workday quote is the title of chapter 2 in Stampp, *Peculiar Institution*.

22. Olmsted, *Back Country*, 73, 83–84.

23. *Papers*, vol. 2: 37n25, 480; *Back Country*, 46–51, quote on 50.

24. *Seaboard States*, 160–61, 163; *Back Country*, 214–15.

25. *Texas*, 93–94; *Back Country*, 246–47.

26. *Back Country*, 214–17.

27. *Back Country*, 29–30; 63–64; *Cotton Kingdom*, 222–23.

28. *Back Country*, 444–46.

29. *Seaboard States*, 190–93; on Cartwright, see *American National Biography*, s.v. "Cartwright, Samuel Adolphus"; and Samuel Cartwright, "Diseases and Peculiarities of the Negro Race," *De Bow's Review* 11, no. 3 (Sept. 1851): 331–38; Raymond A. and Alice H. Bauer, "Day to Day Resistance to Slavery," *Journal of Negro History* 27 (Oct. 1942): 388–419.

30. *Back Country*, 21–22.

31. *Texas*, v, 46, 96.

32. *Texas*, 105–6.

33. *Texas*, 256–58, 314.

34. *Texas*, 323–25.

35. *Texas*, 326–27.

36. Detailed accounts of these years are given in Charles E. Beveridge and David Schuyler, eds., *Creating Central Park, 1857–1861, Papers of Frederick Law Olmsted*, vol. 3 (Baltimore: Johns Hopkins University Press, 1983); and Jane Turner Censer, ed., *Defending the Union: The Civil War and the U.S. Sanitary Commission, 1861–1863, Papers of Frederick Law Olmsted*, vol. 4 (Baltimore: Johns Hopkins University Press, 1986).

37. *Papers*, vol. 4, 560–61.

CHAPTER 2

1. *Texas*, 41.

2. Gwendolyn Midlo Hall, *Africans in Colonial Louisiana: The Development of Afro-Creole Culture in the Eighteenth Century* (Baton Rouge: Louisiana State University Press, 1992), 2–25, 35; Daniel H. Usner Jr., *Indians, Settlers, and Slaves in a Frontier Exchange Economy: The Lower Mississippi Valley before 1783* (Chapel Hill: University of North Carolina Press, 1992), 24–43, 48–49; Thomas N. Ingersoll, *Mammon and Manon in Early New Orleans: The First Slave Society in the Deep South* (Knoxville: University of Tennessee Press, 1999), 3–33; Gilbert C. Din, *Spaniards, Planters, and Slaves: The Spanish Regulation of Slavery in Louisiana* (College Station: Texas A&M University Press, 1999), 2–17; Morris S. Arnold, *Colonial Arkansas, 1686–1804: A Social and Cultural History* (Fayetteville: University of Arkansas Press, 1991), 3–18; Gwendolyn Midlo Hall, *Slavery and African Ethnicities in the Americas: Restoring the Links* (Chapel Hill: University of North Carolina Press, 2005), 97–104; Paul LaChance, "The Growth of the Free and Slave Populations of

French Colonial Louisiana," in *French Colonial Louisiana and the Atlantic World*, ed. Bradley G. Bond (Baton Rouge: Louisiana State University Press, 2005), 252.

3. Hall, *Africans in Colonial Louisiana*, 34–38, 121–27; Usner, *Indians, Settlers, and Slaves*, 164–65, 185, 228–29; Ingersoll, *Mammon and Manon*, 98; Christopher Morris, *The Big Muddy: An Environmental History of the Mississippi and Its Peoples from Hernando de Soto to Hurricane Katrina* (New York: Oxford University Press, 2012), 66–67.

4. On Indian populations generally, see Usner, *Indians, Settlers, and Slaves*, 24–31; Peter H. Wood, "The Changing Population of the Colonial South: An Overview by Race and Region," in *Powhatan's Mantle: Indians in the Colonial South*, revised and expanded edition, ed. Gregory A. Waselkov, Peter H. Wood, and Tom Hatley (Lincoln: University of Nebraska Press, 2006), 96–107. On the Quapaw population, see Kathleen DuVal, *The Native Ground: Indians and Colonists in the Heart of the Continent* (Philadelphia: University of Pennsylvania Press, 2006), 83, 125, 132, 193, 231; and Morris S. Arnold, *The Rumble of a Distant Drum: The Quapaws and Old World Newcomers, 1673–1804* (Fayetteville: University of Arkansas Press, 2000), 158–60, 193, 231. On military and political relationships among French and Indians, see Usner, *Indians, Settlers, and Slaves*, 77–104; DuVal, *The Native Ground*, 70–106, 132–66; Kathleen DuVal, "Interconnectedness and Diversity in French Louisiana," in *Powhatan's Mantle*, 136–59; and Arnold, *Colonial Arkansas*, 98–124, 179–81.

5. Morris, *Big Muddy*, 59–95; John G. Clark, *New Orleans, 1718–1812: An Economic History* (Baton Rouge: Louisiana State University Press, 1970), 19–151; Ingersoll, *Mammon and Manon*, 35–118.

6. David J. Weber, *The Spanish Frontier in North America* (New Haven, CT: Yale University Press, 1992), 198–203, 266–70; Gilbert C. Din, *Populating the Barrera: Spanish Immigration Efforts in Colonial Louisiana* (Lafayette: University of Louisiana at Lafayette Press, 2014), 13–23; Nathalie Nessens, "From Saint Domingue to Louisiana: West Indian Refugees in the Lower Mississippi Region," in Bond, ed., *French Colonial Louisiana and the Atlantic World*, 290–94; Jean-Pierre Leglaunec, "Slave Migrations to Spanish and Early American Louisiana: New Sources and New Estimates," *Louisiana History* 45, no. 2 (Apr. 2005): 202; Hall, *Slavery and African Ethnicities in the Americas*, 58; Jean-Pierre Leglaunec, "*'Un Nègre nommeé* [sic] *Lubin no connaissant pas Sa Nation'*: "The Small World of Louisiana Slavery," in Cécile Vidal, *Louisiana: Crossroads of the Atlantic World* (Philadelphia: University of Pennsylvania Press, 2014), 119; and Albert W. Haarmann, "The Spanish Conquest of British West Florida, 1779–1781," *Florida Historical Quarterly* 39, no. 2 (Oct. 1960): 107–34.

7. Adam Rothman, *Slave Country: American Expansion and the Origins of the Deep South* (Cambridge, MA: Harvard University Press, 2005), 45–54. The largest slave merchant in New Orleans was the American consul, Daniel Clark, who sold more than twice as many bondspeople than his nearest competitor; see Douglas B. Chambers, "Slave Trade Merchants of Spanish New Orleans, 1763–1803: Clarifying the Colonial Slave Trade to Louisiana in Atlantic Perspective," *Atlantic Studies* 5, no. 3 (Dec. 2008): 335–46.

8. Palmer, *Through the Codes Darkly*, 49–54; Hans W. Baade, "The Law of Slavery in Spanish Louisiana, 1769–1803," in *Louisiana's Legal Heritage*, ed.

Edward F. Haas (Pensacola, FL: Pelican Press, 1982), 43–86. Thomas N. Ingersoll discounts the humanitarian aspects of the code; see "Slave Codes and Judicial Practices in New Orleans, 1724–1807," *Law and History Review* 13, no. 1 (Spring 1995): 24–62. Arnold, *Colonial Arkansas*, 125–70, discusses the operation of both French and Spanish law at Arkansas Post. See also Carl J. Ekberg, *French Roots in the Illinois Country* (Urbana: University of Illinois Press, 1998), 148–49.

9. Din, *Spaniards, Planters, and Slaves*, 29–31. For the text of the regulations, see Charles Gayarré, *A History of Louisiana*, vol. 2 (New York: Redfield, 1854), 361–67. See also Jack D. Holmes, ed. and trans., "O'Reilly's Regulations on Booze, Boarding Houses, and Billiards," *Louisiana History* 6, no. 3 (Summer 1965): 293–300.

10. Din, *Spaniards, Planters, and Slaves*, 42–44; Ingersoll, *Mannon and Manon*, 221–23; Powell, *Accidental City*, 279–84.

11. The importance of race-mixing and of a free black population in colonial Louisiana is based on Hall, *Africans in Colonial Louisiana*, 258–74; on Kimberly S. Hanger, *Bounded Lives, Bounded Places: Free Blacks Society in Colonial New Orleans* (Durham, NC: Duke University Press, 1997), 14–15, 18–26; and Powell, *Accidental City*, 287–92. Thomas N. Ingersoll vigorously dissents from this view; see "Free Blacks in a Slave Society: New Orleans, 1718–1812," *William and Mary Quarterly* 48, no. 2 (Apr. 1991): 173–200; and *Mammon and Manon*, 139–42, 213–20, 326–34. See also Paul F. Lachance, "The Formation of a Three-Caste Society: Evidence from Wills in Antebellum New Orleans," *Science and Society* 18, no. 2 (Summer 1994): 211–42.

12. Din, *Spaniards, Planters, and Slaves*, 42–44. Thomas N. Ingersoll argues that neither the Spanish law nor its administration made significant changes in the treatment of slaves or the structure of society from what they were under the French, see *Mannon and Manon*, 211–39.

13. Hall, *Africans in Colonial Louisiana*, 142–50; Usner, *Indians, Settlers and Slaves*, 136–40.

14. Thomas D. Morris, *Southern Slavery and the Law, 1619–1860* (Chapel Hill: University of North Carolina Press, 1996), 340–46; Sally E. Hadden, *Slave Patrols: Law and Violence in the Carolinas* (Cambridge, MA: Harvard University Press, 2001), 6–40, esp. 38.

15. The articles of the code dealing with runaways are 32, 34, 35, and 36. Charles Gayarré, "Regulations of Police," *A History of Louisiana*, vol. 2 (New York: Redfield, 1854), 361–67, nos. 24 and 30.

16. Gayarré, "Regulations of Police"; Records of the Superior Council of Louisiana, *Louisiana Historical Quarterly* 9, no. 3 (July 1926): 530–31; ibid., 16, no. 3 (July 1933): 505.

17. Records of the Superior Council, *Louisiana Historical Quarterly* 9, no. 3 (July 1926): 530–31; ibid., 16, no. 3 (July 1933): 505; ibid., 9, no. 2 (Apr. 1926): 299; ibid.,19, no. 4 (Oct. 1936): 1095.

18. Records of the Superior Council, *Louisiana Historical Quarterly* 19, no. 4 (Oct. 1936): 1087–88; ibid., 19, no. 3 (July 1936): 768–71; Ingersoll, *Mammon and Manon*, 198.

19. Records of the Superior Council, *Louisiana Historical Quarterly* 3, no. 1 (July 1925): 493–94.

20. Ingersoll, *Mammon and Manon*, 88–89.

21. Ingersoll, *Mammon and Manon*, 91; "Index of Spanish Records of Louisiana," *LHQ* 8, no. 3 (July 1925): 27–28.

22. Din, *Spaniards, Planters, and Slaves*, 11–12, 45–46, 58–62, 74–75.

23. See Din, *Spaniards, Planters, and Slaves*, for an account of the episode from the perspective of the government, 91–107, 111–15, 134–35; Diouf does the same for the maroons, *Slavery's Exiles*, 166–92; and Hall, *Africans in Colonial Louisiana*, 202–36, places the Bas de Fleuve group within the context of what she sees as widespread marronage in colonial Louisiana.

24. Hall, *Africans in Colonial Louisiana*, provides a detailed account of the event, 344–74.

25. This account is based on Robert L. Pacquette, "'A Hoard of Brigands?': The Great Louisiana Slave Revolt of 1811 Reconsidered," *Historical Reflections* 35, no. 1 (Spring 2009): 72–96; but see also Rothman, *Slave Country*, 106–7, and Daniel Rasmussen, *American Uprising: The Untold Story of America's Largest Slave Revolt* (New York: HarperCollins, 2011). Pacquette and Rothman both de-emphasize the revolutionary context, so also does Ingersoll, *Mammon and Manon*, 291–94; while Rasmussen describes a revolutionary conspiracy that is hard to prove based on existing evidence. On the immigration of slaves after 1803, see Paul F. Lachance, "The 1809 Immigration of Saint-Dominique Refugees to New Orleans," *Louisiana History* 29, no. 2 (Spring 1988): 109–41; and Leglaunec, *Slave Migrations*, 204–9. On the fear of slave rebellion, see James H. Dorman, "The Persistent Specter: Slave Rebellion in Territorial Louisiana," *Louisiana History* 18, no. 5 (Autumn 1977): 389–404; and Paul F. Lachance, "The Politics of Fear: French Louisianans and the Slave Trade, 1786–1809," *Plantation Society* 1, no 2 (June 1979): 162–97. John Thornton argues that African-born slaves were noted for military-like resistance to slavery but less so for revolutionary attempts to overthrow the institution itself; see *Africa and Africans in the Making of the Atlantic*, 272–303. See also *Afro-Louisiana History and Genealogy, 1719–1820*, www.ibiblio.org/laslave/ (accessed Aug. 20, 2018), a database collected under the direction of Gwendolyn Midlo Hall, which includes separate subsets of enslaved people listed in records dealing with "Revolts and Runaways."

26. Louis Moreau-Liset, comp., Black Code (June 7, 1806), in *A General Digest of the Acts of the Legislature of Louisiana Passed from the Year 1804–1827*, 2 vols. (New Orleans: Benjamin Levy, 1828), 1:100–129, sections 23, 25–37, deal with runaways. Palmer, *Through a Glass Darkly*, cites an earlier version that is shorter and was passed on March 9, 1807; see *Acts of the Second Session of the First Legislature of the Territory of Orleans*, chap. 10, 82–86, March 9, 1807. Judith Kelleher Schafer points out that in the antebellum period the entire code was gradually altered in ways that made it conform more closely to those of other southern states; *Slavery and the Civil Code*, 4–10.

27. Civil Code of the State of Louisiana (New Orleans: J. C. De St. Romes, 1825), Articles 2496–511, pp. 804–8. Johnson, *Soul by Soul*, discusses redhibition and its influence on trading in the New Orleans slave market, 12, 169–70, 183–86. See also Morris, *Southern Slavery and the Law*, 104–13, and Schafer, *Slavery, the Civil Law, and the Supreme Court of Louisiana*, 126–32; Thomas Gibbes Morgan, comp.

and ed., *Civil Code of the State of Louisiana: With the Statutory Amendments, from 1852 to 1853, Inclusive; and References to the Decisions of the Supreme Court of Louisiana to the Sixth Volume of Annual Reports* (New Orleans, J. B. Steel, 1861).

28. Arthur H. De Rosier Jr., *The Removal of the Choctaw Indians* (Knoxville: University of Tennessee Press, 1970), 53–69, 116–47; Robert Gudmestad, *Steamboats and the Rise of the Cotton Kingdom* (Baton Rouge: Louisiana State University Press), 2011, 102–3. See also Amanda L. Paige, Fuller L. Bumpers, and Daniel Littlefield Jr., *Chickasaw Removal* (Norman: University of Oklahoma Press, 2010), and Greg O'Brian, *Choctaws in a Revolutionary Age, 1750–1830* (Lincoln: University of Nebraska Press, 2002).

29. Gudmestad, *Steamboats*, 14–18, 26–29, 32–43, 70, 122–25, 157–60; Louis C. Hunter, *Steamboats on Western Rivers: An Economic and Technological History* (Cambridge, MA: Harvard University Press, 1949), 32–34, 101–2, 537–42, 644; see also Walter Johnson, *River of Dark Dreams: Slavery and Empire in the Cotton Kingdom* (Cambridge, MA: Harvard University Press, 2013), 87–96.

30. Gudmestad, *Steamboats*, 140–42, 150–52; Robert Gudmestad, "Steamboats and the Removal of the Red River Raft," *Louisiana History* 52, no. 4 (Fall 2011): 392–94, 400–402, 405–8, 415–16.

31. "Impressions of New Orleans by a Foreigner," *De Bow's Review* 4, no. 4 (Dec. 1847), 556; Richard Campanella, *Lincoln in New Orleans: The 1828–1831 Flatboat Voyages and Their Place in History* (Lafayette: University of Louisiana at Lafayette Press, 2010), 252–60, 272.

32. Charles Sealsfield, *The Americans as they Are: Described in a Tour through the Valley of the Mississippi* (London: Hurst, Chance, and Co., 1828), 52, 110, 112–17, 118–20. The year of Sealsfield's journey may have been 1826 rather than 1827. On Sealsfield, see Walter Grunzweig, *Charles Sealsfield* (Boise, ID: Boise State University Western Writers Series, 1985).

33. The quote comes from D. C. Glenn, "Mississippi," *De Bow's Review* 7, no. 1 (July 1849): 42–43. For the statistics here, see John Hebron Moore, *The Emergence of the Cotton Kingdom in the Old Southwest: Mississippi, 1770–1860* (Baton Rouge: Louisiana State University Press, 1988), 118, 120, 124–26; James C. Cobb, *The Most Southern Place on Earth: The Mississippi Delta and the Roots of Regional Identity* (New York: Oxford University Press, 1992), 7–28.

34. Moore, *Emergence of the Cotton Kingdom*, 196–98; Morris, *Becoming Southern*, 114–31.

35. Gerald M. Capers, *Biography of a River Town: Memphis: Its Heroic Years*, 2nd ed. (New Orleans: Tulane University, 1966), 23–33, 49, 56–59, 73, 76–77, 91–95, 101–2; T. Harri Baker, *The Memphis Commercial Appeal: The History of a Southern Newspaper* (Baton Rouge: Louisiana State University Press, 1971), 12; see also Carolyn Pittman, "Memphis in the Mid-1840s: Memphis before the Mexican War," *West Tennessee Historical Society Papers* 23 (1969): 30–44; Edward F. Williams III, "Memphis' Early Triumph over Its River Rivals," *West Tennessee Historical Society Papers* 22 (1986): 2–27; Ronald W. Waschka, "Early Railroad Development at Memphis," *West Tennessee Historical Society Papers* 46 (1992): 1–12; Ronald Waschka, "River Transportation at Memphis before the Civil War," *West Tennessee Historical Society Papers* 45 (1991): 1–18; "Memphis and its Manufacturing Advantage," *De Bow's Review* 10, no. 5 (1851): 525–29.

36. Andrew S. Edson, "How Nineteenth-Century Travelers Viewed Memphis before the Civil War," *West Tennessee Historical Society Papers* 24 (1970): 39–40; Frederic Bancroft, *Slave Trading in the Old South*, intro. Michael Tadman (Columbia: University of South Carolina Press, 1996), 250–58. See also Steven Deyle, *Carry Me Back: The Domestic Slave Trade in American Life* (New York: Oxford University Press, 2005).

37. On the geography and ecology of the Arkansas Delta, see Thomas Foti, "The River's Gifts and Curses," in *The Arkansas Delta: Land of Paradox*, ed. Jeannie Whayne and Willard B. Gatewood (Fayetteville: University of Arkansas Press, 1993), 30–51; and Jeanelle Collins, ed., *Defining the Delta: Multidisciplinary Perspectives on the Lower Mississippi Delta* (Fayetteville: University of Arkansas Press, 2015); also Ted R. Worley, "Helena on the Mississippi," *Arkansas Historical Quarterly* 13 (Spring 1954): 1–3, 10.

38. S. Charles Bolton, *Arkansas, 1820–1860: Remote and Restless* (Fayetteville: University of Arkansas Press, 1998), 4–21; Carl H. Moneyhon, *The Impact of the Civil War and Reconstruction on Arkansas: Persistence in the Midst of Ruin* (Baton Rouge: Louisiana State University Press, 1994), 1–39. See also Donald P. McNeilly, *The Old South Frontier: Cotton Plantations and the Formation of Arkansas Society, 1819–1816* (Fayetteville: University of Arkansas Press, 2000); Carolyn Earle Billingsley, *Communities of Kinship: Antebellum Families and the Settlement of the Cotton Frontier* (Athens: University of Georgia Press, 2004).

39. Sealsfield, *The Americans as They Are*, 123, 143; D. Clayton James, *Antebellum Natchez* (Baton Rouge: Louisiana State University Press, 1968), 136–37, 183–216; William L. Richter, "Slavery in Baton Rouge, 1820–1860," *Louisiana History* 10, no. 2 (Apr. 1969): 126–27.

40. Follett, *The Sugar Masters*, 19, 21, 26–27, 30–31. A detailed account of the economic success of one sugar plantation in the 1850s is J. Carlyle Sitterson, "The McCollams: A Planter Family of the Old and New South," *Journal of Southern History* 6, no. 3 (Aug. 1940): 347–67.

41. Campbell Gibson, "Population of the 100 Largest Cities and Other Urban Places in the United States: 1790–1990," United States Census Bureau (June 1998), tables 5–9, https://www.census.gov/population/www/documentation/twps0027/tab04.txt (accessed Apr. 7, 2017).

42. J. D. B. De Bow, "The Destiny of New-Orleans," *De Bow's Review* 10, no. 4 (Apr. 1851): 444–45, quote on p. 444. James E. Winston, "Notes on the Economic History of New Orleans, 1803–1836," *Mississippi Valley Historical Review* 1, no. 2 (Sept. 1924): 200–226; R. B. Way, "The Commerce of the Lower Mississippi Valley in the Period 1830–1860," *Mississippi Valley Historical Association Proceedings* 10 (1918): 57–68; Moore, *Emergence of the Cotton Kingdom*, 285.

43. The census figures given here are for the Orleans Parish, which was conterminous with the City of New Orleans. See Richard Campanella, *Geographies of New Orleans: Urban Fabrics before the Storm* (Center for Louisiana Studies, 2006), 9–13. On the Irish in the city, see the same source, pp. 227–45; the Germans, 247–58; and the blacks, 227–45. The 1850 immigration figures are from J. D. B. De Bow, *A Statistical View of the United States* (Washington: A. O. P. Nicholson, 1854), 399.

44. Ira Berlin, *Slaves Without Masters: The Free Negro in the Antebellum South* (New York: Random House, 1964), 128–32, 172–74, 230–33); Wade, *Slavery in the*

Cities, 243–46; Claudia Dale Goldin, *Urban Slavery in the American South, 1820–1860* (Chicago: University of Chicago Press, 1976), 123–27.

45. Sealsfield, *The Americans as They Are*, 27–28.

46. Quoted in Eric Foner, *The Fiery Trial: Abraham Lincoln and American Slavery* (New York: W. W. Norton, 2010), 11–12. On the behavior and attitudes of enslaved males, see Lussana, *My Brother Slaves*, 62–64, 96–97.

47. G. W. Featherstonhaugh, *Excursion through the Slave States: From Washington on the Potomac to the Frontier of Mexico; with Sketches of Popular Manners and Geological Notices* (New York: Harper & Brothers, 1844), 36; Bancroft, *Slave Trading in the Old South*, 60–61, 284–85; Mungo Park, *Travels in the Interior Districts of Africa* (London, 1816), vol. 2, chap. 24, page no. not clear.

48. Featherstonhaugh, *Excursion through the Slave States*, 37–38.

49. Harriet Beecher Stowe, *Uncle Tom's Cabin* (1852; New York: Barnes and Noble, 2003), 3–9.

50. Tadman, *Speculators and Slaves*, 6–7, 12, 131–32; Deyle, *Carry Me Back: The Domestic Slave Trade in American Life* (New York: Oxford University Press, 2005), 42–44, 283–89. For an excellent account of slave traders and their business, see Johnson, *Soul by Soul*, 47–57.

51. *John Rist v. John Hagan*, 8 Robinson 106 (1844); *John Rist v. John Hagan*, HRSCL.

CHAPTER 3

1. *Revised Code of the Statutes of the State of Mississippi* (Jackson, MS: E. Barksdale, 1857), 238. Earlier Mississippi had defined a runaway as a slave twenty miles from home without a pass but only for those turned over to a justice of the peace. Similarly, Arkansas used eight miles in that context only. See A. Hutchinson, *Code of Mississippi* (Jackson, MS: Price and Fall, 1848), 528; and Josiah A. Gould, *Digest of the Statutes of Arkansas* (Little Rock, AR: Johnson and Yerkes, 1858), 1029. J. Steele and J. M'Campbell, comps., *Laws of Arkansas Territory* (Little Rock, Arkansas Territory: J. Steele, 1835), 523.

2. There are very useful accounts of runaway slaves in Charles S. Sydnor, *Slavery in Mississippi*, intro. John David Smith (1933; Columbia: University of South Carolina Press, 2013), chap. 6; and in Orville W. Taylor, *Negro Slavery in Arkansas*, intro. Carl H. Moneyhon (1958; Fayetteville: University of Arkansas Press, 2000), 208–32.

3. *New York Daily Times*, Jan. 20, 1823. The date of Olmsted's article was February 16, 1853, McLoughlin, *Papers of Olmsted*, 2, 459.

4. Solomon Northup, *Twelve Years a Slave: A Narrative of Solomon Northup: A Citizen of New-York, Kidnapped in Washington City in 1841, and Rescued in 1853 from a Cotton Plantation Near the Red River in Louisiana* (Auburn, NY: Derby and Miller, 1853), xv; Solomon Northup, *Twelve Years a Slave*, ed. Sue Eakin and Joseph Logsdon (Baton Rouge: Louisiana State University Press, 1968). *Twelve Years a Slave*, directed by Steve McQueen (Fox Searchlight Pictures, 2013), was based on this book.

5. Anthony E. Kaye, *Joining Places: Slave Neighborhoods in the Old South* (Chapel

Hill: University of North Carolina Press, 2007), 31–42, 120–28; Northup, *Twelve Years a Slave*, 90–97.

6. Northup, *Twelve Years a Slave*, 108, 150–51.

7. Northup, *Twelve Years a Slave*, 184–90, 254–60, 188–90.

8. Northup, *Twelve Years a Slave*, 240–46.

9. Northup, *Twelve Years a Slave*, 246–49.

10. Northup, *Twelve Years a Slave*, 157–59.

11. Northup, *Twelve Years a Slave*, 237–40.

12. Northup, *Twelve Years a Slave*, 140–45.

13. This section of Northup's book led Eugene Genovese to believe that swamps were a hindrance to escapes rather than an aid. See *Roll Jordon Roll, The World the Slaves* (New York: Random House, 1976), 651.

14. Genovese, *Roll Jordon Roll*, 127.

15. Edward Adams Davis, ed., *Plantation Life in the Florida Parishes of Louisiana, 1836–1846, As Reflected in the Dairy of Bennet H. Barrow* (New York: Columbia University Press, 1943), 165; on Barrow himself, see 10–15. Thomas C. Buchanan discusses rascality and black pride in *Black Life on the Mississippi*, 128–31.

16. Davis, ed., *Plantation Life*, 16–21, 99, 102–3, 110, 112, 157.

17. Davis, ed., *Plantation Life*, 173–75.

18. Davis, ed., *Plantation Life*, 239, 242–43.

19. Davis, ed., *Plantation Life*, 261, 264, 277, 288.

20. Davis, ed., *Plantation Life*, 359, 369–70.

21. John Spencer Bassett, *The Plantation Overseer as Revealed in His Letters* (1935; New York: Negro Universities Press, 1968), 35–39, 35–39.

22. Bassett, *Plantation Overseer*, 57–60.

23. Bassett, *Plantation Overseer*, 61–68, 77–81.

24. Bassett, *Plantation Overseer*, 44-45,106–7.

25. Bassett, *Plantation Overseer*, 111, 129–32, 145–46.

26. Bassett, *Plantation Overseer*, 153–60.

27. Bassett, *Plantation Overseer*, 176–77, 189–90, 203–4, 212–17.

28. "Nègres Maroons," *Le Meschacebe* (Bonnet Carre, LA), Dec. 3, 1854; *Daily Advocate* (Baton Rouge, LA), Jan. 8, 1856.

29. *New Orleans Mercantile Advertiser* and quoted in the *Woodville Republican*, Nov. 24, 1827.

30. "Singular Adventure," *DP*, Feb. 13, 1841. "Runaway Negroes," *DP*, Mar. 21, 1843. "Runaway Negroes," *DP*, July 23, 1845.

31. "A Hungry Burglar," *Daily True Delta* (New Orleans), June 14, 1859.

32. "A Daring Runaway," *Memphis Eagle*, Aug. 21, 1852, reprinted in *DP*, Aug. 26, 1852.

33. "Runaway Negroes Caught in a Cave," *DP*, Aug. 31, 1856.

34. Harry, *Mississippi State Gazette [MSG]* (Natchez), Sept. 30, 1818; Ned, *MSG*, Apr. 29, 1820; Solomon and Abraham, *Arkansas Gazette [AG]* (Little Rock), Oct. 28, 1832.

35. Anthony and Sam, *Mississippi Free Trader [MFT]* (Natchez, MS), Mar. 13, 1850; Bent, *Memphis Appeal [MA]* (Memphis, TN), May 7, 1857; Simon, *MSG*, Oct. 21, 1820.

36. "The Cruelty of Slavery," *Philanthropist* (Cincinnati, OH), June 16, 1837.
37. Phill, *AG*, Oct. 17, 1826; Henry, *AG*, Mar. 26, 1825.
38. Robert, *DP*, Aug. 18, 1841; Noah and Lige, *MA*, Apr. 19, 1860; Tom, *Arkansas Advocate* (Little Rock), Feb. 12, 1838; Luke, *AG*, June 27, 1826.
39. LSU Libraries Special Collections, Slavery Collection, Mss. 1618, folder 7, New Orleans Municipal Records, extract, St. Martinville, July 9, 1822.
40. Rosalie Schwartz, *Across the Rio to Freedom, U.S. Negroes in Mexico* (N.P.: Texas Western Press, 1975), 3–32; Ronnie C. Tyler, "Fugitive Slaves in Mexico," *Journal of Negro History* 57, no. 1 (Jan. 1972): 1–4; Sarah E. Cornell, "Citizens of Nowhere, Fugitive Slaves and Free Africans in Mexico, 1833–1857," *Journal of American History* (Sept. 2013): 354–69; Sean Kelly, "'Mexico in His Head': Slavery and the Texas-Mexico Border, 1810–1860," *Journal of Social History* 37, no. 3 (Spring 2004): 710–18.
41. Henry, *Austin City Gazette* (Austin, TX), July 8, 1840; Anthony, *The Red-Lander* (San Augustine, TX), Oct. 14, 1841; James, *The Red-Lander* (San Augustine, TX), Sept. 30, 1841; Peter, *Texas Democrat* (Houston, TX), May 6, 1846, *Democratic Telegraph and Texas Register* (Houston, TX), Nov. 2, 1846; Jim, *Texas State Gazette* (Austin, TX), Dec. 7, 1850; Doshy Wallace and Elizabeth, *Texas State Gazette*, Jan. 27, 1855; "Not Quite so Fast," *Trinity Advocate* (Palestine, TX), Feb. 9, 1859.
42. Harry, *Austin City Gazette*, Nov. 10, 1841; Harry, *Daily Bulletin*, Jan. 1, 1842; Tom, *Texas Democrat*, Oct. 11, 1848; Levi, *Texas State Gazette*, Mar. 8, 1851; Joe, *State Gazette* (Austin, TX), Dec. 20, 1856.
43. "Capture of Runaway Negroes—Dreadful Extremity Produced by Hunger," *Northern Standard* (Clarksville, TX), Apr. 12, 1851, reprinted from the *San Antonio Western Texan*, Mar. 20, 1851.
44. On the geographic movement of enslaved Arkansans, see S. Charles Bolton, *Fugitives from Injustice: Freedom-Seeking Slaves in Arkansas* (National Park Service, 2006), 27–68; and Kelly Houston Jones, "Chattels, Pioneers and Pilgrims for Freedom: Arkansas's Bonded Travelers," *Arkansas Historical Quarterly* 75, no. 3 (Winter 2016): 319–35. Jess, *AG*, June 28, 1828; Jesse, *AG*, Mar. 4, 1829; John, *Southern Shield* (Helena, AR), July 23, 1842; Mike and Henry, *AG*, Nov. 12, 1856.
45. James Patrick Morgans, *The Underground Railroad on the Western Frontier: Escapes from Missouri, Arkansas, Iowa and the Territories of Kansas, Nebraska and the Indian Nations, 1840–1865* (Jefferson, NC: McFarland, 2010), 175–82; Conevery Bolton Valenčius, *The Lost History of the New Madrid Earthquakes* (Chicago: University of Chicago Press, 2013), 95–99; S. Charles Bolton, "Jeffersonian Indian Removal and the Emergence of Arkansas Territory," in Patrick Williams, S. Charles Bolton, and Jeannie M. Whayne, eds., *A Whole County in Commotion: The Louisiana Purchase and the American Southwest* (Fayetteville: University of Arkansas Press, 2005), 84–90; Austin, *AG*, Apr. 7, 1821; Celia, *AG*, Oct. 14, 1823, Ben, *AG*, Nov. 9, 1833; Spencer, *AG*, Aug. 26, 1836; Colin and David, *AG*, Jan. 24, 1834.
46. Simon, *AG*, Nov. 18, 1837; Billy, Washington, Hartwell, and Will, ibid., Feb. 24, 1839; Harry, ibid., Apr. 21, 1834.
47. Ephraim, *AG*, Feb. 7, 1833; and May 15, 1833.
48. "A Runaway Caught and Delivered Up," *Daily True Delta*, Dec. 26, 1860.
49. "Gathered Items," *Portage County Democrat* (Ravenna, OH), Feb. 14, 1855.
50. Jerry, *AG*, Oct. 25, 1830.

51. Harry, *MFT*, July 7, 1847.
52. Deborah Gray White, *Ar'n't I a Woman?: Female Slaves in the Plantation South*, rev. ed. (New York: W. W. Norton, 1999), 73–79; Stephanie M. H. Camp, *Closer to Freedom: Enslaved Women and Everyday Resistance in the Plantation South* (Chapel Hill: University of North Carolina Press, 2004), 40–47.
53. D. Clayton James, *Antebellum Natchez* (Baton Rouge: Louisiana State University Press, 1968), 171–73.
54. White, *Ar'n't I a Woman*, 70–74; Camp, *Closer to Freedom*, 36–37; and Kaye, *Joining Places*, 146–47. Isabella, *AG*, Oct. 1, 1838; Martha, *Memphis Enquirer*, May 3, 1839; Melinda, *AG*, Mar. 17, 1841.
55. Flora, *The Ariel* (Natchez), Oct. 18, 1828; Matilda, *The Ariel*, Dec. 19, 1825.
56. Lucy, *Statesman and Gazette* (Natchez), Aug. 7, 1828; Maria, *Statesman and Gazette*, Jan. 31, 1829; Jane and Lydia, *VG*, Jan. 1, 1835; Betsy, *Statesman and Gazette*, Sept. 11, 1828; Harriet, *VG*, May 14, 1835; Matilda, *VG*, May 14, 1835; Mary, *VG*, June 25, 1835; Letitia, *VG*, Oct. 8, 1835; Emaline; *Memphis Enquirer*, Aug. 30, 1839.
57. Ned and Maria, *AG*, June 10, 1840.
58. Dave and wife, *Statesman and Gazette*, Aug. 14, 1828; $10 Reward, *MSG*, Nov. 11, 1824.
59. John, *AG*, Dec. 30, 1844; John, *AG*, Dec. 29, 1845; Polly, *AG*, Dec. 22, 1844; Polly, Dec. 29, 1845.
60. Jemima, *AG*, Jan. 9, 1837.
61. Grace and Paul Guire, *VG*, Nov. 28, 1832.
62. Henry, John, Ann, and Bridget, *Ariel*, Oct. 10, 1825; Randal and Maria, *AG*, Feb. 18, 1836; Joe, Moriah, and Fielding, *AG*, July 13, 1837.
63. Jack, Robert, and Winey, *AG*, Sept. 5, 1838; Charlotte and Sam, *AG*, Nov. 9, 1841; Gregory, Warner, Cressy Ann, Mary Jane, Joe, and Charles, *VG*, May 7, 1835; "$200 Reward," *Memphis Enquirer*, May 17, 1839.

CHAPTER 4

1. Herbert Quick and Edward Quick, *Mississippi Steamboatin'* (New York: Henry Holt and Company, 1926), 250. On the role of music in slave culture, see Lawrence W. Levine, *Black Culture and Black Consciousness: Afro-American Folk Culture from Slavery to Freedom* (1977; New York: Oxford University Press, 2007), 30–55, 190–94. On music and steamboat workers, see Buchanan, *Black Life on the Mississippi*, 8, 54–55, 77–79, 89, 105.
2. In addition to the following pages, steamboat escapes are discussed in Buchanan, *Black Life on the Mississippi*, 101–21, and Johnson, *River of Dark Dreams*, 135–50.
3. Lettuce, *MSG*, Nov. 6, 1824, Ben, *MSG*, Nov. 27, 1824; Anderson, *MSG*, Nov. 27, 1824.
4. George, *MSG*, Feb. 5, 1825; Toby et al., *MSG*, Mar. 19, 1825.
5. Jim and Hannah, *Port Gibson Correspondent* (Port Gibson, MS), Aug. 22, 1822.
6. George and Thomas, *The Natchez*, Feb. 10, 1832; "A Runaway Negro Caught," *DP*, Feb. 11, 1848.
7. Dick, *MSG*, Mar. 26, 1825.

8. *Owen v. Brown*, No. 4927, 12 La. Ann. 172 (1857); Schafer, *Slavery, the Civil Law*, 112–13; Bragg, *Historic Names on the Lower Mississippi*, 146.

9. Giles, *Woodville Republican* (Woodville, MS), June 2, 1831.

10. William Ransom Hogan and Edwin Adams Davis, ed., intro. William L. Andrews, *William Johnson's Natchez: The Ante-Bellum Diary of a Free Negro* (Baton Rouge: Louisiana State University Press, 1993), 72n33; 185, 188, 203, 224–25.

11. Thomas Peters, *The Natchez*, July 24, 1830.

12. Buchanan, *Black Life on the Mississippi*, 45–47; Wade, *Slavery and the Cities*, 330.

13. Hunter, *Steamboats on Western Waters*, 443–56.

14. On the racial makeup of steamboat crews, see Buchanan, *Black Life on the Mississippi*, 10–12, 181–84; for a survey of urban opportunities, 23–50, and for chances to earn money, 90–95.

15. *McMaster v. Beckwith*, No. 2017, 2 La. 329 (1831).

16. Bill or Will, *AG*, July 4, 1837; Ben, *AG*, June 5, 1839; Anderson, *AG*, May 22, 1847.

17. Tom, *MSG*, Oct. 9, 1824; Bill or Will, *Natchez Courier*, June 14, 1833; Billy, *VG*, July 31, 1834; Paschael, *Randolph Recorder*, Mar. 23, 1836.

18. "Caution to Ship and Steamboat Masters," *DP*, May 14, 1844; "Secreting a Slave," *DP*, May 13, 1848; "A Runaway," *DP*, July 24, 1849; "City Intelligence," *DP*, Mar. 26, 1850; "New Orleans Runaway in Louisville," *DP*, Mar. 29, 1854.

19. See "To the Editors of True Delta," a letter from Haldeman reprinted in the *MFT*, June 12, 1850.

20. The story was reprinted in the *DP*, Nov. 3, 1841, under the heading "Important to Slaveholders."

21. "Look Out for Rogues," *DP*, Sept. 7, 1845; *Beverley v. Captain and Owners*, 15 La. Ann. 432 (1860).

22. "A Cunning Darkie," *DP*, Feb. 6, 1838; "City Intelligence," *DP*, Sept. 18, 1949.

23. An example of a slave who made use of his color was Winn, a "bright mulatto" who tried to pass as a white man and a member of the Choctaw Nation, *AG*, May 20, 1853; see also Ned, *Mississippian*, Nov. 7, 1834. Norbon, *Natchez Courier and Journal*, Aug. 5, 1836; and William, *VG*, Oct. 31, 1836; Benjamin Drew, *The Refugee: A North-Side View of Slavery* (1856; Reading, MA: Addison-Wesley, 1969), 85–92. Whiteness was so useful in escapes that purchasers were leery of buying people with light skin; see Johnson, *Soul by Soul*, 151.

24. *Williamson v. Norton* (Western World), No. 2427, 7 La. Ann. 393 (1852).

25. Peggy, *The Natchez*, June 12, 1830; Zabette, *AG*, July 20, 1831; Diana, *Memphis Enquirer*, Apr. 24, 1840; "A Runaway," *DP*, July 24, 1849.

26. Harry, *AG*, Sept. 19, 1832; "Runaway Negro," *Helena Spy*, May 28, 1838; Charles, *Natchez Courier*, Apr. 26, 1833.

27. "Another Runaway Negro Retaken," *DP*, June 21, 1840.

28. The case is *Dr. H. Daret v. Captain A. G. Gray*; see Schafer, *Slavery, the Civil Law*, 111–12.

29. Drew, *A Northside View of Slavery*, 183–85.

30. Henry A. Bullard and Thomas Curry, comps., *A New Digest of the Statute Laws of the State from the Change of Government to 1841* (New Orleans: E. Johns, 1842), 253; see for example, Rueben, *Ariel*, May 12, 1828.

31. *McMaster v. Beckwith*, No. 2017, 2 La. 329 (1831); *McMaster v. Beckwith*, HRSCL; Schafer, *Slavery, the Civil Law*, 98–100.

32. *Slater v. Holton*, No. 3894, 19 La. 39 (June 1841); *Slater v. Holton*, HRSCL.

33. *Winston v. Foster*, No. 4617, 5 Rob. 113 (La. 1843); *Winter v. Foster*, HRSCL. For the fine provision, see Meiner, *The Louisiana Digest, 1804–1841*, sec. 1450, p. 213.

34. *Buel v. New York*, No. 3689, 15 La. 251 (1840), *Buel v. New York*, HRSCL; *Hurst v. Wallace*, No. 2402, 5 La. 98 (1833). Schafer, *Slavery, the Civil Law*, 105–6, 108.

35. *George A. Botts v. Cochrane*, No. 1013, 4 La. Ann. 35 (1849); "Supreme Court of Louisiana, Condensed Decisions," *DP* Jan. 27, 1849; "Another Runaway Negro Brought Home," *DP*, July 27, 1840.

CHAPTER 5

1. Paul D. Lack, "An Urban Slave Community: Little Rock, 1831–1862," *Arkansas Historical Quarterly* 41, no. 3 (Autumn 1982): 279.

2. Lack, "An Urban Slave Community," 272–74. On Matilda Fulton, see Jessica Parker Morgan, "'Keeping All Hands Moving': A Plantation Mistress in Antebellum Arkansas," *Arkansas Historical Quarterly* 74, no. 3 (2015): 257–76. Of the fourteen slaves she supervised, five, including two women, were hired out part of the time, and two more made regular trips into Little Rock to pick up the mail. Ibid., 262. See also Michael Pierce, "The Mechanics of Little Rock: Free Labor Ideas in Antebellum Arkansas, 1845–1861," *Arkansas Historical Quarterly* 67, no. 3 (2008): 221–44, esp. 262.

3. Lack, "An Urban Slave Community," 275–79; Henry, *AG*, May 17, 1836; John, *AG*, Nov. 9, 1841; Moses, *AG*, Aug. 20, 1844; Tom, *AG*, Apr. 6, 1857.

4. Richter, "Slavery in Baton Rouge," 134–41; "Louisiana Legislature," *Daily Advocate* (Baton Rouge), May 12, 1857, 1.

5. *William Johnson's Natchez*, 80, 90–91, 135, 137–38, 225.

6. *William Johnson's Natchez*, 276, 303, 321–22, 327, 331, 347.

7. *William Johnson's Natchez*, 446, 450–51.

8. *William Johnson's Natchez*, 468–70; On slavery in Natchez, see Ronald F. L. Davis, *The Black Experience in Natchez, 1720–1880*, rev. ed. (Natchez National Historical Park, 2008), 1–124.

9. James, *Antebellum Natchez*, 172–73.

10. *Dunbar v. Skillman*, 9 Martin's Reports, 285 (1828); *Dunbar v. Skillman*, HRSCL.

11. "An African Bandit in Natchez," *MFT*, June 14, 1848; "The Bandit 'Sol,'" *MFT*, 21, 1848.

12. An Act to Incorporate into One Act the Several Acts Incorporating the City of Memphis and the Town of South Memphis, Dec. 3, 1849, L. J. Dupree, *A Digest of the Ordinances of the City of Memphis, From the Year 1826 to 1857: Together with All Acts of the Legislature of Tennessee that Related Exclusively to Memphis* (Memphis, TN: Memphis Bulletin Company, 1857), 27–37; *Seventh Census of the U.S.*, 575; *Population of the U.S. in 1860*, xxxii, 467; Capers, *Biography of a River Town*, 77–78, 101; Dupree, *Digest of Ordinances*, 197–98; "Summary of Minutes of City Council, Board of Health, etc.: City of Memphis, Part I: 1826–1855," typescript, Memphis Public Library, 64.

13. "Negroes in the City," *Memphis Daily Eagle*, Nov. 8, 1849.

14. Race & Slavery Petitions Project, University of North Carolina, at Greensboro, PAR 11484205 (accessed Aug. 23, 2018); "Summary of Minutes of City Council," 64; Martha, *Memphis Enquirer*, May 3, 1839; Amanda, *Memphis Daily Appeal*, Jan. 1, 1857; Mulatto Girl, *Memphis Daily Appeal*, Sept. 19, 1857.

15. Dupree, *Digest of Ordinances*, 122–26.

16. "Summary of Minutes of City Council," 17, 26–30, 34, 71, 91, 93, 131, 194; Dupree, *Digest of Ordinances*, 162–65; Smith P. Bankhead, *Digest of the Charters and Ordinances of the City of Memphis, from 1826 to 1860 inclusive, Together with the Acts of the Legislature Relating to the city, and municipal corporations generally* (Memphis: Saunders, Oberly, & Jones, 1860), 346–60. On runaways, see Patterson, *The Negro in Tennessee*, 41–43.

17. Memphis Police Blotter, 1858–1860, Shelby County Archives, Memphis, Tennessee.

18. Meigs and Cooper, eds., *Code of Tennessee, 1857–8*, 505–6. For Memphis ordinances dealing with slavery, see Dupree, *Digest of Ordinances*, 122–23; and Bankhead, *Digest of Ordinances*, 360–64.

19. Memphis Police Blotter, 1858–1860, Shelby County Archives, Memphis, Tennessee.

20. [Joseph Holt Ingraham], *The Southwest: by a Yankee* (New York: Harper & Brothers, 1835); "Joseph Holt Ingraham," s.v., *American National Biography Online* (New York: Oxford University Press, 2000).

21. Ingraham, *Southwest by a Yankee*, 1:99–103.

22. Ingraham, *Southwest by a Yankee*, 1:92–94, 100.

23. James Silk Buckingham, *The Slaves States of America* (London: Fisher & Son, 1842); *Oxford Dictionary of National Biography*, s.v. Buckingham, James Silk.

24. Buckingham, *Slave States*, 1:327.

25. Buckingham, *Slave States*, 1:331–33, 337, 340–42.

26. Buckingham, *Slave States*, 1:360; B. M. Norman, *Norman's New Orleans and Environs: Containing a Brief Historical Sketch of the Territory and State of Louisiana and the City of New Orleans* (New York: D. Appleton & Co., 1845), 49–50, 76–80.

27. John Kendall, *History of New Orleans* (Chicago: Lewis, 1922), 70–73, 138–39, 172–75; Robert C. Reinders, *End of an Era: New Orleans 1850* (New Orleans: Pelican, 1964), 51–55; Joseph G. Tregle Jr., *Louisiana in the Age of Jackson: A Clash of Personalities and Culture* (Baton Rouge: University of Louisiana Press, 1999), 307–8; Richard Campanella, *Geographies of New Orleans: Urban Fabrics before the Storm* (Lafayette: University of Louisiana at Lafayette Press, 2006), 211–13, 250–53.

28. Buckingham, *Slave States*, 1:335, 355–56, 375–77.

29. "Kaleidoscopic View of New Orleans," *DP*, Sept. 23, 1843; Olmsted, *Cotton Kingdom*, 233; Campanella, *Geographies of New Orleans*, 9–13; US Census, *Population of the United States in 1860*, 194–96; Earl J. Niehaus, *The Irish in New Orleans, 1800–1860* (Baton Rouge: Louisiana State University Press, 1965), 37–57.

30. James Stuart, *Three Years in North America* (Edinburgh: Robert Cadell, 1833), 2:194–95, 206.

31. Judith Kelleher Schafer, "New Orleans Slavery in 1850 as Seen in Advertisements," *Journal of Southern History* 47, no. 1 (Feb. 1981), and John W. Blassingame, "The Negro in Antebellum New Orleans: Background for

Reconstruction," 348, in Carolyn N. De Latte, ed., *Antebellum Louisiana 1820–1860: Part A, Life and Labor, Louisiana Purchase Bicentennial Series in Louisiana History* (Lafayette: University of Louisiana at Lafayette Press, 2004), 348. "Monthly Passes to Negroes," *DP*, Oct. 22, 1859; "Master and Slave," *DP*, Jan. 27, 1859.

32. The New Orleans advertisement numbers are based on Schafer, "New Orleans Slavery in 1850," 43; the percentages of females are from Virginia Meacham Gould, "'The House that was Never a Home': Slave Family and Household Organization in New Orleans, 1820–1850," *Slavery and Abolition* 18, no. 2 (Aug. 1997): 93, 95–96; data on Lower Mississippi Valley advertisements come from LMVRS. See also Franklin and Schweninger, *Runaway Slaves,* 210.

33. Lucy Brown, *DP*, Sept. 17, 1841; George Anderson, *DP*, Feb. 5, 1848; Gus or Gustus, *DP*, June 10, 1848; Ellis, *DP*, June 13, 1848; Betsy, *DP*, Oct. 19, 1848; Dennis, *DP*, Jan. 19, 1855; Ben Nash, *DP*, May 18, 1855; Susan, *DP*, Mar. 20, 1855; Ben, *DP*, Mar. 30, 1855; Philina, *DP*, June 3, 1855; Oscar Dunn, *DP*, Dec. 9, 1841; Isaac, *DP*, Apr. 14, 1848; George Allen Blackson, *DP*, Jan. 6, 1855; John Cunningham, *DP*, Mar. 4, 1841; Isom Bondy, *DP*, Jan. 2, 1848.

34. Dan, *DP*, Jan. 16, 1848; Morris Butler, *DP*, Aug. 8, 1848; Brazile, *DP*, Mar. 1, 1848.

35. Sarah, *DP*, Sept. 13, 1848; Calip, *DP*, Jan. 18, 1848; Bill, *DP*, May 28, 1848; Dan, *DP*, Sept. 25, 1855.

36. Lislet, *A General Digest of the Acts of the State of Louisiana*, sec. 1, p. 100; ibid., sec. 30, pp. 107–6.

37. Leovy, *Ordinances of the City of New Orleans*, nos. 750–58, pp. 257–62.

38. Dennis C. Rousey, *Policing the Southern City: New Orleans, 1805–1889* (Baton Rouge: Louisiana State University Press, 1996), 14–19, 25–38; Dennis C. Rousey, "Cops and Guns: Police Use of Deadly Force in Nineteenth-Century New Orleans," *American Journal of Legal History* 28, no. 1 (Jan. 1984): 43–51, esp. 47n15; Reinders, *End of an Era*, 63–65; Kendall, *History of New Orleans*, 1:70–73. See also Stacy K. McGoldrick, "The Policing of Slavery in New Orleans, 1852–1860," *Journal of Historical Sociology* 14, no. 4 (Dec. 2001): 397–417.

39. "The City: Runaway Negroes," *DP*, Oct. 27, 1858; "Picking Pockets," *DP*, Dec. 28, 1843; "City Council, Second Municipality Council," *DP*, June 19, 1850.

40. "The City: Runaway Negroes," *DP*, Oct. 27, 1858.

41. "City News: Strayed Cow and Caged Negro," *DP*, May 28, 1856; "The City: Overdoing Things," *DP*, Oct. 1, 1857.

42. "John Otto Green," *DP*, Dec. 9, 1843; "The City: Before recorder Ramos," *DP*, May 8, 1856.

43. "Office of the Chief of Police," *DP*, Nov. 16, 1854, "Office of the Chief of Police," *DP*, June 15, 1854. The data for this period is generally consistent with monthly reports that newspapers printed from time to time. See *DP*, "City Intelligence," Dec. 8, 1852; "Office of the Chief of Police," *DP*, Mar. 18, 1855; "Office of the Chief of Police, *DP*, Feb. 24, 1855; *Daily Creole*, Aug. 5, 1856.

44. "Recorder Baldwin's Court," *DP*, Aug. 10, 1849; "City Intelligence, Arrests," Jan. 1, 1851; "City Intelligence: Third Municipality," *DP*, Nov. 16, 1851; "City Intelligence," *DP*, Mar. 22, 1854.

45. "City Intelligence," *DP*, Sept. 9, 1858; "The Courts, Stealing Cigars," *DP*, June 15, 1855; "City Intelligence," *DP*, Nov. 16, 1853; "The City, Police Matters," *DP*,

Oct. 16, 1855; "City Intelligence, Runaway," *DP*, July 9, 1853; "The City, Suspected Negro," *DP*, Dec. 1, 1858.

46. Dan, *DP*, June 30, 1841; Ann, *DP*, Jan. 26, 1848; Dennis, *DP*, Jan. 19, 1855; Dennis, *DP*, June 9, 1855; Robert, *DP*, Dec. 7, 1841; Elizabeth, *DP*, June 22, 1841.

47. Peter, *DP*, June 17, 1841; Louisa, *DP*, July 20, 1841; Daphne, *DP*, Dec. 9, 1841.

48. "City Intelligence," *DP*, Jan. 21, 1852.

49. "City Intelligence: Charge of Harboring a Slave," *DP*, Mar. 11, 1852; "City Intelligence: Harboring a Runaway," *DP*, May 6, 1851.

50. "A Runaway Caught," *DP*, Mar. 7, 1843; Hal, *DP*, Feb. 9, 1843.

51. "Police Matters," *Daily True Delta*, July 28, 1859; "Dangerous Assault," *DP*, Sept. 8, 1840; "Attempt to Murder," *DP*, May 23, 1843; "Negro Audacity," *DP*, Nov. 19, 1840.

52. "Fired On," *DP*, Mar. 20, 1845; *Evening Post* (New York), Oct. 31, 1836; "Murdered," *DP*, Dec. 22, 1843.

53. Henry C. Castellanos, *New Orleans as It Was: Episodes of Louisiana Life* (1976; Baton Rouge: Louisiana State University Press, 2006), 209–16; Bryan Wagner, "Disarmed and Dangerous: The Strange Career of Bras-Coupee," *Representations* 92, no. 1 (Fall 2005): 124–25.

54. Notice, *Courrier de la Louisiane*, Apr. 15, 1822, *Louisiana Advertiser*, quoted in *Spectator* (New York), vol. 39, issue 46, p. 4; "Breaking Up a Gang of Negroes," *DP*, Oct. 30, 1846; "Runaway Negroes' Camp," *DP*, Mar. 30, 1848.

55. The most reliable sources on Bras Coupee are the obituaries in *DP*, "Squire—The Outlaw!" *DP*, July 19, 1837, and in *Bee*, "Death of Squire," July 20, 1837. Castellanos's account adds details but is congruent with those in the newspapers.

CHAPTER 6

1. Peter H. Wood, *Black Majority: Negroes in Colonial South Carolina from 1670 through the Stono Rebellion* (New York: Alfred A. Knopf, 1974), 239; and Thomas D. Morris, *Southern Slavery and the Law, 1619–1860* (Chapel Hill: University of North Carolina Press, 1996), 340–41.

2. *State v. William Thompson, alias Robinson, and S. J. Baer*, 13 A. N. Ogden, 515, 516 (1858). That most slaves were stolen by people who intended to sell them is the author's impression based on evidence collected for this study, but see also Larry Gara, *The Liberty Line: The Legend of the Underground Railroad* (1961; Lexington: University Press of Kentucky, 1996), 85–86.

3. The now commonly used "friends of the fugitive" term comes from Gara, *The Liberty Line*, 93.

4. Morris, *Southern Slavery and the Law*, 2, and throughout; the double character term was coined in 1858 but is elaborated in Ariela J. Gross, *Double Character: Slavery and Mastery in the Antebellum Southern Courtroom* (Athens: University of Georgia Press, 2000), 3, and throughout; on the Arkansas cases, see J. W. Looney, *Distinguishing the Righteous from the Roguish: The Arkansas Supreme Court, 1836–1874* (Fayetteville: University of Arkansas Press, 2016), 141, 148. While slaves could be punished for their crimes against the state, owners were sometimes required to make restitution for the property damages they had caused; in Arkansas they could sometimes make restitution and then punish the slaves themselves to avoid losing

the labor of the slave. When slaves were executed for murder, owners were often reimbursed for the loss of property. See Morris, *Southern Slavery and the Law*, 253–61; and Looney, *Distinguishing the Righteous from the Roguish*, 140.

5. *The Revised Statutes of Louisiana*, U. B. Phillips, comp. (New Orleans: John Claiborne, 1856), Black Code, sec. 31, p. 54.

6. *A Digest of the Statutes of Arkansas*, E. H. English, comp. (Little Rock: Reardon & Garrett, 1848), 337–40; *The Revised Code of the State of Mississippi* (Jackson, MS: E. Barksdale, 1857), Articles 190, 192, pp. 603–4; Josiah Gould, *A Digest of the Statutes of Arkansas: All Laws of a General and Permanent Character in Force at the Close of the General Assembly of 1856* (Little Rock, AR: Johnson & Yerkes, 1858), 341–42, 344–45; Return J. Meigs and William F. Cooper, eds., *The Code of Tennessee Enacted by the General Assembly 1857–58* (Nashville: E. G. Eastman, 1858), 514; *Revised Statutes of Louisiana*, Black Code, sec. 21, p. 52.

7. *State v. Thompson, alias Robinson, and S. J. Baer*, 13 A. N. Ogden, 515 (1858).

8. Sophy, *MSG*, June 10, 1820; Octavia, *MSG*, Apr. 29, 1820; Toby, Maley, and Eliza, *MSG*, Mar. 19, 1825; Bill, Ann, and Lucy, *Ariel*, June 28, 1828.

9. "500 Reward," *Woodville Republican* (Woodville, MS), about Sept. 16, 1834; Hogan, *William Johnson's Natchez*, 79.

10. Featherstonhaugh, *Excursion*, 95; Looney, *Distinguishing the Righteous from the Roguish*, 205–26; Philip D. Jordan, *Frontier Law and Order: Ten Essays* (Lincoln: University of Nebraska Press, 1970), esp. chap. 2, "The Mississippi: Spillway of Sin." On Arkansas geography, see chap. 2, above.

11. "300 Reward," *AG*, Aug. 2, 1836; Judge William F. Pope, *Early Days in Arkansas, Being for the Most Part the Personal Recollections of an Old Settler* (Little Rock, AR: Frederick W. Allsopp, 1895), 206–11.

12. Abraham, *AG*, Mar. 19, 1822; James, *AG*, Mar. 23, 1823; William, *AG*, Sept. 4, 1835.

13. Hannah, *Randolph Recorder*, Sept. 25, 1835. See also "Arrest of a Rogue," *DP*, Aug. 11, 1841.

14. Bill and Family *AG*, Oct. 26, 1831; Shadrach and Isham, *AG*, Jan. 25, 1833; Willis and Stephen, *AG*, Apr. 19, 1832.

15. "Another Murder," *AG*, Oct. 21, 1828.

16. On Latham and Randolph, see Williams, "Memphis' Early Triumph," 15–22; "Arkansas Robbers," *Randolph Recorder* (Randolph, TN), June 21, 1834.

17. "Robbers and Counterfeiters," *Randolph Recorder*, Sept. 16, 1834. The enslaved man belonging to "Beanford" may have been Jack who ran away from James K. Polk's overseer Ephraim Beanfield in 1834, see above chapter 3.

18. "Kidnappers and Horse Thieves," *AG*, Mar. 10, 1835, reprinted in *Randolph Recorder*, Mar. 20, 1835; "Alarming Murder," *AG*, Mar. 31, 1835; *AG*, Apr. 7, 1835; *AG*, Apr. 14, 1835.

19. "Jail Delivery," *AG*, Apr. 7, 1835.

20. "Murderers and Thieves," *Randolph Recorder*, Apr. 24, 1835; "Arkansas Freebooters—Murder," *Randolph Recorder*, June 19, 1835.

21. The book was subtitled: *Together with his system of villainy, and plan of exciting a Negro rebellion. And a catalogue of the names of four hundred-five of his mystic clan, fellows and followers, and their efforts for the destruction of Virgil A. Stewart, the young man who detected him. To which is added a biographical sketch of Mr. Virgil A.*

Stewart. The author is given as Augustus A. Walton. The opening line is: "It has been a notorious fact, for a number of years past, that negroes and fine horses are frequently missing from the farms of planters and the citizens of the Mississippi Valley." James Lal Penick Jr., *The Great Western Land Pirate: John A. Murrell in Legend and History* (Columbia: University of Missouri Press, 1981), is the standard treatment of its subject; but the relevant portion of Joshua D. Rothman, *Flush Times and Fever Dreams: A Story of Capitalism and Slavery in the Age of Jackson* (Athens: University of Georgia Press, 2012), is now also required reading, particularly for its illuminating analysis of Virgil Stewart. On Murrell's early career, see Penick, 9–31; and Rothman, 29–35.

22. Rothman, *Flush Times and Fever Dreams*, 249.

23. Walton, *Great Western Land Pirate*, 14.

24. Walton, *Great Western Land Pirate*, 24–25.

25. Walton, *Great Western Land Pirate*, 20–22, 31–32, 43.

26. The court agreed that both men were guilty of the crime but reversed the conviction of Morehead because his confession was coerced in the presence of prosecuting attorney Tagert. *Morehead and Bryant v. The State* (Apr. 1849), 28 *Tennessee Reports*, 391–94.

27. H. R. Howard, comp., *The History of Virgil Stewart: and his adventure in capturing and exposing the Great 'Western Land Pirate' and his Gang in Connexion with the Evidence and also of the Trials, Confessions, and Execution of a Number of Murrell's Associates in the State of Mississippi during the Summer of 1835 and the Execution of Five Professional Gamblers by the Citizens of Vicksburg* (New York: Harper & Brothers, 1836), 26, 50, 99–102, 162–63; Penick, *Great Western Land Pirate*, 69–70.

28. Penick, *Great Western Land Pirate*, 86–96; Rothman, *Flush Times and Fever Dreams*, 59–65.

29. *AG*, June 2, 1835; "The Western Land Pirate," *AG*, Aug. 18, 1835, reprinted from the *Natchez Courier and Journal*.

30. See "The Projected Conspiracy," in *AG*, Sept. 1, 1835; and "Murrell the Insurrectionist," in *The Long-Island Star*, published in Brooklyn, Aug. 17, 1835. On the Madison County episode, see below, chap. 7.

31. Bill, *AG*, June 22, 1837; Lewis, *AG*, Feb. 1, 1839; "Jail Breaking," *DP*, Feb. 6, 1852.

32. A. B. Chambers, ed., *Trials and Confessions of Madison Henderson, alias Blanchard, Alfred Amos Warrick, James W. Seward, and Charles Brown, Murderers of Jesse Baker and Jacob Baker, as Given by Themselves; and a Likeness of Each Taken in Jail Shortly after their Arrest* (St. Louis: Chambers and Knapp, 1841). A full account of the episode is given in Mary E. Seematter, "Trials and Confessions: Race and Justice in Antebellum St. Louis," *Gateway Heritage* 12 (Fall 1991): 36–47. See also, Buchanan, *Black Life on the Mississippi*, 122–47, which puts the men and their story in the context of its subject; and Thomas C. Buchanan, "Rascals on the Antebellum Mississippi: African American Steamboat Workers and the St. Louis Hanging of 1841," *Journal of Social History* 34, no. 4 (Summer 2001): 797–816.

33. Chambers, ed., *Trials and Confessions*, 14–15.

34. Chambers, ed., *Trials and Confessions*, 18.

35. Chambers, ed., *Trials and Confessions*, 20–23.

36. Chambers, ed., *Trials and Confessions*, 23–24. On the Buels, see "Criminal Court," *DP*, Jan. 31, 1841; and "Arrest of Burglars," *DP*, Sept. 13, 1840.

37. Timothy F. Reilly, "Slave Stealing in the Early Domestic Trade as Revealed by a Loyal Manservant," *Louisiana History* 55, no. 1 (Winter 2014): 11n8, 15n15, 16n16, 18n19, 24n30; Frederick Bancroft, *Slave Trading in the Old South*, intro. Michael Tadman (Columbia: University of South Carolina Press, 1996; orig. publ. 1931), 58–65; and Wendall Holmes Stephenson, *Isaac Franklin: Slave Trader of the Old South* (Baton Rouge: Louisiana State University Press, 1938); "Arrest of Burglars," *DP*, Sept. 13, 1840.

38. Buchanan, *Black Life on the Mississippi*, 125–31; and Lee Sandlin, *Wicked River: The Mississippi When It Last Ran Wild* (New York: Pantheon Books, 2010), 84–90.

39. Chambers, ed., *Trials and Confessions*, 64–68.

40. Chambers, ed., *Trials and Confessions*, 69–70.

41. "Brown's Confession [to Bullard]," *Daily Missouri Republican*, July 10, 1841; "Brown's Confession," *Daily Missouri Republican*, July 14, 1841.

42. Quotes from "The Confessions of the Murderers," *DP*, July 20, 1841; see also "The Executions at St. Louis," *DP*, July 20, 1841, and "The Confessions of Brown," *DP*, July 29, 1841; "Free Negroes," *DP*, Aug. 22, 1841.

43. "Free Negroes," *DP*, Aug. 22, 1841.

44. "Caution to Steamboat and Ship Masters," *DP*, May 14, 1844.

45. "Negro Stealing," *DP*, Jan. 7, 1848; see also *State v. Banton*, 4 Robinson 31 (1849).

46. Bordewich, *Bound for Canaan*, 309–12.

47. "City Intelligence," *DP*, Nov. 11, 1848.

48. "Negro Stealing," *Daily True Delta* (New Orleans), Mar. 19, 1858, reprinted from the *Madison American*.

49. "Abolition Kidnappers," *DP*, Dec. 9, 1841.

50. "Caution to Steamboat and Ship Masters," *DP*, May 14, 1844; "Sentence for Slave Stealing," *DP*, Feb. 14, 1842; "An Abolitionist," *DP*, Feb. 11, 1842.

51. "Slave Stealing," *DP*, July 4, 1842.

52. Calvin Fairbank, *The Rev. Calvin Fairbank during Slavery Times: How he "Fought the Good Fight" to Prepare "the Way"* (n.p: R. R. McCabe & Co., 1890), 34-44, 46, 50; Fergus M. Bordewich, *Bound for Canaan: The Underground Railroad and the War for the Soul of America* (New York: HarperCollins Publishers, 2005) 209-211. See also "Glorious Old Thief," *Chicago Tribune*, Jan. 29, 1893., p. 33; and "Appeal for Help," *The Inter Ocean* (Chicago, IL), Mar. 21, 1889, p.5

53. "Runaway Negroes," *DP*, May 9, 1855.

54. "Slave Stealing," *DP*, Jan. 28, 1841; "Enticing Away Slaves," *DP*, Aug. 14, 1852.

55. "Slave Stealing," *DP*, Sept. 9, 1843; "The Case of Slave Stealing," *DP*, Sept. 14, 1843.

56. "Charge of Slave Stealing," *Daily Atlas* (Boston, MA), Nov. 16, 1846, reprinted from the "Bill Curtis," in *New Orleans Delta*, Nov. 6, 1846; "Charge of Negro Stealing," *DP*, Mar. 16, 1849.

57. Tilly, Nanny, and six children, *AG*, Oct. 8, 1838; Ann, *Memphis Appeal*, May 1, 1857.

58. "500 Reward," *AG*, Apr. 26, 1843.

59. "A Friendly Transaction," *DP*, Aug. 4, 1841.

60. "Charge of Slave Stealing," *DP*, Aug. 12, 1841.

61. "Charge of Slave Stealing," *DP*, Aug. 12, 1841; "A Liberal Reward," *Woodville Republican*, about Aug. 14, 1830.

62. "Escaped from Jail," *MFT*, Apr. 14, 1852, orig. in *Lauderdale Republican*, Mar. 27, 1852.

63. "Cool," *DP*, Oct. 3, 1847, taken from the *Alexandria Democrat*.

64. *Daily Advocate*, May 9, 1859, reprinted from the *Bayou Sara Ledger*.

CHAPTER 7

1. "Miscellaneous Records of a Tour among the Slave Plantations," *Frederick Douglass' Paper* (Rochester, NY), June 30, 1854.

2. Theodore D. Weld, *American Slavery As It Is: Testimony of a Thousand Witnesses* (New York: American Anti-Slavery Society, 1839), 62–63, 72–74; Ellen Gruber Garvey, "Nineteenth-Century Abolitionists and the Databases They Created," *Legacy: A Journal of American Women Writers* 27, no. 2 (2010): 356–59.

3. On fighting, see Elliot J. Gorn, "'Gouge and Bite, Pull Hair and Scratch': The Social Significance of Fighting in the Southern Backcountry," *American Historical Review* 90, no. 1 (Feb. 1985): 18–43; and Lussana, *My Brother Slaves*, 64–69. A study of Mississippi slave advertisements indicates that evidence of physical damage owing to accidents was roughly equal to that caused by punishment. See Eva Wade, "Contested Space, Mississippi Runaway Slave Advertisements, Violence and the Body," *Journal of Mississippi History* 75, no. 2 (Summer 2013): 108.

4. The original patrol law was passed in 1825; the provisions here are from an amended version passed in 1853. *Acts of the Territory of Arkansas* (1825), 15–17; Josiah Gould, *A Digest of the Statutes of Arkansas* (1856), 822–23. The quote from the Arkansas Supreme Court is in *Henry v. Armstrong*, which contains an extended discussion of the patrol law, 15 Ark. 162 (1854), 164. See also J. W. Looney, *Distinguishing the Righteous from the Roguish: The Arkansas Supreme Court, 1836–1874* (Fayetteville: University of Arkansas Press, 2016), 142–43; Orville W. Taylor, *Negro Slavery in Arkansas*, intro. Carl Moneyhon (1958; Fayetteville: University of Arkansas Press, 2000), 209–11. On patrols in general, see Sally E. Hadden, *Slave Patrols: Law and Violence in Virginia and the Carolinas* (Cambridge, MA: Harvard University Press, 2001), especially pp. 106–21 on duties and activities; Lankford, *Bearing Witness*, for the song, 105, and in general pp. 11, 87, 124, 185–86, 375–76, as well as other examples from the index. The large number of references suggest that some interviewers asked specifically about patrols and the KKK—which were sometimes conflated in the testimony, itself a telling error.

5. Levi Peirce, ed., *The Consolidation and Revision of the Statutes of the State . . . (1852)*; Hutchinson, *Code of Mississippi*, 527–30; Meigs and Cooper, *Code of Tennessee Enacted by the General Assembly of 1857–8*, 502.

6. *Henry v. Armstrong*, the quote is on p. 169.

7. *A. Duperrier v. B. Dutrieve et al.*, 12 La. Ann. 664 (1856).

8. The supreme court overturned the decision on a technicality. *Loussard v. Hartman, et al.*, 16 Curry 117 (1840).

9. *Thompson v. Young*, 30 Miss. 17 (Dec. 1855); English, *Digest of Arkansas*

Statutes, 944; Franklin and Schweninger, *Runaway Slaves*, 150–52; Morris, *Southern Slavery and the Law*, 163–71.

10. *Allain, f.m.c. v. Young*, No. 537, 9 Mart. (O.S.) 221 (La. 1821).

11. *J. B. Arandez v. Thomas B. Lawes*, 5 La. Ann. 127 (1850); see also Schafer, *Slavery, the Civil Law*, 46.

12. "Notes of Travel," *MFT*, Sept. 12, 1849.

13. "Runaway Negroes from Louisiana," *Pine Bluff Republican*, reprinted in *DP*, Oct. 13, 1851.

14. *DP*, Aug. 13, 1850, 1; *DP*, Sept. 5, 1850; *DP*, Oct. 14, 1852, 2; *DP*, Apr. 15, 1852, 2; "Runaway Shot," *MFT*, June 14, 1853; "From the Country," *DP*, Oct. 29, 1853.

15. "Death of a Runaway Negro," *Weekly Advocate*, Sept. 20, 1855.

16. *Albany Argus* (Albany, NY), Oct. 31, 1826; "Items, Melancholy Accident," *Liberator* (Boston, MA), June 25, 1841; "Painful Rumor," *DP*, Aug. 5, 1851.

17. "An Awful Tragedy," reprinted from a Cincinnati paper that had compiled the story from Memphis newspaper sources, *Sandusky Register* (Sandusky, OH), Jan. 22, 1851.

18. Elias Boatner, *Statesman and Gazette* (Natchez), Aug. 14, 1828.

19. "Horrid Murder," *DP*, Oct. 24, 1841, and "Captain De Hart's Murderers," *DP*, Nov. 3, 1841; Ann Patton Malone, *Sweet Chariot: Slave Family and Household Structure in Nineteenth-Century Louisiana* (Chapel Hill: University of North Carolina Press, 1992), 82–84; "Louisiana Items," *DP*, Mar. 27, 1852.

20. "Negro Villainy," *DP*, Aug. 5, 1840; "Daring Attempt," *DP*, Sept. 5, 1840.

21. "Murder by a Slave," *DP*, Sept. 18, 1941.

22. "Murder," *DP*, Aug. 19, 1842.

23. *DP*, July 17, 1844, 2; "Diabolical Murder," *DP*, Feb. 8, 1845; "Horrible Affair," *DP*, Oct. 18, 1845; "Atrocious Murder," *DP*, July 22, 1848.

24. "Louisiana News," *DP*, Apr. 26, 1853.

25. "Dreadful Tragedy," *MFT*, Nov. 29, 1853.

26. "A Desperate Runaway," *DP*, June 2, 1850; "Louisiana Legislature," *DP*, Mar. 24, 1853; "From the Empire Parish," *DP*, July 18, 1854; "Louisiana Intelligence," from the *Monroe Register*, *DP*, June 26, 1857; "Conspiracy Discovered," *Memphis Daily Appeal*, Aug. 14, 1856.

27. "Killed by a Runaway Negro," from the *Memphis Avalanche*, *Frederick Douglass' Paper*, Sept. 17, 1858.

28. *DP*, Aug. 28, 1840, 2; "Runaway Negroes," *DP*, June 23, 1842; "Runaway Negroes, *DP*, Mar. 21, 1843; "An Armed Runaway Arrested," *DP*, June 30, 1843.

29. "To be Hanged," *DP*, Aug. 27, 1852.

30. *Caddo Gazette*, reprinted in *DP*, Oct. 31, 1853.

31. "Arrest of a Daring Outlaw in Lafourche Parish," *DP*, Sept. 28, 1854.

32. "Things About Town, Arrest," *Daily Advocate*, Aug. 20, 1855.

33. "The Eighth of January" and "Desperate Negroes Armed to the Teeth," *Daily Advocate* (Baton Rouge), Jan. 8, 1856.

34. "Arson and Robbery," from the *Weekly Magnolia* of Plaquemine Parish, *Daily True Delta*, Oct. 18, 1859.

35. "Runaway Negroes," *DP*, July 23, 1845; "Capture of Runaway Negroes," reprinted from the *Vicksburg Whig*, *DP*, Dec. 12, 1856.

36. John Hope Franklin, *The Militant South: 1800–1860* (Cambridge, MA:

Harvard University Press, 1956), 34. On the white response to the danger of slave revolts, see Bertram Wyatt-Brown, *Southern Honor: Ethics and Behavior in the Old South* (New York: Oxford University Press, 1982), chap. 15, "Policing Slave Society: Insurrectionary Scares."

37. The most thorough account of these events is in Rothman, *Flush Times and Fever Dreams,* 91–152; but see also Johnson, *River of Dark Dreams,* 46–58. Most of the documentary evidence on the Madison County events are in "Proceedings at Livingston," in Howard, *History of Virgil Stewart,* 221–62.

38. Alice Bayne Windham Webb, ed., *Mistress of Evergreen Plantation: Rachel O'Connor's Legacy of Letters, 1823–1845* (Albany: State University of New York Press, 1983), 37.

39. Webb, ed., *Mistress of Evergreen Plantation,* 62–63, 184. See also Judith Kelleher Schafer, "The Immediate Impact of Nat Turner's Insurrection on New Orleans," *Louisiana History* 21, no. 4 (Autumn 1980), 362–64.

40. "A Negro Revolt," *DP,* Sept. 1, 1840; "Negro Insurrection in Lafayette," *DP,* Sept. 2, 1840; "The Lafayette Insurrection," *DP,* Sept. 22, 1840. "From the *Attakapos* [sic] *Gazette,*" *Liberator* (Boston), Feb. 26, 1841; "Murder Frustrated," *DP,* June 13, 1841.

41. "The Insurrection," *DP,* July 29, 1841. See also *DP,* Aug. 12, 1841, 2; and *North American* (Philadelphia, PA), Aug. 3, 1841, 2.

42. Davis, ed. *Plantation Life,* 236–37.

43. "Negro Insurrection," *DP,* Nov. 17, 1842, "Runaways," from the *St. Francisville Chronicle, Alexandria Gazette* (Alexandria, VA), May 2, 1844.

44. Davis, ed. *Plantation Life,* 323, 341–43.

45. Hadden, *Slave Patrols,* 8–14, 17–20, 30–32, 35–38, 208–11; Lankford, ed., *Bearing Witness,* 201, 321.

46. Kelly Houston Jones, "'Doubtless Guilty': Lynching and Slaves in Antebellum Arkansas," in *Bullets and Fire: Lynching and Authority in Arkansas, 1840–1950,* ed. Guy Lancaster (Fayetteville: University of Arkansas Press, 2018), 17–34; and Vincent Vinikas, "Thirteen Dead at St. Charles: Arkansas's Most Lethal Lynching and the Abrogation of Equal Protection," Lancaster, ed., *Bullets and Fire,* 103–30.

CHAPTER 8

1. Stanley Harrold, *Border War: Fighting over Slavery before the Civil War* (Chapel Hill: University of North Carolina Press, 2010), 2–12; Manisha Sinha, *The Slave's Cause: A History of Abolition* (New Haven, CT: Yale University Press, 2016), 382.

2. For more on this issue, see Thomas F. Harwood, "The Abolitionist View of Louisiana and Mississippi," *Louisiana History* 7, no. 4 (Autumn 1966): 281–308.

3. John C. Calhoun, Address of the Hon. John C. Calhoun, in the Senate of the United States, Slavery: [read for him by Hon. Mr. Mason, March 4, 1850] (Washington, 1850).

4. Don E. Fehrenbacher, *The Slaveholding Republic: An Account of the United States Government's Relations to Slavery* (New York: Oxford University Press, 2001), 33–36, 205–9; Paul Finkleman, *Slavery and the Founding Fathers: Race and Liberty in the Age of Jefferson* (Armonk, NY: M. E. Sharpe, 2014), 83–91.

5. Paul Finkleman, "The Kidnapping of John Davis and the Adoption of the Fugitive Slave Law of 1793," *Journal of Southern History* 56, no. 3 (Aug. 1990): 397–422.

6. Harrold, *Border War: Fighting over Slavery*, 2–12; Morris, *Free Men All*, 51–52, 55–56. Recent work on the fugitive slave issue: Bordewich, *Bound for Canaan*; Steven Lubet, *Fugitive Justice: Runaways, Rescuers, and Slavery on Trial* (Cambridge, MA: Harvard University Press, 2010); and Foner, *Gateway to Freedom*.

7. The Holmes and Davis letter to Mayor Watson and his reply to them, his letter to Walker, and his public letter to the people of Philadelphia are all in *Ariel*, Mar. 2, 1827. The "Narrative of Lydia Smith" is also in the same *Ariel* story, but the "Narrative of Peter Hook" is not. It did appear in the *Poughkeepsie Journal* (Poughkeepsie, NY), on Jan. 31, 1827, and probably many other papers as well. Those two accounts as well as one by Samuel Scoup, who was rescued at Rocky Springs, appear in John W. Blassingame, *Slave Testimony: Two Centuries of Letters, Speeches, Interviews, and Autobiographies* (Baton Rouge: Louisiana State University Press, 1977), 178–84. The Mississippi events and the history of the Cannon-Davis gang are discussed by Carol Wilson, *Freedom at Risk: The Kidnapping of Free Blacks in America, 1785–1865* (Lexington: University Press of Kentucky, 1994), 23–30.

8. *Jack, a negro man, v. Mary Martin*, 12 Wendell 311 (1834); *Jack, a negro man, v. Mary Martin* 14 Wendell 507 (1835), quotes on 530 and 532; "Jack, a Negro Man, vs. Mary Martin," *Journal of Commerce* reprinted in the *Evening Post*, Aug. 18, 1835; "In the Court of Errors," *Evening Post*, Aug. 19, 1835; "Case of a Runaway Slave," *Journal of Commerce*, reprinted in the *Liberator*, Sept. 7, 1833. Morris, *Free Men All*, 64–69, discusses these cases; on the efforts of New York abolitionists on behalf of fugitive slaves, see Foner, *Gateway to Freedom*, esp. 51–56.

9. *Prigg v. Com. Of Pennsylvania 41 U.S. 539* (1842); Paul Finkleman, "*Prigg v. Pennsylvania* and Northern State Courts: Anti-Slavery Use of a Pro-Slavery Decision," *Civil War History* 25, no. 1 (1979): 6–14; Fehrenbacker, *Slaveholding Republic*, 219–22. See also Paul Finkleman, "Story Telling on the Supreme Court: *Prigg v. Pennsylvania* and Justice Joseph Story's Judicial Nationalism," *Supreme Court Review* (1994): 274–91.

10. Here and below, unless otherwise indicated, the Hannum narrative comes from "The Case of Captain Hannum" (which includes Hannum letter of Sept. 11), *DP*, Sept. 25, 1846; "The Kidnapper Captain" (which includes the Hannum letter of Sept. 16), *Pennsylvania Freeman* (Philadelphia, PA), Nov. 5, 1846; and "Great Meeting at Faneuil Hall," *Boston Courier*, Sept. 28, 1846.

11. "To the Public," *Liberator* (Boston, MA), Jan. 1, 1831; Leonard W. Levy, *The Law of the Commonwealth and Chief Justice Shaw* (Cambridge, MA: Harvard University Press, 1957), 72–85; Morris, *Free Men All*, 111–16, quote on 116.

12. "To the Public," *Liberator* (Boston, MA), Jan. 1, 1831; Levy, *The Law of the Commonwealth*, 72–85; Morris, *Free Men All*, 111–16, quote on 116; *Revised Statutes of the Commonwealth of Massachusetts* (Boston, 1836), chap. 125, sec. 20.

13. Quote from "The Kidnapper Captain."

14. "Charge of Kidnapping," from the *Boston Traveller, Commercial Advertiser* (New York), Sept. 11, 1846, quote from "The Kidnapper Captain."

15. "Great Meeting at Faneuil Hall," *Boston Courier*, Sept. 28, 1846.

16. "The Kidnapper Captain," *Pennsylvania Freeman*, Nov. 5, 1846 (comment

relates to Sept. 11 letter). "The Fugitive Slave Case," *Daily Atlas* (Boston, MA), Oct. 1, 1846; *DP,* Oct. 2, 1846; "Captain Hannum," letter of Sept. 22, reprinted from *DP, The Liberator,"* Oct. 23, 1846. "The Kidnapper Captain," *Pennsylvania Freeman,* Nov. 5, 1846.

17. "A Runaway Brought Back," *DP*, Oct. 13, 1846; "The Case of Captain Hannum," *Boston Evening Transcript* (Boston, MA), Sept. 26, 1841; Foner, *Gateway to Freedom*, 112–14.

18. "'Another Douglass' in the Field," *Emancipator and Republican* (Boston, MA), Aug. 25, 1847.

19. "Running Off a Slave," *DP*, June 24, 1842.

20. "A Scene on the Mississippi," *North Star* (Rochester, NY), Dec. 29, 1848.

21. "More Disclosures in Regard to the Murder of Mr. Todd," *Concordia Intelligencer* (Vidalia, LA), June 11, 1842, reprinted in "The Slave Murders and the Executions at Union Point, Louisiana," *MFT*, Feb. 28, 1854.

22. "Horrible Murder by Negroes," *DP*, June 1842.

23. "A Tale of Horror," *Philadelphia Inquirer*, June 18, 1842.

24. "Horrible Murders by Negroes," *New York Tribune*, June 18, 1842; "Horrible Murders by Negroes," *Evening Post* (New York), June 18, 1842; "Horrible Murder by Negroes," *Spectator* (New York), June 22, 1842; "Horrible Murder by Negroes," *Commercial Advertiser* (New York), June 18, 1842. Other papers that carried the story include *Painesville Telegraph* (Painesville, OH), June 29, 1842; *Sentinel of Freedom* (Newark, NJ), June 21, 1842; *Massachusetts Spy* (Worcester, MA), June 22, 1842; *New-Bedford Mercury* (New Bedford, MA), June 24, 1842; *Republican Farmer* (Bridgeport, CT), June 21, 1842; *Jamestown Journal* (Jamestown, NY), June 30, 1842; *Southern Patriot* (Charleston, SC), June 16, 1842; *Norfolk Democrat* (Dedham, MA), June 24, 1842; *Alexandria Gazette* (Alexandria, VA), June 18, 1842; *Maine Cultivator and Hallowell Gazette* (Hallowell, NH), July 2, 1842; *Easton Gazette* (Easton, MD), July 2, 1842; *Wisconsin Enquirer* (Madison, WI), July 23, 1842; *Adams Sentinel* (Gettysburg, PA), June 27, 1842; *Hillsborough Recorders* (Hillsborough, NC), June 30, 1942; *Wisconsin Express* (Madison, WI), July 21, 1842; *Tarboro Press* (Tarboro, NC); *Southport Telegraph* (Southport, WI), July 13, 1942; *Sunbury American* (Sunbury, PA), June 25, 1842; *Wilmington Chronicle* (Wilmington, NC), June 22, 1942; *Newark Daily Advertiser* (Newark, NJ), June 18, 1842; *Sentinel of Freedom* (Newark, NJ), June 21, 1842; *North Carolina Star* (Raleigh, NC), June 22, 1842.

25. "Fiendish Barbarity !!!," *Liberator*, July 1, 1842.

26. Both the letter and the *Tribune* are given in "Abolition Falsehood," *MFT*, Feb. 28, 1854. The *Free Trader*'s response is given in "Singular Misrepresentation," *Washington Star* (Washington, DC), Mar. 8, 1854. Other papers that carried the same article as the *Tribune* included the *Herald of Freedom* (Wilmington, OH), Feb. 17, 1854; *Albany Evening Journal* (Albany, NY), Feb. 2, 1854; and *New York Evening Post*, Feb. 3, 1854.

27. "Abolition Falsehood," *MFT*, Feb. 28, 1854.

28. "Correction," *New York Tribune*, Mar. 6, 1854.

29. "Explosion of a Humbug," *Brooklyn Daily Eagle*, Mar. 10, 1854; *Newport Mercury*, (Newport, RI), Mar. 11, 1854; *Journal of Commerce* reprinted in *Dispatch* (Richmond, VA), Mar. 7, 1854; "Abolition Falsehood," *Tri-Weekly Commercial* (Wilmington, NC), Mar. 4, 1854; "Correction," *New York Tribune*, Mar. 6, 1854;

"Explosion of a Humbug," *Brooklyn Daily Eagle*, Mar. 10, 1854; *Newport Mercury* (Newport, RI), Mar. 11, 1854; *Journal of Commerce* reprinted in *Dispatch* (Richmond, VA), Mar. 7, 1854; "The New Orleans Bulletin," *Pittsburgh Gazette* (Pittsburgh, PA), Mar. 10, 1854.

30. "Abolition Slanders and Southern Savages," *Washington Sentinel* (Washington, DC), Mar. 10, 1854. Other newspapers included *Democratic Pioneer* (Elisabeth City, NC), Mar. 21, 1854; *Brooklyn Daily Eagle* (Brooklyn, NY), Mar. 10, 1854; and the *National Era* (Washington, DC), Mar. 8, 1854.

BIBLIOGRAPHY

BOOKS

Abbot, Benjamin Vaughn, ed. *United States Digest: A Digest of Decisions of the Various Courts Within the United States from the Earliest Period to the Year 1870.* Vol. 12. Boston: Little, Brown, and Company, 1879.

Allain, Mathé. *"Not Worth a Straw": French Colonial Policy and the Early Years of Louisiana.* Lafayette: University of Louisiana at Lafayette Press, 1988.

Arkansas Territory. *Acts Passed at the Fourth Session of the General Assembly of the Territory of Arkansas: Which Was Begun and Held at the Town of Little Rock, on Monday, the Third Day of October, and Ended on Thursday, the Third Day of November, One Thousand Eight Hundred and Twenty-Five.* Little Rock: Wm. E. Woodruff, Printer to the Territory, 1826.

Arnold, Morris S. *Colonial Arkansas, 1686–1804: A Social and Cultural History.* Fayetteville: University of Arkansas Press, 1991.

———. *The Rumble of a Distant Drum: The Quapaws and Their World, 1673–1804.* Fayetteville: University of Arkansas Press, 2000.

———. *Unequal Laws Unto a Savage Race: European Legal Traditions in Arkansas, 1686–1836.* Fayetteville: University of Arkansas Press, 1985.

Asbury, Herbert. *The French Quarter: An Informal History of the New Orleans Underground.* New York: Basic Books, 2003. Originally published 1936.

Baker, T. Harri. *The* Memphis Commercial Appeal: *The History of a Southern Newspaper.* Baton Rouge: Louisiana State University Press, 1971.

Bancroft, Frederick. *Slave Trading in the Old South.* Columbia: University of South Carolina Press, 1996.

Bankhead, Smith P. *Digest of the Charters and Ordinances of the City of Memphis, from 1826 to 1860 inclusive, Together with the Acts of the Legislature Relating to the city, and municipal corporations generally.* Memphis: Saunders, Oberly, & Jones, 1860.

Baptist, Edward E. *The Half Has Never Been Told: Slavery and the Making of American Capitalism.* New York: Basic Books, 2014.

Bassett, John Spencer, and James K. Polk. *The Southern Plantation Overseer as Revealed in His Letters.* New York: Negro Universities Press, 1968.

Beckert, Sven. *Empire of Cotton: A Global History.* New York: Random House, 2015.

Berlin, Ira. *Many Thousands Gone: The First Two Centuries of Slavery in North America*. Cambridge, MA: Harvard University Press, 1998.

———. *Slaves Without Masters; The Free Negro in the Antebellum South*. New York: Pantheon Books, 1974.

Beveridge, Charles E., and Charles Capen McLoughlin, eds. *The Papers of Frederick Law Olmsted: Slavery and the South, 1852–1857. Vol. 2*. Baltimore: Johns Hopkins University Press, 1983.

Beveridge, Charles E., and David Schuyler, eds. *The Papers of Frederick Law Olmsted: Creating Central Park*. Vol. 3. Baltimore: Johns Hopkins University Press, 1983.

Billingsley, Carolyn Earle. *Communities of Kinship: Antebellum Families and the Settlement of the Cotton Frontier*. Athens: University of Georgia Press, 2004.

Blassingame, John W. *The Slave Community: Plantation Life in the Antebellum South. Rev. and Expanded*. New York: Oxford University Press, 1979.

———. *Slave Testimony: Two Centuries of Letters, Speeches, Interviews, and Autobiographies*. Baton Rouge: Louisiana State University Press, 1977.

Bolton, S. Charles. *Arkansas 1800–1860: Remote and Restless*. Fayetteville: University of Arkansas Press, 1998.

———. *Fugitives from Injustice: Freedom Seeking Slaves in Arkansas, 1800–1860*. National Park Service, 2006.

Bond, Bradley, ed. *French Colonial Louisiana and the Atlantic World*. Baton Rouge: Louisiana State University Press, 2005.

Bordewich, Fergus. *The Underground Railroad and the War for the Soul of America*. New York: HarperCollins, 2005.

Bragg, Marion. *Historic Names and Places on the Lower Mississippi River*. Vicksburg: Mississippi River Commission, 1977.

Brasseaux, Carl. *Steamboats on Louisiana's Bayous: A History and Directory*. n.d.

Bry, Hon. H. "Ouachita Country, III." *De Bow's Review* 3, no. 5 (May 1847): 407–11.

Buchanan, Thomas C. *Black Life on the Mississippi: Slaves, Free Blacks, and the Western Steamboat World*. Chapel Hill: University of North Carolina Press, 2004.

Buckingham, James Silk. *The Slave States of America*. London: Fisher & Son, 1842.

Calhoun, John C. *Speeches of Hon. John C. Calhoun on the Subject of Slavery: In the Senate of the United States, March, 1850: [read for him by Hon. Mr. Mason, March 4, 1850]*. Washington, 1850.

Camp, Stephanie M. H. *Closer to Freedom: Enslaved Women and Everyday Resistance in the Plantation South*. Chapel Hill: University of North Carolina Press, 2004.

Campanella, Richard. *Geographies of New Orleans: Urban Fabrics before the Storm*. Lafayette: University of Louisiana at Lafayette Press, 2006.

———. *Lincoln in New Orleans: The 1828–1831 Flatboat Voyages and Their Place in History*. Lanham, MD: Garrett County Press, 2012.

Capers, Gerald. *Biography of a River Town: Memphis: Its Heroic Year*s, 2nd ed. New Orleans: Tulane University, 1966.

Castellanos, Henry C. *New Orleans as It Was: Episodes of Louisiana Life.* 1976; Baton Rouge: Louisiana State University Press, 2006.

Celinski, David S. *The Waterman's Song: Slavery and Freedom in Maritime North Carolina.* Chapel Hill: University of North Carolina Press, 2001.

Censer, Jane Turner, ed. *Defending the Union: The Civil War and the U.S. Sanitary Commission, 1861–1863. Papers of Frederick Law Olmsted.* Vol. 4. Baltimore: Johns Hopkins University Press, 1986.

Chambers, A. B., ed. *Trials and Confessions of Madison Henderson, alias Blanchard, Alfred Amons Warrick, James W. Seward, and Charles Brown, Murderers of Jesse Baker and Jacob Weaver; as Given by Themselves; and a Likeness of Each Taken in Jail Shortly after their Arrest.* St. Louis: Chambers and Knapp, 1841.

Clark, John G. *New Orleans, 1718–1766: An Economic History.* Baton Rouge: Louisiana State University Press, 1970.

Cobb, James C. *The Most Southern Place on Earth: The Mississippi Delta and the Roots of Regional Identity.* New York: Oxford University Press, 1992.

Collins, Jeanelle, ed. *Defining the Delta: Multidisciplinary Perspectives on the Lower Mississippi Delta.* Fayetteville: University of Arkansas Press, 2015.

Cramer, Zadok. *The Navigator: Containing Directions for Navigating the Monongahela, Alleghany, Ohio, and Mississippi Rivers, with an Ample Account of These Much Admired Waters . . . and a Concise Description of Their Towns.* Pittsburgh [PA]: Published and sold by Cramer, Spear and Eichbaum, 1814.

Dabney, Thomas Ewing. *One Hundred Great Years: The Story of the* Times-Picayune *from its Founding to 1940.* Baton Rouge: Louisiana State University Press, 1944.

Dahlinger, Charles William. *Pittsburgh. A Sketch of Its Early Social Life.* New York: G. P. Putnam's Sons, 1916.

Davis, Edward Adams, ed. *Plantation Life in the Florida Parishes of Louisiana, 1836–1846, As Reflected in the Dairy of Bennet H. Barrow.* New York: Columbia University Press, 1943.

Davis, Ronald L. F. *The Black Experience in Natchez, 1720–1880.* Natchez National Historical Park, rev. ed., 2008.

De Rosier, Arthur H. *The Removal of the Choctaw Indians.* Knoxville: University of Tennessee Press, 1981.

Deyle, Steven. *Carry Me Back: The Domestic Slave Trade in American Life.* Oxford: Oxford University Press, 2006.

Diaof, Sylviane A. *Slavery's Exiles: The Story of American Maroons.* New York: New York University Press, 2014.

Din, Gilbert C. *Populating the Barrera: Spanish Immigration Efforts in Colonial Louisiana.* Lafayette: University of Louisiana at Lafayette Press, 2013.

———. *Spaniards, Planters, and Slaves: The Spanish Regulation of Slavery in Louisiana.* College Station: Texas A&M University Press, 1999.

Din, Gilbert C., and John E. Harkins. *New Orleans Cabildo: Colonial Louisiana's First City Government, 1769–1803.* Baton Rouge: Louisiana State University Press, 1996.

Drew, Benjamin. *The Refugee: A North-Side View of Slavery.* 1856. Reading, MA: Addison-Wesley, 1969.

Dupree, L. J., comp. *A Digest of the Ordinances of the City Council of Memphis from the Year 1826 to 1857, together with all Acts of the Legislature of Tennessee which related exclusively to the City of Memphis.* Memphis, TN: Memphis Bulletin Company, 1857.

DuVal, Kathleen. *The Native Ground: Indians and Colonists in the Heart of the Continent.* Philadelphia: University of Pennsylvania Press, 2006.

Eakin, Sue, ed. *Solomon Northup's* Twelve Years a Slave*: And Plantation Life in the Old South.* Lafayette: University of Louisiana at Lafayette Press, 2007.

Ekberg, Carl J. *French Roots in the Illinois Country: The Mississippi Frontier in Colonial Times.* Urbana: University of Illinois Press, 1998.

English, E. H. *A Digest of the Statutes of Arkansas, Embracing All Laws of a General and Permanent Character in Force at the Close of the Session of the General Assembly of 1846: Together with Notes of the Decisions of the Supreme Court Upon the Statutes.* Little Rock: Reardon & Garritt, 1848.

Fairbank, Calvin. *The Rev. Calvin Fairbank during Slavery Times: How he "Fought the Good Fight" to Prepare "the Way."* N.p.: R. R. McCabe & Co., 1890.

Featherstonhaugh, G. W. *Excursion through the Slave States: From Washington on the Potomac to the Frontier of Mexico; with Sketches of Popular Manners and Geological Notices.* New York: Harper & Brothers, 1844.

Fehrenbacher, Don Edward, and Ward McAfee. *The Slaveholding Republic: An Account of the United States Government's Relations to Slavery.* New York: Oxford University Press, 2001.

Finkleman, Paul. *Slavery and the Founders: Race and Liberty in the Age of Jefferson.* Armonk, NY: M. E. Sharpe, 2014.

Fogel, Robert William. *Without Consent or Contract: The Rise and Fall of American Slavery.* New York: W. W. Norton, 1989.

Fogel, Robert William, and Stanley L. Engerman. *Time on a Cross: The Economics of American Negro Slavery.* New York: W. W. Norton, 1989.

Follett, Richard J. *The Sugar Masters: Planters and Slaves in Louisiana's Cane World, 1820–1860.* Baton Rouge: Louisiana State University Press, 2007.

Foner, Eric. *Gateway to Freedom: The Hidden History of America's Fugitive Slaves.* New York: W. W. Norton, 2015.

Franklin, John Hope. *The Militant South: 1800–1860.* Cambridge, MA: Harvard University Press, 1956.

Franklin, John Hope, and Loren Schweninger. *Runaway Slaves: Rebels on the Plantation.* New York: Oxford University Press, 2000.

Frazier, Harriet C. *Runaway and Freed Missouri Slaves and Those Who Helped Them.* Jefferson, NC: McFarland, 2004.

Gara, Larry. *The Liberty Line: The Legend of the Underground Railroad.* Lexington: University Press of Kentucky, 1996.

Gayarré, Charles. *A History of Louisiana.* Vol. 2. New York: Redfield, 1854.

Genovese, Eugene. *Roll Jordon Roll: The World the Slaves.* New York: Random House, 1974.

Goldin, Claudia Dale. *Urban Slavery in the American South, 1820–1860.* Chicago: University of Chicago Press, 1976.

Gould, Josiah. *A Digest of the Statutes of Arkansas: All Laws of a General and Permanent Character in Force at the Close of the General Assembly of 1856.* Little Rock, AR: Johnson & Yerkes, 1858.

Gross, Ariela J. *Double Character: Slavery and Mastery in the Antebellum Southern Courtroom.* Athens: University of Georgia Press, 2000.

Grünzweig, Walter. *Charles Sealsfield.* Boise, ID: Boise State University Press, 1985.

Gudmestad, Robert H. *Steamboats and the Rise of the Cotton Kingdom.* Baton Rouge: Louisiana State University Press, 2011.

Gutman, Herbert G. *Slavery and the Numbers Game: A Critique of Time on the Cross.* Urbana: University of Illinois Press, 1975.

Hadden, Sally E. *Slave Patrols: Law and Violence in Virginia and the Carolinas.* Cambridge, MA: Harvard University Press, 2001.

Hahn, Steven. *A Nation Under Our Feet: Black Political Struggles in the Rural South from Slavery to the Great Migration.* Cambridge, MA: Harvard University Press, 2003.

Hall, Gwendolyn Midlo. *Africans in Colonial Louisiana: The Development of Afro-Creole Culture in the Eighteenth Century.* Baton Rouge: Louisiana State University Press, 1992.

———. *Slavery and African Ethnicities in the Americas: Restoring the Links.* Chapel Hill: University of North Carolina Press, 2005.

Hanger, Kimberly S. *Bounded Lives, Bounded Places: Free Black Society in Colonial New Orleans, 1769–1803.* Durham, NC: Duke University Press, 1997.

Harrold, Stanley. *Border War: Fighting over Slavery before the Civil War.* Chapel Hill: University of North Carolina Press, 2010.

Hogan, William Ransom, and Edwin Adams Davis, ed. *William Johnson's Natchez: The Ante-Bellum Diary of a Free Negro.* Introduction by William L. Andrews. Baton Rouge: Louisiana State University Press, 1993.

Howard, H. R., comp. *The History of Virgil A. Stewart and His Adventure in Capturing and Exposing the Great "Western Land Pirate" and his Gang in Connexion with the Evidence; and also the Trials, Convictions, and Execution of a Number of Murrel's Associates.* New York: Harper & Brothers, 1836.

Hunter, Louis C., and Beatrice Jones Hunter. *Steamboats on the Western Rivers: An Economic and Technological History.* Cambridge, MA: Harvard University Press, 1949.

Ingersoll, Thomas N. *Mammon and Manon in Early New Orleans: The First Slave Society in the Deep South*. Knoxville: University of Tennessee Press, 1999.

[Ingraham, Joseph Holt]. *The Southwest: by a Yankee*. 2 vols. New York: Harper & Brothers, 1835.

James, D. Clayton. *Antebellum Natchez*. Baton Rouge: Louisiana State University Press, 1968.

Johnson, Walter. *River of Dark Dreams: Slavery and Empire in the Cotton Kingdom*. Cambridge, MA: Harvard University Press, 2013.

———. *Soul by Soul: Life Inside the Antebellum Slave Market*. Cambridge, MA: Harvard University Press, 1999.

Jordan, Winthrop. *Tumult and Silence at Second Creek*. Baton Rouge: Louisiana State University Press, 1993.

Jordon, Philip D. *Frontier Law and Order: Ten Essays*. Lincoln: University of Nebraska Press, 1970.

Kaye, Anthony E. *Joining Places: Slave Neighborhoods in the Old South*. Chapel Hill: University of North Carolina Press, 2007.

Kendall, John. *History of New Orleans*. Vol. 1. Chicago: Lewis Publishing Company, 1922.

King, William W., Levi Peirce, and Miles Taylor. *The Consolidation and Revision of the Statutes of the State of a General Nature, Prepared by L. Peirce, M. Taylor, W. W. King, Commissioners Appointed by the State. Feb. 5, 1852*. 1852.

Kolchin, Peter. *American Slavery, 1619–1877*. New York: Hill and Wang, 2003.

Lankford, George E. *Bearing Witness: Memories of Arkansas Slavery: Narratives from the 1930s WPA Collections*. Fayetteville: University of Arkansas Press, 2003.

Levine, Bruce. *The Fall of the House of Dixie: The Civil War and the Social Revolution That Transformed the South*. New York: Random House, 2014.

Levine, Lawrence W. *Black Culture and Black Consciousness: Afro-American Folk Thought from Slavery to Freedom*. New York: Oxford University Press, 1977.

Levy, Leonard W. *The Law of the Commonwealth and Chief Justice Shaw*. Cambridge, MA: Harvard University Press, 1957.

Lewis, Peirce F. *New Orleans: The Making of an Urban Landscape*. 2nd ed. Santa Fe, NM: Center for American Places, 2003.

Libby, David J. *Slavery and Frontier Mississippi, 1720–1835*. Jackson: University Press of Mississippi, 2004.

Looney, J. W. *Distinguishing the Righteous from the Roguish: The Arkansas Supreme Court, 1836–1874*. Fayetteville: University of Arkansas Press, 2016.

Louisiana, and Edward Livingston, Louis Moreau Lislet, P. Derbigny, and Joseph Charles de St. Romes. *Civil Code of the State of Louisiana*. New Orleans: Printed by J. C. de St. Romes, 1825.

Louisiana, and Meinrad Greiner. *The Louisiana Digest, Embracing the Laws of the Legislature of a General Nature, Enacted from the Year 1804 to 1841, Inclusive, and in Force at This Last Period. Also, an Abstract of the Decisions of the Supreme Court of Louisiana on the Statutory Law, Arranged Under the Appropriate Articles in the Digest.* New Orleans: B. Levy, 1841.

Lussana, Sergio. *My Brother Slaves Friendship, Masculinity, and Resistance in the Antebellum South.* Lexington: University Press of Kentucky, 2016.

McDonald, Roderick A. *The Economy and Material Culture of Slaves: Goods and Chattels on the Sugar Plantations of Jamaica and Louisiana.* Baton Rouge: Louisiana State University Press, 1993.

McLaughlin, Charles Capen, and Charles E. Beveridge, eds. *The Papers of Frederick Law Olmsted: The Formative Years 1822–1852.* Vol. 1. Baltimore: Johns Hopkins University Press, 1983.

McNeilly, Donald P. *The Old South Frontier: Cotton Plantations and the Formation of Arkansas Society, 1819–1816.* Fayetteville: University of Arkansas Press, 2000.

Maio, Irene S. Di., ed. and trans. *Gerstacker's Louisiana: Fiction and Travel Sketches from Antebellum Times through Reconstruction.* Baton Rouge: Louisiana State University Press, 2006.

Malone, Ann Patton. *Sweet Chariot: Slave Family and Household Structure in Nineteenth-Century Louisiana.* Chapel Hill: University of North Carolina Press, 1992.

Martin, Jonathan D. *Divided Mastery: Slave Hiring in the American South.* Cambridge, MA: Harvard University Press, 2004.

Meigs, Return J., and William Cooper, eds. *Code of Tennessee Enacted by the General Assembly of 1857–'8.* Nashville, TN: E. G. Eastman and Company, 1858.

Metcalf, Theron, and Horace Mann. *The Revised Statutes of the Commonwealth of Massachusetts Passed November 4, 1835: To Which Are Subjoined, an Act in Amendment Thereof, and an Act Expressly to Repeal the Acts Which Are Consolidated Therein, Both Passed in February 1836, and to Which Are Prefixed the Constitutions of the United States and of the Commonwealth of Massachusetts.* Boston: Dutton & Wentworth, State printers, 1836.

Mooney, Chase C. *Slavery in Tennessee.* Westport, CT: Negro Universities Press, 1971.

Moore, John Hebron. *The Emergence of the Cotton Kingdom in the Old Southwest: Mississippi, 1770–1860.* Baton Rouge: Louisiana State University Press, 1988.

Moreau Lislet, Louis. *A General Digest of the Acts of the Legislature of Louisiana: Passed from the Year 1804 to 1827.* New Orleans: Benjamin Levy, 1828.

Morgan, Philip D. *Slave Counterpoint: Black Culture in the Eighteenth-Century Chesapeake and Lowcountry.* Chapel Hill: University of North Carolina Press, 1998.

Morgan, Thomas Gibbes. *Civil Code of the State of Louisiana: With the Statutory Amendments, from 1852 to 1853, Inclusive; and References to the Decisions of the Supreme Court of Louisiana to the Sixth Volume of Annual Reports.* New Orleans: J. B. Steel, 1861.

Morgans, James Patrick. *The Underground Railroad on the Western Frontier: Escapes from Missouri, Arkansas, Iowa and the Territories of Kansas, Nebraska and the Indian Nations, 1840–1865.* Jefferson, NC: McFarland, 2010.

Morris, Christopher. *Becoming Southern: The Evolution of a Way of Life, Warren County and Vicksburg, Mississippi, 1770–1860.* New York: Oxford University Press, 1999.

———. *The Big Muddy: An Environmental History of the Mississippi and Its Peoples from Hernando do Soto to Hurricane Katrina.* New York: Oxford University Press, 2012.

Morris, Thomas D. *Free Men All: The Personal Liberty Laws of the North, 1780–1861.* Baltimore: Johns Hopkins University Press, 1974.

———. *Southern Slavery and the Law, 1619–1860.* Chapel Hill: University of North Carolina Press, 1996.

Mullin, Gerald W. *Flight and Rebellion: Slave Resistance in Eighteenth-Century Virginia.* New York: Oxford University Press, 1972.

Niehaus, Earl J. *The Irish in New Orleans, 1800–1860.* Baton Rouge: Louisiana State University Press, 1965.

Norman, Benjamin Moore. *Norman's New Orleans and Environs: Containing a Brief Historical Sketch of the Territory and State of Louisiana, and the City of New Orleans, from the Earliest Period to the Present Time: Presenting a Complete Guide to All Subjects of General Interest in the Southern Metropolis; with a Correct and Improved Plan of the City, Pictorial Illustrations of Public Buildings, Etc.* New Orleans: Published by B. M. Norman. New York: D. Appleton & Co., 1845.

Northup, Solomon. *Twelve Years a Slave: A Narrative of Solomon Northup: A Citizen of New-York, Kidnapped in Washington City in 1841, and Rescued in 1853 from a Cotton Plantation Near the Red River in Louisiana.* Auburn, NY: Derby and Miller, 1853.

Northup, Solomon. *Twelve Years a Slave.* Edited by Sue L. Eakin, and Joseph Logsdon. Baton Rouge: Louisiana State University Press, 1968.

Novak, Shannon A. *House of Mourning: A Biocultural History of the Mountain Meadows Massacre.* Salt Lake City: University of Utah Press, 2008.

O'Brian, Greg. *Choctaws in a Revolutionary Age, 1750–1830.* Lincoln: University of Nebraska Press, 2002.

Olmsted, Frederick Law. *The Cotton Kingdom: A Traveller's Observations on Cotton and Slavery in the American Slave States, 1853–1861.* New York: Mason Brothers, 1861.

———. *The Cotton Kingdom: A Traveller's Observations on Cotton and Slavery in the American Slave States, 1853–1861.* Edited by Arthur M. Schlesinger. New York: Alfred A. Knopf, 1953.

———. *A Journey in the Seaboard Slave States, with Remarks on their Economy.* New York: Mason Brothers, 1861.

———. *A Journey to the Back Country.* New York: Mason Brothers, 1861.

———. *A Journey Through Texas; or, A Saddle-trip on the Southwestern Frontier.* New York: Dix Edwards and Company, 1857.

———. *Walks and Talks of an American Farmer in England*. New York: G. P. Putnam, 1852.

Paige, Amanda L., Fuller L. Bumpers, and Daniel Little Jr. *Chickasaw Removal*. Norman: University of Oklahoma Press, 2010.

Palmer, Vernon Valentine. *Through the Glass Darkly: Slave Law and Civil Law in Louisiana*. Clark, NJ: Lawbook Exchange, 2012.

Park, Mungo. *Travels in the Interior Districts of Africa*. London, 1816.

Penick, James Lal, Jr. *The Great Western Land Pirate: James A. Murrell in Legend and History*. Columbia: University of Missouri Press, 1981.

Phelps, Alonzo. *Confession of Alonzo Phelps: The Rob-Roy of the Mississippi*. Jackson, MS: G. R. & J. S. Fall, 1834.

Phillips, U. B. *The Revised Statutes of Louisiana*. New Orleans: J. Claiborne, State printer, 1856.

Phillips, Ulrich Bonnell. *American Negro Slavery: A Survey of the Supply, Employment of Negro Labor as Determined by the Plantation Regime*. Baton Rouge: Louisiana State University Press, 1966.

Pope, William F. *Early Days in Arkansas, Being for the Most Part the Personal Recollections of an Old Settler*. Little Rock, AR: Frederick W. Allsopp, 1895.

Powell, Lawrence N. *The Accidental City: Improvising New Orleans*. Cambridge, MA: Harvard University Press, 2012.

Quick, Herbert, and Edward Quick. *Mississippi Steamboatin': A History of Steamboating on the Mississippi and Its Tributaries*. New York: H. Holt and Co., 1926.

Rasmussen, Daniel. *American Uprising: The Untold Story of America's Largest Slave Revolt*. New York: HarperCollins, 2011.

The Revised Code of the Statute Laws of the State of Mississippi. Jackson, MS: E. Barksdale, State Printer, 1857.

Roper, Laura Wood. *FLO: A Biography of Frederick Law Olmsted*. Baltimore: Johns Hopkins University Press, 1983.

Rothman, Adam. *Slave Country: American Expansion and the Origins of the Deep South*. Cambridge, MA: Harvard University Press, 2005.

Rothman, D. Joshua. *Flush Times and Fever Dreams: A Story of Capitalism and Slavery in the Age of Jackson*. Athens: University of Georgia Press, 2012.

Rousey, Dennis C. *Policing the Southern City: New Orleans, 1805–1889*. Baton Rouge: Louisiana State University Press, 1996.

Rybczynski, Witold. *A Clearing in the Distance: Frederick Law Olmsted and America in the 19th Century*. New York: Scribner, 1999.

Sandlin, Lee. *Wicked River: The Mississippi When It Last Ran Wild*. New York: Pantheon Books, 2010.

Schafer, Judith Kelleher. *Slavery, the Civil Law, and the Supreme Court of Louisiana*. Baton Rouge: Louisiana State University Press, 1997.

Schudson, Michael. *Discovering the News: A Social History of American Newspapers.* New York: Basic Books, 1978.

Schwartz, Rosalie. *Across the Rio to Freedom: U.S. Negroes in Mexico.* El Paso: University of Texas Press at El Paso, 1975.

Sealsfield, Charles. *The Americans As They Are; Described in a Tour Through the Valley of the Mississippi.* London: Hurst, Chance and Co., 1828.

Seck, Idbrahima. *Bouki Fait Gombo: A History of the Slave Community of Habitation Haydel (Whitney Plantation) Louisiana, 1750–1860.* New Orleans: University of New Orleans Press, 2014.

Sellers, James B. *Slavery in Alabama.* Tuscaloosa: University of Alabama Press, 1950.

Sinha, Manisha. *The Slave's Cause: A History of Abolition.* New Haven, CT: Yale University Press, 2016.

Smith, Thomas Ruys. *River of Dreams: Imagining the Mississippi River before Mark Twain.* Baton Rouge: Louisiana State University Press, 2007.

Stampp, Kenneth M. *The Peculiar Institution: Slavery in the Ante-Bellum South.* New York: Random House, 1956.

Steele, John, and James M'Campbell. *Laws of Arkansas Territory.* Little Rock: J. Steele, 1835.

Stephenson, Wendall Holmes. *Isaac Franklin: Slave Trader of the Old South.* Baton Rouge: Louisiana State University Press, 1938.

Stowe, Harriet Beecher, and Amanda Claybaugh. *Uncle Tom's Cabin.* New York: Barnes & Noble Classics, 2003.

Stuart, James. *Three Years in North America.* Edinburgh: Robert Cadell, 1833.

Sydnor, S. *Slavery in Mississippi.* Introduction by John David Smith. 1933; rpt., Columbia: University of South Carolina Press, 2013.

Tadman, Michael. *Speculators and Slaves: Masters, Traders and Slaves in the Old South.* Madison: University of Wisconsin Press, 1996.

Taylor, George Rogers. *The Transportation Revolution, 1815–1860.* New York: Harper & Row, 1951.

Taylor, Orville W. *Negro Slavery in Arkansas.* Fayetteville: University of Arkansas Press, 2000.

Thornton, John. *Africa and Africans in the Making of the Atlantic World.* 2nd ed. New York: Cambridge University Press, 1998.

Twain, Mark. *Life on the Mississippi.* New York: Modern Library, 2007.

United States. *Old River Control.* New Orleans: US Army Corps of Engineers, New Orleans District, 2009.

United States, and J. D. B. De Bow. *Statistical View of the United States: Embracing Its Territory, Population—White, Free Colored, and Slave—Moral and Social Condition, Industry, Property, and Revenue: the Detailed Statistics of Cities, Towns and Counties; Being a Compendium of the Seventh Census, to Which Are Added the Results of Every Previous Census, Beginning with 1790.* Washington, DC: B. Tucker, Senate printer, 1854.

Usner, Daniel H., Jr. *Indians, Settlers, and Slaves in a Frontier Exchange Economy: The Lower Mississippi Valley before 1783.* Chapel Hill: University of North Carolina Press, 1992.

Valenčius, Conevery Bolton. *The Lost History of the New Madrid Earthquakes.* Chicago: University of Chicago Press, 2015.

Vidal, Cécile. *Louisiana: Crossroads of the Atlantic World.* Philadelphia: University of Pennsylvania Press, 2014.

Wade, Richard C. *Slavery in the Cities: The South 1820–1860.* New York: Oxford University Press, 1964.

Walton, Augustus Q. *A History of the Detection, Conviction, Life and Designs of John A. Murel, the Great Western Land Pirate.* 1835.

Waselkov, Gregory, Peter H. Wood, and Tom Hatley. *Powhatan's Mantle: Indians in the Colonial South.* Revised and expanded. Lincoln: University of Nebraska Press, 2006.

Webb, Allie Bayne Windham. *Mistress of Evergreen Plantation: Rachel O'Connor's Legacy of Letters, 1823–1845.* Albany: State University of New York Press, 1983.

Weber, David J. *The Spanish Frontier in North America.* New Haven, CT: Yale University Press, 1992.

Weld, Theodore Dwight. *American Slavery As It Is: Testimony of a Thousand Witnesses.* New York: American Anti-Slavery Society, 1839.

White, Deborah Gray. *Ar'n't I a Woman?: Female Slaves in the Plantation South.* Rev. ed. New York: W. W. Norton, 1999.

Williams, Patrick, S. Charles Bolton, and Jeannie M. Whayne, eds. *A Whole County in Commotion: The Louisiana Purchase and the American Southwest.* Fayetteville: University of Arkansas Press, 2005.

Wilson, Carol. *Freedom at Risk: The Kidnapping of Free Blacks in America, 1780–1865.* Lexington: University Press of Kentucky, 2009.

Wood, Peter H. *Black Majority: Negroes in Colonial South Carolina from 1670 through the Stono Rebellion.* New York: Alfred A. Knopf, 1974.

Wyatt-Brown, Bertram. *Southern Honor: Ethics and Behavior in the Old South.* New York: Oxford University Press, 1982.

ARTICLES

Baade, Hans W. "The Law of Slavery in Spanish Louisiana, 1769–1803." In *Louisiana's Legal Heritage*, edited by Edward F. Haas, pp. 43–86. Pensacola, FL: Pelican Press, 1982.

Bauer, Raymond A., and Alicia H. Bauer. "Day to Day Resistance to Slavery." *Journal of Negro History* 27, no. 4 (1942): 388–419.

Beasley, Jonathan. "Blacks—Slave and Free—Vicksburg, 1850–1860." *Journal of Mississippi History* 38, no. 1 (1976): 1–32.

Berlin, Ira, and Herbert Gutman. "Natives and Immigrants, Freemen and Slaves:

Urban Working Men in the Antebellum South." *American Historical Review* 88, no. 5 (Dec. 1983): 1175–1201.

Blassingame, John W. "The Negro in Antebellum New Orleans: Background for Reconstruction." In *Antebellum Louisiana 1820–1860: Part A, Life and Labor, Louisiana Purchase Bicentennial Series in Louisiana History,* Vol. 4, edited by Carolyn N. De Latte, 344–58. Lafayette: University of Louisiana at Lafayette Press, 2004.

Brasseaux, Carl A. "The Administration of Slave Regulations in French Louisiana, 1724–1766." *Louisiana History* 21, no. 2 (1980): 139–58.

Buchanan, Thomas C. "Rascals on the Antebellum Mississippi: African American Steamboat Workers and the St. Louis Hanging of 1841." *Journal of Social History* 34 no. 4 (Summer 2001): 797–816.

Carriere, Marius, Jr. "Blacks in Pre-Civil War Memphis." *Tennessee Historical Quarterly* 48, no. 1 (1990): 3–14.

Cartwright, Samuel. "Diseases and Peculiarities of the Negro Race." *De Bow's Review* 2, no. 3 (Sept. 1851): 331–38.

Chambers, Douglas B. "Slave Trade Merchants of Spanish New Orleans, 1763–1803: Clarifying the Colonial Slave Trade to Louisiana in Atlantic Perspective." *Atlantic Studies* 5, no. 3 (2008): 335–46.

Chenault, William W., and Robert C. Reinders. "The Northern-born Community in New Orleans in the 1850s." *Journal of American History* 51, no. 2 (1964): 232–47.

Cornell, Sarah E. "Citizens of Nowhere: Slaves and Free African Americans in Mexico, 1833–1857." *Journal of American History* (Sept. 2013): 351–74.

Cowles, Lynn A. "Absconded: Enslaved Women, Escape, and Mississippi Runaway Slave Advertisements." *Mississippi Journal of History,* 75, no. 2 (Summer 2013): 163–71.

De Bow, J. D. "The Destiny of New-Orleans." *De Bow's Review* 10, no. 4 (Apr. 1851): 444–45.

———. "Impressions of New Orleans by a Foreigner." *De Bow's Review* 4, no. 4 (Dec. 1847): 556.

———. "Texas." *De Bow's Review* 23, no. 2 (1857): 113–32.

Dessens, Nathalie. "From Saint Domingue to Louisiana: West Indian Refugees in the Lower Mississippi Region." In *French Colonial Louisiana in the Atlantic World,* edited by Bradley G. Bond, 288–309. Baton Rouge: Louisiana State University Press, 2005.

Dorman, James H. "The Persistent Specter: Slave Rebellion in Territorial Louisiana." *Louisiana History* 18, no. 5 (Autumn 1977): 389–404.

DuVal, Kathleen. "Interconnectedness and Diversity in French Louisiana." In *Powhatan's Mantle: Indians in the Colonial South.* Revised and Expanded, edited by Gregory Waselkov, Peter H. Wood, and Tom Hatley, 136–59. Lincoln: University of Nebraska Press, 2006.

Edson, Andrew S. "How Nineteenth Century Travelers Viewed Memphis Before the Civil War." *West Tennessee Historical Society Papers* 24 (1970): 30–40.

Ermus, Cindy. "Reduced to Ashes: The Good Friday Fire of 1788 in Spanish Colonial New Orleans." *Louisiana History* 54, no. 3 (2013): 292–331.

Finkleman, Paul. "The Kidnapping of John Davis and the Adoption of the Fugitive Slave Law of 1793." *Journal of Southern History* 56, no. 3 (1990): 397–422.

———. "*Prigg v. Pennsylvania* and Northern State Courts: Anti-Slavery Use of a Pro-Slavery Decision." *Civil War History* 25, no. 1 (1979): 5–35.

———. "Story Telling on the Supreme Court: *Prigg v. Pennsylvania* and Justice Joseph Story's Judicial Nationalism." *Supreme Court Review* (1994): 247–94.

Foti, Tomas. "The Rivers Gifts and Curses." In *The Arkansas Delta: Land of Paradox*, edited by Jeannie Whayne and Willard B. Gatewood, 30–51. Fayetteville: University of Arkansas Press, 1993.

Garvey, Ellen Gruber. "Nineteenth-Century Abolitionists and the Databases They Created." *Legacy: A Journal of American Women Writers* 27, no. 2 (2010): 357–66.

Germenis, Matthew. "Runaway Slave Advertisements in Mississippi, Violence and Dominion." *Journal of Mississippi History* 75, no. 2 (Summer 2013): 97–105.

Gibson, Campbell. "Population of the 100 Largest Cities and Other Urban Places in the United States: 1790–1990." United States Census Bureau (June 1998).

Glenn, D. C. "Mississippi." *De Bow's Review* 7, no. 1 (July 1849): 38–44.

Gorn, Elliott J. "'Gouge and Bite, Pull Hair and Scratch': The Social Significance of Fighting in the Southern Backcountry." *American Historical Review* 90, no. 1 (Feb. 1985): 18–43.

Gould, Virginia Meacham. "'The House that was Never a Home,' Slave Family and Household Organization in New Orleans, 1820–1850." *Slavery and Abolition* 18, no. 2 (Aug. 1997): 90–103.

Greer, Matthew. "Carrying the Tools for Freedom: Negotiating the Environments of Mississippi in Slavery and Escapes." *Mississippi Journal of History* 75, no. 2 (Summer 2013): 121–32.

Hand, Shane. "As White a Servant as Any in the State: Near White Mississippi Runaways, 1800–1860." *Journal of Mississippi History* 75, no. 2 (Summer 2013): 193–204.

Harwood, Thomas F. "The Abolitionist Image of Louisiana and Mississippi." *Louisiana History* 7, no. 4 (1966): 281–308.

Holmes, Jack D., ed. and trans. "OReilly's Regulations on Booze, Boarding Houses, and Billiards." *Louisiana History* 6, no. 3 (Summer 1965): 293–300.

Ingersoll, Thomas N. "Free Blacks in a Slave Society: New Orleans, 1718–1812." *William and Mary Quarterly* 48, no. 2 (1991): 173–200.

———. "Slave Codes and Judicial Practices in New Orleans, 1724–1807." *Law and History Review* 13, no. 1 (1995): 24–62.

Jones, Kelly Houston. "Chattels, Pioneers, and Pilgrims for Freedom: Arkansas's Bonded Travelers." *Arkansas Historical Quarterly* 75, no. 3 (Winter 2016): 319–35.

———. "'Doubtless Guilty': Lynching and Slaves in Antebellum Arkansas." In *Bullets and Fire: Lynching and Authority in Arkansas, 1840–1950*, edited by Guy Lancaster, 17–34. Fayetteville: University of Arkansas Press, 2018.

Kelly, Sean. "'Mexico in His Head': Slavery and the Texas-Mexico Border, 1810–1860." *Journal of Social History* 37, no. 3 (Spring 2004): 709–23.

Lachance, Paul F. "The Formation of a Three-Caste Society: Evidence from Wills in Antebellum New Orleans." *Social Science History* 18, no. 2 (1994): 211–42.

———. "The Growth of the Free and Slave Populations in French Colonial Louisiana." In *French Colonial Louisiana in the Atlantic World*, edited by Bradley G. Bond, 250–87. Baton Rouge: Louisiana State University Press, 2005.

———. "The Politics of Fear: French Louisianians and the Slave Trade, 1786–1809." *Plantation Society* 1, no. 2 (1979): 162–97.

———. "The 1809 Immigration of Saint-Dominique Refugees to New Orleans in 1709: Reception, Immigration and Impact." *Louisiana History* 29, no. 2 (1988): 109–41.

Lack, Paul D. "An Urban Slave Community: Little Rock, 1831–1862." *Arkansas Historical Quarterly* 41, no. 3 (1982): 258–87.

LeGlaunec, Jean Pierre. "Slave Migrations in Spanish and Early American Louisiana: New Sources and New Estimates." *Louisiana History* 46, no. 2 (2005): 185–209.

———. "'Un Nègre nommeé [sic] Lubin no connaissant pas Sa Nation': The Small World of Louisiana Slavery." Cécile Vidal, *Louisiana: Crossroads of the Atlantic World*. Philadelphia: University of Pennsylvania Press, 2014.

Louisiana Historical Society. "Calhoun, Meredith." *Dictionary of Louisiana Biography*, lahistory.org (accessed July 6, 2015).

McFarland, Kenneth. "The Travels of Frederick Law Olmsted in the Antebellum South." *Magnolia* 20, no. 4 (2006): 1, 3–10.

McGoldrick, Stacy K. "The Policing of Slavery in New Orleans, 1852–1860." *Journal of Historical Sociology* 14, no. 4 (Dec. 2001): 397–417.

Mangipano, John. "Social Geography of Interstate Escape: Runaway Slaves from Louisiana to Mississippi, 1801–1860." *Journal of Mississippi History* 75, no. 2 (Summer 2013): 133–49.

Moore, Jessica Parker. "'Keeping All Hands Moving': A Plantation Mistress in Antebellum Arkansas." *Arkansas Historical Quarterly* 74 (Autumn 2015): 257–76.

Olmsted, Frederick Law. "A Voice from the Sea." *American Whig Review* 14 (Dec. 1851): 525–35.

Olney, James. "'I was Born': Slave Narratives, Their Status as Autobiography and History." In *The Slave's Narrative*, edited by Charles T. Davis and Henry Louis Gates Jr., 148–74. New York: Oxford University Press, 1985.

Paquette, Robert L. "'A Hoard of Brigands': The Great Louisiana Slave Revolt of 1811 Reconsidered." *Historical Reflections* 35, no. 1 (2009): 72–96.

Patterson, Caleb Perry. "The Negro in Tennessee, 1790–1865." *University of Texas Bulletin*, no. 2205 (1922): 1–222.

Pierce, Michael. "The Mechanics of Little Rock: Free Labor Ideas in Antebellum Little Rock, 1845–1861." *Arkansas Historical Quarterly* 67, no. 3 (2008): 221–44.

Pittman, Carolyn. "Memphis in the Mid-1840s: Memphis before the Mexican War." *West Tennessee Historical Society Papers* 23 (1969): 30–44.

Reilly, Timothy F. "Slave Stealing in the Early Republic as Revealed by a Loyal Manservant." *Louisiana History* 55, no. 1 (Winter 2014): 5–39.

Reilly, Tom. "The War Press of New Orleans: 1846–1848." *Journalism History* 13, nos. 3–4 (Autumn–Winter 1986): 86–95.

Richter, William L. "Slavery in Baton Rouge, 1820–1860." *Louisiana History* 10, no. 2 (Apr. 1969): 125–45.

Rousey, Dennis C. "Cops and Guns: Police Use of Deadly Force in Nineteenth-Century New Orleans." *American Journal of Legal History* 28, no. 1 (Jan. 1984): 41–64.

Sanson, Jerry Purvis. "More Than Twelve Years a Slave: The Enduring Legacy of Solomon Northup." *Southern Studies: An Interdisciplinary Journal of the South* 22 no. 1 (2015): 1–15.

———. "Memphis and its Manufacturing Advantage." *De Bow's Review* 10, no. 5 (1851): 525–29.

Schafer, Judith Kelleher. "New Orleans Slavery in 1850 as Seen in Advertisements." *Journal of Southern History* 47, no. 1 (1981): 33–56.

———. "The Immediate Impact of Nat Turner's Insurrection on New Orleans." *Louisiana History: The Journal of the Louisiana Historical Association* 21, no. 4 (1980): 361–76.

Seematter, Mary E. "Trials and Confessions: Race and Justice in Antebellum St. Louis." *Gateway Heritage* 12 (Fall 1991): 36–47.

Sitterson, J. Carlyle. "The McCullum's: A Planter Family of the Old and New South." *Journal of Southern History* 6, no. 3 (1940): 347–67.

Steuckgrath, Prof. George. "Historical Collections of Louisiana—Baton Rouge." *De Bow's Review: Agricultural, Commercial and Industrial Resources* 26, no. 4: 439–44.

Tyler, Ronnie C. "Fugitive Slaves in Mexico." *Journal of Negro History* 57, no. 1 (1972): 1–12.

Vinikas, Vincent. "Thirteen Dead at St. Charles: Arkansas's Most Lethal Lynching and the Abrogation of Equal Protection." In *Bullets and Fire: Lynching and Authority in Arkansas, 1840–1950*, edited by Guy Lancaster, 103–30. Fayetteville: University of Arkansas Press, 2018.

Wade, Eve. "Contested Space: Mississippi Runaway Slave Advertisements, Violence and the Body." *Journal of Mississippi History* 75, no. 2 (Summer 2013): 107–19.

Wagner, Bryan. "Disarmed and Dangerous: The Strange Career of Bras-Coupee." *Representations* 92, no. 1 (Fall 2005): 117–51.

Waschka, Ronald W. "Early Railroad Development at Memphis." *West Tennessee Historical Society Papers* 46 (1992): 1–12.

———. "River Transportation at Memphis before the Civil War." *West Tennessee Historical Society Papers* 45 (1991): 1–18.

Way, R. B. "The Commerce of the Lower Mississippi Valley in the Period 1830–1836." *Mississippi Valley Historical Association Proceedings* 10 (1918): 57–68.

White, Dan F. "A Connecticut Yankee in Cotton's Kingdom." *Olmsted South: Old South Critic/New South Planner*, edited by Dana F. White and Victor A. Kramer, 12–49. Westport, CT: Greenwood Press, 1979.

Williams, Edward F., III. "Memphis's Early Triumphs over Its River Rivals." *West Tennessee Historical Society Papers* 22 (1986): 2–27.

Winston, James E. "Notes on the Economic History of New Orleans, 1803–1836." *Mississippi Valley Historical Review* 11, no. 2 (1924): 200–226.

Wood, Peter H. "The Changing Population of the Colonial South: An Overview by Race and Region." In *Powhatan's Mantle: Indians in the Colonial South*, revised and expanded, edited by Gregory Waselkov, Peter H. Wood, and Tom Hatley, 66–134. Lincoln: University of Nebraska Press, 2006.

Worley, Ted R. "Helena on the Mississippi." *Arkansas Historical Quarterly* 13, no. 1 (1954): 1–15.

COURT CASES

Dunbar v. Skillman, 9 Martin's Reports, 285, 1828.

McMaster v. Beckwith, No. 2017, 2 La. 329, 1831.

Hurst v. Wallace, No. 2402, 5 La. 98, 1833.

Jack, A Negro Man, v. Mary Martin, 12 Wendell 311, 1835.

Jack, A Negro Man, v. Mary Martin, 14 Wendell 507, 1835.

Buel v. New York, No. 3689, 15 La. 251, 1840.

Loussard v. Hartman, et al., 16 Curry 117, 1840.

Slater v. Holton, No. 3894, 19 La. 39, June 1841.

Prigg v. Com. Of Pennsylvania 41 U.S. 539, 1842.

Winston v. Foster, No. 4617, 5 Rob. 113, 1843.

George A. Botts v. Cochrane, No. 1013, 4 La. Ann. 35, 1849.

Morehead and Bryant v. The State, 28 Tennessee Reports 391–94, Apr. 1849.

State v. Banton, 4 Robinson 31, 1849.

J. B. Arandez v. Thomas B. Lawes, 5 La. Ann. 127–31, 1850.

Henry v. Armstrong, 15 Ark. 162, 1854.

Thompson v. Young, 30 Miss. 17, December 1855.

A. Duperrier v. B. Dutrieve et al. 12 La. Ann. 664–65, 1856.

State v. William Thompson, alias Robinson, and S. J. Baer, 13 La. Ann. 515, 1858.

FREQUENTLY USED NEWSPAPERS

Ariel (Natchez)

Arkansas Gazette (Little Rock)

Daily Picayune (New Orleans)

Memphis Appeal (Memphis)

Mississippi Free Trader (Natchez)

Mississippi State Gazette (Natchez)

The Natchez (Natchez)

New York Times (New York)

Randolph Recorder (Randolph, TN)

Vicksburg Register (Vicksburg, MS)

Woodville Republican (Woodville, MS)

WEBSITES

Digital Library on American Slavery, Race & Slavery Petitions Project.

Documenting Runaway Slaves (University of Southern Mississippi). Runaway Slaves in Mississippi (1800–1860): Series 1. Edited by Douglas B. Chambers and Max Grivno. (Feb. 2013). Arkansas Runaway Slaves (1800–1860). S. Charles Bolton (Feb. 2013).

Historical Archives of the Supreme Court of Louisiana (University of New Orleans).

Texas Runaway Slave Project, East Texas Research Center.

INDEX

Aberdeen, Mississippi, 89
abolition, 46, 85
abolitionists, 15, 184, 207, 213, 216–21;
   fomenting revolt, 202; as slave
   stealers, 172, 175–76, 210
Abraham (slave of James Daswell), 82
Abram (slave, in Baton Rouge) 86
Abram (slave of Edwin Eppes), 68
Adams, Charles Francis, 219
Adams County Jail (Mississippi), 92,
   98, 108
Adams, John Quincy, 218
Addison (slave of James K. Polk),
   78–79
Adele (slave of Mr. Faisons), 108
advertisements for runaways, 101, 137,
   143, 161, 233–35; *Arkansas Gazette*,
   90, 94, 119, 153, 154; *Daily Picayune*,
   84, 113; for female fugitives, 91–93,
   127, 144; for groups of fugitives,
   125; for stolen slaves, 151–52; in
   New Orleans, 135–36; in Texas, 86;
   Memphis Appeal, 178; *Mississippi
   Free Trader*, 3, 91; *Mississippi State
   Gazette*, 82; *Natchez Courier*, 100;
   Woodville Republican, 99
African-born slaves, 8, 36–38, 45, 46, 86
agriculture, plantation 56
*Aiming for Pensacola: Fugitive Slaves on
   the Atlantic and Southern Frontier*, 5
Alabama, 26–27, 81, 82, 88, 89
Albert (slave of James K. Polk), 91
Albert (slave of John B. Nevitt), 122–23
Albert (slave of John P. Tagart), 162
alcohol consumption by slaves, 82, 118,
   120–21
Alexandria, Louisiana, 174

Alexandria Parish, Louisiana, 180
Alexandria, Virginia, 60
Amanda (slave), 127
American Anti-Slavery Society, 170–72
American Slavery As It Is, 184
American Whig Review, 14
Amite County, Mississippi, 104, 193
Anderson, George, 136
Anderson, James, 105
Anderson (slave in Fayette County,
   Kentucky), 98
Anderson (slave of Henry Borrough),
   104
Andry, Manuel 47–48
Ann (slave in Petit Gulf, Mississippi),
   94
Anthony (slave in Bienville Parish,
   Louisiana), 83
Anthony (slave of Madame Cloutier),
   86
Anthony (slave of James J. Vickers),
   3, 10
anti-white activities, 69
anti-slavery sentiment, 15, 19–20, 55, 133
Antony (slave of William Ford), 68
Archy (slave of E. Peal), 222–23
Arkansas, 50, 51, 65, 90, 92; cotton
   crops in, 55–56, 58; criminal activity
   in, 152–65; escape from, 83, 87, 98;
   escape through, 77, 87–89; escape to,
   89, 84, 94; laws concerning slavery,
   150–51; outlaw gangs, 154–55. *See also*
   Mystic Clan; slave patrols, 185–86;
   slave stealing, 152–65; sold in, 61, 89
Arkansas Gazette, 154, 156–57, 164;
   advertisements for runaways, 90,
   94, 119, 153, 154

Flush Times & Fever Dreams: A Story of Capitalism and Slavery in the Age of Jackson, 7
Foche, M., 84
Follett, Richard, 7
Ford, E. M., 105
Ford, Osborn, 92
Ford, William, 66, 67–68, 71
Foreman, Colonel (counterfeiter), 157
Foreman, Stephen W., 155–56
Forrest, Nathan Bedford, 55, 83
Forsyth, John, 82
Fort Gibson, Oklahoma, 89
Fort Smith, Arkansas, 90
Foster, R. W., 113–14
Fowler, Jesse, 108
Fox, Samuel S., 195
France, 35–40
Frances (slave of McMasters), 170
Francoise (slave), 44
Franklin and Armfield (slave traders), 60
Franklin County, Mississippi, 92
Franklin, Isaac, 169
Franklin, John Hope, 5, 201
Franklin, Louisiana, 198
Franklin Parish, Louisiana, 195
free blacks: assisting slaves, 42, 66, 108, 125, 135, 145, 150; as slave catchers, 46, 141, 175; as slave owners, 100–101, 120–21, 178; kidnapped, 20, 208, 209, 210–12, 214; in Memphis, 127–28; in Mexico, 30, 32; in New Orleans, 41, 58–59, 134, 139, 142–44, 173; living conditions, 22–23, 119; on steamboats, 97, 102, 103, 106, 111, 127, 173; passing as, 8, 92, 98, 113, 115, 177; rights of, 39–40
free papers: forged, 104, 106, 170; ignored, 108
French and Indian War, 35
French language, 22, 86, 99
French National Assembly, 46
French Revolution, 46
friendships between slaves, 67, 84, 103
fugitives: diet, 43–44; short term vs. long term, 33

Fugitive Slave Act of 1850, 15, 33, 207
Fugitive Slave Law of 1793, 209–15
fugitivism, 4–5, 8
Fulton, Matilda, 118–19
Fulton, William, 118–19

Gaines, Edmund Pendleton, 54
Garčon, Pierre, 43
Garner, John I., 78
Gayden, Griffin, 151–52
Gentilly Road, 80
geography in avoiding capture 32, 41, 44
George (slave), 98
Georgetown, Kentucky, 90
Georgia, 18, 21–22, 83
German Coast, Louisiana, 47, 80
Germans, 55, 59
Gilbert (slave of James K. Polk), 78–79
Giles (slave of Bennett H. Barrow), 99–100
Gill, William H., 87
Goodloe, Edwin R., 17
Grace (slave of Henry Knox), 94
Grandissimes, The, 147
Grand Prairie, 84
Gray, Mayo, 205
Gray, Sampson, 90
Great Dismal Swamp, 20–21, 26
Great Lakes region, 58
Great Raft, 51, 56, 86
Green, John Otto, 141
Greenock, Arkansas, 88
Grimké, Angelina, 184
Grimké, Sarah, 184
Grooms, Richard, 103–4
Grundy County, Tennessee, 174
Guedry (Iberville, Parish), 192
Guire, Paul A., 94
Gus (slave, carpenter), 136

Hadden, Sally E., 206
Hagan, John, 62–63

Negro news, 79
Negro Speculation, 62
Nelly (slave), 69
Nelson, Robert J., 123–25
Ne-ta-ki-jah, 89
Netherland, J. W., 165
Nevels, Bill, 79
Nevitt, John B., 91, 122–23
New Madrid Earthquake, 88
New Orleans Commercial Bulletin, 228
New Orleans Delta, 222
New Orleans Gas Light Company, 151
New Orleans, 47, 84, 103, 129–48,
    212–14; city regulations, 138–39;
    criminal law in, 140–142; descrip-
    tion of, 57–58, 131–33; escaping from,
    45–46, 92, 99, 170, 215–21, 223; free
    blacks in, 22–23, 41–42; occupations
    of fugitives, 136–37; Parish and City
    Court of, 110; police department,
    139–42, 173, 174; slave behavior in,
    40; slave trade, 66–68; sold in, 67,
    93–94; steamboat escapes from, 103,
    107; stolen slaves in, 166–72, 177–78
New Orleans proclamation of 1753, 43
New Orleans Mercantile Advisor, 80
New Orleans (steamboat), 50
New River, 60
New Spain, 38, 85
*New York Daily Times. See New York
    Times*
New York Daily Tribune, 17
New York Journal of Commerce, 228
New York, New York, 112–14, 212–14
New York (steamboat), 115
New York Times, 13–15, 17, 66, 67
New York Tribune, 223–27
Newport Mercury, 228
Niagara (ship), 99, 216–17, 218, 220
Nicholls, William H. (free black), 177
Nichols, Henry, 145
Noah (slave), 84
Norbon (slave, Kentucky), 107
Norman's New Orleans, 132
North: escape to, 79, 89, 94; as destina-
    tion, 20, 95, 109, 166, 170–72, 175–77;
    southern belief about, 222

North Carolina, 26, 93
North Star, 223
northern United States, 66
Northup, Henry B., 67
Northup, Solomon "Platt", 66–72, 86,
    97, 229

O'Connor, Rachel, 202
Octavia (slave in Natchez,
    Mississippi), 152
O'Hanlon, Doyle, 63
Ohio, 90, 173
Ohio Anti-Slavery Society, 170–72
Ohio River, 50, 90, 102, 101–12, 171;
    escaping on, 98, 99, 107, 115, 177
Ohio Valley, 39, 58
Oklahoma, 50, 89
Olmsted, Frederick Law, 13–35, 66, 183,
    185; early life, 13–14; later life, 33–34;
    publications about the south, 17;
    travel route, 16–17
Olmsted, John H., 14, 16–17, 25,
    30–31, 35
Ontario (Canada), 107
Opelousas, 37
Opelousas Courier, 192
opinion of the south: by New
    Englanders, 13–35, 129–31;
    by the English, 131–34
O'Reilly, Alejandro, 41
Ottoman (ship), 215–16
Ouachita County, Arkansas, 186–87
Ouachita Parish, Louisiana, 95, 192
Ouachita River, 51, 55, 56, 104
outlaw fugitives, 48, 66, 125–26
overseer, 25–26, 74, 75–77, 81, 91, 94;
    use of lethal force, 24
Owen, Shapley, 99
owner, slave, 62
owner efforts to recapture, 100
owner, financial losses for runaways, 74
owners, Louisiana, 86
owner responsibility, 66
ox driver slave occupation, 95
Ozark highlands, 55, 93

S. Charles Bolton is professor emeritus of history at the University of Arkansas at Little Rock and the author of several books on colonial religion and early Arkansas.